AF552547

COMPARATIVE ETHICS IN HINDU AND BUDDHIST TRADITIONS

Comparative Ethics in Hindu and Buddhist Traditions

RODERICK HINDERY

MOTILAL BANARSIDASS PUBLISHERS
PRIVATE LIMITED • DELHI

2nd Reprint : Delhi, ***2017***
Second Revised Edition : Delhi, 1996
First Edition: Delhi, 1978

ISBN: 978-81-208-0866-9

MOTILAL BANARSIDASS
41 U.A. Bungalow Road, Jawahar Nagar, Delhi 110 007
8 Mahalaxmi Chamber, 22 Bhulabhai Desai Road, Mumbai 400 026
203 Royapettah High Road, Mylapore, Chennai 600 004
236, 9th Main III Block, Jayanagar, Bengaluru 560 011
8 Camac Street, Kolkata 700 017
Ashok Rajpath, Patna 800 004
Chowk, Varanasi 221 001

Printed in India

by RP Jain at NAB Printing Unit,
A-44, Naraina Industrial Area, Phase I, New Delhi–110028
and published by JP Jain for Motilal Banarsidass Publishers (P) Ltd,
41 U.A. Bungalow Road, Jawahar Nagar, Delhi-110007

To
my parents
ANN *and* RICHARD HINDERY,
and my parents-in-law
VERONICA *and* LEONARD INGOLDSBY

FOREWORD

I take great pleasure in offering a "word before" the contents of this significant achievement in comparative ethics. The reader will find this volume to be a major resource in which to explore the moral traditions of some major human civilizations. Some of its values lie in the primary sources it makes available—many of which are either overlooked or excluded by the canons guiding other authors' selections. Other values include the canons for the selections in this work, criteria guaranteed to give an accurate and comprehensive description of Hindu and Buddhist ethics, and fullsome enough to include the "popular" as well as the more formal sources of moral imagination and judgment. As if these were not enough, there are still other benefits for those who would wish to consider these sources from normative and metaethical perspectives. Although Professor Hindery has not himself sought to perform these kinds of inquiries into the materials he has so ably and sensitively assembled, he has made it possible—indeed, probably necessary—for ethicists of all stripes to look into Hindu and Buddhist ethics once again, but now with the aid of a more complete picture of their many-sided and sometimes conflicting sources of moral wisdom. Resisting the ease of a high road from which to scan the whole of a tradition through the prism of but one of its parts, Professor Hindery has assumed the challenge of a more adventurous journey through the complex web of informal as well as philosophically elegant texts. In so doing, however, he has given readers of the English language a sometimes startling, but always informative antidote with which to oppose conventional assumptions about the "other-worldly" or the overly spiritualized interpretations of Asian forms of moral imagination and judgment.

Professor James F. Smurl,
Indiana-Purdue University

Indianapolis

PERMISSIONS

I wish to thank the following for their permission to include here extracts from the books listed.

Oxford University Press, Oxford:
for excerpts from *Hymns from the Rigveda*, translated by A. A. Macdonell; *The Thirteen Principal Upanishads*, translated by R. E. Hume; *The Laws of Manu*, translated by Georg Bühler; and *The Vedānta Sūtras of Bādarāyaṇa with Commentary by Śaṅkara*, translated by George Thibaut.

Columbia University Press, New York:
for excerpts from *Twenty Plays of The Nō Theatre*, edited by Donald Keene, 1970.

Harvard University Press, Cambridge, Mass.:
for excerpts from *The Bhagavad Gītā : Translated and Interpreted* by Franklin Edgerton, copyright 1944, 1972 by Eleanor Hill Edgerton.

CBS International Publishing, New York, and Eliot Deutsch:
for excerpts from *The Bhagavad Gītā*, translated by Eliot Deutsch, 1968.

Shanti Sadan, London:
for excerpts from *The Rāmāyaṇa of Vālmiki*, translated by H. P. Shastri.

John Murray, Ltd., London:
for excerpts from *Vedic Hymns*, translated by Edward J. Thomas.

V.V.S. Krishnamurthy Aiyar (copyright):
for excerpts from *The Kural or the Maxims of Tiruvalluvar*, translated by V.V.S. Aiyar (Madras : Jupiter Press, 3d ed., 1952).

Bhandarkar Oriental Research Institute, Poona:
for excerpts from P. V. Kane's *History of Dharmaśāstra*, Vol. II, I.

Asia Publishing House, Bombay:
for excerpts from *Six Sanskrit Plays*, edited by Henry W. Wells.

Sahitya Akademi, New Delhi:
for a translated excerpt in S. Sen's *History of Bengali Literature*. Rev. ed., p. 264.

Motilal Banarsidass, Delhi,:
for excerpts from *The Hymns of the Ṛgveda*, translated by R.T.H. Griffith. Rev. ed. 1973.

I would also like to thank the following journals for permission to repeat or use excerpts from some of my writings which they published first or concurrently :

Journal of Religious Ethics, "Hindu Ethics in the *Rāmāyaṇa*;" *Insight : A Journal of World Religions*, "Hindu Ethics as Reflected in Some Popular Indian Classics;" *Journal of Religious Studies*, "Ethics in the *Bhagavad Gītā*;" and *The Journal of Ecumenical Studies*, "Ethics and Esthetics in Confucianism."

CONTENTS

ABBREVIATIONS

Rv	Rigveda
Ups	The Upanishads
Manu	The Laws of Manu
Ry	The Rāmāyaṇa
Gitā	The Bhagavad Gītā
Mbh	The Mahābhārata
Av	The *Advaita Vedānta* or non-dualistic philosophical "point of view" or system, especially Śaṅkara's
VS	The Vedānta Sūtras with Commentary by Śaṅkarācārya
TB	Theravāda Buddhism
MB	Mahāyāna Buddhism

PREFACE TO THE SECOND EDITION

If I could reword this volume's title, I would delete the adjective "comparative" and speak simply of "Ethics in Hindu and Buddhist traditions." Because for some the term "comparative" seems to be inexorably evaluative, I emphasize my conscious intention to draw comparisons only at the descriptive level of ethical structure, not at the evaluative level of ethical appraisal. My descriptive comparisons, which are explained in the first chapter and summarized in Appendix II, report empathetically what others claim. They do not assess the validity or rank the quality of those claims.

Evaluative comparisons entail philosophical, metaethical structures which rest on previous individual assumptions, on cultural worldviews, and probably on vested interests. I attempt to avoid such conscious and direct, philosophical appraisals, not because they lack supreme importance or urgent practical significance, but because ethical evaluations can be constructed more fruitfully if they are first grounded on informed and structured descriptive collations and analyses. My goal of descriptive neutrality, of course, can only be approximated. Overtly historical observations carry evaluative overtones, to which one may be deaf both culturally and subconsciously. My fifth and final methodological inquiry (p. 5), for example, about how individuals relate to societal institutions, might convey an emphasis which would appear individualistic from the perspective of cultures and personal backgrounds more communitarian than my own.

One way to defuse the impact of whatever evaluative assumptions function covertly, and therefore harmfully, for freedom, is to lay them on the table. A primary presupposition of my own, for example, has long been alarm at the extent to which the structures of organized religions have often diminished the values which I assume to be primary. These goods include interpersonal liberty, dignity, justice, love, and the right of all persons, not just elites, to carve out their own spiritual identities and sainthood. Twelve years after the initial publication of this book, I now recognize how its composition both expressed and strengthened my esteem for these values. Just as the inmost heartbeats of organized religions have incalculably inspired the realization of these goods, some religious structures have simultaneously destroyed the ability of persons to think and feel for themselves. In my view, other-centered love and justice may be impossible to practice without at least implicit religious motivation, but I also feel that their religious grounding and cultivation gets confused with indoctrination.

Indoctrination diminishes freedom and the realm of the ethical by manipulating human reason, feeling, or both at the same time. The most destructive manipulation is often the most innocent and unintended. Unconscious indoctrination may be more poisonous than conscious propaganda. Because I have experienced indoctrination simultaneously with the admirable effects and inspiration of religion from within my own Christian tradition, readers interested in Hindu, Buddhist, and other ethics are forewarned about my personal preoccupation. To some degree it probably influenced and helped motivate my choice of the structure and content of this study.

In sum, what neutralizes indoctrination in general also applies to efforts like this one, namely, the disclosure of presuppositions and perspectives which might unintentionally modify descriptive findings. Precisely to protect this book's descriptive worth, I have divulged my primary values and preoccupations, like the need to think for one's self while avoiding logical and emotive manipulation by the tyranny of custom, institutions, or individual leaders. While the present work strives to remain within a descriptive context, its implications about the value of compassionate love and about institutional threats to human liberty are ripe for evaluative explorations.

Comparative philosophical evaluations of ethics will become more helpful if they too are prefaced by similar search for and disclosure of their own individual and cultural assumptions. They will progress fruitfully as they fulfill two other conditions. First, they should utilize the cross-cultural data and new horizons already available. Second, because ethics is both science and art, philosophical comparisons should avoid endless or circular talk about methodology and get on with the practical art of comparison. One learns piano composition and playing not by thinking alone, but also in the performance.

Comparative ethics, perhaps better renamed pluralistic ethics, both in its descriptive and evaluative senses, is as socially and politically crucial as ethics itself. An ethics constructed without intercultural perspective is no longer feasible. All the eminent Western, Eastern, and other religious and ethical classics require reinterpretation and assimilation from intercultural points of view.

The future of comparative religion and ethics should not be confined to mere conversation among religious ethical systems. It should expand to the dialogues between religion and science in general and between the disciplines of ethics and the social sciences. Stimulated by awareness of these new vistas, my own interests have moved from doing further volumes in history and theory to interdisciplinary study of practical issues in contemporary ethics. I am especially interested in an ethics which asks less about what responsible persons *must* do and more about how much they *can* do. It is time, I think, to retrieve and intensify the symbiotic relationship between ethics and spirituality. I hold the maxim "not to grow is to wither" to be especially true in an ethical dimension, true for persons, institutions, and religious organizations and cultures.

PREFACE

Although this book is addressed primarily to people with moral and political interests, it should prove more widely helpful to teachers, students, and larger audiences attracted simply to literatures, philosophies, and religions of other cultures. These wider groups might be especially interested in the opening theory on method and its appended synopsis of historical Hindu mysticism and external Hindu moral structures (a systematic glossary of terms). While the highly complex chronological order of Hindu texts and their consequent pluralism is respected through chapter divisions by texts, the second of the book's two appendices supplies a short diagram of topical parallels and contrasts which run through these sources. When future research can extend this diagram through several other religions and cultures, constructive ethical philosophers will be better prepared to discern or reject the viability of a residual cross-cultural ethics.

I have begun this practical inquiry into descriptive comparative ethics with Hindu materials, because some Hindu traditions are chronologically prior to and have had genealogical impact on other major moral traditions. Except for a brief addition on Buddhist moral texts, my investigation stops with Hindu traditions only because of the limitations of time and space. But in Hinduism I found competing and complementary traditions which usually interacted and moved people non-linearly. They were communicated in forms which Max Weber has called emotively "charismatic," and which others would label "esthetic." From this finding I build an opening chapter on method which is offered as theoretically seminal both for the analysis of this volume and for fuller comparative studies in the future. After initial scrutiny of the kinds of questions which comparative ethics might fruitfully ask, the seven subsequent chapters address those queries to classical primary sources of morality, both formal and popular. The ninth chapter summarizes Hindu ethics and adds an epilogue. The tenth chapter introduces the groundwork for further comparative study of Buddhist moral cultures in India, China, and Japan.

Since there are large gaps in historical data about India and, as I have been told by her philosophers, an abiding disinterest there in ethical reflections, it has been necessary throughout to offer a variety of interpretive options without pinning the reader down to interpretations which are just getting their first testing. My own preferences, when undisguised or stated in chapter nine's epilogue, remain necessarily tentative due to the present stage of ethical description. That chapter contains both a summary and a short epilogue on motivating ethical judgments. For those interested, the appendices deal with more critical textual materials about the two major epics, the *Rāmāyaṇa* and the *Mahābhārata,* and with the topical diagram (referred to above) which looks for parallel statements in various Hindu sources on ethoses like compassion, giving, or ascetical life-negation. Like the glossary of chapter one, this device may be employed either prior to or throughout the use of the volume.

For additional background, readers may turn to the most recent and objective of many works on Hindu morality, *The Evolution of Hindu Ethical Ideals,* published by Professor Cromwell Crawford of the University of Hawaii in 1974 (Calcutta: Firma K.L. Mukhopadhyay). Dr. Crawford graciously allowed me to study his book while it was still in manuscript form in the summer of 1974. This lucid treatise is especially helpful on the ethical ramifications of the *darśanas* or philosophical systems. Seeking to complement rather than replace or repeat Crawford's work, the present study employs an analysis which is comparative and materials which are largely popular. Either general information or specific inspiration to study ethical traditions in the people's classics were personally and gratefully received in interviews with Professors Surama Dasgupta, J. Sharma, K.N. Upadhyaya, Eliot Duetsch (the latter three at the University of Hawaii), from Professors R. S. Sharma, R. C. Pandeya, and Margaret Chatterjee of the University of Delhi, and from Professor Bibhuti Yadav of Temple University, each of whom would probably disagree with various judgments of my own. The transfer value of various conversations with specialists in other traditions at Temple University and around the world awaits acknowledgment in chapter ten. I hope that this book will encourage others to compose volumes on comparative (pluralistic) ethics in other major religions and scientific disciplines. Those who affirm the unity of nature and grace will grasp the need for connecting ethics to scientific disciplines without falling into the deterministic errors of natural law theory.

The initial research for the Buddhist section of a possible second volume is appended here as chapter ten, and a smaller seed for the Confucian section was published in the *Journal of Ecumenical Studies* 15:2. Reference to my work in Muslim and Christian ethics appears in the bibliography. The disadvantages of including chapter ten in the present volume may be discerned in the chapter's title. It is merely an introduction to Buddhist moral texts which evince potentially pluralistic meanings, a project which has not been attempted previously. Although comparisons with Hindu moralities remain minimal or largely implicit, nonetheless, analysis by others may establish more lucidly that according to the popular and widespread claims of many Buddhists, intellectuals included, morality is not merely a dispensable scaffold for faith, mind-culture, or enlightenment. It is rather their symbolic (dual/non-dual or transdual) embodiment and in some sense their verification. In an at least one principal Buddhist ethos wisdom and compassion are one. In the event that future contingencies should not allow me to complete volume two, chapter ten's inclusion and accessibility within book form and within the same volume may better encourage others to develop, integrate, analyze, and evaluate the practical worth of cross-religious comparisons and contrasts in moral ideals and inspirations. To strengthen the possibility that this unfinished venture may be continued, I have dared to include my addendum about Buddhist moral texts within both the book and the title. Its presence may serve as a further reminder that the ethics of Hindu traditions alone (or any other culture) may be viewed paradigmatically for implicit instruction or enlightenment about one's own moral roots, tradition, and heritage of human rights.

In addition to acknowledging assistance and inspiration from administrative and teaching colleagues and from students at Temple University, and especially from my spousal research assistant and indispensable critic, Sheila Hindery, I wish to express special appreciation for the support, encouragement, and criticisms of my parents, Ann and Richard Hindery, and of generous friends and colleagues like Daniel Carney, Phylis Sturm, Cromwell Crawford, James Smurl, and others to whom I have referred above or in chapter ten, note 1.

CHAPTER I

METHOD IN COMPARATIVE ETHICS

Abstract. A. Type of readers. B. The priority of the descriptive and five forms of its questions. *C. The limited function of textual exposition* within interdisciplinary comparative ethics; criteria of textual selections. *D. Hindu ethics*: paradigm for cross-cultural descriptions. *E. Populist-Elitist dialectics*: competitive or complementary? *F. Synopsis* of a Hindu mystical tradition. *G. A systematic glossary* of external structures in Hindu morality NOTES.

The cross-cultural and populist/elitist background of this ethical inquiry necessitates some preliminary statements about terms and method. One concerns the verbal equation of morality and ethics (as practice and reflection, both descriptive and normative), both terms employed to refer to some freedom and other-directedness. In spite of helpful analytical attempts to distinguish morality's concrete and normative dimensions from the analytical and descriptive, the term "moral" is generally equated in usage, even by professional ethicians at times, not only with practice or reflection on the normative, but also with second-order "ethical" or "metaethical" reflection on the meaning and justification of moral conduct. Therefore, in this chapter, the author will surrender to the synonymous equation of the concepts of "moral" and "ethical" cooperation and altruism. Nevertheless, they will be used most directly in the sense of *descriptive* collation and analysis of the overtly *normative* prescriptions which people allege.[1]

The words for morality have also been confused historically with words meant to convey "love". The degree to which the family cognate "morality" equals "love" towards self and others can be nearly total, at least from certain logically idealistic or ideological perspectives. The author makes this idealistic identification, in spite of linguistic poverty and confusion in the area.

In short, in the author's idealistic usage as well as in frequent historical practice, both "self-love" and "other-love" have been employed as life-affirming self-acceptance and non-egotistical other-regard. Unfortunately, in other historical practice the terms have simultaneously designated narcissistic pride, sentimental possessiveness, and self-surrendering *Liebestod/thanatos* (the sometimes exhilarating and illusory thrill of the instinct and love of death). This disastrous confusion of language mirrors as even more regrettable pattern of behavior. These latter, "non-idealistic," equations play no part in this volume. Thus, in admittedly idealistic language, attention-seeking self-pity, self-aggrandizement, or various forms of slow, sudden, ritualistic, or stark suicidal finales are not here designated as authentic self-and other-loves, but as their counterfeits, if not their very contradictions : hostility and hatred. This judgment does not at all imply that such counterfeits are moral rather than psychological or cognitive problems.

Aside from these and future "methodological" clarifications in this chapter, the immediate and primary objective of the present work as a whole is to discuss moral *content* rather than *assumptions, terms, and method* in comparative ethical analysis. Stronger methodological interpretations and comparisons urgently await more thorough literary, descriptive, and expository analysis of historical moral claims. This priority of substantive descriptive ethics has been largely ignored, partly because of centripetal and premature discussions about method, isolated from substance.

A. *Types of Readers.* This volume's specific focus centers on the transfer- or cross-cultural values (moral or other) of Hindu ethical systems, both philosophical and popular. The question is not merely how peoples came to *decide* on certain moral ethoses or normative ideals about right and wrong. Rather it asks how they claimed *to move* themselves beyond the inner, solipsistic world of mere aspirations to the stirring world of social action. In other words, the focal inquiry concerns religious as well as esthetical and emotive wellsprings of human relations. Properly scientific and socio-psychological analyses, which are so vital, must heed first the historical records of the people's own claims. This motif is so critical to this volume that this chapter in particular will develop it and redevelop it in concentric circles.

While the book's most particular thrust is thus directed to the motivating grounds of moral and political activity in Hinduism, its wider ambit speaks to readers and students of literature, historical events, and their interactions through the visions of various social sciences. The latters' concerns are less ethical than general.

They seek to understand others through their literature, history, or social structures. Others may extend and apply these concerns beyond analytical *description* to overt *normative inferences* about international detente, cross-cultural enrichment (not imitation), or additional political, humanistic, and religious goals.[2] The new subfield of descriptive, comparative ethics is not automatically and judgmentally normative. Its findings may be utilized, for better or for worse, even by those who reject "a moral point of view" as in Marxian or other philosophically agnostic ("scientific") perspectives.

B. *The Priority of Descriptive Ethics and Five Sets of Questions Which It May Ask.* On the other hand, whether comparative ethics operates intra- or inter-culturally, it cannot remain an abstract chronicle of a myriad of unrelated moral claims. It must restrict the unlimited scope of its subject to some tentative classifications of analytical inquiry. To begin is to limit. For whatever moral or non-moral ends or means the reader may intend to employ the findings of descriptive ethics, the author presupposes that the following five sets of questions must be addressed to every moral assertion of textual or oral traditions. The first three are epistemological: *how* do you know ? The last two are substantive: *what* do you say you know ?

1. In contrast with mores, morality is generally understood to entail some minimum of free volition which reaches beyond entirely deterministic customs, conventions, class traditions, laws, or social forces. Morality or mores ? The former is thought to extend to a norm which "ought" to be freely embraced. In brief, if morality is present, why ? *Why be moral* ? Why be other- as well as self-centered ? In the final analysis is morality realized through knowledge (*vidyā*) or some free volition ?

2. More specifically : *is ethical behavior based on anthropologies or worldviews* like one or more of the following ? a) Moral cooperation is in some way always self-compensating or karmic, either in this life or in another form of existence. This view supports itself directly from the effects or fruits of human action or perhaps by additional analogical argumentation from "laws of nature," like ecological feedback. Disputes arise when analogies are interpreted literalistically, as in the debates about the control of human life, which range from artificial birth control to the termination of some forms of that life. b) *Conduct is*

grounded—humanistically or religiously—*in either alleged mystical experiences or beliefs* in the unity of all beings. Such worldviews are "divinely" supported either by alleged revelations or by the grace to "leap" beyond what is humanly invisible or doubtful. c) *Morality stems from a previous intuition* (insight without logical inference) *into altruism or else a working postulate* that no one can be "human" without a willingness to sacrifice self-interests. Sometimes even life itself is exacted, both in mutually cooperative and in purely altruistic love for others. For the sake of convenience, the three worldviews may be dubbed the *cooperative*, the *mystical*, and the *altruistic*. They shall be referred to again, either directly or through the Hindu symbols of Rāma, Shankara, and Sītā.

3. Whether or not *ethical behavior* is validated by worldviews—experienced, intuited, believed, or postulated—*is it also justified by other separate or integrated appeals*, such as a) trust in *collective experience*, which authoritative laws and customs finally encapsulate;[3] b) a comparable resort to logical, common-sense reasoning from the "useful" *consequences of actions* on combined self- and other-interests; or c) a Confucian-like anthropological presupposition that all human beings are not merely rational, but also emotive, "thinking hearts" ? From this outlook people are moved to the good only through the esthetical and sometimes charismatic "*value-feeling*" for living beings, or their various artistic expressions, or even for the beauty and other qualities of nature as such. The term "esthetical" is here re-expanded beyond rather recent Western notions of visual spectatorship to include: hearing, feeling, perceiving, imagining, moving, building, creating, playing, laughing, crying, loving, embracing, sharing, just being, etc. Parasitical inner lives of passive onlooking are thereby fused with outgoing, non-vicarious symbols of touch, movement, and action. This last ancient and cross-cultural stress on the esthetical resembles contemporary returns to a morality of character or model persons. It also reflects both classical and now renewed efforts to unify the ethical with the esthetical, the right, true, and good with the beautiful. In particular, it coincides with an age-old Hindu predilection for the unity of devotion (*bhakti*) and esthetical tastes and feelings (*rasas*).[4]

As previously indicated, this question of esthetical motivation is the central issue of the present comparative exploration. It leads to a substantive query which receives equal attention.

4. *What ethos or ethoses are central in explicit moral systems or implicit moral worldviews* ? "Ethos" here means the moral or non-moral virtues or values which assume paramount priority and importance in popular moral systems (unelaborated people's philosophies). Ethoses may also function pivotally in the explicit and systematic constructions of professional philosophers. Further, ethos may denote a single virtue like compassion or a whole gestalt of interrelated values like life-affirmation, love, and non-violence. In any case, the search for ethos has become more than a quest for values which are endowed with merely verbal centrality. Rather it is the pursuit of what most effectively *instigates* people or inspires (breathes into) them to move from professed ideals to actual performance. The question of ethos, therefore, seems inseparable from the previous question about esthetical motivation. Some religious people would also add that it is inseparable from the question of grace. In either case, what is revealed as false is a neat dualism between substantive, objective moral content and subjectively moving and propelling forms of moral ethoses. Action and its actors are perceived as one.

5. The last inquiry is also substantive. *What are the fundamental attitudes about relationships between individuals and societal conventions or institutions* ? Do individual egos sometimes grow fat and sassy or societies discriminatory or aggressive in such areas as sexist discrimination, violence, economics, racial differences, or simple human respect ? Fully pursued, this question would lead to intricate histories of laws and customs.[5] Here, it is limited simply to signs of prevailing attitudes. It thereby remains most closely related to the continuing investigation of ethos and esthetical motivations (taken widely, as above, and already examined in questions three and four above).

C. *The Limited Function of Textual Exposition Within Interdisciplinary Comparative Ethics*; *Criteria of Textual Selections.* Just as a fully scientific ethics is intrinsically cross-cultural or comparative, it is also essentially interdisciplinary. Even taken by itself, *textual* analysis cannot flower until professional linguists, linguistic analysts, and historians complete their work, which is so crucial for more adequate social scientific inquiry (psychological, sociological, economic, political, etc.). The present volume summarizes and joins in some rather primitive ethical analyses of texts, simply because these have not been done from the perspective of comparative ethics. Like most scientific work, therefore, the present analysis is tentative. Not only are many textual tools still primitive, but texts have not yet been well envisaged contextually or with the cooperation of other disciplines.

Therefore, the present enterprise remains largely expository, certainly not by choice, but by force of circumstances. But it does defend documented expositions as one necessary part of a much broader project. True, the modern field anthropologist or sociologist may see, hear, and feel his or her way through the present into the past, and by means of individuals or smaller circles into wider segments of society. But even these feelings must eventually be recorded on tape or in print. All field results become finally textual.[6]

Criteria of selection. On the other hand, authentic textual emphasis seeks maximal or "democratic" exposure to ethical allegations, because descriptive ethics is intrinsically scientific and therefore cross-cultural, both in terms of time (history, ancient and recent) and space (cultural geography). Arriving, then, at the criteria for textual selections, one thrives more vigorously on *primary* sources, not only for reasons of maximal exposure, but because the contradictory interpretations or findings of *secondary* sources[7] betray the defensive or revisionistic spirits with which they were sometimes composed—a fault to be attributed in India, as elsewhere, to histories of both interior and imperialistic military, economic and other cultural oppressions. The assumption will be increasingly clarified that primary classics, moreover, include not only samples from formal scriptures, authoritative religious commentaries, or canonical, legal and philosophical treatises, but also selections from peoples' classics, records of those multiple smaller circles of traditions which seldom lack profound philosophical wisdom about morality. What they needed was not wisdom, but the wealth, literacy, force, or power which facilitates the recognition of wisdom.

In any case, the wide "democratic" hunt for maximal records leads to a derivative criterion which could be called the "republican" factor, that is, the set of criteria by which either formal or popular texts may be "classical" in a "representative" sense.

What are these factors ? Intrinsic quality, consensual popularity, historical impact, utilization by power elites—or various mixtures ? If consensual popularity fits into the landscape, the elusive historical goal is to find those works which were most heard by and were most appealing to most people. This objective is especially impeded in the Indian subcontinent, where historiography's primary purposes were admittedly didactic rather than factual. Indeed, it is a highly ambitious venture anytime and anywhere, given the historical complexities in discerning causes and effects.

As regards this volume's selections of classics, the choices of both popular and formal ones rely more on unquestioned tradition than on proven polls, more on uncriticized, surviving custom (*sadācāra*) than on palpable demonstrations that they were really heard by and influenced large groups of people. This admission seems all the more necessary today when competitive materials such as mass-produced films are available in most cities and villages. In other words, what is taken as representative may be shifting today, but it may have been mobile in the past as well. The actual influence of even a major work like the *Rāmāyaṇa* must be questioned. Aristocratic controls, links with vested interests, and manipulations of power elites were probably not as likely to have undermined its genuinely widespread popularity and effectiveness, but the hypothetical nature of this inference invites future scientific attention. While popularity cannot always be shouted down, it can often occur by accident or by a mass contagion, or it can be manufactured. For example, for centuries of publication of the Chinese novel, *The Water Margin*, obscene, sadistically pornographic, and narcotizing elements have been provided with maximal publicity by those in the best positions to reap economic benefits.[8]

To minimize arbitrariness and to attain some semblance of representativeness in the following selections, it has been necessary to travel and to confer at length with a whole league of textual and other scholars in Asia, America, the Middle East, and Europe. It seemed similarly imperative to confront a humbling mass of histories of literature, anthologies, critical editions of primary texts, and secondary references in the cross-cultural, as yet unwritten, history of ethics. During this period the problem of aristocratic influence locked in a third tactical hypothesis, the necessity of suggesting interpretive options. This postulate entails neither promise nor threat of detailed speculations or professional exegeses. The latter remain presently tentative. As was stated before, familiarization with the methods of professional textual exegesis is an ongoing process. Its maturity is correlative with still pending scientific information and interpretations of contextual situations. Meanwhile the variety of options must be exposed and retained.

One final point should be made about the use of data. From Marxian and other purportedly amoral points of view, morality is merely superstructual or epiphenomenal to deeper economic and other social forces. From these perspectives, efficiency would require, therefore, that the descriptive investigation of moral behavior be relegated to the teamwork of historians, social scientists, and specialists in literary forms and composition. As an independent subject of inquiry, ethics, like religion, is a feudalistic anachronism. Away with its books, journals, classes, and learned societies. Polar to these Marxian assumptions are those of Max Weber.[9] This great historiographer of cultures and herald of an interdisciplinary future felt fewer economic and other deterministic forces at work in the world. Thus, room was allowed for a moral dimension, based on universal insight and charged with magnetic attraction. But the depiction of this dimension was to be left to the prophet and the artist. In spite of this humble conviction, Weber's own synthetic foray into a "history of cultures" encapsulated several layers of directly ethical observations, which probably sprang somewhat spontaneously from his trans-disciplinary overview. As an alternative to Marxian economic interpretations of human behavior, Weber granted systems of worldviews and beliefs a *direct* impact on conduct, coequal, in fact, with the causality of conditions like the economic or political.

Weber's genius, however, lay not in his talent as a directly descriptive ethicist. To repeat, for him ethical behavior was reputedly incapable of direct description. His own intellectual contribution crystallized rather in his talented conjunction of the viewpoints and methods of history, law, sociology, and economics. Concretely, he demonstrated that these and other disciplines, like anthropology or political science, are best navigated through channels which are both multi-disciplinary and cross-cultural. Like the encyclopedic Greeks, scholastics, or the fourteenth century Arab genius, Ibn Khaldun (1332-1406), Weber foresaw that all data are both wholes and parts. Brought to an impressive stage of completion, his synthetic master-voyage demonstrated that all the "disciplines" of human behavior are interconnected in a world which is round and whose mappings have been barely begun in present disciplines or new integrations yet to be created.[10] However, even from Weber's cross-disciplinary though only semi-moral *weltanschauung*, the *history* of ethics demands a distinct, if never isolated, description and analysis apart from the further contributions of social sciences and humanistic or religious philosophies. This verdict is all the more appropriate if one agrees with the naturalistic or neo-naturalistic "moral cooperator" that the ethical hypothesis simply appears to function more fruitfully than the semi- or amoral one, even if it cannot be firmly anchored.

D. *Hindu Ethics: A Paradigm For Cross-Cultural Descriptions.* If the Orient or India is not the only place to initiate a cross-cultural kind of descriptive survey, it seems to be a justifiable and productive point of departure on three scores. First, in contrast to the histories of so-called Western cultures and religions, those of Asia are relatively less cluttered with inward spinning, inbred, and repetitive analyses by Western philosophical clubs ("members only"). As a result, work in Indian ethics can progress more manageably, if with regrettably inexperienced analytical strength and accuracy. A second fortunate by-product of beginning in Asia is that with the availability of new Asian linguistic vistas, trained Anglo-American teams of linguists need no longer queue up for what Kai Neilsen censured as ethnocentric, if not narcissistic, glances at slides which capture only Anglo-American ethical words and syntaxes.[11] Third, the Orient is a reasonable springboard because in the still unrefuted view of F.S.C. Northrop,[12] P. T. Raju,[13] and others, it is in Asia that religions, esthetics, and ethics have remained better integrated. Attempts to isolate any one of them are refuted by new synthetic outlooks which are aware that the closest equivalents to these terms are mere analogues. In the absence of the Latin and English terms "religio" and "religion," one finds counterparts like "teachings" or "ways" (*dharma*, *chiao*, or *tao*). In Asia the links between ways of living, seeing, and relating to life's ultimate issues are not simply moral. The appreciation or creation of the beautiful, moreover, is not merely utilitarian as it was in the Maoist regime. Beauty is not merely dispositive to the ethical, in the sense that art and the beautiful happen to bring people together. Rather sensitivity to the beautiful, even in what is *prima facie* ugly, is said to be the very fabric of morality and human life. In Northrop's theory, the Asian "non-dualistic" or unitive perception of the interwovenness of the self with nature and other selves is a "non-atomistic" awareness of the "undifferentiated aesthetic continuum" of life.[14] The point behind these groping phrases is the alleged experience of non-dualism, especially in East Asian traditions.

The author has never intended to limit his comparative goals to Asia or India alone, but to stay in touch with several other cultures. Although the frustration of not yet being able to collate and publish numerous identifications of other ethical materials —some newly discovered—and their interpretations is painful, a fourfold value of being temporarily waylaid in the further description and assessment of Hindu ethical traditions can be passed on to the reader.

First, the delay in that vast historic sea of time and texts stimulates the conclusion that Hindu ethics is itself both diachronically and synchronically (past and present) pluralistic. In short, comparative description is feasible not only across cultures but also within them. This observation becomes nearly tautological for those sympathetic with current trends towards intracultural ethnic self-awareness.

Second, the realization that most Hindus still acculturate themselves in non-linear forms of communication, together with the recollection of customary reliances on elaborate chains of oral recitations and dramatizations, encourages the present exploration of method in descriptive ethics. Possible latent benefits in the project must be generously ascribed to the inspiration of critics and reviewers who have insisted that the author should not compose his descriptive themes without first explaining his method of procedure.

Third, the awareness that Indian classics, both canonical and popular, encounter one another not only in complementary relationships, but also in vibrant competitions, raises the possibility that this phenomenon may be paradigmatic for everywhere.

In India, China, the Soviet Union, etc., therefore, a most crucial descriptive opener must be: "To which populaces am I listening, and what were they up to ?"

Finally, it was in attending a theatrical Hindi performance of the ancient *Rāmāyaṇa* in Delhi that the author was moved to a recognition of what should have been already transparent. The application of descriptive ethics to the realm of popular drama, the charismatic, the esthetical, or to whatever else may move people morally and inside-out (freely), gives a new dimension to descriptive ethics: it must ascertain what stirs activity as well as what merely convinces internally. It bears repeating that the possible humanitarian uses and totalitarian abuses of such knowledge will beget a Faustian power for those who would move beyond description to evaluative and normative prescriptions. On the other hand, ever since Goebbels and Hitler attempted to repeat the marvels of American consumer seduction, the abuses of motivation have thrived increasingly—weeds which may need grass to prevent their perennial return.

As it was indicated in note one, the author had published elsewhere a number of assumptions seemingly prerequisite for any endeavor which presumes to step ahead normatively with minimal bias or partisanship.[15] He has also reflected there at length on the commonly employed meaning of "religious" ethics. Therefore, little will be added here about the problems of normative constructions or that most delicate and circularly regressive question about "religion": does a "religion" or set of teachings like Hinduism embody cultural forces, or *vice versa*, or both ? Unless otherwise specified, "religion" is here understood simply as a second-order reflection on what many peoples seem to have meant by it and its cousins: ways of living, seeing, and worshipping, with general reference to trans- or super-human forces (theistic or non-theistic). If anyone should be convinced, like John Dewey was long ago, that reference to a "beyond" in any form is simply a developmental stage in the evolution of humanistic behavior, then one's next step is to ferret out mythological, symbolic and humanistic substitutes for what religious rituals, dramas, and worldviews have long offered to human understanding and motivation.

In delineating Hindu religious ethics in particular, it is impossible to abstract entirely from Hindu religious rituals, devotion (*bhakti*), or beliefs about Brahman, gods, and cosmologies. This is due to the actual or at least asserted connections drawn between these factors and modes of behavioral cooperation. However, in the light of copious volumes penned in those more metaphysical and cosmological directions about ways of "seeing," and also with *aspiring* respect for brevity and simplicity, the present correlations between ethical norms and religious cosmologies and ritual will be kept in the lowest profile possible. However, they cannot be ignored entirely, because of the social and ethical functions and dysfunctions of religious ways of being, seeing, and behaving ritually. From a functionally agnostic point of view, there is no conscious, premature attempt here to defend or disqualify Hindu or other religious beliefs. The goal rather is to view them empathetically or, in proper jargon, with phenomenological *epoche*, that is from their point of view or at least from a truth-bracketing "detached within." Other less agnostic and explicitly religious comparative efforts may also proceed fruitfully and scientifically, as long as their religious presuppositions stay visible and their methods remain critically scientific.

Why be moral ? From Hindu and other religious traditions, this question has been asked from three separate or sometimes integrated levels, those of moral cooperation, moral mysticism, and moral altruism. At any level today's personal and social crises about why one should be moral are related not only to holocausts or to accelerating consciousness of global starvation and suffering, but also to the growing eclipse of *religious* belief in a cosmic network supporting general welfare here or hereafter. For many people, the cosmos no longer seems to orbit in a harmonious waltz around the Dantesque divine Love or Natural Law which moved the sun and the stars.

The cooperator's view. At first it was "religiously" surmised that "natural law," Hindu *rita* (rite become right or cosmic order), or the Chinese "way of heaven" could be salvaged if they were conceived not merely as *telos* (goal) or *deon* (duty), but in interpersonal, I-Thou, interwovenness. Further, modern neo-naturalists came to distrust pure altruism because of its notorious counterfeits—like literal "disinterested love," sadomasochism, or *"ressentiment."* Still, in seeking to justify some minimum of other-regard at self expense, they could not forego such models as the

Pauline members/body or the Platonic participations/whole. In striving for the good of the other and the whole, even at apparent loss to the self, somehow one was still judged as never excluding the good of all the members, including the self.[16] Put biologically, this model would not allow for amputations, whatever the diagnosis. Aside from these models, at least one could always offer "good reasons" (beyond intuition and belief) as to why the cooperative citizen should impartially postulate both justice and benevolence as the functional keys to social survival and growth.[17] What determines a "good" reason ? This question will reappear in this chapter's model of concentric development, just as the notion of counterfeit loves like sentimental narcissism or death-seeking hatred has already reappeared at this point.

The altruist. Dissatisfied with the factual conflicts of interest which disrupt such harmonious thinking in an increasingly complex world, others have courageously turned from the model of reasonable cooperation to sheer altruism, even if it means total self-sacrifice or the "humble acceptance of death, chance, transcience, nothingness."[18] In the West, Camus has recalled Sisyphus to the stage as a mythic symbol of blind courage for others. In Asian models, the dogged, chin-up geist of Sisyphus is replaced by warm personifications of loving compassion. In Buddhism, they are *bodhisattvas* (literally, enlightened sentient beings) who forego ultimate "enlightenment" in endless rebirths to save others, mainly spiritually, but also materially. In Hinduism, as chapter five illustrates, the Rāmāyaṇic heroine, Sītā, in spite of her belief in heavenly and endless continuation of this life and its loves speaks strongly of compassion. She embodies it with such non-attachment (undergoing ordeal by fire for the sake of others) that she may be the most likely Hindu candidate for a model of altruism.

Unconvincingly, for many, some altruists have employed reason to validate their position. They either deny or bracket the fact that the Kantian kind of reason of which they speak is probably not isolated in splendid abstraction, but is a reason which its defenders have "phenomenologically" experienced as already altruistic.[19] Similarly, others like G. E. Moore and Max Scheler returned early in the twentieth century to a basic intuition of "the good" and even to multiple intuitions. The latter venture was particularly frightening for people bothered by the facts of conflicting intuitions. At any rate, inanely or not, intuitional altruists were convinced that there is a non-inferential shortcut to moral cognition. Simultaneously, other followers of Moore rejected the idea that the "good" could be cognitively known at all and that it only expresses preferences which people support with "good" reasons—a return to the cooperative world-view. To avoid circularlity, of course, the "good reasons approach" has to resort to a kind of pragmatic assumption that people everywhere must aspire to at least one value which is linked to a kind of chain or network of values. The present writer has explained this theory in detail elsewhere, although his position now integrates it with those of the mystic and the altruist as is explained in the epilogue.[20]

To return to the intuitional altruist, some of them have hoped for insights into Wachian "types" (after the comparative religionist, Joachim Wach) or into Joseph Campbell's mythical hero with a thousand faces, the representative paradigm for everyone. That magic particular within which the universal may be easily intuited provides the self-evidence for altruistic morality. Surely, one profound moral experience, like the philosopher Kierkegaard's "existential" sacrifice of not marrying his beloved Regina, outweighs a multitude of acts which are neither intensely felt nor brilliantly examined. The intuitional justification of morality lives on, in spite of conflicting intuitions and (for others) the seemingly unverifiable pontifications and postures of moral supremacy.

Validation by direct insight is not only modern but ancient, in Asia as well as in Greece. In addition to Hindu claims, that of the Confucian Mencius (370-290 B.C.E.) deserves mention in this opening chapter because of the clarity of his illustration. Mencius declared that whoever is not naturally moved to action from a heart of compassion at the sight of a child about to fall into a well is not even human. Even if not clearly intuitional, altruism can be similarly traced to the earlier Confucian *Analects*' (15.8) assertion that in arriving at perfect sagehood (*Sheng-jen*) or at human-heartedness (*jen*) "one would rather sacrifice his life in order to realize humanity." If this declaration should be interpreted not intuitionally but as a working postulate necessary in the pragmatic and in the "good reasons" approaches to the moral life, some intuitionists would insist that this kind of postulation of other-love is too rationalistically bloodless to stir anyone. They point to the Confucian anthropology of people as "thinking hearts" and are willing to surrender or negotiate intuitional allegations beyond the basic one having to do with "why be moral ?" or "why love ?"

The mystical and religious moralist. Many people are confused in the face of the above claims of ethical cooperation and altruism until they turn either to mystical experience or to religious belief for, literally, moral support. Both phenomena have prevailed in Hinduism, in spite of the rapid growth of secularizing processes in contemporary India. Even Max Weber, whose knowledge of Hinduism was immense, was unable to abandon what were ultimately religious appeals for morality. Neither could Weber surrender his fascination with emotive charisma, considered above in terms of esthetical motivation. In this dilemma, Weber passed on another version of one last problem to be considered in this chapter. Comparative ethics confronts it as the problem of the interrelationships between aristocratic elites and democratic majorities.

E. *Populist-Elitist Dialectics: Competitive or Complementary ?*

When Weber addressed the cultural denouement of early twentieth century rationalism in Western cultures, he issued a final verdict which was curious or at least equivocal for one who had remained so rationalistic: "Specialists without spirit, sensualists without heart; this nullity imagines that it has attained a level of civilization never before achieved."[21] For Weber, all rational thought seemed to be finally based on experiential or intuitive value or faith judgments of the good and the holy.[22] The articulation of these judgments Weber chose to reserve to artists and prophets. His final evaluation of the non-rational basis of the rational, therefore, seemed to confirm the non-rational. He felt that there was an undeniable non-rational aspect to life. Even if the magical and religious parts of the non-rational world were sometimes dysfunctional for practical rational conduct, still the affectional, traditional, and charismatic qualities of life were positive in both group leadership and mass attraction.[23] As a rationalist who kept his ties with Kant as well as Nietzsche, with similar paradox Weber joined the non-rational, charismatic dimension of life to the aspect which seemed rational and universally heroic. Affectional charisma was associated with Weber's own moral protests against life's imperfections and against those power-elites and in-groups of Brahmins and Confucian literati who seemed to Weber to have served the power of corrupt states.[24] Ironically, if not mysteriously, the authenticity of non-rational charisma was judged by its conformity with the rationally ethical and its struggle with the sinful.

In David Little's intricate analysis of Weber's approach to religious ethics, he correctly discerned that Weber's categories of the rational and charismatic call for further refinement and elasticity. This is particularly true in handling human struggles personified in Nietzsche's resuscitation of the Apollonian and Dionysian models of rational goodness and mysterious, even demonic, moral energy. By themselves, the affectional and the rational constitute a framework incapable of describing the tensions symbolized by *eros/thanatos* (love/death) or the Hindu gods of life and life-giving destruction, Krishna and Shiva.[25]

Weber's consciousness of these limitations may have been at work in his demand for much more extensive studies in ethnography and folklore, a gap unfilled by his own aborted work in the sociology of religion.[26] In analyzing Weber's paradoxically rational fondness for what he considered irrationally charismatic, David Little may have overstated his point that for Weber charisma equals seizure or arbitrary authority with no transsubjective court of appeal.[27] But Little probably captured Weber's *angst* or unease before irrational chaos, those subterranean, prereflective, unconscious, and sometimes quasi-demonic forces which would seem to thwart, if not terrorize, objective attempts to classify and clarify moral behavior. Where could Weber turn without middle-ground synthetic categories which he lacked? Without a Schelerian value-feeling which claimed to reach outside objects cognitively or without a continuum of emotivist- "good reasons", functional approaches, Weber was left with split personality structures like the charismatic and the rational. Such uses were equated by many, if not clearly by Weber, with the chasm between the thinking and controlling elites and the emotional masses.

The negative view of mass charisma: fear of 1) *the irrational and* 2) *vulgar tastes.* 1. *The irrational.* Reluctantly Weber could not cast charisma aside, because it brought social morality to life. Yet, he foresaw its foreboding connection with mass contagion long before the arrival of Jacques Ellul's apocalyptic, gloomy, but still brilliant analyses of propaganda. Ellul was to censure the forms and sources of hypnotic mob suggestivity and of contemporary, scientifically planned propagandas. He saw them as geared toward political and economic exploitation of human beings as citizen puppets and programmed consumers. Passive, impulsive, chain-reactivity to charismatic "fuhrers" was to reach politics, religion, entertainment—eventually portraying itself as a scientific "industry"—and social conduct in all other areas of life.

For Ellul the scene of emotional crowds was capable of projecting even further horror. The timid, imitative rabble could be transfigured into aggressive armies. Meanwhile, the high volume of their madness might be drowned out by piped in music or by mechanical sounds sold as music. The meaning of what the invisibly aggressive masses produced would be covered by other cultural facades as well. But citizens of the world—East, West, and South, conscious only of their good citizenship were to be manipulated into tax-supporting or working collaborators of totally militarized industrial complexes. Increasingly accustomed tohomicide by the media, their profits would stem mainly from the potential of further holocaustal murder and the benign, homicidal neglect of starving millions in need of help to help themselves.

2. *Vulgar tastes*. With the touch of a more Orwellian scenario, the same collectivity can be desensitized to the lowest and most vulgar common denominators of esthetical tastes and moral and intellectual consciousness. A background figure lingers in the shadows. Whatever the mass predisposition to the cheap or the cruel, however low the common denominator of its narcotized awareness, the pusher is never far away. Note the fate of *The Water Margin*, referred to above. Popularized by a small group for vested economic interests, it is still an irritant to the government of the People's Republic of China.[28]

A similar elitist origin may be attributed to the Japanese attraction to *samurai* plays about the Bushidō or warrier ethic of absolute loyalty. From an outsider's viewpoint, *Chūsingura* and other Kabuki dramas of Chikamatzu seem to evoke a distorted sense of "face" or "honor" at the expense of respect for life. In a possibly circular causal chain between elites and multitudes, where have the most chilling historical agents of atavistic regression to the cruel arisen ? Out of the masses or out of elites ? The point concerns not only China, Japan, or India. It is difficult to recall a civilization which has lacked its colliseums of placatory bread and tranquillizing circuses. When these controlling and often enslaving powers are assumed, are not smaller, better organized cliques, in-groups, exclusive philosophical clubs, or traditions exposed more nakedly to the temptations of vested interests and the absolute power which corrupts power elites so absolutely ? Upper caste Hindu Brahmins, Buddhistic monastic elites, and Confucian literati have been partly replaced by new secular reichs, bureaucracies, or agencies of esoteric, higher, or central intelligence. So much for negatively apocalyptic characterizations of charismatic masses and the parasitical power elites which live off their backs. The interrelation thus far depicted is one which is mutually destructive and competitive.

The positive view. Alternatively, if both masses and elites are forever with humankind, their relationships may be less competitive than interactional or complementary. This more optimistic ideal would coincide with Confucian and populist teachings elsewhere that every human person is a potential "lover of wisdom," a philosopher-sage, capable of reflecting on direct and second-order experiences of life's more ultimate issues concerning meaning and morals. In this view it is unrealistic to surmise that philosophical elites will cease to exist. But the function of their wisdom might complement rather than literally outclass popular wisdom. Alone, either group will miss part of a varied, pluralistic human wisdom. The lesson is that one should inform oneself about both popular and elitist wisdoms, neither dismissing nor hastily canonizing either. One should accept both refining and productively clarifying ethical analyses and earthy, esthetical, and loving moral characterizations which spark, stir, and wake up the world to moral action.

Together with the more formal, scriptural, philosophical and legal classics, one accordingly searches the popular classics of fables, poetry, stories, dramas, and their current framing within contemporary artistic genres. Both types of sources allow access to the archives of collective moral experience. As for popular classics in particular, even when they are spelled out unsystematically, or with almost no conscious reflection, chapters five and seven will demonstrate that they still offer systemic rationales and justifications for most moral enigmas troubling humankind.

Above all, their esthetical portrayal of model characters, both real and artistic, leads the way to actual social motion. Even reputedly life- and social action-denying groups among Indian Brahmins or Advaitic (non-dualistic) mystics were surprisingly eager to use appeals to Indian *rasas* or esthetical feelings like love, compassion, or abhorrence.

F. *Synopsis of A Hindu Mystical Tradition.*

To imply that one may isolate one Hindu mystical tradition from a plurality may be to speak more theoretically than historically. With this much admitted, one can go on to deal with the soul of Hinduism's structure, according to the conventional opinion, Brahminic mysticism.

Age-old, classical debates fuel still-burning controversies about whether beauty exists only in the eye of the beholder or in the face of the Apollo or Helen beheld. In its most diffuse meaning, does the esthetical experience exist only in the subject ? Does the taste of Beatrice's kiss exist only in the mind of Dante ? The debates have suggested all varieties of fusional compromises which explain how outside harmony, symmetrical variety, and multiple forms achieve reality beyond, or only within the subject.[29] It is hard to deny that it is within the person who perceives that these and other components of the beautiful achieve their integrational metamorphosis as "the beautiful." In those cases of downright filth, ugliness, pain, misunderstanding, tragedy, or the Sartrean nausea of being the object looked at or the subject who stares, it is in the encounter of subject and object that even those components attain both transfiguration and transvaluation.[30] From this perspective the author has previously written that esthetic perception

> is empathetic. It feels oneness with whatever it encounters, without denying its otherness. Since consciousness is not dominated or darkened by the glasses of hostility, it is a "Look-looking" at others which embraces, caresses, and confirms; not a staring which scalds and instrumentalizes. Refusing to judge what is other for its otherness, it projects no judgement on itself.[31]

From a view—note the recurring visual limitation of that metaphor—not far from Buddhistic or Hindu Advaitic ones, lives are an emptiness, a playful *māyā* (illusion), a meaningless theatre of the absurd, endless waitings, transient and even comic reflections of a single moon beyond the light of human comprehension. As the celebrated *Nō* play figure, Matsukaze, Buddhistically announced: "The moon above is one; Below it has two, no three reflections which shine in the flood tide tonight."[32] Her feeling mirrored the historical Buddha's first noble truth about life, that all is *duḥkha*, Dachau, meaningless suffering: "The sufferings of life, old age, sickness, and death—All these in the end shall be destroyed ! May you quickly find salvation."[33] Even for the Buddha's Brahminic predecessors, human ennoblement and bliss (*ānanda*), therefore, consisted not in archetypal integration with one's primal forces, not in the persevering or chained noble dignities of Sisyphus or Prometheus, and not in the expanded mind and heart of Aeneas which was magnified by sufferings and hardships.

From Hindu and other mystical mountaintops, the only natural dynamo for movement either into moral compassion or life's other significant dimensions, is not only trans-sensual and trans-visual, but trans-subjective, that is, beyond the basic illusory duality (*moha*) between the "self" and the other. Neither merely cathartically escapist or individually self-fulfilling, the esthetical experience of the mystic is said to be an inside-out awakening, a joyous, liberating *ecstasis*, that all is one self, one *Ātman*-Brahman, an odyssey beyond space, possible in any time or millennium. At least in some Buddhist, and probably Brahminic Hindu teachings,[34] this *cognitive* awakening comprises four *volitional* dispositions (*brahmavihāras*): love, compassion, sympathetic joy, and impartial, all-loving detached spiritual equanimity towards all forms of life in their tragic illusoriness.

The noble being, whether a Hindu hermit living through the mystical perfection of the last of life's four stages or a Buddhist become *arahant* or *bodhisattva*, is not merely a televolitional well-wisher. Admittedly though, such an attitude was indeed given the most solemn primacy and was thought to be efficacious for others. In particular, the bodhisattva sought *also* to lessen *any* kind of suffering, great and small, every pain, every hunger, even, finally, the thirst for justice. What greater meaning to life than to lighten the staggering sum of its sufferings ?[35] But in the worldview of *samsāra*, the cyclic wheel of endless births of all sentient beings, the great *duḥkha* or misery of every human being is the wheel of life itself. It follows that the cardinal noble truth and the epitome of moral altruism is the extinction of craving, of attachment even to life itself. At the surface, one may say that rebirth into suffering is occasioned by the *karma* (action as breeding its own moral compensation) of one's previous existence. *Karma*, as moral reward and punishment for the past, explains not only pain itself, but its disturbingly inequitable distributions.

The surprise evoked from those who live in those relatively few cultures which have rejected the "rebirth of all people for millennia," may possibly be alleviated by introspective readings of "Western" philosophers from Plato to Jacques Maritain. These thinkers have insisted that a preconscious intuition of some form of pre-existence is undeniably universal. In addition, trans-cultural forms of arts and symbols, universal, psychical and mythic archetypes, ideas, and syntactical processes, the great collective heroes, wishes, dreams and dramas of humankind—all of this evidence, one can argue, is not merely symptomatic of subjectively conscious functions. Rather it constitutes an argument for the reality of reincarnation and, for better or for worse, endless lives.

One may react incredulously to such intense and persistent claims about human existences and cite the comparable universality of superstition. Still the relentless facticity of the claim of previous and continuing lives does not fade away unless or until one can prove that the supposed universality is a ruse, elitist or otherwise. A related but separable conviction attributed to the Hindu masses is that the peak of moral altruism or love and the perfection of all moral cooperation is to occasion for self and others the "self"-awakening which extinguishes the final cause of every evil, namely, attachment to life. Further in some quarters the simplistic reduction of this realization to sleep, "eternal rest," or literal extinction (*nirvāṇa, nibbāna*) meets a hornet's nest of Hindu, Buddhist, and other denials.

To repeat, what is primary about Hindu mystical moral compassion in life is its concern about release from life itself as people now know it. Programs of social ethics and welfare are not thereby bypassed. Rather, every compassionate alleviation of suffering has its relative importance. But programs of social ethics and welfare are merely by-products of life's really noble truths.

In either Hindu or Buddhist mysticism the attenuation and deification of the ultimate teachings about life to sheer morality is a travesty. It is also self-defeating. To cultivate a taste for music, art, beauty, existence or mystical enlightenment as a merely instrumental acculturation of life's essentially moral function is as inane as focusing on a dim star in an attempt to obtain the brightest light for the naked eye. Due to its make-up, it is only when the groping eye is allowed to relax and absorb a wider perspective that it captures what was dim in a fuller brightness. In teachings deemed conventionally Buddhist and Hindu, the focus on morality partakes of a similar fate. One can try too hard. The same seems to be true in Taoism. First, take care of the life of contemplation (an experience not limitedly visual). Then, morality and love will take care of themselves. Those banqueters for whom the taste of morality is first will be the last to be seated.

So much for an outsider's attempted synopsis of what is conventionally called the mystical heart of Hinduism. It is hoped that the reader will tolerate this schema's coarse binding of Hindu and Buddhist teachings, which became so intertwined through centuries of coexistence. This integration was meant to accentuate more clearly the cross-cultural prevalence of the long celebrated and purportedly "good news": if people seek first the kingdom of God, then all other things, morality included, will be added unto them.

Pros and cons. Even outsiders and agnostics may contend that the contemplative worldview's grandeur has not been disqualified, because it has never been fairly tried. Further, as for those who claim the mystical vision as their own, their repeated warning is that "transcendental" insight is incommunicable, at least verbally or conceptually. They add that its possession is achieved only by autonomous, inside-out exertion, even if that be called utterly gratuitous grace. Their critics may formulate the query: "Is it that you are unable to express your experience to others, or that you were never sure or clear about its reality or content for yourself—whether it is illusory or real ?" But the Seer may respond that the question presupposes that experience is real only if it can be rearticulated to oneself in some fashion, notionally, poetically, etc. He points to the analogy of the forgotten moment of beauty or love which a recovered letter or picture may reassure one were once real. When outsiders attempt to repeat what they think they hear mystics saying, they must allow for their own misunderstanding or misinterpretation. Perhaps by such an admission, they may draw a step closer to truth or honesty than what is allowed by mere pretense of grasping the mystical.

On the other side, one may say that claimants of transcending mystical experience suffer a triple temptation: 1) self-deception, 2) selling one's mind to another person, or 3) being swept aloft by the exuberant power and glory which mystical visions imply and inspire. Mystics have often accused their critics of a different temptation : fleeing, refusing, or losing visions once glimpsed or within grasp through egoistic or other defaults. Such accusations are always liable to backfire in a projection of the accuser's own self-judgment. Finally, the sympathetic outsider may conjecture that perhaps the reality of the mystical comes down to whether mystical and moral "intuitions" are ultimately a univocal or single notion. Perhaps they are not reducible to the sudden, creative recognition of a field or profile that was always there. Within Zen Buddhism as well as elsewhere, the most solemn battles have been engaged over whether "transcendental" insight is sudden or gradual, infused or acquired, evolves passively, or is courted actively. Possibly, both alternatives are extremes of a lengthy spectrum. Maybe there are many kinds of intuition. Depending on context, on subjective temperament, on attentiveness, on the frequency, quality, or recentness of preparatory experiences like love and suffering, or, lastly, on the long, laboratory hours of endless inductions, the integrated recognition of fields, minute and large, may happen in a host of individual ways. All of these paths of intuitive recognition may be as different from one another as the singularity of every fingerprint or the uniqueness of every vocal pattern.

As the author has intended no final put-down of mystical insight grounding morality, he makes no final case for it either. But he does caution that to verify or disqualify *some* of its forms the scientific spirit calls for intense descriptive and analytical collaboration. To complete a picture previously sketched in the plea for the priority of the descriptive, if there should be other stellar systems which operate in the more immediate environment of this universe, they cannot be recognized with binoculars alone, but through the painstaking syntheses created by a thousand giant telescopes. Put negatively, if the universe is to be finally scrubbed clean of mystical intuitions, the scientific descriptivist must warn that the repudiation of some forms is not yet the automatic dismissal of all. From a scientific perspective, an overall mystical grounding for morality has been dismissed prematurely. Meanwhile, more systematic collaborations would seem to be the call of the hour. There is the fear, one hopes unfounded, that the question may be closed down by analytical academics, politburos, or the communication programs of international corporations and industries, which direct and control human life and consumption with increasingly computerized, "fraternal" concern.

In sum, not all moral or mystical insights have been dismissed simply because some of them were erroneous, self-contradictory, or contrived. Conventional mystical grounds for morality like historical Hindu mysticism need a fairer cross-examination. 1) Does conventional Hinduism exist conjointly or correlatively with other kinds of Hinduism, like a populist, charismatic life-view which sounds not life-denial but a *l'hayyim* (cheer for life) of its own ? If so, is the latter entirely non-mystical ? 2) Might a fuller description of both populist and conventionally mystical moralities prepare the way for new and more positive syntheses ? Some think not. They feel that Hindu, if not all, mysticism is "constitutionally incapable of moving toward" life-affirmation or modernization. While this verdict may be historically true, it neglects the possibility that if Hindu mysticism is to be taken as the heart of Hindu morality, it might be susceptible, at least theoretically, to reinterpretations, which remain faithful to aspects of a highly pluralistic tradition. If positive mysticisms need not instrumentalize themselves before humanism alone, might they not seek their own goals and the humanistically moral at the same time ? This question, to wich the epilogue will address itself, concerns both the "if" and the "how". In other words, the question of grounding morality in mysticism or elsewhere raises the question of how to *move* on these grounds and whether one can learn anything practical, like morality, without doing it.

G. *A Systematic Glossary of External Structures in Hindu Morality*[36]

For the newcomer to the study of Hindu morality, the number

four can be helpfully mnemonic: four historical periods of Hinduism, four *Goals* of life, four developmental *Stages* of life, four *Classes* of people, and, as this volume will endeavor to demonstrate, at least four pluralistic *Moralities* which became finally two. In this conventional framework of foursomes, only in the last frame will the mold of ordinary interpretations be stretched beyond recognition, reasons for the departure being adduced from the conclusions of each chapter to follow. Not all Hindus would agree with the subsequent diagram of four central *Paths*, four key *Virtues*, four *Vices*, or four *Philosophical Means to Knowledge*, but many would. The fourfold division of *Deities* and *Philosophical Schools* is even more arbitrary, but, again, it is a pedagogical beginning.

A. *Four Goals (Purushārthas) of Life*:

1. *artha*: wealth and power;
2. *kāma*: pleasure and love;
3. *dharma*: teachings in their moral aspect including class teachings (*varṇadharma*) and also general or trans-class morality (*sādhāraṇadharma*), such as the ten general virtues recommended in *The Laws of Manu* for all classes or the four virtues listed below (in F);
4. *moksha* (and *nirvāna*): liberation from the present form of life; the latter term has a variety of sub-meanings.

According to some Hindus, the first three goals (as *trivarga*) operate alone, without the fourth goal.

B. *Four Stages (Āśramas) of Life*:

1. *brahmacarya*: youth-student stage;
2. *grihastha*: householder, married and earning stage;
3. *vānaprastha*: forest ascetic stage, alone, with spouse, or with groups;
4. *sannyāsa*: ascetical-mystical stage, the final stage leading to the goal of *moksha*.

C. *Four Classes (Varṇas) of Society*:

1. *brahmins*: priests, definers of reality, custodians of the royal treasury, and confirmers of royal authority; until the final chapter, the conventional connotations of Brahmins and neo-Brahmins will be respected. Then, it will be suggested that early Brahminism in the Vedic and priestly sense became already *neo-*

Brahminic and life-denying in the mystical and "anti-Vedic" *Upanishads* rather than at later periods.

2. *kshatriyas*: rulers and soldiers;
3. *vaiśyas*: farmers, business people, etc;
4. *śūdras*: the lowest caste or class.

The top three classes have retained power and discrimination mainly against *śūdras* and outcastes until the illegality (at least theoretically) of discriminatory caste (*jāti*) in recent times. Even the reformer M. K. Gandhi was prepared to rationalize the four *varṇas* as traditional, meaningful, and socially functional divisions, vaguely resembling the Pauline metaphor of the parts of the body—all with different but equally important functions. But the many *jātis* in the strict sense were severely, if not effectively, condemned.

D. *Four Competing Moralities* (*Finally Reducible to Two*):

Life-Affirming:

1. Vedic sources: this-worldly morality from the period between 1500 and 1300 B.C.E.; affirmation is especially apparent in the *Rigveda*;
2. Epic, folk, secular, and popular literary sources: epics, devotional literature, dramas, poetry, secular treatises (*śāstras*);

Life-Denying:

3. Legal sources: those *śāstras* which were lawbooks, and Brahminized layers of 1. and 2. above;
4. Priestly and philosophical sources: the four *Vedas*:
   a. the *Rigveda*,
   b. the *Atharvaveda*: on magic formulas;
   c. the *Sāmaveda*: on melodies;
   d. the *Yajurveda*: on sacrificial formulas.

Of the *Vedas*, which were basically collections of sayings (*saṃhitās*), both a. and b. had moral implications, especially the former. The *Vedas* went through three stages of further evolution after their initial influence (giving them a *four-fold* life span.) They were eventually related to the priestly *Brāhmaṇas*, which were prose commentaries on sacrificial rites. The *Brāhmaṇas* evolved into the *Upanishads*, which word literally means "secret documents". Finally, a fourth stage of their existence can be posited since the *Upanishads* were systematized into short sayings or *sūtras* called the *Brahma*

Sūtras or the *Vedānta Sūtras* (*vedānta* means "end of the *Vedas*"). While some writers limit the term *Veda* to the first stage (a.—d.), others extend it to include the *Upanishads*. For the discussion of Vedic interpretations, see J. below.

E. *Four Paths* (*mārgas*) *of Life*:

1. *karma mārga*; the path of action; this is called by some *karma yoga*;
2. *bhakti mārga*; the path of devotion;
3. *jñāna mārga*: the path of knowledge or contemplation;
4. *yoga* or *rāja-yoga*: the path of yoga; not all accept the inclusion of this as a *mārga*.

F. *Four Virtues*:

1. *ahimsā*: non-injury; this was made famous by Gandhi's program of non-violence;
2. *dāna*: giving;
3. *satya*: truthfulness;
4. *niṣkāma karma*: non-attached action; this was promoted by the *Gitā*, Gandhi, and other religions.

There are of course many more cardinal virtues, but these four were selected because of their importance to this study. It should be noted that *dāna* is connected with *dayā* (compassion), and may also be related to the *four* compassionate virtues (*brahmavihāras*) which are of Hindu as well as Buddhist origin:

a. *maitrī*: loving friendliness;
b. *karuṇā*: compassion;
c. *muditā*: sympathetic joy;
d. *upekṣā*: equanimity; this was the highest of all for the early Buddhist, but simply one of an integral four for others.

G. *Four Vices*:

1. *himsā*: injury of any sentient being;
2. *ahaṃkāra*: too much ego;
3. that engendered by *avidyā* (non-knowledge) or *moha* (delusion): thinking of this world as finally real instead of illusory *māyā*;
4. that engendered by lack of *dama*: lack of self-restraint or application.

As with the virtues, there are many other vices. Number 3 is considered a vice because only Brahman, with whom each individual is to be identified, is real—at least in formal, canonical, philosophical, and especially Vedāntic thought.

H. *Four Gods or Manifestations of Brahman* (*Avatārs*):

1. Brahman: the Absolute, conceived personally/theistically or impersonally/non-theistically;

Manifested in:

2. Brahmā: creator;
3. Īśvara;
4. Vishṇu, and the duos Rāma/Sītā, Krishna/Rādhā, and Śiva/Kālī.

Actually, there is a god for every household, but these reappear most frequently in this study. Other famous gods who took their turns (henotheistically) in the devotional limelight were Varuṇa, god of moral order (*ṛta*, *rita*), *Ṛta*, sometimes personalized, Prajāpati, and the war-god, Indra.

I. *Four Philosophical Means to Knowledge* (*Pramāṇas*):

1. *pratykṣa*: perception (intuition ?);
2. *anumāna*: reason or inference by consequences;
3. *śabda* and *sadācāra*: human authority and custom;
4. divine authority.

Divine authority passed on mystically/theistically/devotionally is originally transmitted orally (*śruti*). Divine authority initially passed on through texts and orally is called *smṛti* (recollection or tradition). But this method of transmission sometimes functions equally with *śruti,* that passing of texts orally or the process through which a text is "heard" (not externally revealed but inwardly realized).

J. *Philosophical Schools* (*Darśanas*):

1. *Nyāya-Vaiśeṣika*;
2. *Sāṃkhya and Yoga*;
3. *Pūrva Mimāṃsā*;
4. *Uttara Mimāṃsā or Advaita Vedānta*: the latter being the "non-dualistic end of the *Vedas*".

See D. above. The *Vedānta Sūtras*, rather than the four earliest *Vedas*, became, along with the *Upanishads* and the later, more devotional *Gītā*, the main topic of commentary by the philosophical schools or *darśanas* (literally, "points of view"). Six principal schools have been called orthodox (*āstika*). For the sake of pedagogical fourness, they are here compressed to four. Unlike Buddhism or Jainism, they attribute authority to the *Vedas*, even while disagreeing on some basic interpretative points. The most powerful school, *Advaita Vedānta*, with its greatest exponent, Śaṅkara, is the topic of chapter eight. Non-dualism refers to lack of duality between Brahman and finite reality. Accordingly, every being or self (*ātman*) is really Self or *Ātman*, being identical with Brahman—if one could only shelve delusion and realize this. Of the two greatest Advaitic philosophers, Śaṅkara and Rāmānuja, the latter attempted to qualify his non-dualism by reattributing personality or attributes to Brahman. In so doing, he lost popularity in the more modern philosophical revival.

NOTES

1. For the unconscious and philosophically normative assumptions which usually, or perhaps always, underlie attempts at purely descriptive ethics, see Douglas Sturm, "The Priority of the Philosophical Question: A Response to David Little on Max Weber," *Journal of Religious Ethics* 2,2 (Fall 1974), 41-52. It is left to the reader to decide if my five sets of questions put to descriptive materials are philosophically normative or are ones which can be asked with no norms in view. For purposes of objective clarity, if not creative contribution, I divulge my own normative preferences or assumptions in the epilogue, just in case the reader will not have guessed them already (for example: creative life-affirmation, the priority of the death-instinct as the greatest of evils, and preferential openness to those mystical claims which, without instrumentalizing themselves, coequally lead to cooperative social action). I have analyzed elsewhere a number of prerequisites for explicit endeavors which presume to move from descriptive ethics to prescription. See Roderick Hindery, "Exploring Comparative Religious Ethics," *Journal of Ecumenical Studies* 10,3 (Summer 1973), 552-74. As for the actual usage of the ambivalent term "religion," the same essay delineates its persevering connections with trans-humanistic symbol systems about meaning, identity, and human behavior. The same applies to East Asian analogues for "religion" like *dharma, tao, or chiao*, which refer additionally to ethics and esthetics.

2. At a recent national symposium, lawyers and other specialists generally argued together that international law cannot function viably without some inter-cultural ethical agreements. Such a principle might be exemplified in Francisco de Vitoria's (c. 1492-1546, the theoretical father of international law) cutely rhetorized maxim: "What if the American Indians had 'discovered' Europe? Quid tunc? (What then?)" See D. P. O'Connell, "The Role of International Law" in *Conditions of World Order*, ed. Stanley Hoffman (Boston: Houghton Mifflin Company, 1968). For a summary of these trends and related bibliography see M. P. Golding, "History of the Philosophy of Law," *The Encyclopedia of Philosophy* VI, ed. Paul Edwards (New York: Macmillan Pub-

lishing Co., Inc. and the Free Press, 1967), 254-264. One may also consult the bibliographies of fifteen sister or cross-referenced articles in this encyclopedia; as well as John N. Hazard, *Communists and Their Law: A Search for the Common Core of The Legal Systems of The Marxian Socialistic States* (Chicago: The University of Chicago Press, 1969), esp. pp. 519-28; and Ghita Ionescu, *Comparative Communist Politics* (London: The Macmillan Press, 1972) and *Philosophy East and West: Symposium on Law and Morality: East and West* 21, 4 (October 1971).

3. When the authority of either vertical or contemporary consensus of opinion is isolated from its lifeblood, that is, from the distillation of collective experience, it begins to function as physical or psychological force—authority as authority. Consequently, descriptive ethics is particularly alert when authorities commence to act in various coercive forms. Even assent to religious authority, which invests collective groups, hierarchies, or individuals with the mark of infallibility, must finally recognize that authoritative claims are not self-evident. Otherwise, no need for the authoritative. Neither can an allegation of inerrancy be traced circularly to the original claimant's inerrancy, as it has been historically attempted. If authority's superior titles are not bestowed solely by majority vote (since majorities can be wrong), neither can they escape individual assent. In other words, personally generated decision for or against authority is intransigently its own "hound of heaven," a point of conscience taught by the historical Buddha long before the English poet, Francis Thompson, or Vatican II, or, in part, Martin Luther. In short, no authority is inerrant for anyone, unless one has *a priori* or previously determined that the authority is incapable of error. However, one could not reasonably decide on the "authority's authority," apart from its fruits, an immediate insight or a wider, alleged "experience" of the true or the holy.

4. See John C. Plott, *A Philosophy of Devotion* (Delhi: Motilal Banarsidass, 1974), pp. 281-83 and 336-60.

5. Beneath the oceans of laws in which practically free individuals swim at their peril, there is evidence that customs and laws have been only feebly enforced, broken, and unable to extinguish irrepressible individual aspirations which inspired and recorded themselves in collections of popular classics. The struggle between the individual and social structures is incompletely narrated by formal religious and legal classics alone. The latter's escalating sanctions, threats, and repetitiveness betray the survival of individual freedom, even in the most totalitarian circumstances—a point illustrated in recent Soviet and Chinese writings. Aware of these phenomena, the ethical descriptivist is similarly attentive to the difference between narration and didactic approval of oppressions of freedom, civil, sexual, etc.

6. In field interviews persons can become so impressed with the interrelational complexity of the real, non-bookish situation, that, even as amateurs, they can quickly begin to suspect certain pitfalls for interviews. The first one is to assume, without due warrant, that "a single informant may be taken as representative of the group." The second most obvious enticement is the delusion that months or years of field experience can wash away the taint of outside spectator and confer the grace of cultural insider efficaciously. Third

is one which professional field workers would avoid scrupulously: the neglect of the written word or symbol for the tape recorder and the camera. The vast majority of human beings are no longer living and available for taped interview. Moreover, even living persons, Marshall McCluhan included, still choose to record some of their most examined reflections in the style of characters, pictographs, or words which can be made linear by others. The urban graffiti explosion is a mere token of the irrepressibility of the linear.

7. See, for example, findings which arise from the chiefly secondary sources of Edward E. Westermarck's (1862-1939) *The Origin and Development of Moral Ideas* II (London: Macmillan and Co., Limited, 1917), 755-835. This sociologist's categorically subjectivistic and emotivist ethical views, together with his emphasis on basic cross-cultural divergences, might have been more accurately qualified, if his ethical resources had been more representatively primary.

8. The popular impact of this sadistic novel appears in the need felt by the Chinese Communist Press to continue to censure it for its imperialistic and allegedly "Confucian" ethos. For a summary and commentary confer C. T. Hsia, *The Classic Chinese Novel* (New York: Columbia University Press, 1968).

9. See above all Weber's *Ancient Judaism*, 1952 and *The Religion of India*, 1958, both trans. by H. H. Gerth and D. Martindale (Glencoe, Illinois: Free Press); *Protestant Ethic and The Spirit of Capitalism*, trans. Talcott Parsons (New York: Charles Scribner's Sons, 1958), *Sociology of Religion* trans. F.H. Knight (New York: Collier Books, 1961); and *The Religion of China*, trans. H. H. Gerth (New York: The Free Press, 1951).

10. To borrow Hume's metaphor about the need for painters as well as anatomists, other central contributions will spring up from people more directly oriented to subject syntheses, the painters. If every reality, like every atom, is both a subspecies and yet a universe for its own components, both part of a macrocosm and also a microcosm, then creative new syntheses will continue to emanate from concrete realities or topical subjects. Perhaps some day universities will rename some of their departments and schools after realistic topics like "studies in propaganda," "the department of studies in consumer exploitation," or "the school of global starvation." Clear and productive thinking towards any imaginative overview presupposes experience cultivatible within present fields. But the interdisciplinary generalist's concentration may shift from his or her original arena to topical subjects of concern, particularly if the latter, say a real issue in religion or ethics, should achieve more than epiphenomenal recognition.

11. See Kai Nielsen's verdict on the limitedly Anglo-American and normative character of Stephen Toulmin's analysis of moral language in "History of Ethics," *The Encyclopedia of Philosophy* III. In this lengthy article, Nielsen's summation of twentieth-century ethics and the representativeness of the "good reasons approach" is as instructive as his subsequent work on "Problems of Ethics," ibid., 117-34.

12. See his *The Meeting of East and West: An Inquiry Concerning World Understanding* (New York, Macmillan Co., 1946).

13. Among Raju's several works see his *Introduction to Comparative Philosophy*

(Carbondale, Illinois: Southern Illinois University Press, 1962), pp. 280,311, and 317-18. This work is a rare, if not unique, improvement over the dated work of Masson-Oursel, *Comparative Philosophy* (London Kegan Paul, Trench, Trubner, and Co., 1926).

14. Just as many East Asians would reject endeavors to distinguish ethics, esthetics, and religion, others would play down populist-elitist divisions. This volume's comments on religion are summarized in n. 1 and later in this chapter. In addition to Joachim Wach's classics on comparative religion and "types," see Joseph M. Kitagawa's classification in "Primitive, Classical, and Modern Religions" in *The History of Religions*: *Essays on The Problem of Understanding*, ed. J. M. Kitagawa (Chicago: The University of Chicago Press, 1967) and a similar entry of diverse essays co-edited with Mircea Eliade in 1959. Wach treats his types (charismatic leader, Seer, Audience, pp. 331-73) most immediately in his *Sociology of Religion* (Chicago: University of Chicago Press, 1944), along with reference to the much earlier typologies of the comparative pioneers, William James and Friedrich Hegel; see pp. 9 and 45. More recent classifications of the term "religion" may be found in David Little and Summer B. Twiss, Jr., "Basic Terms in the Study of Religious Ethics," in *Religion and Morality*, ed. by Gene Outka and John P. Reeder, Jr., (Garden City New York: Anchor Press/Doubleday, 1973), pp. 60-61 and James Smurl's *Religious Ethics*: *A Systems Approach* (Englewood Cliffs, New Jersey: Prentice-Hall, Inc. 1972). Like Smurl, Little and Twiss take the term "religion" in its interpretational or meaning-giving function. In particular they see religion dealing with three interpretive problems of life: nature, suffering and death, and human conduct. Patrick Burke adds Marxian fourth, the problem of social structures, in his *Searching in the Syntax of Things*, co-authored by M. Friedman and S. Laeuchli (Philadelphia: Fortress Press, 1972), pp. 39-51 and in his *The Reluctant Vision* (Philadelphia: Fortress Press, 1974), pp. 62-69.

15. See my article referred to above n. 1, and also Roderick Hindery, "Pluralism in Moral Theology: Reconstructing Universal Ethical Pluralism," in *CTSA Proceedings*, 1973, 71-94.

16. I was brought to defend this thesis in my doctoral dissertation entitled *The Disinterested Love of God*...., (Rome: Academia Alfonsiana/Lateran University, 1962).

17. Various rationales for the "good reasons approach" and representative proponents are discussed by Kai Nielsen in his "History of Ethics," 110, for example: Phillipa Foot, A. I. Melden, Kurt Baier, Georg von Wright, and John Rawls. Although some philosophers like Bertrand Russell, and, more recently, Joseph Margolis, modestly insist that all personal and cultural valuations are simply partisan convictions, they defend personal positions and manifestos quite vigorously. These spring from human disagreements about what is good to the consequent normative necessity of non-interference with the decisions of others. From this initially *laissez-faire* premise, a whole moral system can be built as was done by J. S. Mill in the nineteenth century. See Margolis, *Values and Conduct* (New York: Oxford University Press, 1971), pp. 211-12.

18. Iris Murdoch, *The Sovereignty of Good* (New York: Schocken Books,

1971), p. 103. See also Richard S. Peters, *Reason and Compassion* (London and Boston: Routledge and Kegan Paul, 1973).

19. Thomas Nagel, like Kant and Nagel's influential and immediate mentor, John Rawls, attempted to build altruism not on intuition but on so-called "rationality" in *The Possibility of Altruism* (Oxford: Clarendon Press, 1970), p. 144; David Little did the same in "Comparative Religious Ethics," in *The Study of Religion in Colleges and Universities*, ed. Paul Ramsey and John Wilson (Princeton, New Jersey: Princeton University Press, 1970), pp. 229-230. In his *Agape: An Ethical Analysis* (New Haven: Yale University Press, 1972), Gene Outka summarizes the problem in the context of twentieth century *Christian* contributions to this age-old controversy about the meaning of *agape* or "disinterested love." He examines the thought of theorists like Barth, the Niebuhrs, Nygren, Gilleman, D'Arcy, and Johann. The debate's long history had been summarized magisterially by Anders Nygren, *Eros and Agape* trans. P. S. Watson (New York: Harper and Row, 1969), within the framework of *agape* entailing a kind of self-hatred and realization of one's human sinfulness. Continuing divergences about the possibility of love or *agape* in the present life may be related to conflicting anthropologies of how evil or good people are. In my opinion, apocalyptic and other notions of human depravity have been worked to death, even if for ecumenical or rhetorical purposes only. A restoration of the human self-image is long overdue.

20. Reference in fn. 15 above.

21. Weber, *Protestant Ethics*, p. 182.

22. See ibid., pp. 29-31 and Weber's *Ancient Judaism*, pp. xii-xiii.

23. See *Protestant Ethic*, p. 281 n. 105 and David Little "Max Weber and the Comparative Study of Religious Ethics," *Journal of Religious Ethics* 2,2 (Fall 1974), 28.

24. See, for example, *Ancient Judaism*, pp. 397-98.

25. Little described Weber's rational ethic as a this-worldly consequentialism, (*Zweckrationalität*), either absolutistic or relativistic, especially the latter. See "Max Weber," 6,7, 15, 20, 24, and 26.

26. Weber, *Protestant Ethic*, pp. 30 and 186 n. 11.

27. "Max Weber," 32.

28. Hsia, *The Chinese Novel* p. 82.

29. See Monroe Beardsley, "Aesthetics, History of;" and John Hospers, "Aesthetics, Problems of," *The Encyclopedia of Philosophy* I, 18-55.

30. See Jerome Stolnitz, "Ugliness," *The Encyclopedia of Philosophy* VIII, 174-76.

31. Roderick Hindery, "Marcuse's Eroticized Man," *Christian Century*, February 4, 1970.

32. Donald Keene, ed., *Twenty Nō Plays of The Nō Theatre* (New York: Columbia University Press, 1970) pp. 25 and 29.

33. Ibid., p. 47.

34. See the Hindu *Yogasūtra of Patañjali* 1.33 and the Buddhist *Dīgha Nikāya* III. 1.224 and IV.76.233.

35. This inversion of the nineteenth century British utilitarian principle of the greatest happiness for the most people has been used by Iris Murdoch and Stephen Toulmin. It was carefully explained to me from this Buddhist

point of view by the well known writer about living Buddhist experiences, John Blofeld.

36. Aside from direct quotations, which employ many conflicting and inconsistent systems, Sanskrit and Pali transliteration in this volume sometimes extends that employed by Wm. T. de Bary, ed., *Sources of Indian Tradition* I (New York: Columbia University Press, 1958), pp. 521-24. This volume's employment of the abbreviations following the table of contents now begins in chapter two. Further inquiries into specific topics may be pursued through tool-books like Charles J. Adams, *A Reader's Guide to the Great Religions* (New York: The Free Press, 1965); the works of Wm. T. de Bary referred to *passim* and *International Bibliography of The History of Religions*, ed. by *Numen's* C. J. Bleeker and compiled by H. Boas and S. H. Alish (Leiden, Netherlands: Brill, 1952-1975). The eighteen volumes survey the years 1952-71.

CHAPTER II

ETHICS IN THE RIGVEDA

Abstract. A. Introduction: (1) the moral relevance of Vedic antiquity: the principle of historical proportionality in Vedic reasoning from consequences of behavior like gambling; application and antiquity as such; (2) antiquity as authority: human authority, collective experience. *B. Classes.* Traces of racial and sexual slavery ? *C. Morality or mores?* Three views: either or both. *D. The Ethos of giving* (*dāna*) and the effects of not giving; (2) *The life-affirmative ethos* of the "Hymn to Dawn" as opposed to later stress on mystical liberation from this life (*moksha*). *E. The evolution of moral justification* from a resort to *rita* as impersonal order and then as divine authority. *F. Conclusion.* The pre-Aryan and pre-priestly Vedic senses of sin (*pāpa*) and life-affirmation. Is sin integral to a moral point of view ? The transition to the mystical morality of the *Ups*, from ritual action to Upanishadic questions. NOTES.

A. Introduction: 1) *The Moral Relevance of Vedic Antiquity*: *The Principle of Historical Proportionality in Vedic Reasoning From Moral Consequences.* "Provincial," "nationalistic," and "chauvinistic" are designations which variously convey the unwarranted exclusion of a broader understanding of people and life. What a term like "provincial" evokes through the image of space, "passee" describes in time, but with a denotation limited to what focuses on the past. Less precise are linguistic and conceptual tools for expressing what "provincially" fixates on the present and the future. To enshrine the past is to embalm it. But to ignore the past or to peer at it narcissistically, as a mere preview of the present, does not enhance the future. It narrows it.

For persons who wish to make space for literary antiquity within their particular walls of time, a good test case would be a study of the Vedic collections (*saṃhitās*) of hymns and rituals called *mantras* or *maṇḍalas* (mystical phrases, 1500-1300 B.C.E.), especially the most ancient *Rigveda* (*Rv*) or *Songs of Praise.* Preliminary to an inquiry into their moral content, the *Vedas* may be used to illustrate two innate hermeneutical or interpretive problems concerning the relevance of documents which are especially ancient. These obstacles will be met in all but the last chapter of the present work. The first obstacle concerns application to the present; the second, antiquity as such.

Application. Granted that a more cosmopolitan acquaintance with past peoples and cultures is worthwhile in itself, not all persons wish to prescind indefinitely from what is going to be "done" with knowledge and understanding of the past. They are persuaded that they are digging for utilitarian lessons under the rocks of history's mistakes, if not its successes. As a result, the logic of avoiding diffuse pursuits compels them to ask, recurrently and with increasing precision, what they are searching for and why. They inquire whether their quest is to support the status quo, to change it, or to satisfy other preoccupations. Further, when ancient behavioral guidelines are discovered, the utilitarian students of history must ask if these are to be retraced and transferred literally, fundamentalistically. Or are they to be redrawn only analogously, with a feel for relativity, proportionality, or the paradigmatic "as" and "so"? *As* the Trojan horse concealing Greek soldiers brought surprise and destruction to the people of Troy, *so* what constitutes Trojan horses for people today?

When the historical quest is directed to guidelines which are moral, this fundamental interpretive or hermeneutical principle of historical proportionality is particularly important. The ancient Rigvedic ballad of the gambler illustrates this, while offering the reader an immediate introduction into the moral reasoning found in this collection (*Rv* X. 34. 1-11).

The Vedic gambler lists several consequences of his behavior which bring him sadness. The contemporary moral interpreter can thereby navigate in two directions, by letter or by spirit. Literally, the gambler is one who risks *wealth* to gain more wealth. Analogously, he is simply one who takes unwarranted risks. In the latter view he barters many things: safety for additional time, future health for present productivity, the growth of personal relationships for a more illustrious career, etc. For either of these readings the literal effects of the gambling described in the *Rv* appear surprisingly contemporary: financial debts and destruction, harm to spouse and relatives, rejection by the same, continuing fear, and compulsive gambling in spite of increasing problems.

Dice, verily, are armed with goads and driving-hooks, deceiving and tormenting, causing grievous woe.
They give frail gifts and then destroy the man who wins, thickly anointed with the player's fairest good.
The gambler's wife is left forlorn and wretched;....
In constant fear, in debt, and seeking riches....
Play not with dice; do cultivate thy corn-land. Enjoy the gain, and deem that wealth sufficient (X.34.7, 10,13).[1]

Aside from the interest of this picture for those who would learn from it normatively, one sees immediately an ancient Vedic method of verifying moral claims: by reasoning from consequences (consequentialism).

Antiquity. Another basic interpretive problem concerns antiquity, or rather its supposedly inherent authority. At first impression it is easy to infer from historical studies of morality that antiquity engenders accuracy. For some critics, the trouble with this inference stems from the obvious flaws or contradictions in many age-old action guides. Pauline injunctions curtail slavery without abolishing it. Muslim *shariáh* improved the social conditions of women without liberating them. Ancient religious codes proscribed the excesses of wars rather than their causes. Therefore, if age bears a relationship to moral reliability, the correlation has to be analogously directional rather than literal. With this limitation in view, the axiom that antiquity symbolizes moral accuracy may operate out of a rationale like the following.

First, the age of a norm attests to its lack of parochialism in terms of time. A norm has functioned "cross-culturally" by way of chronology, if not cartography. What has worked cross-culturally in a time-crossing, trans-temporal, or diachronic sense may be more prone to succeed again. Or, what has failed less frequently in a variety of situations is thought to have a better chance when repeated.

Second, the longevity of an action guide's existence can be indicative of the respect it factually commands from increasing numbers of people and, as a result, is an argument from a chronologically vertical consensus. Of course, as was indicated in chapter one, if unanimity of opinion is taken simply as a form of classical disputation by authority, like all arguments from authority as such, it is the weakest of rationales. But it contains and often conceals the more profound realization that an individual might enrich personal or first-order experience by appropriating that of other individuals or groups. If the generation of three and a half millennia have assented to and passed on the tale of the gambler in the *Rv* as reflective of lessons they too have learned, then an individual today might profit from that considerable accumulation of human knowledge in contrast to his or her own limitations. Although even that total composite of experience remains as fallible as the human components which constitute it, the point emphasized here is that appeal to antiquity is primarily, radically, or in its literal roots, an argument from experience rather than from authority as such. One may insist that the Vedic gambler has no authority of his own, either human or divine. Nevertheless, it is his experience of behavioral effects which one is invited to assimilate or reject.

It is true that at some undetermined point the *Rv* was recognized as possessing the credentials of divinely inspired *śruti* (that which is inwardly heard or realized, the Hindu equivalent for "scriptures"). At that point *śruti* began to function as a validation of moral action which was more complex than a mere appeal to experience. The lingering presence of this appeal gainsays the generalization of Max Weber that legitimation "by the sanctity of tradition is the most universal primitive case," but it also supports the position that ancient justifications of morality call for an analytical apparatus more sensitive and complex than Weber's.

2. *Antiquity as authority*. As was just implied, Hindus' references to Vedic knowledge or wisdom eventually became the grounds for their claims of orthodoxy against Buddhists, Jainists, and others who rejected them. Their own authority was a mysterious or even numinous sense of religio-moral realization within the Seer. Those anonymous Seers, (*Rishis*), or Nobles (*Aryas*) who handed down the *Vedas* are said to have disclaimed personal authorship. Implicitly, at least, a trans-human source of moral and religious truths was affirmed. It was indistinguishable both from the original Seers and from the later Upanishadic Brahmins who would claim succession to the Seers' reputedly divine authority. In theoretical contrast to later classical texts like *Manu*, the epics, or the *Vs*, the *Vedas* are not mere "recollections," "equivalent tradition," or elaborations

of truths (*smritis*). They are alleged to be truths heard (*śruti*) or, in an inside-out sense, revealed. Not "revealed" in the sense of divine, outside intervention, they were—in non-Hindu language —inwardly inspired.

In their dimension as divinely binding commands, the *Vedas* were called laws or *śāstras*. As traditions they were called *āgamas*. It is conceivable that some Hindus attributed a divine origination to the Vedas simply as an attempt to express their great antiquity and the considerable value which antiquity can sometimes reflect. Conversely, greater age than evidence duly warrants may have been assigned to them to symbolize belief in their supra-human genesis. In either case, for early Hindus, the age of the *Vedas* was related to their divine authorship and authority.

The divinities who speak within or sanction the Vedic sayings are many. They are sinless models for human conduct, especially the god Varuṇa. Further, they are the final source of cosmic *rita*: rite become right, the right and the literally "straight" as opposed to the "crooked" ("crooks" in the modern personal form, IV. 23). The Āryan idea of a divine moral ruler was also held by pre-Indic Āryans, including the followers of Zoroaster (628-551 B.C.E.). The relationships of the Āryan devotees to gods were not merely obediential, but theistic/polytheistic, personally devotional (prefiguring *bhakti*), and even familial (*Rv* VIII. 47.2 and X.42.9). Devotional and moral behavior were to win devotees heavenly resurrection. Such positive ethical symbols underscore the life-affirmative nature of the *Vedas*. In contrast to the later Upanishadic revitalization of pre-Vedic asceticism (*śramaṇism*), there is definite hostility to asceticism as in *Rv* VIII, 3.9. It seems as though there is only one *āśrama* (stage of life), the householder's. Even Brahmins, who were then still far more priestly than mystical or philosophical, were highly conscious of the importance of progeny.

The point at hand behind these introductory remarks about Vedic content is that antiquity was employed as a device meant to lend authority to the Vedic prescriptions—at least for Hindus. For outsiders, the alleged antiquity typifies recourse to primal experience (rather than authority) in its deepest and most reliable sense. Even for non-Hindu observers, it must be admitted that the question of the *Vedas*' vintage is independently exciting. In the contention of many scholars, they comprise the oldest literary—if not archaeological—monuments in the planet's history.

Part of the musty, mysterious, and seemingly numinous atmosphere of the *Vedas* may stem from cryptic formulations capable of plural meanings. It may also derive from religious and mythopoeic contents and legends. But the *Vedas*' ancestry is still impressive, even if—according to more conservative estimates—they can only be traced back to 1500-1300 B.C.E. Since critical textual evidence has not yet helped scholars to disentangle the various chronological layers of the *Vedas*, a scrupulously scientific judgment has to steer clear of fixed dates. On the authority of the respected Moriz Winternitz, the development of Vedic literature can be scientifically situated between the outside dates of 2500 and 500 B.C.E. This dating would not be as exact as the current conjectures about the earliest layers of the Hebrew Pentateuch in the ninth and eighth centuries B.C.E. Furthermore, if Venkatarama Raghavan is correct that Vedic religious concepts originated in a common heritage shared by the Āryans, the Hittites (c. 2000 B.C.E.), and the Mitannis of Asia Minor (fifteenth-fourteenth centuries B.C.E.), the outside possibility of a common cross-cultural moral legacy may also be inferred by those interested in doing so.

In the present phase of critical studies of the *Vedas*, it seems less possible to affirm moral ideas in high profile than to question those who see previews there of all the major seminal ideas of Hindu ethics. Morality, of course, like amorality and beauty, exists partly in the eye of the beholder. One's subjective presuppositions or interpretive models color one's findings. As is true of many ancient and cryptic or polyvalent texts like the *Vedas* or the Chinese *Tao Te Ching*, it is possible to see the *Rv* at several points along a spectrum which ranges from moral statements to amoral rituals. For those operating with an evolutionary model, all the key, embryonic concepts of Hindu ethics are allegedly discernible. The more spiritual goals (*puruṣārthas*) and stages (*āśramas*) of life, as well as *saṃsāra-karma* (the wheel of rebirth with moral compensation from previous lives), are proclaimed to be as visible as universal commands, virtues, and detachment from egoism.[2] Few have yet taken the trouble to challenge, let alone refute such contentions with critical evidence.

However, data here will indicate that, apart from giving (*dāna*) and some common-sense moral logic, those elements may be visible only to the x-ray sight of revisionistic eyes.

On the other hand, of several ideas basically affecting Hindu ethics and possibly visible in low profile, two should be singled out: 1) class, and 2) sin in a moral sense. Subsequently, the reader's attention will be turned to three additional moral notions whose positive presence is more striking, namely: giving, life-affirmation, and *rita*.

B. *Classes* (*varṇas*, literally colors, as distinguished from the innumerable *jātis* or more clearly discriminatory castes).

Interpreters who function out of reformist presuppositions would herald the absence or infrequent occurrence of certain materials in the *Vedas* as a confirmation of their own social ideals. For example, there are no statements denying sexual equality or class equality. Class is wrong, some reformers argue, because it is not positively supported by the *Vedas*. Apparent *Rv* allusions to class as well as to priesthood can be played down as later accretions or as evolutionary mutations never meant to flower within orthodox Hinduism. Contrarily, other reformers have accepted and affirmed the Vedic authenticity of *Rv* statements about class—distinguishing sharply between discriminatory caste (*jāti*) and socially functional and non-discriminatory classes (*varṇas*). I.C. Sharma's attribution of a metaphysical and social necessity for *varṇas* is a typical explanation of the *Rv* hymn about *Purusha* (man typified ?)

> 1. Thousand-headed was the Puruṣa, thousand-eyed, thousand-footed. He embraced the earth on all sides, and stood beyond the breadth of ten fingers. 2. The Puruṣa is this all, that which was and which shall be. He is Lord of immortality, which he grows beyond through (sacrificial) food. 3. Such is his greatness, and still greater than that is the Puruṣa. One fourth of him is all beings. The three fourths of him is immortal in Heaven.[3]

Subsequent verses describe the sacrifice of Puruṣa by other gods.

> From his sacrificed body developed the world, animals, and classes of men. 11. When they divided the Puruṣa, into how many parts did they arrange him ? What was his mouth ? What are his two arms ? What are his thighs and feet called ? 12. The *brahmin* was his mouth, his two arms were made the

> *rājanya* (warrior), his two thighs the *vaiśya* (trader and agriculturalist), from his feet the *śūdra* (servile class) was born (X.90).[4]

Class is of divine origin or part of the very nature of the cosmos. But to identify this single passage as a Vedic justification for later forms of caste discrimination would be as precipitous as to utilize the Pauline passage about the body's parts and their different functions (1 Cor. 12:4-31) as grounds for justifying current maldistribution in the ownership of the means and fruits of production. P. V. Kane attempts to argue that Vedic classes or varṇas were opposite to castes (*jātis*) which were more unquestionably discriminatory (as in *Manu* I.118 and VII.41). Vedic classes emphasized not hereditary, unjust rights, but duties based on profession, culture, and, as Kane put it, race.[5]

Interestingly, Kane indicates that the four groups referred to in *Rv* X.90 are not really specified as "*varṇas*" although in subsequent history they acquired that nomenclature. The authentic *varṇas* of Vedic origin are not four but two. They are to be literally understood as classes based on the color of the skin. In *Rv* I.104.2, a scene emerges where two groups oppose one another: the nobles or Āryas supported by the god, Indra, and the native, dark-skinned *dāsas*.

> (I.104.2). These men have come to Indra for assistance; shall he not quickly come upon these pathways ? May the Gods quell the fury of the Dāsa, and may they lead our folk to happy fortune.[6] (I.130.8). Indra in battles helps his Āryan worshipper, he who hath hundred helps at hand in every fray, in frays that win the light of heaven. Plaguing the lawless he gave up to Manu's seed (i.e., man), the dusky skin; Blazing, 'twere, he burns each covetous man away, he burns the tyrannous away.[7]

If neither classes nor discriminatory castes (*jātis*) are yet present, the foundations for racial prejudice seem ineluctably manifest, although the notion is missing in Weber's detailed account of Indian caste.[8] The same may be affirmed of sexual differentiation and sexual slavery, if not of slavery in general: "A gift of fifty female slaves hath Trasadasyu given me, Purukutsa's son, Most liberal, kind, lord of the brave" (*Rv* VIII.19).[9] The Vedic approval of female slavery is not as vigorous, however, as the general approval of slavery recorded in the extant copy of the Mesopotamian *Code of Hammurabi.* (The dating of this text is much later than Hammurabi's reign between 1728 and 1686 B.C.E.). While the latter's code may mirror only part of the culture's general civilization, it records minimal regard for women in general and a detailed sense of equity concerning male property rights which were textually buttressed by the death penalty.[10]

As for the Vedic teaching on slavery, one of its more solemn ramifications is that it did not extend morality beyond the Aryan in-group. Either the *dāsas*, and women in some respects, are disqualified as human beings, or else moral responsibility embraces only the Āryan elite instead of all persons. While one cannot clearly infer yet that the whole of the *Vedas* is oriented merely to the in-group, neither is there adequate evidence to the contrary. The phenomenon of in-group morality is, of course not limited to ancient societies. Neither does it relegate those civilizations to a lower stage of moral development. Even today, the phenomenon of the in-group or elite may help explain how the annual global starvation of over sixty million persons—ten *yearly* "holocausts" also needing publicity—can be practically ignored, tolerated, or nearly obliterated from public consciousness. This is to say nothing of other inter-group or international evils perpetrated against the resources and rights of present and future generations.

C. *Morality With Sin or Mere Mores*? If, as is sometimes claimed, Vedic mores leave morality, and especially sin, in the background, are they necessarily amoral? Even moralistic people admit the existence of social infractions which are not sinful in a moral sense. But sin as an evil harmful to self/others, not finally reducible to mere ignorance, freely and responsibly willed by an individual, is a highly problematic notion in Asian religions in general. It is particularly slippery in the cryptic *Rv* where it is not entirely clear that sin is always perpetrated consciously.[11]

> If we, as gamblers cheat at play, have cheated, whether in truth or without knowing, all that loose from us, O God. So may we be dear to thee, O Varuṇa. Whatever sin is found in me, whatever evil I have wrought, If I have lied or falsely sworn, Waters, remove it far from me (V.85.8).

Furthermore, the prayer for divine retribution on enemies

who are thieves expresses less outrage for a sin against justice than fear that the enemy may strike again. "The friend, Oh Agni (God of fire), who designs to injure the essence of our food, kine (archaic plural for cows), steeds, or bodies, May he the adversary, thief, and robber, sink to destruction, both himself and offspring" (VII.104).

Early in this century Edward Westermarck questioned the moral nature of Vedic sin and of the deity, Varuṇa, whom it was thought to offend. His reasoning was that devotees of Varuṇa also sought forgiveness from Indra who favored only his devotees and destroyed those who neglected him. Westermarck concluded that the Vedic religion was preeminently ritualistic and implicitly immoral.[12] Applied strictly, this assertion might disqualify the Jewish Yahweh, as well as Indra and Varuṇa, as guardians of a moral world. However, its point is met elsewhere in more tempered form. Surama Dasgupta emphasized sin as an external pollution transferable to others.[13] Two *Rv* passages lend credence to her externalistic interpretation. "Let the prayer-haters bear our sin to every side. We crave this gracious favor of the Gods today" (*Rv* X.36.9). Conversely, *Rv* VI.51.7 expressed the prayer: "Let us not suffer for the sin of others nor do the deed which ye, O Vasus, punish. Ye Universal Gods ! are all controllers; may he do harm unto himself who hates me."

One's own sin is not only imputable to others, but it seems forced upon people by factors other than their own will or else through ignorance or "heedlessness.". "Not our own will betrayed us, but seduction, thoughtlessness, Varuṇa ! wine, dice, or anger. The old is near to lead astray the younger; even sleep removeth not all evil-doing" (*Rv* VII. 86.6). "Whatever transgressions (*abhidroha*) we who are mere men have practiced as against the divine hosts and whatever *dharmas* (note the term's early use) laid down by you we may have confounded through our ignorance (or heedlessness) do not destroy us on account of the guilt (*enas*)" (*Rv* VII.89.5).[14] But ancient texts like these are too obscure and contain too many chronological layers to support the neat conclusion that sin is amoral or deterministically karmic. They prove no more, for instance, than an isolated reference to the Pauline passage about the will's helplessness proves the prevalence of fatalism in the Christian

New Testament. The tidy hypothesis of Vedic amorality leaves a clutter of contrary passages, such as the section on giving.

D. 1. *The Ethos of Giving.*

Among many Vedic songs which rank giving in high esteem (e.g., *Rv* I.125 and 126.1-5 and V. 61), this hymn is not clearly circumscribed within an egotistically consequentialistic ethic or amorality. In fact, it looks like a backdoor entry into the world of the moral. It is not only the giver's actions which are judged, but the giver himself. The indictment is delivered from a point of view which may transcend that of the giver's exclusive self-interest. Vedic giving conforms to the divine, cosmic order and does effect desirable consequences for the self like continued wealth, an open heart, success, helpful friendships, love, and neutralization of loneliness and guilt. But are Vedic giving and guilt moral and immoral rather than amoral ?

1. The riches of the liberal never waste away, while he who will not finds none to comfort him.
2. The man with food in store who, when the needy comes in miserable case begging for bread to eat, Hardens his heart against him—even when of old he did him service—finds not one to comfort him.
3. Bounteous is he who gives unto the beggar..and feeble. Success attends him in the shout of battle. He makes a friend of him in future troubles... Let the rich satisfy the poor, implore, and bend his eye upon a longer pathway. Riches come now to one, now to another, and like the wheels of cars (chariots) are ever rolling. 6. The foolish man wins food with fruitless labour; that food—I speak the truth—shall be his ruin. He feeds no trusting friend, no man to love him. All guilt is he who eats with no partaker (X.117).[15]

Whether giving and guilt are manifestly moral concepts may be viewed comparatively through the Christian Pauline norm: "Love seeks not its own interests," a line which was to spark an intense age-old Christian debate, still unsettled. "Let each of you look not only to his own interest, but also to the interests of others" (Philippians 2:4). From this text one may hypothesize a moral world in which human needs are organically and interdependently related. According to this *weltanschauung*, one's welfare is automatically other-regarding, taking into account the other's stance, because life is either revealed or seen to be constructed in that harmonious structure. The medieval Christian theologian, Thomas Aquinas, explained this ecological kind of self-feedback through the Greco-Platonic concept of participation.

In the Thomistic theology, persons love God as parts love the whole, only for the interest or motive of the whole; but, thereby, they inevitably love themselves.[16] Most Christian attempts to explain the apparent paradox are based on the assumption of a logic-crippling mystery, that of divine immanence. Contrary to the Muslim Sunni view, God, who is wholly or transcendently other, is so unlimitedly other that he can totally pervade the being of a creature without threatening its identity or his own transcendence. Paradoxically, divine fear for transcendence would compromise it. Balancing on the "edges of language," the belief in immanence and a polar creaturely participation is barely distinguishable from the concept of identification. In fact, in their attempt to explain love as motivated by both self- and other-interest, some mystics and theologians of Semitic-born religions have come so close to positing "identification" that their explanations sound surprisingly like the Hindu doctrine of *Ātman* treated below. "It is wrong to accuse Christian love of not loving man for himself; on the contrary it is the only love capable of this, because it is directed to that which is imperishable in him."[17] However, church and other religious officials always made sure that the mystics expressed qualified affirmations of God's separate or "dualistic" existence.

From the above perspective of divine immanence or near-identification, those painful, if sporadic, situations of conflicting interests can be depicted as merely apparent or transitory. The Christian worldview requires the sacrifice of self-interest, but only at a surface level. The model for this sacrifice is Jesus' death on the cross, a death which also happened to promote his own exaltation and lordship according to verses following the one quoted above (Philippians 2:4-11). Similarly, from self-motivated, self-sacrificing actions which are manifestations of God's gratuitous grace, Christians expect ultimate rewards or benefits which happen to accrue to their eternal self-regard. If only unconsciously, other-love has become instrumental for unending self-perfection. Even the love of God has become a means for the sanctification of one's self. Christians and others who cannot affirm a certain belief in a *literal* heaven or in tangible this-worldly compensations may be at least assured that, in some unfathomable way, they are holier, more faithful, or more developed persons. Entrusting not only the present, but even the endless future (their very existence) to a beneficent God, they simply cannot lose. *They* manifest the soundest faith.

In the *Rv* perspective, one which also includes gods who send temporal punishment, the hymn to *dāna* offers a sanction quite like, and perhaps no less moral than the Christian one. Not to share food or one's self brings sin, guilt, or diminishment in having lost a more important self-interest for an immediate and lesser one. However self-compensating, Vedic giving is a simple and lofty ideal, unless one assumes that self-hatred and revulsion toward self-reward is a prerequisite for other-love. Like Christian *agape*, this eminent Vedic virtue provides no magic solution to routine, concrete, or critical clashes of human interests. Yet, it seems to include other-regard with self-love just as "ethically" as Christian tradition.

Proceeding from a contrary position, Max Weber paid no heed to Vedic allusions to giving, guilt, or *rita*. He theorized that the *Vedas* "do not contain a rational ethic." "The ethical world of the Vedas," he continued, "is simply that of all heroic ages, as expressed by singers dependent upon gifts from kings and heroes—singers who did not fail to emphasize their own power and the powers of the gods they might magically influence."[18] As previously noted, it can be concluded from David Little's analysis of Weber's work in comparative ethics that Weber's notion of ethics is complex and difficult to grasp.[19] Weberian morality seems to favor the more diffuse notion of "practical" or consequentialist justification, relativistic conduct oriented toward action and goals. Opposing this is a stricter and more traditional meaning of ethics which Weber is said to reject, a system of absolute principles which transcend the arbitrary mores of individual societies (*Gesinnungsethik*).

Whether Little's more general thesis about Weber's rejection of principles is overstated or not, the Vedic hymn about the effects of giving would belie Weber's thesis that the *Vedas* are not ethical. In the absence of a positive indication that beneficiaries must belong only to a given society or that the Seers intended to delimit the application of their messages to a given in-group, it can be plausibly theorized that the antipodes of giving and guilt extend beyond the Sages' immediate elites. In other words, the overturning of this likelihood would necessitate the impossible uncovering of passages which encourage non-Brahmins to selfishness, gambling, theft, lying etc. Thus, the *Vedas* express morality rather than mere mores. Prescinding from Weber's relativistic interpretation, it can also be held that the Bards sang of conduct which even Weber would call moral, that is rational, consequentialist, action-oriented behavior.

2. *The Life-affirmative Ethos of the "Hymn to Dawn."*

To his credit, Weber accurately signaled the Vedic absence of some basic "Hindu" ideas with pessimistic moral dimensions like karmic retribution.[20] As was noted above, these ideas were more probably pre-Vedic. On a different level, another gap noted by Weber was the later Hindu prohibition of beef consumption.[21] Weber may be forgiven his inaccurate judgment that the *Vedas* contain no heavenly moral sanction.[22] He formulated this position from his insight that the *Vedas* are also devoid of allusion to *nirvāṇa* and to what some would call pessimistically ascetical traits. This discovery is supported by the lack of a Vedic reference to the mystical and other worldly goal of *moksha*. Weber realized that the *Vedas* affirmed this life and its values, even though he was disposed to ignore their proclivity to rational, common sensical moral action.

Weber's passing suggestions that the *Rv* world is life-confirming can be justified from direct evidence, not only by the *Rv*'s general mood of praise for life, but by very specific passages. For example, *Rv* I.113.5-6 mentions a variety of ends which include *artha* (wealth) and *kāma* (as pleasure and love). But other-worldly liberation (*moksha*) which came to predominate Upanishadic Hinduism is lacking. Of the four goals (*purushārthas*) which came to crystalize classical Hinduism's central aims of life, it is the three more life supportive ends (*tri-varga*) which are Vedic: wealth or *artha*, *kāma*, and *rita* (as predecessor or *dharma*).

5. Rich Dawn, she sets afoot the coiled-up sleeper, one for enjoyment, one for wealth or worship. Those who saw little for extended vision. All living creatures hath the Dawn awakened.

6. One to high sway, one to exalted glory, one to pursue his gain, and one his labour:
All to regard their different vocations, all moving creatures hath the Dawn awakened (*Rv* I.113, and see X.10, 31.2, and 191.2).

Similarly missing are more other-worldly stages of life (*āśramas*), while diversity of vocations is thought praiseworthy. The entire "Hymn to Dawn" (*Rv* I.113.1-20) is a typical example of the positive *Rv* attitude towards living.

15. Briging all life-sustaining blessings with her, showing herself she sends forth brilliant lustre...
16. Arise ! the breath, the life, again hath reached us; darkness hath passed away and light approacheth. 17... Shine then today, rich Maid, on him who lauds thee, shine down on us the gift of life and offspring.

Vedic acclaim for life includes strong approval of both life and erotic life as in *Rv* X.10. *Rv.* X.95 records a hymn-dialogue between King Purūravas and his beloved Urvaśī which was to become a *leitmotif* throughout the ages, for example, in the popular dramatic poetry of Kālidāsa and others (fourth-fifth centuries C.E.) which will be treated in chapter seven. The hymn to Dawn concludes with the King's loving pursuit of Urvaśī. Yet he lacked assurance that she loved him or that they would be reunited. Possibly, aside from the story-telling or theatrical dimension, there is a dialectic here of two competing themes: simultaneous commendation and suspicion of erotic love as symbolized by women. If so, the hymn is a harbinger of a tension which will reappear in Vālmīki's *Rāmāyaṇa* (*Ry*) and in other dramas which have sustained its strength throughout the history of Hindu culture(s).

Weber's picture of a Vedic life-affirming world without an implicit ethical system is correct only if he meant a *developed* system. But his supposition that the *Rv* is clearly sinless and therefore wholly amoral incurs obstacles. Although ideas of sin and misfortune are still confused in the later *Atharvaveda*, apparently moral crimes and expiations abound there. The *Rv* itself mentions several kinds of conduct in more than an amoral sense: lying, incest, seduction, conjugal infidelity, induced abortion (at least in reference to female embryos), theft, and non-payment of debts. "O king (Varuṇa) may I not live by the wealth acquired by others. For many a dawn has gone by, but not for me always thinking of debts." "O Varuṇa...may I not be deprived of rightly earned riches" (II.28.11).

Final substantiation of whether moral sin is present in the *Rv* would have to take into account the use of many synonyms for sin like *āgas*, *enas*, and *pāpa*.[23] It would also necessitate an evaluation of the possible moral meaning of each of these terms. Meanwhile, aside from the above hymns about gambling and giving, it is Vedic testimonials to *rita* and to corresponding functions of gods like Varuṇa and Mitra which constitute the most cogent evidence that the Vedic milieu is plausibly a moral one. This picture seems likely, even if it should also reveal partly immoral and amoral dimensions.

E. *The Evolution of Moral Justification by a Resort to Rita as Impersonal Order and then as Divine Moral Authority.*

Rita, etymologically related both to rite and right, refers variously to order at three levels: 1. nature (cosmic order), 2. sacrificial or ritual order, and 3. the order of human conduct.[24] In the last context, it has usually been translated into English as order, law, or eternal law. *Rita* is established through human activity (*Rv* X.125.5) and its violation is associated with sin, offenses against gods like Agni, Varuṇa, and Mitra, the god of loyalty and promise-keeping. In their historical (henotheistic) turns as the most popular or leading divinities, these gods protect *rita*, assist (X.66.4) and reward humans who observe it, and free from sin those who have offended it (*Rv* I.24. 14-15). "The winds waft sweets, the rivers pour sweets, for the man who keeps the law..." (*Rv*, I. 90.6). Infraction of *rita* evokes divine punishment. "Thrice, Agni, let thy noose surround the demon who with his falsehood (*anrita*) injures Holy Order (*rita*)" (X.87.11). In subsequent literature, *rita* will yield to the primary Hindu moral term, *dharma*, itself already found in *Rv* VII.89.5.

Among its more general meanings, *dharma* also refers to a whole way of life rather than to mere doctrines or moral teachings alone. Along with Weber's insistence that *dharma* is merely group or caste-oriented mores, his denial that it is a universal morality will be examined in chapter four. But the following passages gather texts which seem to position Vedic *rita* in ethically normative contexts which are universal.

[Agni] Mark the Law, thou who knowest, yea, observe it;
send forth the full streams of eternal Order.
I use no sorcery with might or falsehood;
the sacred Law of the Red Steer [Agni] I follow (*Rv* V.12.2).

In *Rv* X.87.11, quoted in the preceding paragraph, and in other passages like the following, *rita* is either equated with or entails another term which became basic in Hindu thought, truth (*satya*). Opposed both to *rita* and *satya* is falsehood (*anrita*). "What indeed we never did before (shall we do it now); shall we who have spoken *rita* (so far) now speak *anrita* ? (X.10.4.)[25] Other identifications of *rita* and truth/truth-speaking can be observed in *Rv* X.113.4 and I.105.12.

Sometimes *rita* seems to be addressed personally as one of the gods.

Aditi, Heaven and Earth, the great eternal Law, Indra, Viṣṇu, the Maruts, and the lofty Sky. We call upon Ādityas, on the Gods, for help.... (X.66.4).[26] Eternal Law hath varied food that strengthens thought of eternal Law, removes transgressions.[27] The praise-hymn of eternal Law, arousing, glowing, hath oped (sic) the deaf ears of the living. 9. Firm seated are eternal Law's foundations, in its fair form are many splendid beauties....10. Following eternal Law he (Indra) too, upholds it;...(IV. 22-9-10).

O Agni, for we offer sacrifice to Mitra and Varuṇa
to gods and to the great (*bṛhat*) *ṛta* (*Rv.* I.75.5).

This deification of *rita* and the presence of many other deities may portray either a moralization of the gods or the deification of different ideals or values alleged to have occurred later in the *Brāhmaṇas*, the ritual documents which succeeded the *Vedas*. The point at hand, however, is that *rita's* share in the process of deification renders it comparable to the analogous notion of "*lex aeterna*" and cosmic moral order in Western thought. In both instances, the course of human conduct may be divulged in a system beyond one which human beings themselves impose, a system which approximates a concept of divine moral immanence. "Dweller in noblest place, mid men,...he is holy Law" (IV.40.4-5).[28]

There are many other hymns concerning *rita* which may

allude exclusively or primarily to its *cosmic* signification. But due to its frequent link with human behavior, it is rarely, if ever, clear that its reference to cosmic order *excludes* that of human deportment (as in *Rv* IV.23.10 above and VI.51.3). Admittedly, the correlation of human activities like truth-telling with *rita*, a divine or divinely sustained order, is not yet final demonstration that human conduct includes inalienable responsibility. Nor does it prove that it proceeds morally/immorally rather than amorally from ignorance or from factors intrinsically or extrinsically deterministic. But *rita's* additional association with the themes of reward and punishment, developed in later literature, evinces a trend in a rationally moral direction, notwithstanding the contrary evidence already adduced.

F. Conclusion and Qualification

The author's conclusion about *Rv* morality is the same as it would have to be for other equally ancient and cryptic texts in present stages of research. There is not (and may never be) sufficient textual evidence to prove or disprove that the Vedic world was exclusively or primarily moral in the strict, free, and other-concerned senses of the term. However, the evidence for at least a *partly* moral outlook is surprisingly not much more tenuous than that of much later, intercultural, and more complex religio-ethical documents. Given the multiple authorship and the various chronological strata of the *Vedas*—that perspective quite irrelevant to devotional (including Hindu devotion) approaches—,it may be reasonably supposed that there are concurrent instances of the moral, the amoral, and the tensions between them. Or, if one insists on taking the *Vedas* as some kind of cohesive whole, then it is most logically inferred that the moral, amoral, and their mixtures are all dialectically/complementarily present.

Weber's theory that Vedic Hinduism is amoral, therefore, is a conjecture whose principal strength is derived from the powerful, systemic integration of his awe-inspiring general gestalt, rather than directly from Vedic data. Talcott Parsons rightly estimated that Weber's structural analysis was "most intimately associated with great ranges of historical and comparative material, mastered extraordinarily well."[29] Correct as a comprehensive assessment, this praise should not be allowed to obscure the fact that much fewer data were available in Weber's day. Consequently, his formulation about Vedic morality, including sin, can be turned exactly upside down in a plausible schema like the following.

"Sin" does not dominate the *Vedas*. But, among the strata of Vedic ruins, one finds a city intensely moral at several levels. These could have inspired activity which was moral, industrial, and economic—social ethoses like those which *finally* (belatedly ?) spring up in Europe. Had it not been for later historical contingencies, the *Vedas* might have offered foundation blocks for civilizations far more socially, technologically, and morally oriented than those now witnessed in the West. Since the *Vedas* lacked the ascetical self-consciousness of human depravity and self-hatred—which Weber saw as part of the Protestant ethic, but which had regularly reappeared in vast movements from the early Manicheans to Neo-Puritans—they affirmed this-worldly, non-Manichean values in a manner which might have propelled rather than impeded a social ethic. Put at its boldest, the dynamics of the life-confirming Vedic religions might have been more conducive to a world-building mentality than the ascetical religio-ethical "Christian" systems which were historically infected with outside Manichean and Puritanical life-denial, with enigmatic self-hatred (thanatos), or, in psychological terms, with sado-masochistic death instincts. Perhaps Albert Schweitzer was more correct than Weber. Given the negative historical forms assumed by Christianity, which were more Manichean or non-Christian than Christian, the West became partly humanized not because of "Christianity," but in spite of it. In contrast, vibrant Vedic loves of the world, life, children, spouses, and friends steered clear of hedonism, eudaemonism (self-happiness hang-ups), egoism, or idleness, because they were coupled with respect for the ideals of sharing (*dāna*), truth (*satya*), and *rita*. Likewise, if Schweitzer's indictment of later Hindu "life-denial" is allowed to stand, it cannot be applied to Vedic Hinduism, a pre-reflective, intelligent moral mentality potentially more conducive to humanistic and constructive human justice and sharing than historical Western forms of the ethics of "competition, consumption, and success, whatever the cost for the future."

However, data does not warrant that this benign interpretation, so diametrically opposed to Weber's conscious analysis, can be adhered to without qualification. If the Vedic landscape is moral in the judgment of some, its colors need a bit of Utopian brightening. Divine punishments were invoked upon enemies. Racial oppression was authenticated by divine approval. Sexual discrimination went uncensured. Slavery was approved. The exaltation of life and love were partly ambiguous. Sporadic admissions existed that moral responsibility was transferable and stemmed not from volition, but from ignorance or other causes. In the extant texts, some of the traditionally respected Hindu norms seem to be missing, like celebrated Hindu non-violence (*ahiṃsā*).[30]

To conclude with a comparative and necessary digression, insistence on reading sin, or much sin, into the *Vedas* may flow from an assumption which is not self-evident to all peoples: if there is no possibility of *willing evil* (malice), there is none for willing good. In Christian traditions, for instance, this presupposition has never been satisfactorily squared with beliefs that human beings and angels truly love God in the "freedom" of heaven, where they are absolutely unable to do otherwise. This same separation of moral goodness from the necessary cooption of willing evil has been attributed to Hinduism by Frederick Underwood.[31] Even if God were envisioned finitely, as some religions have done in limiting his power with his intelligence. etc., or as a helpless agent of evil holocausts and "meaningless suffering," given his will to share life with free creatures, would this limitation of moral goodness necessarily portray God as a malicious agent who *wills evil* ? The dilemma has been symbolized by intercultural and ambiguous moral deities or deific pairs in many religions.

At a "deeper" structural level, anxiety about an amoral world may be bound up with a rationale about self-worth. If there is no situation where unequal talents and graces may be democratized now or in heaven by sheer goodness or strength of will, then persons are doomed to the status quo of their relatively lower levels of emotional, intellectual, or other talents and worldly gifts, a situation which might breed "*ressentiment.*" Further incentives to rise from weakness or to strive for uprightness would appear to be enervated. If life is sheerly a matter of amoral cooperation for mutual benefits, where morality is neither rewarded nor compensates for present inequalities, then both individuals and societies seem to be threatened. Present and foreseeable distribution of benefits is undeniably hierarchical. Heavenly redistribution, however, seems terribly tenuous or far off to many. In short unless one is automatically better or holier than another thou by sinning less, then the meaningful interpretability of life itself seems jeopardized. Like religious holiness for some, morality as an equalizer of the unequal human condition seems necessary to others for justice and ultimate meaning.

Joining the scenarios of counter-rationales to all "moral points of view" lies a theory in which even those convinced of ample freedom to do good feel that a co-ability to will evil does not protect a moral world, but endangers it. For others, the theory of moral one-upmanship, like the theory of *willing evil*, is only a sado-masochistic expression of "man against himself," a way of venting self-hatred. Rather, humans are naturally good in the Confucian, pre-reflective sense, unless they are programmed by inward or outward forces like self-hatred or propaganda. In this view, the abolition of either sin or even volitionally moral responsibility does not neutralize human goodness, which is primarily a pre-reflective concern of mind/will or a reflective concern of mind alone. At any rate, the "death of sin" at least, would be liberation in a human evolutionary process which unleashes natural and spontaneous human goodness which death-minded civilizations have repressed. Humanly constructed "morality," obstructs the premoral goodness which is "beyond freedom and dignity."

Whereas morality should at least be feasible without the unthinkable option of willing evil or sin as evil, it should not be conceived of as an equalizer of human worth, since human beings are as incomparably unique as the stars and the lilies of the valley, or odiously and meaninglessly comparable like brown and white or yellow and Christmas. In sum, to employ morality, or holiness, as an equalizer is self-defeating. Even if such a result should occur, one could intend it only by conquering one's own purposes. Altruism, human-heartedness, or non-egoistic love cannot be willed to "get ahead morally" (egoistically). On the other hand, true love and morality would only be devastated if it were confused with the rejection of self-love" or the tangible love of others. What seems to end as a final "puzzlement" or mystery will be readdressed in the epilogue.

The purpose of this chapter's concluding digression is the

crucial one of reminding or trying to convince readers that there are both pros and cons for not prejudging the issues of sin and morality in themselves, and to encourage them to listen further to other enriching insights within Hinduism, Buddhism, and Chinese religions. Moreover, the arguments are not unrelated to critical, modern and painfully relevant debates about the meaning of punishments in the fields of law and psychology, or the meaning of rewards in economic and social motivation. It is hoped that the preceding data, if not the digression which they inspired, have established that the hymns of the Vedic world, even if thought to be divinely inspired, dialectically included levels which probably were moral, amoral, and mixed in the conventional meanings of the terms. Second, those who bracket the *Vedas*' divine inspiration and who are, therefore, less inclined to see them as an integral, normative whole may see both morality/immorality and amorality arising from different sources and periods of composition. Those who would derive clearer and more systematic, normative *weltanschauungs* from Vedic history must continue their search elsewhere than in this volume.[32] In the interim, whether one evaluates the Vedic vista as strictly moral or amoral, some topics unquestionably deal with issues which reach the terrain of what human beings usually call moral issues: class, slavery, sin, giving, life-affirmation, and justifications for conduct by the various paths of reasoning from consequences or appealing to divine and human authority or cosmic order or group experience.[33] If such a moral landscape is not clearly *altruistic* or *mystically* grounded, it provides a type of practical, *naturalistic cooperation* or system of partly other-regarding agreements which one might admit are moral in the sense of "Everyperson's" common sagehood. The question of the next chapter is whether the Vedic interpretations remained "moral" and life affirmative through the period of the *Upanishads* (*Ups*) (800-500 B.C.E.).

NOTES

1. Unless otherwise specified, translations are taken from *The Hymns of The Ṛgveda*, trans. Ralph T. H. Griffith (rev. ed.; Delhi: Motilal Banarsidass, 1973). See also M. R. Gopalacharya, *The Heart of the Rigveda* (Bombay and New Delhi: Somaiya Publications Pvt Ltd, 1971; *Hymns of The Atharva-Veda* I trans. R. T. H. Griffith (Benares and London: E.J. Lazurus & Co., and,

Luzac and Co., 1895); and *Hymns of The Vedas* (all four Vedas), trans. A. C. Bose (Bombay and New York: Asia Publishing House, 1966). Although the *Atharvaveda* may affirm *kāma* as love more strongly, this chapter restricts itself to the more ancient and explicitly moral *Rigveda* (*Rv*). Since chronological specification of Indian documents has not yet ceased its up-dating movement, I have selected the time-conjectures which are closer to the present, without assuming that future scholarship will not revise them even further. The historian, Moriz Winternitz, *The History of Sanskrit Literature*, Vol. I, 1 (2nd. ed., Calcutta: University of Calcutta, 1959), 64-65) indicates that extant Vedic verses may reflect a mere fraction of what once existed. He also attests: "So much is certain, that, whatever the practical value of the songs of the Ṛgveda may be, there exists no more important source for the investigation of the earliest stages in Indian religion. . mythology. . indeed, of peoples in general, than these songs of the Ṛgveda" (see also p. 101). Except for the hymn to *dāna* or giving (*Rv* X.117, a later passage), Winternitz would not concur with I. C. Sharma that ethics comprise the main theme of Vedic thought. See Sharma, *Ethical Philosophies of India*, ed. and rev. by S. M. Daugert (New York: Harper Torchbooks, 1965), p. 60. Aside from John McKenzie's quite biased *Hindu Ethics* (London: Oxford University Press, 1922) and the latest studies of Surama Dasgupta (not her historian-husband Surendra Nath), *Development of Moral Philosophy in India* (New York: Frederick Ungar Publ. Co., 1961) and Cromwell Crawford's previously mentioned *Hindu Ethical Ideals*,—the best secondary work on Hindu ethics, especially on the Vedas and the *Rv*, is the pioneer first class study of the Sanskrit specialist, W. E. Hopkins, *The Ethics of India* (New Haven: Yale University Press, 1924). It is important especially for its references to *rita* and heavenly reward, as on pp. 9, 10, and 50. A descriptive compilation of contemporary data and ethical bibliography has been compiled by Creighton Lacy, *The Conscience of India* (New York: Holt, Rinehart, and Winston, 1965).

2. See Sharma, *Ethical Philosophies*, pp. 73 and 87 and N. V. Banerjee, *The Spirit of Indian Philosophy* (New Delhi: Arnold-Heinemann Publishers, 1974), p. 39.

3. See also the introduction and translations of P. T. Raju in *The Great Asian Religions* by Wing-tsit Chan, Isma'il Rāgī al Fārūqi, et al (London: Collier-Macmillan Limited, 1969), pp. 1-29, esp. pp. 21-22; and the Thomas translation in S. Radhakrishnan, *A Sourcebook in Indian Philosophy* (Princeton, New Jersey: Princeton University Press, 1957), p. 19.

4. Thomas translation in Radhakrishnan, ibid.

5. See Pandurang Vaman Kane, *History of Dharmaśāstra* Vol II, I (Bombay: Bhandarkar Oriental Research Institute, n.d. (1930's), p. 84; see also pp. 25-27.

6. Kane's trans., ibid. p. 25. See also *Rv* I.104.2.

7. Another racial reference in Kane (*Rv* IX.71.2) seems too obscure to understand.

8. Weber, *The Religion of India*, pp. 29-133.

9. On slavery see Kane's *History* II,I, 180-87.

10. See James B. Pritchard, ed., *The Ancient Near East*, Vol. I (London and Princeton, New Jersey: Princeton University Press, 1958), pp. 138-67.

11. Compare with Henry Lefever, *The Vedic Idea of Sin* (London and Travancore, India: Mission Press, 1935), p. 7.

12. Westermarck, *The Origin and Development of Moral Ideas*. See also his *Ethical Relativity* (New York: Harcourt, Brace, and Company, Inc., 1932).

13. Dasgupta, *Development of Moral Philosophy*, pp. 59-60.

14. Kane's trans., *History* II,I, p. 5.

15. Macdonell trans., as in Radhakrishnan, *Sourcebook*, p. 389. The last line is translated: "He eats alone, and he alone is guilty." "Is guilty"- "reaps sin" in Kane's *History* IV,I—and in Gopalacharya, *The Heart of the Rigveda*, p. 389.

16. "....caritas attingit ipsum Deum ut in ipso sistat, non ut eo aliquid nobis proveniat." (Loosely translated: divine love in people reaches at God for his own sake, not for any self gain); Thomas Aquinas, *Summa Theologica* II,II, q. 23. a. 6c.

17. "C'est bien à tort que l'on accuse l' amour chretien de ne pas aimer l'homme pour lui-meme; il est au contraire le seul qui en soit capable, parce qu'il s'addresse à ce qui en lui est inamissable" (Yves de Montecheuil, "Le ressentiment dans la vie morale et religieuse d'apres Max Scheler," *Rescherches de Science Religieuse*, April 1937, 147-48; see also Dominique Nothombe, *Le Motif Formel de La Charité envers Le Prochain*, Paris 1952, pp. 24-28 (Doct. diss. Angelicum).

18. Weber, *The Religion of India*, p. 261; see also p. 337.

19. Little, *Max Weber*, 6-7,20, 33-34.

20. While some scholars infer karmic notions from pre-Vedic sources, or, less plausibly, the Vedic inescapability of sin, others place its genesis in the Ups. (See Kane, *History* IV, p. 56 and Weber, *The Religion of India*, p. 28).

21. Weber, ibid., p. 28.

22. See Kane, *History* IV, 153-60, esp. 156 for direct *Rv* references to heavenly reward.

23. See ibid., pp. 5-8.

24. See M. Hiriyanna, *Outlines of Indian Philosophy* (London: George Allen & Unwin Ltd., 1932), p. 33 and C. A. F. Rhys David's commentary on the Buddhist *Dīgha Nikāya* (*The Long Dialogues of the Buddha*), *Dīgha* III (London, Pali Text Society): "The meaning of the word (*rita*) would" seem to have evolved from "motion, rhythmic motion, order, cosmic order, moral order, the right....a long period must be postulated for the growth and consolidation of such ideas..back to the third millennium before Christ. The use of the word died out in India before the time of the rise of Buddhism... It has not been traced in either the Buddhist or the Jain canonical literature."

25. Trans. in Kane, *History* IV, 4.

26. ibid.

27. "Crooked acts," according to Kane, ibid., IV, 27.

28. Confer also I.75.5 as in the Kane trans., ibid., 5.

29. Parsons, *Societies: Evolution and Comparisons* (Englewood Cliffs: New Jersey: Prentice-Hall, Inc., 1966), p. 111.

30. The virtue is lacking in the comprehensive index of Kane's *History*, IV.

31. In later Hinduism, as in Christianity, *jīvanmukti* (that stage of life

prior to death which is the perfected Hindu's foretaste of *moksha* or final liberation) is believed to transcend morality. "The saint has gone beyond considerations of good and evil in the sense that his goodness is innate...such goodness is no longer goodness if such goodness is held necessarily to imply the possibility of evil" (pp. 64-65). "*Jīvanmukti* is non-moral because to perform a moral act, the possibility of performing an immoral act has to remain. In the conception of *jīvanmukti* the possibility has been transcended. ." (p 65); Frederick B. Underwood, "Notes on Conscience in Indian Tradition," *Journal of Chinese Philosophy* II,1 (December 1974). "Non-moral" in one sense of *jīvanmukti* is "neither amoral nor immoral" (p. 64); it transcendentally includes the moral.

32. Holding out for a morality which is differently based, Max Scheler felt the contrary, namely that craving for equal moral worth expressed "*ressentiment*" and the "labor theory of value." See Alfons Deeken, *Process and Permanence in Ethics*: Max Scheler's *Moral Philosophy* (New York, N.Y.: Paulist Press: 1974).

33. Readers who wish to pursue the moral aspect of *bhakti* will find a *Rv* reference in I.8.32. Although I cannot confirm his claim, Banerjee, *The Spirit of Indian Philosophy* finds *ahimsā* there, p. 291. Winternitz's amoralistic interpretation of the *Rv* may be contrasted with Venkatarama Raghavan's idea of continuing if not developing morality. See the latter's "Hinduism" in Isma'īl Rāgī al Fārūqī, ed., *Historical Atlas of The Religions of the World* (New York: Macmillan Publishing Co., Inc., 1974), pp. 73-76.

Chapter III

ETHICS IN THE UPANISHADS

Abstract. A. A Chronological Graph. B. A Mystical-Moral Worldview. The *Ups* justify moral action through a basically mystical world-view and new proclamation that every individual is one and the same *Atman*-Brahman, if it could only be realized (in *moksha*). A corollary proclamation is more negative in its view that any existence short of *moksha* is ultimately valueless and illusory. *C. Morality or mores?* The deceptive realities of individual existence and rebirths are caused by *avidyā* (ignorance), so that sin is lutimately a matter of intellection rather than volition. Although not everyone agrees that a real capacity to will evil is necessary for moral freedom, many are bewildered by Upanishadic efforts to describe a trans-moral world "beyond good and evil" which is still implicitly moral, and certainly not immoral. In his use of this phrase to describe a radically new and opposite life-affirmative ethos, Nietzsche offered the clue that the concept of "beyond" (*trans*) does not deny morality, but proposes an utterly new and superior ethics in a confusing linguistic strain. He also bombarded the ascetical and less social virtues of the *Ups* and of all religions, in spite of their verbal acceptance of more positive and general virtues. *D. The Ascetical Ethos.* Like Nietzsche, Schweitzer crystallized the Upanishadic spirit of life-negation, thinking that he had to demand the abrogation of the whole of Hinduism. But the question arises as to whether Upanishadic and other mysticisms *logically* necessitate world-denial or have simply done so in some of their historically embodied forms. A practical or working solution is offered in the Upanishadic *āśrama* (stages) system in which the negatively ascetical ethos still prevails. *E. Ethical validation.* The Upanishadic Seers and Brahminic philosophers validated the supremacy of their spirit by identifying their own authority with the divine. *F. Class structures and the individual.* With divine and Brahminic authority, the four *varṇas* and Brahminic supremacy were said to be divinely created. As legislated in *Manu*, the rules for these classes would allow sparse room for individual conscience. NOTES.

A. Chronological graph.

The fourteen principal *Upanishads* (*Ups*), whose anonymous and multiple composition from a scientific view is of no interest to the pious believer (as in other religions) are listed in the chronological order conventionally attributed to them (800-500 B.C.E.). Currently, their pre-Buddhistic origin is debated and even the earliest or first of the three groups below (1-6) is known to contain later layers. The second group includes numbers 7-9, 12, and 14; the third series is comprised of 10, 11, and 13. The central ethical references are located in numbers 1-3, 5, 7-9, 12, and 13. Those who posit a Buddhist influence point to the *Ups*' non-Vedic and ascetical opposition to or deemphasis of theism, priestly rituals and devotions, sacrificial violence, and the Vedic *tri-varga* of wealth, love, and moral *dharma*.

Abbreviations	*Upanishads*
Bṛ.	1. *Bṛahadāraṇyaka*
Chānd.	2. *Chāndogya*
Taitt.	3. *Taittirīya*
Ait.	4. *Aitareya*
Kauṣ.	5. *Kauṣītaki*
Kena	6. *Kena*
Kaṭha	7. *Kaṭha*
Īśa	8. *Īśā*
Muṇḍ.	9. *Muṇḍaka*
Praśna	10. *Praśna*
Māṇḍ	11. *Māṇḍūkya*
Śvet.	12. *Śvetāśvatara*
Maitri	13. *Maitri*
Mhny	14. *Mahānārāyaṇa*

B. The Mystical Worldview as Grounds for Morality.

"Whoever knows he is deep strives for clarity; whoever would like to appear deep to the crowd strives for obscurity" (Friedrich Nietzsche). If Nietzsche's condemnation does not plainly apply to the thirteen or fourteen principal *Ups* listed above, their obvious obscurities cannot be denied. The *Ups* were literally mysteries or secrets learned in confidential oral tradition while "sitting down near someone." Ultimate enigma is the main theme which unifies these texts. They are self-contradictory to some and unsystematic to all: each finite self (*ātman*) is the same higher, one, ultimate Self (*Ātman*) or Brahman (*Chānd.* 6.1ff.). True, in some sections many theistic or personal gods are still active, including Prajāpati, a moral preceptor (*Chānd.* 8.7-12). But in other passages the gods are reduced to the monotheistic Brahma(n) [earlier texts leave off the impersonal "n"]. (*Maitri* 4.5-6 and *Bṛ.* 3.9.1-9) who is often described as *impersonal* or without virtues or attributes (*nirguṇa*). Further, Brahman lacks duality (*a-dvaita*) and is "without a second." Brahman is not separate from the world and human beings (*Māṇḍ.* 7; *Bṛ.* 4.3.30; 2.4.14; 1.45 and 3.7.3-23). Subject and object are no longer distinct from one another (*Chānd.* 6.13.1-3), just as salt is invisibly pervasive in water. In some passages, however, Brahma(n) still appears theistically, endowed with personality and attributes (*saguṇa*).[1]

In either event, the intriguing identification of the individual self with Brahman is a metaphysical motif whose ethical implications are profound. The knowledge or intuition of this coalescence with the *Ātman* in every creature is itself life's first mandate. Its natural consequence is the rejection of thought and actions dualistically expressive of mine and thine. "In thinking 'This is I' and 'that is mine,' he binds himself with his self, as does a bird with a snare" (*Maitri* 3.2). Put positively, the moral consequences of oneness with other beings in the one *Ātman* is love for *Ātman's* sake.

In the well known Upanishadic dialogue attributed to Yājñavalkya and his wife, Maitreyī (*Bṛ.* 2.4.5) the former reveals the formula for immortality. "Then, said he: 'Lo, verily, not for love of the husband is a husband dear, but for love of the Ātman a husband is dear."[2] Similar verses predicate the same about the love of a wife, sons, wealth, "Brāhmanhood," "Kshātrahood," the gods, and beings in general. This theme of identification is so specifically essential to the Upanishadic tradition and so radically different from the *Vedas* that one immediately wonders about its moral ramifications. The conventional outsider's reaction was exemplified in Weber's charge of moral quietism. In contrast, a more sympathetic outlook does not agree with Weber that the *Ups* contain not universal morality, but caste mores. Further, it develops a rationale for the *Ups*' mystical stance as follows, seeing it as an idealistic sort of justification which responds to the question "why be moral ?"

First, dualistic worldviews which affirm the reality of subject and object are said to teach that others are to be loved less for themselves than for the sake of a deity or savior. As a result the recipients of benevolent actions suffer humiliating doubts as to whether they are loved for themselves or as mere means to the spiritual welfare of their benefactors.

Second, to be loved because one's true self is the *Ātman* is not necessarily to be exploited egotistically by others who thereby love the same *Ātman* in themselves. For it is theoretically supposed that the agent of altruistic action is not a higher manifestation of *Ātman* than the recipient, but simply one among potential spiritual equals. In addition, it can be maintained that non-dualistic love of others avoids both the pitfalls of what is now called psychological transference and the concomitant perils of neglecting authentic self-love. From this position the Upanishadic merger with others is the only way out of the loveless no-exit or Sartrean corner into which human beings are painted—condemned to love, but only with possessive stares. Non-dualistic identification with others in *Ātman* is thereby conceived as the simplest, most satisfactory answer to long debated problems about love and self-interest resurrected by modern "philosophical egotism" —what is naturally good for yourself or for General Motors is naturally good for the whole country. Simultaneously, it satisfies an ultimate need in regard to the meaning of life (called "religious interpretability"). Existence is not transitory. Meaning does not collapse when the face of death is confronted. Rather, the spectre of death is checkmated in the realization that one's true self involves an eternal and blissful state of awareness. The knowledge that one's individual consciousness will cease is no cause for trauma. Rather the discontinuance is envisioned as liberation (*Śvet.* 6.76). Awareness that one's real self is *Ātman* is a joyous or "blissful" release from the cycle of rebirths, which cycle is a fate worse than death.[3]

C. *Morality or mores ? "Beyond Good and Evil."*

Besides the rationale outlined above, Weber's judgment also necessitates a less speculative inquiry into whether the Upanishadic attitude is truly moral. The following data gathered under Nietzsche's title "Beyond Good and Evil" may be read from two contrary points of view. Those who are convinced that morality is non-existent if it excludes the capability of *willing evil* might conclude that there is an amoral stance in the *Ups.* Others may draw the opposite inference, based on their assumption that there exists a kind of non- or trans-moral ethics, neither amoral nor immoral, which does not depend on the volitional capacity for sin.

Sin as avidyā (ignorance). M. Hiriyanna typified both classical and modern interpretations of sin in Hinduism when he commented that the foundations of Upanishadic ethics are to be discovered in the evolution of sin from ritual disorder or exterior offenses against gods to a dualistic *ignorance* of the identity of every individual with Brahman.[4] In the *Vedas* sin, and especially the meaning of sin, had remained in dim and blurred focus.[5] Similarly, it was hardly a principal topic of conversation for Upanishadic Seers.

To discern first hand whether sin in the *Ups* is finally a matter of wrong willing or wrong seeing, one must examine the key term for the root of sin, *avidyā*, a counterpart to the principle of mystical non-dualism. The *Ups* describe *avidyā* cognitively and non-volitionally as blindness (*Bṛ*. 4.4.10) and delusion (*Kaṭha* 2.5). It exists in "unwise" and "stupid" people who desire wealth and what is pleasant (*Kaṭha* 2.1.6). "Heedless' and "deluded" they come "again and again" under the control of death. In *Kaṭha* 2.6, a personification of death speaks of delusions about wealth and the permanence of the present world. But ignorance abides also in "doers of deeds" who neglect the ways of the ascetical life and make sacrifice and merit central. They too will suffer rebirth (*Muṇḍ*. 1.2.8-10).[6] In addition to this depiction of sin as non-volitional ignorance, the second and more confusing motif relevant to morality is the Upanishadic injunction to "shake off good and evil." How ?

Beyond Good and Evil. Since the real identity of individuals is the *Ātman*, in that ultimate existence they are literally beyond good and evil and unconcerned about good and bad action (*sādhu* and *pāpa*, as in *Taitt*. 2.9).

> Verily, he is the great, unborn Atman, who is this (person) consisting of knowledge among the senses. In the space within the heart lies the ruler (*Ātman*) of all..He does not become great by good action nor inferior by bad action....The Ātman is not this, it is not that (*neti, neti*)....It is unattached, for it does not attach itself....One is not stained by evil action.... Evil does not overcome him; he overcomes all evil....Free from evil,....he becomes a Brahman (*Bṛ*.4.4.22-23).

A similar teaching is attributed to the god, Indra. "So he

who understands me—by no deed whatsoever of his is his world injured, not by stealing, not by killing an embryo, not by the murder of his mother, not by the murder of his father; if he has done any evil (*pāpa*), the dark color departs not from his face [he does not grow pale]" (*Kauṣ.* 3.1).

Unless these declarations are isolated from wider contexts, they do not condone immorality, but simply affirm its illusoriness along with the whole of the present life.[7] This "shaking off good and evil" (*Muṇḍ.* 3.1.2.) flows naturally from the *intuitive* awareness of one's identity with Brahman. Most significantly, it comes only to those who live a new and supreme stage of life which is ascetical and beyond the householder's works (*Muṇḍ.* 1.2.12).

> They who practice austerity (*tapas*) and faith (*sraddhā*) in the forest,
> The peaceful (*śānta*) knowers who live on alms.
> Depart passionless (*vi-rāga*) through the door of the sun.
> To where is that immortal Person (*Purusha*) e'en the imperishable Atman" (*Muṇḍaka* 1.2.11).

A linguistic clue to the meaning of this amoral or trans-moral perspective may be found in the *weltanschauung* of Friedrich Nietzsche. After slow initial recognition, awareness of Nietzsche's enduring significance has grown imperceptibly but surely, thanks in part to his impact on Freud, Sartre, Buber, and Scheler. Likewise he influenced Max Weber and Albert Schweitzer, two thinkers like himself who were directly concerned with Hindu ethics. If Nietzsche's opinion of Upanishadic Seers was severe, it was because he felt that they, like all "priestly" ascetics, threatened the authentic way of life which is imperative for superior human beings (Supermen or *Übermenschen*). This higher life was positively depicted through biological and esthetical images like health, strength, beauty, and nobility. These qualities were jealously devalued as "evil" by weak or "bad" people who lacked them. For such persons Nietzsche wrote the epitaph : "..inability for revenge is called [by them] unwillingness to revenge."[8]

Out of his unique life experience, Nietzsche had concluded that the kinds of good and evil which Hindu and other religious moralities proposed were radically infected with the sickness of *ressentiment*, however spiritually conceived. As a denial of what is other

> this need to direct one's [other-rejecting] view outward

> instead of back to oneself—is of the essence of *ressentiment* : in order to exist, slave morality always first needs a hostile external world; it needs, physiologically speaking, external stimuli in order to act at all—its action is fundamentally reaction.[9]

In Nietzsche's position the Upanishadic "shaking off" or going beyond good and evil was an idea common to all of India, including its Hindu and Buddhist traditions. These religions, like Christianity, denied that salvation was attainable through moral virtue. Quoting his friend Paul Deussen's (1845-1919) translation of the non-dualistic philosopher, Śaṅkara (788-829 C.E.), Nietzsche observed that union with Brahma(n) was acquired neither by fewer faults nor an increase of virtue. Aspects of this and other religio-moral teachings which Nietzsche condemned were linked by him to a pessimistic weariness of life. This *ressentiment* was said to have found its chief expression in the life-denying self-castigation of the ancient, power-hungry Brahmins, a group through whom Nietzsche criticized life-denying ascetics of every age and religion.[10] Although he respected strength and discipline, including self-discipline, he found Brahminic asceticism self-contradictory and ridden with "a *ressentiment* without equal, that of an insatiable instinct and power-will that wants to become master not over something in life but over life itself...."[11]

In the historiography of Nietzsche, "love" hid both *ressentiment* and the drive to possess or exist parasitically in others. "Humility" was a slavish, hidden, and therefore less trustworthy form of the will to power. It was a life-negating spirit of gravity (*Geist der Schwere*). This solemn will or "gravity" was a downward force which made would-be angels fall like demons, as G.K. Chesterton's pun would later scold. Totally disoriented in their pomposity, ascetically religious moralities had turned life upside down. In turn, argued Nietzsche, their ethics had to be overthrown. Their values needed to be "transvalued" beyond good and evil, that is, beyond *counterfeit* goods and evils.[12]

Among the three goals of this comparison of the *Ups* with Nietzsche, the first is to call more attention to the significant bombardment which he sustained against the ascetical morality of the *Ups* and other religious traditions. Second, Nietzsche offers the linguistic clue through which one can perceive whether the Upanishadic virtues comprise amoral mores or universal morality. Like Nietzsche in his own time, the Upanishadic Seers were striving to propose a whole new way of life which was actually revolutionary with respect to previous Vedic tradition. While this lifestyle did not exclude conventional morality from the married stage of life, it sought to transvalue the ascetical *dharma* into a basic attitude which was so morally superior that it was unspeakably so. It went beyond or "shook off" good and evil. Like Nietzsche, the ascetical composers of the *Ups* were straining linguistically to express a new, transcending, or "super" morality, although in content theirs was opposite to Nietzsche's. But whatever its ascetical ethos, this trans-moral world of the *Ups* did not exclude morality from its purview.

Third, neither did the *Ups* go very far in the positive promotion of a universal morality. Rather it focused on the specifically ascetical virtues of a limited group.[13] In a hierarchical model, stages and goals of life other than the ascetical and mystical (*moksha*) functioned as merely developmental prerequisites for the trans-moral life of the ascetic who approached or realized *moksha* in this life (the *jivanmukta*). In medieval times, as chapter eight will delineate, Upanishadic morality underwent further qualification. The philosopher, Śaṅkara, supported the omission of all but the highest, ascetical stage of life and dismissed all human values except mystical *moksha*. But prior to this development, the *Ups* themselves had already stressed ascetical, group virtues to the relative neglect of the social virtues and a universal ethic. In recent times, the "supermen" ethos of the ascetics was described in such Nietzschean language by the modern Hindu reformer, Aurobindo Ghose.[14] Like Kierkegaard's Abraham or Knight of Faith, this supergroup was to transcend and, sometimes, even suspend the esthetical and moral levels of life in a third, supreme level of *śraddhā* (religious faith).[15]

Theoretically, nevertheless, everyone was expected to cultivate universal virtues like giving (especially the householder), compassion, self-restraint (*Bṛ*. 6.2.16) and nonviolence.[16] Additional, general, social norms in negative form prohibited murder, abortion, theft, adultery, and the consumption of alcohol (*Chānd.* 5.10.9; 5.115 and *Kauṣ*. 3.1). Together with the vigorous Upanishadic praise for and equation of truthfulness and the right,[17] this list of proscriptions formed an ancient Hindu analogue for the celebrated five Buddhist precepts.

With further norms to honor parents and not to covet added to the list (*Taitt.* 1.11.2 and *Īśā* 1), the content of universal commandments theoretically equals and surpasses that of the last seven commandments of the Jewish decalogue. True, *dharma* sometimes operates as a mere Brahminic (*Taitt.* 1.11.2) or warrior code (*Bṛ.* 4.14) whereby "the weak control the strong." However, it is equated with *rita* and universalized in several passages.[18] Further, it is identified with Brahman-*Ātman* (*Bṛ.* 2.2.1. and *Śvet.* 6.6). Lastly, it includes love for *Ātman* in every creature (*Bṛ.* 2.4.5 and *Taitt.* 1.11). But for all these verbal affirmations, it is the ascetical ethos which predominates.

D. The Ascetical Ethos.

Contrasted with brief and cryptic stanzas about worldly enjoyment and action (*Īśa* 1 and *Taitt* 1.11.1), wealth, pleasure, beauty, joy, and a long life are said to cause decay and undesirable cyclic rebirth (*Kaṭha* 1.27-28 and *Maitri* 1.4). This ethos was crystallized by Albert Schweitzer as one of world- and life-negation, as opposed to "life-affirmation," a healthy reverence and love for all forms of life. Further, by insisting that this negativism was part and parcel of Hinduism, he implicitly demanded the abrogation of the whole tradition and blocked all continuity with the past.[19]

Among the reactions occasioned by Schweitzer's barrage, Sarvepalli Radhakrishnan's was typical. He replied that a this-world- and life-asserting love has to be rooted in an Upanishadic other-worldliness. Only then can love become authentically disinterested or "other"-interested.[20] This mystical-moral worldview makes sense in the light of the ancient controversy rekindled by modern philosophical egotism—what is best for me and General Motors is naturally or automatically best for the country. In insoluble conflicts of self and other interest, what could make self-sacrificial altruism desirable except divine or other-worldly sanction? In another kind of language: one cannot ground ethical altruism without mysticism. As has been seen, not all ethical altruists agree with that position.

Radhakrishnan's response to Schweitzer has been faulted in turn on two scores.[21] First, the judgment of Indian scholars like the historian, Surendra Nath Dasgupta, coheres with Schweitzer's that non-involvement in nature is characteristic of all Indian "philosophies" except Buddhism. Second, there is no adequate continuity between confirmation of this world and a life whose goal is liberation from this world. This same unworkable discontinuity has been observed about the moral ramifications of Aurobindo Ghose's teachings.[22] But the dilemma or "mystery" of the discontinuous is not unique to Upanishadic or other mystical-moral worldviews. Not even the overarching genius of the Christian Teilhard de Chardin could explain it satisfactorily. Why go on building an earth which is programmed to self-destruct, like every human body, or deflects human beings from their supreme and final goal ? The question deserves more attention in the future. At any rate, although mysticism in the *Ups* and elsewhere has promoted life-negation in historical fact, it is no more compelled to do so logically than is any other world-view which admits the impermanence of this "non-lasting city."

Counterarguments that world-building does not divert but facilitates spiritual growth reflect forms of contemporary humanism. But do they mirror the view of the *Ups* ? The answer of the *Ups* themselves is both yes and no. With the deceptively simple, pragmatic device of *āśramas* a householder can build the world. Later in the forest, he can leave it. He can have his world and leave it too. What remains as a matter of historical complexity is the varying extent to which the forest ethos affected or dominated the rest of Hindu life. Much depended on the form and strength with which Upanishadic Brahmins validated their assertions.

E. *Ethical Validation*

The three-pronged appeal of the *Vedas* to *rita*, divine authority and group experience of undesired consequences of conduct provided implicit answers to the penultimate questions of legitimation that arise in metaethics. In the *Ups*, Vedic validations of morality survive, but in new forms. Vedic argumentation by way of the this-worldly consequences of giving or gambling on oneself or others is replaced with an estimate of their effects on future rebirth and *moksha*. The Upanishadic shift away from a rational analysis of this-worldly effects redistributes the burden of ethical validation to other principal sources which are said to ground ethical claims, namely, arguments from 1) divine authority, 2) divine order, 3) a non-inferential, but divinely inspired realization of *Ātman* akin to intuition, and 4) human authority.

First, it is "the divine voice" of Prajāpati which enjoins a virtuous life of restraint, giving, and compassion (*Bṛ*. 5.2.2). What charts the "path to the world of good deeds" (*Muṇḍ*. 1.1) are the "sacred *mantras*" of the *Vedas*. As in the *Vedas*, appeals to tradition and divine authority eventually merge.[23] Second, *dharma* is apparently still bound up with *rita* or the cosmic divine order, one not limitedly relative to what human consciousness would make of it. Third, since it is uncertain that the entirety of *dharma* is manifest to the unaided human eye, further moral guidance is to be had in observing the virtues of good Brahmins (*Taitt*. 1.112). Fourth, it is the Brahmins who relay and interpret both the Vedic *mantras* and ultimate truths (*Muṇḍ*. 1.2.12). Most significantly, Brahminic discourse itself is to be entitled "*śruti*," truths divinely inspired. Since by divine order, human planning, or chance the canon of *śruti* became theoretically closed precisely with the Upanishadic pronouncements, the potential of Brahminic authority, moral and otherwise, was, in principle, maximal. It was further enhanced by the Brahminic confirmation of four divinely designed classes among which theirs was supreme (*Bṛ*. 1.4.11).

No matter how strongly the Brahmins made verbal claims to moral authority, this fact does not demonstrate that their rule was historically effective, either as regards the *kshatriya* class or the classes in general. Mere analysis of textual claims cannot solve matters of historical fact. However, one can speculate on the psychological theory that strongly authoritative claims often beget effects opposite to those desired. If individuality is suppressed, people may seldom *disobey*, but they may be disposed to a state of inert *non-obedience*.

F. *The Individual and the Class Structure*

What were originally two main classes or *varṇas* (literally colors), dark skinned natives (*dāsas* or *rākṣasas*) and lighter skinned Aryan conquerers from the northwest, become clearly four in the *Ups*. The Āryan Brahmins and *Kshatriyas* split into a third principal group, the *viś* or *vaiśyas*, whereas the natives become a fourth varṇa (*śūdras* or slaves) and also outcastes. If one chooses, like Weber, to minimize the continuing racial significance of these divisions,[24] then their genesis has to be explored in terms of economics, power, religion, or other factors. Religion is the source according to the *Ups*. The *varṇas* are divinely created (*Bṛ.* 1.4.11.-15).

In an Upanishadic anecdote sometimes used to illustrate the ultimate spiritual egalitarianism of the class system, a youth who admits his ignorance about his ancestry receives Brahminic assurance that his truthfulness could emanate only from a Brahmin. While this argument for equality may fail by proving too much, the story does point to a special Brahminic monopoly on the truth, including the truth behind moral judgment. In a dazzling circularity of Anselmian logic, it is maintained that since all truths about morality, caste, or religion are entrusted to the Brahmins, then this claim itself is one whose Delphic truth finds final verification in Brahminic authority. The apparently oceanic leap from the shore of thought to the land of fact is, of course, not peculiar to Upanishadic mysticism or religion. Moreover, it grounds the related and specific ethos of Manu, in which there is little place for individual conscience.

NOTES

1. See Robert Ernest Hume, trans., *The Thirteen Principal Upanishads* (rpt 1975, 2d rev. ed.; London, Oxford, New York : Oxford University Press, 1931), *Śvet.* 6.3.7 and 7.17; *Muṇḍ.* 2.28, and *Kaṭha* 2.23. For example, the theistically inclined *Śvet.* is said to contain the dualistic ideas of *sāmkhya* philosophy and yoga or a mixture of the two as in *Maitri* 6. 7-8.

2. In accord with the suggestion of S. Radhakrishnan, Hume's "soul" is replaced with the original "*Ātman*" or Self.

3. Is this release the same as *nirvāṇa*? Helpful indices notwithstanding, I have not been able to locate "*nirvāṇa*" in the *Ups*. Taken as a non-dualistic concept less positive than *moksha*, the possible absence of the term may signify its Hindu appropriation at a later time, nourished by Buddhist and *Av* influences. Lal Mani Joshi has contested the once accepted opinion of M. Winternitz that the *Ups* were largely pre-Buddhist (except for a few fourth century passages like *Bṛ.* 3.2.12 and 6). See Joshi's *Brahmanism, Buddhism, and Hinduism*, The Wheel Publication 150/151 (Kandy, Ceylon : Buddhist Publication Society, 1970). As was noted in chapter one, Joshi defends the greater antiquity of Buddhism, its *śramanic* or ascetical impact on the *Ups* (*Śrama* means exertion, a term related to the stage or *āśrama* of ascetical exertion, after which

other *āśramas* took their generic nomenclature). Joshi also noted the *Ups*' opposition to the *Vedas* against theism, ritual sacrifice, and life-affirmation. The scriptural canonicity and authority of the thirteen or fourteen main *Ups* (called *Vedānta*, end and goal of the *Vedas*) was confirmed by Śaṅkara and extended to the philosophical aphorisms (*Brahma or Vedānta Sūtras*) which encapsulated them and which provided the bases for later Vedāntic philosophical commentaries.

4. In short, "all evil is traceable to *ahaṃkāra*, the affirmation of a finite [dualistically separate] self-existence; [see *Maitri* 6.28] and the consequent tendency not to live in harmony with the rest of the world..." Hiriyanna, *Outlines of Indian Philosophy*, p. 73.

5. See *Rv* I.89. In a repetition of the Vedic picture of sin as crooked-going (*enas*), the *Ups.* ask the god, Agni, to preserve people from *enas* (*Bṛ.* 5.14.8 and *Īśā* 18). The sun is beseeched to "snatch away my sin" (*pāpa* or evil as opposed to *sādhu* or good, *Kaush.* 2.7 and *Taitt.* 2.9) Vedically equated with *anrita* or falsehood, sin opposes *satya* or truth (*Taitt.* 2.6). Of the several other synonyms for sin given in P.V. Kane's *History of Dharmaśāstra* IV, 5-8, none is indexed in Hume's translation of the *Ups.*

6. See also *Maitri* 7.9. On the *Ups*' deterministic strain, see *Kauṣ.* 38 and Kane's *History* IV, 4 as opposed to *Bṛ.* 3.2.13. As for the utter gratuity of realizing *Ātman*, see *Muṇḍ.* 3.2.3 and *Kaṭha* 2.23.

7. Contrast the seemingly immoral *Bṛ.* 5.14.8 and *Chānd.* 5.10. 9-10 with *Kaṭha* 2.24 : "Not he who has not ceased from bad conduct....can obtain him by intelligence." Consult also the double-truth model of knowledge in *Muṇḍ.* 1.1.4-5: moral knowledge is presently necessary, but finally dispensable. For other verses which seem to approve immorality see *Chānd.* 4. 14.3; *Bṛ.* 3.2.13; *Praśna* 3.7; *Maitri* 3.2 and 4.4, *Kaṭha* 3.7.8 and 5.7; and *Muṇḍ.* 1.3.11.

8. Nietzsche, *Zur Genealogie der Moral* I, 14; trans. Walter Kaufmann, *On the Genealogy of Morals* (New York : Vintage Books, 1969), p. 47.

9. *Ibid.*, pp. 36-37.

10. *Ibid.*, pp. 106-8 and 115.

12. The very phrase is the title of Nietzsche's *Jenseits Von Gut Und Böse*, trans. W. Kaufmann, *Beyond Good and Evil* (New York : Vintage Books, 1966)

13. Virtues dispositive to discipline, meditation, and the "right viewing" of life rather than general "right doing" as in *Maitri* 4.4; *Chānd.* 2.21.1, and *Bṛ.* 6.2.16.

14. A thesis developed in her doctoral dissertation at Temple University by Dr. June O'Connor with whom I was privileged to collaborate as first reader; now published as *The Quest for Political and Spiritual Liberation : A Study in the Thought of Sri Aurobindo Ghose* (Rutherford, New Jersey : Fairleigh Dickenson University Press, 1976).

15. See Soren Kierkegaard on the "Knight of Faith's" "teleological suspension of the ethical" (religious insight prevailing over common morality's precept against killing) in *Fear and Trembling*, trans. Walter Lowrie (Princeton, New Jersey : Princeton University Press, 1941).

16. See *Chānd.* 8.15 and 3.17.4 as opposed to the *Gītā's* (2.19-20) use of *Kaṭha* 2.18-19.

17. Extended assent to social virtues can be located in *Bṛ* 6.2.16; *Chānd.* 2.21.1,3, and 17.4; and *Taitt.* 1.9 and 1.11.2.

18. See *Bṛ.* 1.4.14; *Chānd.* 3.17.4; 6.1.16; 7.1.17; and *Taitt.* 1.9, 11.2; *Bṛ.* 2.5.12; and *Kaṭha* 31.

19. Scheweitzer, *Indian Thought and Its Development*, trans. C.E.B. Russel (rpt. 1960; Boston : Beacon Press, 1936).

20. See Wm. F. Goodwin's review of the Scheweitzer-Radhakrishnan debate in "Mysticism and Ethics.....," *Ethics* 67, 1 (October 1956), 25-41—years before this journal had limited its consideration of the philosophy of ethics to exclude Asian contributions.

21. See Goodwin, *ibid.*

22. Confer note 14 above.

23. As in *Bṛ.* 2.6 and 4.5.

24. Weber, *The Religion of India*, pp. 119, 124, 126, and 351, n.18. For comparative references with the *Rākshashas* of the epics, see Hume's translation of the term in *Maitri* 1.4 and 7.6 as "ogres."

CHAPTER IV

ETHICS IN MANU

Abstract. Chief and most famous of the law codes of India, *The Laws of Manu* (*Manu*)—200 B.C.E.—100 C.E.—survived as a basis for practice until the nineteenth century. For many it remains to this day the key to translating modern Indian civil law into indigenous and effective language. Its numerous and comprehensive injunctions, directed to all castes, were edited and reinforced by ascetical and newly world-concerned Brahmins in their own name and in the name of the Self-existent. A. *Ethical validation by Brahminic authority* superseded every other form of appeal. B. *Structures of ethical significance : the dynamics of classes and stages.* After identifying their authority with divinity, the Brahmins employed it to legitimate both castes and stages of life. The former functioned as a symbol not only for direct societal power over other castes and over law in general, but as a noetic structure for interpreting life itself. The *āśramic* schema exalted the ascetical stages whose ethos overflowed in multiple ascetical regulations for householders. Together these structures reflected a mystical worldview quite concerned with the ethical-legal regulations of social life. C. *Morality or mores?* For all their ascetical tone, the laws of Manu appear not amoral, but moral (or immoral) in that they were universally directed to every class and caste. D. *In search of an ethos* : while the ethoses of giving, caste, and justice are salient, they are submerged in the kinds of relationships which individuals were allowed in their functions as sexual beings, caste members, and parts of society. As for women, they were protected and discriminated against on the grounds of their weakness and seductiveness, if not for other racial and social factors. Outcastes and the lowest castes were immobilized economically, juridically, and socially. For them, in particular, physical punishments were severe; but everyone lacked basic civil rights in court procedures, marriage laws, etc. As a result, even if the institutes of Manu were largely ignored in practice, they may have occasioned a psychological reaction in the direction of inert non-obedience. Whether the ideals of Manu were those of the people can be better verified in the examination of popular literature like the *Rāmāyaṇa* (chapters five and seven). NOTES.

The *Ups* had offered few norms to regulate the complexities of social existence. Therefore, if the principal and most famous Hindu lawbook, the laws (*śāstras*) or institutes of Manu (200 B.C.E.-100 C.E.), was composed by the same Brahminic authors without lay participation, one might at first expect them to carry on in the same asocial vein. On the contrary, not only did they embody a code for forest-destined Brahmins, but they attempted to systematize and repromulgate multiple laws and customs which had dealt with social relationships across all classes. Furthermore, *dharma-śāstra* in general, and the laws of Manu in particular, never acquired the character of "Western" laws which have legally bound judges. However, they remained the sole authority until nineteenth century British rule and contemporary Indian reforms.[1] In the opinion of some Indians, modern civil law will not become effective until it is translated into the language and thought patterns of Manu, so indelible was the impression made by the *śāstric* tradition.

On the other hand, others, like J.M.D. Derrett, point to the gap between Hindu legal aspirations and actual practice. The performance gap, argues Derrett, should not evoke defensive cultural shame, but curiosity.[2] To amplify his observation, how could laws offered under such powerful religious and societal caste-sanctions fail to be effective? It has already been theorized above that customs and laws which were imposed under severe religious threats could have backfired. They could have promoted a psychological disposition to inertia, non-obedience, or even a kind of unintended disposition for Gandhi's more passive forms of resistance. The same speculation would apply equally to laws which were too numerous and intrusive, at least by some contemporary social standards.

By any criteria, the laws of Manu were indeed multiple and most solemnly validated. Ascetical and contemplative Brahmins had undertaken the responsibility of re-promulgating ancient and sometimes conflicting laws in their own name and in the name of Brahman. The laws were ascribed to the first man (*Manu* or humanity personified) who had heard them from the Self-existent. Technically "recollected traditions" (*smriti*) were given divine legitimation as scriptural *śruti* (what was divinely heard or realized, *Manu* I.102 and II.10).

A. *Ethical Validation by Brahminic Authority*

The continuity between the asocial *Ups* and the socially concerned institutes of Manu lay less in their similar resort to divine authority than in the joint identification of that authority with Brahmins themselves. It was only the Brahmins who were to study and interpret the laws of Man, "nobody else" (*Manu* I.103).

> Even that which one Brāhmaṇa versed in the Veda declares to be law, must be considered (to have) supreme legal force, but not that which is proclaimed by myriads of ignorant men (I.113). Thus did that worshipful deity disclose to me [Manu] through a desire of benefiting mankind, this whole most excellent secret of the sacred law (I.117). He who recognizes the universe in the Self [*Ātman*], does not give his heart to unrighteousness (I.118).

Brahminic law superseded the *Vedas*. Since some *Vedas* were lost, doubts could be resolved by following the institutes of Manu. Whatever was there must have also been present in the *Vedas* (*Manu* II.7). Even two conflicting laws were held to be equally Vedic and valid (*Manu* II.14). To scorn universal Brahminic authority was to scorn the *Vedas*. As Nikhilananda would claim in a modern introduction to the *Vedāntasāra*, enlightened gurus are essential for knowing "whether our interpretation of the words of Śruti is correct."[3] The only qualification to Brahminic supremacy over "conscience" was a debated allusion to "self-justification" which may have referred exclusively to *Brahminic* self-satisfaction: "The whole Veda is the first source of the sacred law, next the tradition and the virtuous conduct of those who know the (Veda further), also the customs of holy men, and (finally) self-satisfaction" (*Manu* II.6).

As in the *Ups*, Vedic moral validation by reasoning from consequences was overshadowed by a related, but different, appeal to karmic effects. Without specification, bad conduct was said to effect misfortune, disease, and a short life. Contrarily, virtue brought wealth, longevity (IV.156-58 and 173), fame, and bliss after death (II.2.9). With karmic inevitability "justice being violated destroys; justice being preserved, preserves." "With whatever disposition of mind (a man) performs any act, he reaps its results in a (future) body endowed with the same quality" (XII.83). There were situational exceptions to law, like lying to preserve another's life (VII.104) or some divorce and remarriage (IX.175) but these residually contextualist inferences (XII.105) were reserved only for the professional or official interpreters of the laws. It was they alone who were to decide what was consistent with the *Vedas*.

Endowed with such interpretive power, the Brahmins' potential for defining the meaning and rules of life was to be limited only by their integrity, their fear of karmic effects, or their thirst for "fame" and "unsurpassable bliss after death" (II.9). Thus, the rationale for authority in Manu postulated a steady supply of virtuous teachers whose voices would presumably dominate over false prophets. Meanwhile, the method of moral justification which underpinned Manu was neither human insight nor consequentialist reasoning from conscience, but the invocation of an authority which was both divine and Brahminic. How their decisions fared concretely requires examination in a wider framework : the individual's role within the system of castes, stages, *karma*, and society in general.

B. *Structures of Ethical Significance : Classes and Stages of Life.*

1. *The dynamics of caste.* Reserving chiefly for others the fuller inquiry into possible inequities resulting from caste the present analysis concentrates on the principal motivations and dynamics behind caste. Amid labyrinthine ritual, social, and moral prescriptions in Manu, caste functioned as the superstructure in both the legitimation and delineation of the moral life. Caste was itself divinely legitimated.

> 1.87. But in order to protect this universe He, the most resplendent one, assigned separate (duties and) occupations to those who sprang from his mouth, arms, thighs, and feet. 88. To Brāhmaṇas he assigned teaching and studying (the Veda), sacrificing for their own benefit and for others, giving and accepting (of alms). 89. The Kshatriya he commanded to protect the people, to bestow gifts, to offer sacrifices [note the reappropriation of *himsā* or sacrifice], to study (the Veda) and to abstain from attaching himself to sensual pleasures. 90. The Vaiśya to tend cattle, to bestow gifts, to offer sacrifices, to study (the Veda), to trade, to lend money, and to cultivate land. 91. One occupation only the lord prescribed to the Śūdra, to serve meekly even these (other) three castes. 99. A Brāhmaṇa, coming into existence, *is born as the highest on earth, the lord of all created beings* [emphasis added], for the protection of the treasury of the law. 102. In order to clearly settle his duties and those of the other (castes) according to their order, wise Manu sprung from the Self-existent, composed these Institutes (of the sacred law). 103. A learned Brāhmaṇa....

> must duly instruct his pupils in them, but nobody else (shall do it).

Subjected to a secular mode of interpretation, the significance of caste, particularly the Brahmins' position, might lie in meaning, power, or a combination of these. Weber favored the hermeneutics of meaning. For him, the systematic unity of Brahminic society lay in the structure of classes (*varṇas*) and subcastes (*jātis*) here designated by the convenient umbrella synonyms "class" and "caste." Caste is explained not by economic conditions as in Marxism, argues Weber, but by a projection of "theodicy," a symbol system which produces meaning.

> The combination of caste legitimacy with karma doctrine, thus with the specific Brahmanical theodicy—in its way a stroke of genius—plainly is the construction of rational ethical thought and not the product of any economic "conditions."[4]

The case for a meaning system is an appealing non-Marxist alternative for many philosophers and other macro-theorists like Weber. With explicit reference to the Brahmins, it was also attractive to Nietzsche who theorized that the system was a Brahminic machination meant to instil fear and to satisfy "an even more fundamental need," fear and reverence by others for Brahmins.

Another explication of the caste-*karma* structure so trenchant in Manu relies less exclusively on the "search for meaning" in life and operates from a hermeneutic of *meaning combined with power*. Along with creed (meaning), there are code and cult, both of which can be utilized as instruments of power. The data pointing to this more complex organism are considerable. Segregation in occupation and function is to be strictly enforced by punishments. "The whole world is kept in order by punishment [*daṇḍa*], for a guiltless man is hard to find;. . . ." (VII.22). Without punishment "all castes (*varṇas*) would be corrupted (by intermixture), all barriers would be broken through. . . ." (VII.24). The laws of caste gave the Brahmins power over the ruling and military establishment (VIII.306-9 and 381), the courts (VIII.9) and everyone else as well. As the *Ups* had conceived it, "A weak man controls a strongman by Law" (*Bṛ.* 1.4.14). Through sometimes conflicting injunctions, the Brahmins held the widest options for marriage, other men being unable to marry up the social ladder (III.4-44 and X.31). Other Brahminic benefits included physical protection by everyone, a kind of guaranteed income,[5] access to servants and slaves (IX.235), and prestige bordering on worship (IX.317 and X.3). Not to be overlooked was their power in making, interpreting, and enforcing laws (XI.31-34), and last, but not least, the official and exclusive power of describing and defining reality, that is, the truths of the *Vedas* and the knowledge of Brahmān (X.1). If the latter prerogative seems limitedly spiritual and abstract, one may recall its not inconsiderable attraction to modern, leading definers of other religious, philosophical, cultural, or political worldviews. Whether they are understood as "participations" in divine rights, human mesmerization by ambition, or the drive to control for the sake of other ends, the noetic powers of explaining reality have continued to galvanize leaders in sciences, technology, and the mass media. If the popularity of the role still remains baffling, the puzzle may be partly ascribed to the indistinguishable zone which sometimes lies between the worlds of theoria and praxis, creative imagination and invention, or political vision and fantasy.

So paradigmatically important is the merging of concrete and noetic power in the Brahmins that it merits an attempt to comprehend it by a second and concluding digression. A socialist could aver that money is not power, unless it is butteressed by a capitalistic worldview which decrees that money will symbolize accomplishment and reward. A capitalist could retort that mere symbolic participation in or socialistic proximity to the centers of prestige, influence, and decision-making (the merit badge system) cannot of themselves replace monetary strength without a worldview that so ordains. Either position illustrates the symbiotic relationship between the power of ruling and of defining the meaning of reality.

Brahminic preoccupations with power's defining aspect are discernible in a graphic eschatology which integrates both hells and miserable rebirths—in lower castes or in simpler, living or inanimate creatures (VI. 61-63; XII.15-81). Their nearly Buddhistic reflections on the tortures of repeated separations, old age, suffering and death (XII.78-80) might seem discouraging to Indians who speculated pessimistically on the difficulties of transcending stages of inanimation or animality. (One could conjecture that this pessimism might have driven many to Buddhist worldviews whenever they looked more promising.) In the interim, common Hindu morality fit into the system of *karma*-caste as a pathway to rebirth into higher castes. Higher castes thereby achieved their own teleological significance (IX.335; X.127-28, and XII.9). Conjoined with a more distant ultimate liberation, upward social mobility became the more immediate and palpable goal for all but the highest caste. At a surface level, all but the highest class were to be content with a downstairs level of existence. Upon eventual rebirth into the upper class or upstairs Brahminic level, one was eligible to seek the final height of *moksha*. Meanwhile, there was a double standard of life and morality.

The trans-morality of mysticism was not synthesized but was simultaneously affirmed with a lower morality of *karma*-rebirth. There were, finally, two kinds of existence which required a double standard : "The acts prescribed by the Veda are of two kinds, such as procure an increase of happiness and cause a continuation (of mundane existence, *pravritta*), and such as endure supreme bliss and cause a cessation (of mundane existence, *nivritta*)," (XII.88). The first set of acts results in length of life, children, and wealth as opposed to disease and misfortune (IV.156). The latter kind of acts is performed "without any desire (for a reward), preceded by (the acquisition) of (true) knowledge. . . ." (XII.89). This most excellent knowledge is the recognition of all things in *Ātman* which brings righteousness (XII.85 and 118).

2. *The four āśramas or stages of life.* The entire moral system of *dharma* in Manu was framed within a triangle. Besides caste and *karma*, there were *āśramas* or the stages of life. Theoretically, there were four stages, although the latter two tended to receive combined commentary : 1) the *Brahmacāri* or students who dwell with the ascetics; 2) the *Grihastha* or householder; 3) the *Vānaprastha* or retired ascetic; and 4) the *Sannyāsin*, the mendicant who relinquishes the way of sacrifices and good works (VI.87). As indicated earlier, it was apparent already in the later *Ups* that the *āśramas*, especially the second and third (the worldly and the ascetical) functioned as amazing developmental devices whereby an other-worldly ethics coexisted with another one more affirmative of the present life. Although

descriptions of the successive stages were primarily addressed to Brahmins, they have been extended to all three top Aryan castes, as in the passage just cited about the double moral standard.

The synthesis of the first three *āśramas* was constructed on the basic principle of the three Vedic "debts" or (*ṛṇas*). The debts referred to the education given by the Seers or *rishis*, to the life one has received from one's ancestors, and to gifts from the deities. Correspondingly, they were paid by learning as student, procreating as householder, and sacrificing as student, householder, and ascetic (VI.35-37). Historically, the latter ascetical stages dominated not only in the above-mentioned code of the double standard, but also in the fact that students could serve their ascetical teachers for life as a guarantee of liberation without rebirths (II.244 and 249), a prelude of Śaṅkara's more explicit declaration. However, an opposite this-worldliness prevailed when "in accordance with the precepts of the Veda and of the Smriti, the housekeeper is declared to be superior to all of them; for he supports the other three" (VI.89). The householder's stage was generally obligatory (compare *Manu* VI.37 with 2.244).

The neatness of this polar model is spoiled by a close look at prescriptions for the householder which are both painstakingly numerous and ascetical. Leaving little to the imagination, multiple and detailed directions abound about association with *cāṇḍālas* (outcastes) and *śūdras* (IV.79ff and III.239), ritual, occupations, diet, toiletry, behavior, general life style, and thoughts (as in *Manu*, chaps. or books III-V). As a result, not only did the Brahminic lawgivers legislate total control, but they injected an ascetical tone into the this-worldly stage of life.

C. *Morality or Mores ?*

Preliminary to further inquiry into the value emphases or ethos of Manu is the issue of morality itself. Among conditions frequently demanded as preconditions for authentic morality are those of 1) altruistic motivation, 2) knowledge, 3) volition, and 4) universality. Manu's passing treatment of the first three requirements may be mentioned in brief, but fuller attention is required for universality. 1) A kind of altruistic motivation can be grounded in Manu's belief in everyone's identification with *Ātman* conjoined with the rejection of the desires of individual egos. 2) Equated with ignorance but rarely (XII.26), in Manu sin was intentional (= attention?) (XI.46), although not to the degree of clear volition (*citta*) assumed by later *bhakti* poets like Tulsīdās. 3) Belief in volitional guilt is not the only explanation for the severity of Manu's penalties. On grounds of volition alone, the case for morality in Manu could be pressed in either direction.

4) *Universality*. When Weber insisted that Upanishadic *dharma* was entirely relative to caste and was not universal, he grudgingly admitted the existence of eight "unusually colorless" virtues indispensable for *all* Āryans which became "somewhat more positive" in Manu.[6] This admission is crucial in the debate about whether Brahminic ethics were simply codes of in-group mores or a universally applicable morality. According to Manu itself, the virtues to which Weber refers were ideals which applied to people in every stage of life and explicitly to the members of the three (top) Āryan *varṇas*. In continuity with the moral universalization already evident in the *Ups* and possibly in Vedic *rita*, Manu decreed: "By twice-born [the top three *varṇas* educated or *reborn* in the Veda-knowledge] men belonging to (any of) these four orders, the tenfold-law must be ever carefully obeyed" (VI.91):[7] 1. Contentment, *Dhairya* or *Dhriti*; 2. Forgiveness (*Kṣamā*); 3. Self-control (*Dama*); 4. Abstention from unrighteously appropriating anything (*Asteya*); 5. Obedience to the rules of purification (*Śauca*) [cleanliness]; 6. Coercion of the organs (*Indriya Nigraha*) [control of desire]; 7. Wisdom (*Dhī*); 8. Knowledge of the Supreme *Ātman* (*Vidyā*); 9. Truthfulness (*Satya*); 10. Abstention from anger (*Akrodha*). (*Manu* VI.92).[7] In Cromwell Crawford's opinion, these are ascetical, dianoetic, and unsocial virtues. The point here is that they did not make up the exclusive *dharma* of a particular *varṇa* or *āśrama*, but a common, universal *dharma* (*sādhāraṇa*) which can be called morality.[8]

Even more explicit mention of universality occurs in *Manu* X.63: "Abstention from injuring (creatures), veracity, abstention from unlawfully appropriating (the goods of others), purity, and control of the organs, Manu has declared to be the summary of the law for the four castes." Compared to the commandments in the *Ups* or to the five Buddhist precepts, Manu's "summary" differed by adding control of the organs and by omitting precepts against abortion and alcohol; but these, along with a prohibition against gambling (IX.221), were legislated elsewhere (V.90 and IV.235; see also XI.88).

However, the Upanishadic injunction toward *ahimsā* (nonviolence) was qualified substantively, for example with norms that kings should inflict punishments (*daṇḍa*) previously specified (like the enforcement of contracts) by the compilers of *Manu* and their commentators. The recommended punishments ranged from admonitions and imprisonment to torture, dismemberment, castration, and exile (VIII.24-420). A directly imposed death penalty was prescribed for theft as well as killing (VIII.34). Moreover, one could kill an aggressor to defend one's self, women, friends (VII.165), and to defend Brahmins or to protect the fees of officiating priests (VIII. 3-19).

While none of these textually recorded admonitions tells the reader how effectively kings and rules enforced such norms and violence in actual practice, "punishment alone" was said to govern all created beings (VII.18). "The whole world is kept in order by punishment, for a guiltless man is hard to find" (VII.22, guilt not being clearly *moral* guilt). That kings were not always cooperative with the many strictures on their authority (VII.26-36) might be inferred from the repetitiveness of the commands. A similar judgment could be extended to the frequently enjoined subordination of rulers to Brahmins (VII. 37-58) whose administrative counsel was proposed to be decisive (VII.58), even in matters of war. The plausibility of their noncooperation with the Brahminic version of *dharma*, and of *rāja-dharma* in particular, is strengthened by historical records of the internecine struggles of Indian kings which frequently attracted foreign invasions.[9]

An inquiry into how Manu's counterpoint theme of *ahimsā*, in particular, fared in historical performance would investigate Weber's accusations that "India has been permanently involved in a state of ferocious warfare and unbridled lust of relentless conquest as no land on earth."[10] Gandhi's appropriation of *ahimsā* from pre-Vedic, Jaina, and Buddhist traditions rather than Hinduism could be invoked to bolster the thesis that *ahimsā* has not effectively appealed to more than a small minority.

In addition to the above-mentioned general virtues and norms, including *ahimsā/himsā*, there was one other set of commands in Manu which was addressed universally to all four castes. Categorized in bodily, verbal, and mental divisions, they expressed a new depth of interiorization. They added proscriptions against detraction, idle talk, "heretical" views, adultery, "coveting the property of others," and "thinking in one's heart what is undesirable" (XII.5-7). The first three condemnations render the list redolent of the Buddhist *daśākuśala* (the ten "not right" or evil courses of action). The Buddhist catalog differs only in its prohibition of greed and insults.

The similarity of these norms raises the historian's difficult question about which set of precepts, Hindu or Buddhist, arrived earlier. This problem is inseparable from pending critical assurance as to whether the earliest oral or written transmissions of the *Ups* or *Manu* were or were not, in some measure, Buddhistic. Of course, chronological posteriority by itself would not demonstrate causal dependence without further textual and historical assistance, given the possibilities of a common source (like *sāmkhya*, yoga, or pre-Vedic, ascetical *śrāmaṇism*) and of coincidence.

Prescinding from the reciprocal influences of codes in the *Ups*, Manu, and the Buddhist five precepts and *daśākuśala*, their similarities and differences may be summarized as follows. Manu's lists are distinguished by more social and interiorized qualities which are also found in Buddhism : forgiveness, the control of anger and of detraction, the utility of speech, and the integrity of thought and desire. Equivalents for the last seven commands in the Jewish decalogue occur both in *Manu* and the *Ups*. Whatever else may be inferred, Manu legislates moral ideals not merely for an in-group, but for all members of society. Therefore, in whatever ways universality is prerequisite for morality, the condition is met in the Institutes of Manu. The scope of these all-embracing commands equals and extends beyond those of Sinai.

Shivesh Thakur goes so far as to point to analogues in *Manu* for the Roman/Christian cardinal and theological virtues. However, it is not clear whether he claims to observe in or infer from *Manu* such qualities as courage, universal justice, and *agape*. In that comparative context, he introduces the verdict that the five Hindu values most celebrated and promulgated were "negative" : non-stealing, cleanliness, restraint of the senses, truthfulness, and non-injury or *ahimsā*.[11]

D. *In Search of An Ethos* : *Dāna or Giving*; *Caste-contentment*; *or Justice*.

While the ethoses of giving, caste-contentment, and justice were prominent, it can be briefly demonstrated that they were finally superseded by the discriminatory relationships which individuals experienced within Manu's societal structures.

1. *Dāna*. Giving was a central duty in *Manu*, even if it is not characterized by the interior qualities attributed to Christian love or *agape*. Incumbent on the top three (Āryan) castes,[12] *dāna* involved the stage of the householder in particular : A householder must give (as much food) as he is able (to spare) and to those who do not cook for themselves, and to all beings one must distribute (food) without detriment (to one's own interest)" (IV.43). More than truthfulness and other less positive virtues, *dāna* was a unique candidate for what best describes the ethos of Manu because of its place in the social structure. The socio-economic system was a hierarchical one which would have collapsed without giving. In the absence of both socialistic systems of exchange and capitalistic concentration on ever increasing production for oneself and others (ignoring the infringement on the future raw materials and heritage of later generations), giving in India became practically and ideally indispensable. But other themes appeared even more trenchantly and more frequently.

2. *Contentment with one's caste*. Sometimes moral priorities and tone may be gleaned from lists of so-called unforgivable, mortal, or deadly sins (*mahā-pātaka*). Virtues contrary to those sins reveal values which hold genuine priority. In *Manu*, the key determining factor of a sin's gravity was whether it was injurious in some way to Brahmins.[13] Manu's list of capital offenses includes interesting extensions of previous Brahminic and Buddhist catalogues like the murder of women, infants, and friends, as well as theft, fornication, the consumption of *surā* (alcohol) and forbidden foods (IX.235, XI. 56-59). The most unusual inclusion, pretension to a higher caste (XI.56), exposes a kind of spirit which will be more clearly seen in an overview of Manu's whole system of justice.

3. *Justice.* The authenticity of Manu's quest for social equity is partly manifested in the broad scope of its preoccupations. Collated into eighteen divisions, they include such subjects as sales, debts, wages, honest labor, property, assault, defamation, and inheritance. Other signs of a genuine pursuit of equity emerge in laws about property, about the quality of evidence demanded in court, and about interest taking. "Property stolen by thieves must be restored by the king to (men of) all castes (varṇa)";.... (VIII.40). Whether the *śūdras* shared in these property rights is not clear from the texts alone, since this participation was both denied (VII.417) and affirmed (IX.157). As for testimony in court, "Trustworthy men of all the (four) castes (varṇa) may be made witnesses in lawcourts...." (VIII.63) but not "Dasyus" [native Dāsas] or "men of the lowest castes, although they could give evidence for one another (VIII.66-71). Under the scrutiny of humanistic socio-economic analysis, careful restrictions on interest-taking might compare most favorably with the equity regulated by other cultural, and contemporary legal systems which obscenely *pretend* that "usury" is no longer existent, given new symbolic understandings of currency (see VIII.140-57 and X.117). Interest rates higher than two to five per cent were prohibited—the lower castes paying the higher rates. Lenders should "not take interest beyond the year, nor such as is unapproved, nor compound interest, periodical interest, stipulated interest and corporal interest" (IX.153).

In spite of these distinguished instances of comparably equal treatment under the law, justice is ultimately disqualified as a candidate for the central mood of Manu. The simultaneous presence of unjust discriminatory regulations prohibits such a judgment. They are so numerous as to merit treatment in a separate section which further specifies the issues raised above (stages and classes of life, B) under the heading of ethos of individual and societal relationships.

E. *The Ethos of Society's Priority Over the Individual.*

In a civilization where the distinct existence of individuals is believed by some to be illusory, the realization of oneness with *Ātman* might theoretically take two opposite paths: 1) reverence for the *Ātman* in every creature, and 2) positive disregard for the individual. In *Manu*, manifestations of the latter may be subsumed under three groupings, depending on whether individual identity is sacrificed to 1) sexual function, 2) caste function, or 3) one's role in society as a whole.

1. *Sexual discrimination*. In Manu's culture, women were considered to be weak, wicked, seductive, and always socially dependent on males.[14] "Manu allotted to women....impure desires, wrath, dishonesty, malice, and bad conduct" (IX.17). The marital relationship was hierarchically conceived. By some contemporary standards, it was clearly chauvinistic: "Though destitute of virtue, or seeking pleasure (elsewhere), or devoid of good qualities, (yet) a husband must be constantly worshipped as a god by a faithful wife" (V.154). "....she must never mention the name of another man after her husband has died" (V.157). Furthermore, her rights in court, in divorce cases, or in freedom of association were unequal (III.239; VII.77 and IX. 77-82). Polygamy too was common (IX.149). Prohibitions against polygamy and the possibility of initiating divorce by women were not legalized until the twentieth century. Even *suttee* or widow-burning was legal from the seventh to nineteenth centuries.

Yet women were to be honored. They would brighten their homes "if they are beautiful" (III. 56-62). Part of this protective attitude towards women in *Manu* has been attributed to the great fear of the racial and social effects which might ensue if women could marry or procreate with men of lower castes (VIII.353). Only in rare instances does a counter-theme affirming spousal love and happiness approach the very diverse milieu depicted in the *Vedas*, the core-*Mbh*, or the *Ry* (e.g., in *Manu* IX.28 and 45).

2. *Caste discrimination*. George Orwell's "all men are equal, but some are more equal than others" was applied not only sexually but, as the reader may have noted, to the Brahmins as a class, even if some Brahmins were materially quite poor (for these and others the Brahmins did have a societal mechanism of excommunication). Earlier in this chapter, the concern was mainly to observe the dynamics of the economic, legal, social, and reality-defining power which came to be invested in the Brahmins. Here it is simply to emphasize the obvious conclusion that these inequalities were, by some recent criteria, also inequities.

By caste alone, individuals (especially *caṇḍālas* or outcastes) were "given" unequal rights economically, juridically, socially (by rules of association and marriage), and penally. In particular, all lower castes were subjected to what would be labeled today as the "cruel unusual punishments" of dismemberment and painful deaths. Freedom of speech varied according to caste. Employment was regulated by caste. The slavery of the *Śūdras* was explicitly encouraged (VIII. 412-16). Unequal opportunity insured deterministic social immobility: "A man of low caste who through covetousness lives by the occupations of a higher one, the king shall deprive of his property and banish" (X.96). "No collection of wealth must be made by a Śūdra, even though he be able (to do it); for a Śūdra who has acquired wealth gives pain to Brāhmaṇas" (X.129).

While comparison between social and economic immobility in Manu and existing civilizations may be overdone, C. Wright Mills' famous sociological evidence of contemporary immobility may provide insights into Manu's milieu. He contends that it is chiefly the rich who grow richer. Others do not. Apart from both genuine and dubious benefits which accrue to all members of "developed" societies, few rise above the relative economic standard of their parents. The significance of Mills' observation does not rest chiefly in its application to purely economic norms of living. His model of economic immobility applies rather to the whole world of power. The more one lacks power of any kind (intellectual, linguistic, emotional, or class), the more impossible it is to move "upward" or "forward." Above all, modes and habits of conceptualization are notoriously impervious to change, whether the scene involves patriotism, politics, or religion. Few people have changed themselves through the attraction of logic or ideas alone. It usually takes notable events or experiences to provide the proper setting for such intellectual movement. Thus, some cynics add that almost no one changes or is changed in religious views or world views by appeals to the mind alone. Furthermore, they may continue, those who do alter intellectually tend to stir up the stormiest reactions. Be that as it may, modern experiences of varied forms of immobility offer bases for an empathetic understanding of caste immobility in the society of Manu.

In an extended sense, caste systems, then and now, are eluded with difficulty. In spite of the grossest dysfunctions, they do offer the comfort of security and meaning. With rules and lines made clear, even psychologists point to the lowering of the heat of anxiety or of fear before the unexpected. Caste provides a most unstrenuous tactic in the comfortable search for individual identity: it can be found in a role—even in a uniform or type of garb, or anti-garb. Possibly, Manu's division of the four *varṇas* is still admired by contemporary Indians and others because it is a convenient device for explaining the diversification of functions in the social corpus. Moreover, with an admission of caste's present theoretical illegality and a rejection of its discriminatory dysfunctions, it is alleged that the Hindu division into *varṇas* does not logically necessitate the reduction of individuals to their roles or to any other inequities. Theoretical continuity is thereby retained with a tradition indelibly engraved in Indian peoples from the days of Manu and before, if not from time immemorial.

The strategy of this approach will be recognized by religious and political reformers. It is said that genuine innovations have to be sold in the language of tradition and encapsulated in unalarming epithets like "restoration," "development of doctrine," or "reform." The underlying assumption is that Hindus' and others' needs to conceptualize life in terms of caste are alive and, therefore, deserve continued allegiance. Another more Buddhistic course would carry on the discussion by challenging precisely that supposition. This is not to say that followers of the Buddha were historically able to root out all caste or were immune to occasional compromise.

3. *Social discrimination in general.* For a complete picture of Manu's subordination of the individual to society, a few remarks about the relation of individuals and society as a whole— without references to their sexual, caste, or *āśramic* groupings—are necessary. The observations are, of course, relative, because a process view of cultural evolution forbids one to judge the laws of Manu by the standards of the United Nations Declaration of Human Rights or of modern national constitutions, including that of India. However, while a thorough comparison would be unfair, a few samplings would be enlightening for an understanding of Manu.

In the area of law and order, for instance, the right to remain silent when accused, on grounds of self-incrimination, was rejected by the institutes (VIII.13 and 20). Also, cruel and unusual punishments range from castration for insulting members of higher castes (VIII.371) to amputations, impalement, exile, and painful forms of capital punishment (VIII.379; IX.237-39, and IX.276). Further, laws on surveillance by the state approximated Orwell's "big brotherhood" (IX.265). In the social realm, what is currently called unemployment compensation during sickness was denied. Marriages were pre-arranged by others. Derrett connects this phenomenon with the continuing exodus to bachelorhood in the forest, although this trend may also have pertained to other difficulties associated with providing for a family in crowded and impoverished conditions.[15]

Classification of individuals into *āśramic* groups or stages need not have submerged individual identity under function. But, concretely and quite apart from the ascetical character of the stages, the multiplicity of stage-laws must have been a burden to the human memory, at least to whatever extent they were taken seriously. Together with caste and other encumbrances, stage-laws constituted no small straw on the back of human individuality.

Summary. Physically, individuality was subordinated to social structures. Noetically, it was smothered by the "Vedic" and *smriti* authority invested in or assumed by the Brahmins. Structural circumscriptions of caste and sex were compounded with *āśramic* and other codices said to be more comprehensive than Islamic *shar'iah*.[16] In the very attempt to create some forms of economic and civil equity like fair trials, the Brahminic judicial system ignored or punished individual liberty. In a dimension more noetic than physical, individuals were subjected to the Brahmins' authority and power of defining life in the Brahminic language of *karma-saṃsāra* (rebirth), and final liberation (*moksha*) from illusory individuality.

When European philosophers like Hegel or Mill were first introduced to Asian cultures and ways of thinking, they reacted by asserting that in Asia the "individual has no value in itself,"[17] or that the "complete despotism of custom" is the case everywhere, especially in "the whole East." "Custom is there, in all things, the final appeal. . . ."[18] Indians themselves speak of the "unalterable" conformity which has been demanded of individual persons.[19]

However, sympathizers with these indictments should bear in mind the problematic extent to which the laws of Manu actually mirrored Hindu life and ideals at the times of their formation, codification, and implementation. More importantly, Brahminic beliefs and values have not always reflected the moral mentality of the majority of Hindu believers and mystics. In short, the possibility must be tendered that the Institutes of Manu do not represent the moral ideals of Hindu adherents, taken as a whole. This point can be explored from several angles, including linguistic and literary studies.

Linguistically, an impressive case has been built by Hajime Nakamura. Assuming that linguistic forms are the surest key to modes of consciousness, his thesis is that Sanskrit syntax and expressions in the *Ups* and elsewhere constitute evidence of a non-dualistic consciousness.[20] If correct, this hypothesis would corroborate the position that Manu's legal presuppositions denied value to individuals as such. It could be construed that personal privileges were lacking because they were deemed meaningless. There were no individual rights imply because there were really no individuals. Noticeably, most of Nakamura's illustrations are extracted from the *Ups*, the *Gītā*, or Śaṅkara. A more cogent demonstration would employ—in the measure they are extant—syntactical examples of the Sanskrit and other languages spoken by the people, instead of the language transmitted and recopied for millenia by either a Brahminic hereditary elite or non-dualistic philosophers.

For this reason, an adequate survey of Hindu ethics must search the archives of popular literature, unless it is gratuitously presupposed that Upanishadic or *śāstric* literature alone represents the moral convictions and ideals of early Hindus. Even from a perspective of what beliefs *ought to have been* rather than one of *what they were in fact*, it is difficult to exclude popular literature. Since some popular sources also claimed divine authority or have been granted the authoritative status of *smriti* (tradition), it is imperative to study them, too. Investigation of this kind of material will render possible a fuller and fairer judgment about the representativeness of Manu. If it can be shown that its laws are non-representative or inadequately reflective of most Hindu convictions, then there is an alternative humanistic reaction to the kind of criticism about the tyranny of laws and customs which was registered by the great defender of individual liberty, John Stuart Mill.

In the listing of candidates which best encapsulate the moral ethos of Manu, several elements have been reviewed: *ahimsā*, *dāna*, justice, and indirectly, caste. In the process of eliminating each of these, it has become clear that the functional moral ethos of Manu flows from the premise that the meaning of life is ascetical. Since the Brahmins controlled society totally and defined life in terms of ascetical austerity and other-worldly bliss, the overriding moral tone was that of the forest. The Vedic world-affirmation which had been eclipsed in the *Ups* remained hidden.

With logical integrity, one could stop with this notion of an ascetical spirit and waive the effort to identify it further. One could even work in the opposite direction and insist that an ethos is too complex to be captured by any single epithet—but so is any concept. But a more specific, if bolder, characterization can be drawn from the intricate laws about endless matters, especially caste and Brahminic authority. This judgment flows from a common experience, well articulated by Gandhi, that ends sometimes take on the nature or color of their means. In *Manu*, the ends were liberation and better rebirths. Control was the means. Society's relationship to its members was one of total supremacy and complete control. This instrumental process of control became so supreme and absorbing in *Manu* that, in the world of text if not that of practice, an inversion of means and end transpired.

Taking second place, spiritual goals at least unconsciously yielded to this-worldly means. While Vedic world-affirmation had disappeared, it was replaced with "world-concern." The concern was a moral one for control or power, but also for order, sharing, and some justice. As a result, the moral purview of Manu was as different from that of the *Vedas* or that of the *Ups* as it would be from the vista of the *Ry* or the *Gitā*. Manu's moral ethos of control was a *tertium quid*. It was a qualitatively new creation of its own, revealing evidence of a diachronic moral pluralism in the history of Hindu ethics.[21]

NOTES

1. See *The Laws of Manu*, trans. Georg Bühler (rpt.; New York : Dover Publications, Inc., 1969). This historical thesis on the ineffectiveness of Indian laws has been frequently proposed by the eminent historian J. M. Duncan Derrett, as in *Dharmaśāstra and Juridical Literature* in Vol. IV, *A History of Indian Literature,* ed. Jan Gonda (Wiesbaden : Otto Harrassowitz, 1973) pp. 2-3.

2. For Derrett's disagreement with P. V. Kane on this issue see Derrett, ibid., pp. 63-64 and Derrett, *History of Indian Law* (*Dharmaśāstra*) (Leiden/ Koln : E. J. Brill, 1973), p. 35 where he signals the lack of lay creation or comprehension of *śāstra* and the belated reform of laws about polygamy and divorce in 1955-56 (p. 32). Derrett qualifies his generalization by granting that traditional Indian law, like Manu, specified contracts and criminal penalties which were enforced until British rule. Even after the reforms of 1955-56, the corpus of family laws is said to remain available for consultation and imposition; see Derrett, *Dharmaśāstra*, pp. 8-9.

3. Nikhilananda, *Vedāntasāra or the Essence of Vedānta* (rpt. 1968; Calcutta : Advaita Ashrama, 1949). p. xvi.

4. Weber, *The Religion of India*, p. 131.

5. See *Manu* VII.349; III.45-46; IX.243; X.76; and XI.6 in contrast with X.109-113.

6. Weber refers to an eightfold list in Gautama's lawbook : "forbearance, patience, freedom from envy, purity, tranquility, correct life, freedom from desire, and freedom from covetousness" (p. 172).

7. To Bühler's English translation for the ten virtues in *Manu* VI.92 are added the Sanskrit originals as compiled in Shivesh Thakur, *Christian and Hindu Ethics* (London : Allen & Unwin, 1969). Pending further verification, all but the second and tenth can be readily located in the *Ups*, e.g. in *Ait*.5.2.; *Kena* 33; *Kaṭha*.3.4-5. According to Bühler's synopsis, parallel passages exist in the *Dharma-Sūtra* of Vasishṭha X.30 and *Yājñāvalkya* III.66.

8. It also occurs in a list of five commands which correspond to the following virtues in Manu's tenfold law, numbers four-six and nine with *ahimsā* added. They bind all four classes or all human society as known in Manu. In Bühler's resumé, related sections are found in *Yājñavalkya* I.122; *Gautama* VIII.23; *Āpastamba* 1.23.6; and *Vishnu Smriti* II.16-17.

9. See Derrett, "Rājadharma," *The Journal of Asian Studies* 34.4 (August 1976), who adds : "The brahmins' abnegation of power is a myth. Brahmins took power when they could, as they do still" (p. 603). After Vedic times "vast numbers of brahmins were not priests," (p. 602) just as there were many priests other than brahmins who had more devotional or other than Brahminic convictions. Given the historical brahminic coalition with violent forces and Manu's several passages which favor violence, the several conflicting pro-*ahimsā* sections must reflect the views of different constituencies. On Man's *ahimsā* towards all creatures, see II.159; III.164; IV.148, 170; V.43-52; VI.65, VII.345, and the famous Jaina-like caution not to swallow or breathe insects (VI.68-69).

10. Weber, *The Religion of India*, p.-133.

11. Thakur, *Christian and Hindu Ethics*, pp. 145-46. Thakur finds Patañjali's list more positive (p. 148) and he notes Yājñavalkya's Buddhistic substitution of abstention from sexual intercourse and from alcohol for cleanliness and restraint. He also adverts to Praśastapāda's addition of *bhūtahitatva*, a more socially oriented pursuit of the good of creatures. Without adducing warrants for his conclusion, Thakur further judges that *ahimsā* eventually becomes so prominent as to provide Hindu morality with its specific geist. My analysis is unable to confirm that inference.

12. As in *Manu* I.86; IV.227-35; IX.333; and X.79.

13. See *Manu.* 235 and XI.55. Offences to the Buddhist community of monks (the *saṅgha*) form a comparable backbone in the canon of Buddhist deadly sins (*pañca-anatarya-karmāṇi*).

14. *Manu* II.213; IX. 3-5, 45; and V.148-57.

15. Derrett, *History of Indian Law*, p. 20.

16. See Tara Chand, "The Individual in the Legal and Political Thought and Institutions of India," in *The Indian Mind*, ed. Charles A. Moore (Honolulu : East-West Center Press, 1967), pp. 378 and 383.

17. Hegel, as in Hajime Nakamura, *Ways of Thinking of Eastern People* (Honolulu : East-West Center Press, 1964), p. 12.

18. John Stuart Mill, *On Liberty in the Utilitarians*, J. Bentham and J. S. Mill (Garden City, New York : Doubleday and Co., Inc. 1961), p. 547.

19. Chand, "The Individual," p. 378.

20. See Nakamura's *Ways of Thinking*, pp. 44-48, 60-66, 87-98, and 130-36.

21. The separate endurance of this tradition can be detected in a Vedāntic appropriation of the *Ry* which has been depicted as the "jewel of all works in the Vedānta." See B. L. Atreya, *The Yogavāsiṣṭha and its Philosophy* (rev. ed. : Moradabad : Darshana Printers, 1966), p. 1. The (seventh century C.E. ?) *Yogavāsiṣṭha* (the *Vāsiṣṭha-Rāmāyaṇa* or -*Mahārāmāyaṇa*) was composed for seekers of *moksha*.

Chapter V

HINDU ETHICS IN THE RĀMĀYAṆA

Abstract. This descriptive exposition of Hindu ethics in the *Rāmāyaṇa* (*Ry*), India's most celebrated people's classic, begins with an A) Introduction, including discussions of the 1) importance, 2) plot, and 3) structure of the *Ry*. It then analyzes the Vālmiki version in terms of four ethical questions about B) mores, C) ethos, D) societal structures, and E) forms of ethical validation. The epic's life-affirming ethos, together with its moral education and esthetical persuasion through model characters, is viewed as a pluralistic alternative to forms of Hindu ethics more known in the West. The latter are those implied in Hindu non-dualistic philosophies, mysticism, and an ascetical ethos of world-denial. This study will F) conclude with the suggestion that popular or Rāmāyaṇic ethics can at least complement the ethical implications of philosophical Hindu systems in the quest for religio-ethical and political-economic reform in India.

Appendix I, at the end of this volume, provides data on the *Ry's* historical impact and related textual matters and further information on the role of women in Indian society. NOTES

A. Introduction. The reduction of the age-old pluralistic tradition of Hindu ethics into the small circle of its Brahminic and philosophical versions, especially Śaṅkara's *Advaita Vedānta* (AV)—non-dualism or monism, stems from a complex convergence of historical developments. Many Indian and Hindu reformers whose watchword became the Buddha's basic "noble truth" that "all life must be *duḥkha* (misery)," explain this change as a reaction to overpopulation, famine, disease, poverty, and systems of injustice perpetuated by indigenous power elites, as well as imperialistic intrusions and gross oppression imported from other nations and religions. The cumulative effect of these conditions on Indian self-esteem and confidence was understandably traumatic.

A modern dialectical reaction to these obstacles appeared in 1893 at the Chicago parliament of religions when the Indian reformer and Advaita Vedāntist, Vivekānanda, offered his sophisticated defense of Advaitic neo-Hinduism as the matrix of what was spiritually superior in every religion. Through social and nationalistic reformers like the Tagores, Aurobindo Ghose, Gandhi, and other proponents or charismatic adapters of Vedântic non-dualism, Hindu Indians were transfused with resurging self-respect. Meanwhile, Hindu defenders and critics alike slipped into the reductionism of identifying pluralistic Hinduism with the currently renowned and successful, yet much smaller, tradition of Brahminic and neo-Vedāntic spiritualism. Accordingly, the ancient and diversified heritage of Hindu ethics became stereotyped, especially in the English speaking world, as a passive, negative, world-denying ethos of non-attachment, nonviolence (*ahimsā*), and tolerance of class discrimination. On Brahminic authority, this-worldly love and happiness were seen as merely developmental stages up the path toward ascetical mind-culture and the final goal (*purushārtha*) of life. The goal was better rebirths in the cycle of *karma* (moral compensation) and *saṃsāra* (transmigration), or, ultimately non-dualistic liberation (*moksha*) from the delusion of individual existence. This freedom was thought to accompany the realization of one's true spiritual self (*Ātman*) as Brahman (ultimate Reality). Merely penultimate and relative in value were the social, ethical reforms and devotion (*bhakti*) to various gods which neo-Hinduism so ingeniously incorporated and sponsored.

The present chapter strives to avoid innuendos either for or against the intrinsic spiritual value and ethical ramifications of the Brahminic and neo-Vedāntic traditions. Further, it does not yet deal with estimates, like D. D. Kosambi's and Max Weber's, about the economic and social benefits of Advaitic incorporations of Buddha and other popular deities in the monistic/polytheistic synthesis constructed by the celebrated Advaitic philosopher, Śaṅkara. Instead, it defends the conviction that other Hindu moralities, enshrined in popular classics like the *Rāmāyaṇa* (*Ry*, accent antepenultimate), are not less systemically intricate and coherent than the formally philosophical traditions (*darśanas*) and are qualitatively different.

1. *The Ry's importance*. Regrettably, of the three main volumes on Hindu ethics composed in recent decades only Cromwell Crawford's clear treatise pays the *Ry* the slightest attention.[1] However, if the stature of contemporary plays and musicals is partly evaluated by the length of continuous runs in centers of culture, the representativeness of the epic called "Vālmīki's" *Ry* is similarly measurable—the striking difference being that the latter has perdured not for a few years but for millennia.

"Such absolute and all-commanding sway and influence of literature," states Shantikumar Vyas, "is perhaps unknown in the West with the single exception of the Bible. Even Occidental scholars agree no work of world literature secular (but not separated from the sacred) in its origin has ever exerted so profound an influence on the life and thought of a people as the *Vālmīki-Rāmāyana*."[2] In view of the poem's ancient composition (conjectures range from the third century B.C.E. to the second century C.E.), its enduring moral influence in classical Sanskrit, as well as in popular Hindi, Bengali, Jaina, and Buddhist literature, and its regular public recitations from the second century C.E., the epic stands unparalleled in Indian culture. The prestige of all seven of the books, including Supplementary Book VII, was heightened by the fourth (?), fifth, and eighth century dramatizations of Bhāsa, Kālidāsa, and Bhavabhūti. Equally influential, at least at the so-called plebian level, were religious productions (*Rāmalīlās*), emerging at least by the time of Kamban's Tamil version in the ninth (twelfth?) century, the *bhakti* revival, and Tulasīdās' Hindi version of the sixteenth century. From the fifteenth century, dramatists wrote "only" on the *Ry*.[3] It emerged as the most eminent and ancient poem in every Indian regional language. Its regular recitations and annual religious productions were eventually multiplied in film. Small wonder, therefore, that it has been considered responsible for disseminating in nearly every city and village the Hindu moral values that survive today.[4] One would have to point to the reliving of the Passover or to Christian passion and moral dramaturgy or liturgy to find a non-Indian analogue for an ancient drama which has so captivated or represented a people's feelings. Many think its very recitation works salvifically.

Even abstracting from the thorny and evasive problems of the poem's causal impact on elites or the larger populace as "the national manual of ethics,"[5] and, of populist interplay with the reconstructions and controls of the usual Brahminic custody or frequent appropriation of "literature" and ritual,[6] the above data indicate that the *Ry* is a leading revealer of the pulse of Indian convictions and "has carried traditional Hindu ideals to the youngest and simplest of many generations."[7] Given that most members of past and present Indian civilization(s) have had to absorb all of their education, morals included, in media which are audial or visual rather than linear or "literate" then the epic's significance as a morality play would seem to outweigh that of philosophical systems like Śaṅkara's Advaita which are read by and taught through only a proportionately small elite. To reach the people, ethical philosophy or *dharma* (*s*) would have to be communicated in the forms of poetry, rhythm, song, dance, and, most of all, in what Max Scheler would call the figure of the "ideal model person." Literary documentation of the epic's effect is detailed further in Appendix I below.

2. *Plot.* The moral message and persuasive power of the poem should be judged not only through its explicitly didactic passages but especially through its characters and mythically based events. Unlike its sister-epic, the *Mbh,* the *Ry* consists of a relatively single and simple plot about the love, exploits, and suffering of Prince Rāma, and Princess Sītā. Both characters, particularly Rāma, are divinized, especially in versions composed after the devotional or *bhakti* revival and the version of Tulasīdās. Rāma's actual historical existence is obscure, but it is important, since in the centuries after Vālmīki his divinity is portrayed and believed in an increasingly literal fashion. Like Krishna, Rāma is an *avatār* (manifestation) of the God, Vishnu. In the ninth and sixteenth century versions of Kamban and Tulasīdās, whose plots remain substantially unchanged to the present day (at least up to the episode of Sītā's first reacceptance by Rāma), Rāma deserves worship and unqualified moral emulation. By contrast, in the original *Vālmiki-Rāmāyaṇa,* listeners, viewers, or readers must distinguish for themselves which deeds of Rāma and others are meant to be normative and which are proposed as anti-types. This requirement on the reader may become clearer after a brief glance at the classic's plot. This summation and the ensuing analysis is of necessity tentative because of the lack of commentaries based on critical editions and because of gaps in the form and composition critiques that are so vital for comprehending the ancient writings of other religions and cultures. Intriguing details about which verses were left untouched by Brahmins and other scholiasts (and why) await future attention.

Rāma, eldest son of the polygamous Daśaratha, King of Ayodhya in Northern India, symbolizes from the mythical outset the conquest of good over evil. At his father's request, he and his closest stepbrother, Lakṣmaṇa, provide forest ascetics with physical protection from demons. Early in the story Rāma is portrayed as the future protector of his people and as happily married. By a physical feat which no one else could match, he won marriage with a lovely princess, Sītā, and lived happily with her for twelve years. Meanwhile, King Daśaratha had promised Rāma's stepmother, Kaikeyī, two "boons" in an open-ended style resembling King Herod's vow to Salome recorded in the Christian Gospels. Kaikeyī demanded Rāma's exile to the forest for fourteen years and his replacement as heir to the throne by her son, Bharata. Unless the King's vow functions solely as a literary device meant to launch a dramatic adventure, it constitutes one of the classic's main moral dilemmas. Against priestly and authoritative counsel, Rāma fulfils the two demands voluntarily, and with Sītā and Lakṣmaṇa, his closest half-brother, undergoes exile as a forest ascetic. At this separation King Daśaratha dies of grief and Bharata reluctantly replaces Rāma during the fourteen year interim of Rāma's self-imposed odyssey.

If Vālmīki meant the king's commitment to serve a moral as well as literary objective, then, depending on one's assumptions, it may be viewed either as that true but tragic kind of Kantian principle which must be honored at all costs or else as an abstract, hypnotic, and immoral absolute which is detrimental to individuals within its ambit. In either case Rāma's duty or *dharma* to his father's promise takes priority over his duty or *dharma* to others as ruler and spouse. In a good dramatic fashion, destructive consequences (*karma*) do not occur immediately. Rāma and Sītā spend years of connubial bliss in the forest. Ultimately, Sītā is kidnapped by Rāvaṇa, a figure of more ancient legends now becomes a symbol of evil. Rāvaṇa is king of Laṅkā (Ceylon/Sri Laṅkā or a nearby island). Rāma and Lakṣmaṇa gather allies, conquer Rāvaṇa and Laṅkā, and rescue Sītā. In spite of his beloved's protests that her situation under Rāvaṇa's control was against her "volition," Rāma bends to public opinion and renounces her. Proved innocent of infidelity through ordeal by fire and a divine voice, Sītā returns to Ayodhyā to live happily with Rāma ever after. In later productions, the epic is caught up not merely with first union or reunion, but with the continuing conjugal bliss of the two principal characters.

In some redactions and dramatizations the people's consensus pressures Rāma to a second renunciation and a trial by fire. But Sītā first dies of sorrow or else descends to another life within the earth in a finale of mythic divinization.[8] Except for the Tulasīdās recension, which reserves moral comment about Sītā and rather stresses the general conquest of good over evil, the above summary would indicate that Sītā is more clearly a moral heroine than is Rāma a moral saint. In the Vālmīki plot, Rāma's rejections of Sītā are morally more ambiguous than Sītā's fidelity. Yet, in actual popularity, Rāma seems to have remained the central model of identification for Hindus as the endurer of tragic fate, strengthened like Aeneas in virtue and compassion. Alternative conjectures could center on Rāma as an object of *bhakti* rather than moral emulation or even as that classic figure who is conquered by suffering, though not without dignity.

The Vālmīki rendition reflects moral ideals which may go back as far as Manu in the period following the *Ups.* Didactic sections are thought by some to be later, stricter, and more ascetical or priestly than the original narrative. More expert linguistic and historical locations of them must be ascertained in the future.

3. *Structure.* In its external structure, the *Vālmiki-Rāmāyaṇa* is divided into seven *kāṇḍas* or books, each of which contains brief sections which have been called chapters.[9] For ethical studies books II, VI, and VII are of special interest, not only for their didactic portions, but also for their events and character portrayals, some of which may in themselves impart a moral lesson. Of course, life is more ambiguous and mysterious than any story by itself can convey, and reality lacks the order and necessary or "logical" connections constructed by story-tellers. Nonetheless, narrative was thought to be most important in Indian civilization. Its emphasis on the primacy of the story both in defining reality and in teaching morality concurs with three contemporary approaches to doing ethics.

The first of these stresses the ethic of model persons over abstract norms. Only concrete persons, it maintains, can appeal to the whole person, because human beings are less Aristotelian than Confucian, less rational animals than thinking hearts. The emotive attraction evoked by personified values is not merely blind passion. It may also be an intelligent response in itself. The neat dichotomy between concepts as intelligent and emotions as non-intelligent is rejected.

The second approach seeks to reunite an "ethics of character" with an ethics of decision and command. As a result of various philosophical and religious developments and a growing self-consciousness about responsible decision-making, the being or "character" of moral agents is said to have been eclipsed by attention to acts and decisions (for example, in debates about utilitarian calculus and situation ethics).

The third contemporary emphasis seeks to recover and reconstruct ancient Greek and other combinations of the ethical and the esthetical. But what stirs to moral action is not merely visual beauty but extends to other senses, to outgoing movement, and to the beauty of living moral characterization. In any of these three views scientifically descriptive ethics should include an account of popular classics and their records of the esthetical and rhetorical or persuasive dimensions of moral claims. This thesis presupposes interdisciplinary links between descriptive ethics, psychology, and literature. In the case of more ancient and mythopoeic classics or layers thereof, it does not insist *a priori* that they are amoral.

The lasting truth that all three approaches share with Indian tradition seems to be that a story like that of the *Ry* is the best medium not only for suasion to the moral, but also for conceptualizing it clearly. It was to both persuasive and conceptual aspects that Max Scheler referred when he wrote: "Nothing on earth allows a person to become good so originally and immediately and necessarily as the evidential and adequate intuition (*Anschauung*) of a good person *in* his goodness. This relation is absolutely superior to *any other* in terms of a possible becoming good of which it can be considered the origin."[10]

Morality *via* hagiography can succumb to an imposition of prototypes which lack variety and mobility and which are easily manipulable by political, economic forces or directionless trends. Contrarily, if the *Ry* is taken as suggestive rather than a final statement, its many characters can point the way to a pluralistic and creative morality of diverse models.

B. Morality or Mores? Universality and Volition The following exposition of the classic's moral system analyzes it in terms of four ethical issues: (1) mores, (2) ethos, (3) institutions, and (4) ethical justifications. While the second issue will receive special attention primarily for reasons intrinsic to the text, it also happens to underline the above mentioned contemporary emphases on character, beauty, and persuasion.

Universality. The ethical aspect of *dharma* (a term of many meanings, one of which is the closest Sanskrit analogue for "religion") in the *Ry* is manifestly general (*sādhāraṇa* or *sāmānya*) rather than, as Weber contended, limited or specific to in-groups like family, caste, or stages of life.[11] In contrast to the teaching of the *Gītā*, caste or *varṇa dharma* can yield priority to debts common to all human beings. For example, the three debts (*ṛṇāṇi triṇi*) of sacrifice, study and procreation (II,106) are owed to gods, *rishis* (sages) and ancestors. The ethical criterion of universalizability is notably less strained when applied to the duties and virtues of the *Ry* than to those of *Manu*. The epic's defense of moral responsibilities which extend beyond caste consists partly of worldly consequentialist reasoning (*Zweckrationalität*) to be detailed below. This form of consequentialism supports the position of David Little in his debate with Max Weber about the nature of Hindu religious-ethical validations. Weber stressed the function of traditional and charismatic validation at the expense of reason's role behind the universally ethical.

Volition. Even volition is less problematic in the epic than in the *Ups* or Vedānta philosophies. Sin is not mere ignorance (*avidyā*). As is the case in many popular classics—a phenomenon largely overlooked—sin is volitional. This interpretation is strengthened through the following protest by Sītā in response to her repudiation by Rāma (emphases added):

> Why dost thou address such words to me, O Hero, as a common man addresses an ordinary woman? I swear to thee.... that my conduct is worthy of thy respect! It is the behavior of other women that has filled thee with distrust! Relinquish thy doubts since I am known to thee! If my limbs came in contact with another's, it was *against my will*, O Lord, and not through any inclination on my part, it was brought about by fate. *That which is under my control, my heart,* has ever

remained faithful to thee; my body was at the mercy of another;. . . . If despite the proofs of love that I gave thee while I lived with thee, I am still a stranger to thee, O Proud Prince, my loss is irrevocable ! (VI, 118).

In tension with this confirmation that volition is necessary for sin are statements in the poem which ascribe misfortune to faults committed in ignorance previously in this life.[12] In context, however, the import of these karmic imputations is not to deny the requirement of free volition. They rather attempt to solve problems about evil, injustice, and life's meaning like those raised in the Book of Job. An instance of this is Lakṣmaṇa's argument that the virtuous like Rāma would not "suffer adversity" (VI, 83) if spiritual law really existed. A second example occurs at the death of Rāma's father, King Daśaratha.

He finds an explanation for his grief at Rāma's exile in tracing the loss of his son to an accidental homicide in which as a hunter he had caused a similar sorrow and loss to the aged parents of a young hermit. The distraught father had foretold to the king: "The grief, that this accident has visited my son has caused me, thou thyself will endure on account of thine own son. And it will prove the cause of thy death" (II,64).

While expressions of karmic fatalism are uttered by Rāma, an opposite belief, characterized in Sītā and Lakṣmaṇa, seems to be the *Vālmīki-Rāmāyaṇa's* more dominant communication. Referring to her abduction to Laṅkā, Sītā admits to her ally, Hanumān that "all that has happened to me is on account of an evil fate and the consequence of some fault committed formerly. One reaps the fruits of one's actions " ". . .the path of destiny is inexorable" (VI,115, and see 113). But paradoxically, in a section where Sītā is said to speak as a goddess, she adds:

A superior being does not render evil for evil, this is a maxim one should observe; the ornament of virtuous persons is their conduct. One should never harm the wicked or the good or even criminals meriting death. A noble soul will ever exercise compassion even towards those who enjoy injuring others or those of cruel deeds when they are actually committing them who is without fault ?" (VI,115).

When Rāma insists that inscrutable human loss, suffering, frustration, and death result from the mystery of *karma* (contrast II, 23 with III, 63), Lakṣmaṇa retorts: "If thou attributest this matter to the decree of fate, this thought is unpleasing to me and should be rejected. The weak and cowardly are subject to fate, but valiant souls, who are masters of themselves, do not bow to destiny. That hero, who by his spirited efforts does not fail in his undertakings, destiny is powerless before him" (II,23). The fact that, in the *Vālmīki-Rāmāyaṇa*, Rāma utters no rebuttal, but only a tearful pledge of continued obedience to his father's promise, can be taken as a verdict against determinism and fatalism. However, since the fatalistic viewpoint was so strong as to germinate and propel the central dynamics of the epic and to merit enunciation by Rāma himself, it may have been an actual historical attitude far more prevalent than the ideal of exertion here proposed. On the horizon of aspirations, at any rate, the *Vālmīkī-Rāmāyaṇa* teaches that fate cannot succeed without human cooperation.[13] The concept of *karma* does not foster complete determinism, therefore, any more than existentialist convictions that human agents become identified with their actions, that they are what they do. *Karma* means that while Rāma retains his freedom, he does not merely perform a heroic action—he becomes a heroic character. But his character does not compel or decide his fate deterministically. Rather it gives it direction. Human freedom and, consequently, morality itself prevail.

Every spectator or reader of the *Ry* can, of course, choose to be the arbiter of its meaning. One can make of Rāma what one wills, master of his destiny or puppet. Thus the reading of Vyas is fatalistic.[14] But his direct point is not determinism, but simply that it is the suffering of the human Rāma which has always attracted the masses. Nevertheless, the people did not feel that Rāma was the cause of his own suffering. They regarded him as great-souled or magnanimous. The source of his pain was, in John Stuart Mill's phrase, the tyranny of custom.[15]

C. Ethos. Vyas' portrayal of Rāma as the model sufferer of custom and fate may highlight a central theme in the ethos of the *Ry*. But there are other motifs. One which calls for special notice is Vālmīki's social protest against the subordination of individuals (women in particular) to societal attitudes and mores. Among the remaining motifs are 1) truth, 2) Rāma, paragon of virtues, and 3) life-affirmation. The latter two will characterize the specific ethos of the Vālmīkian drama.

1. *Truth.* It is possible to diagnose the *Ry* as a kind of Kant-

tian celebration of truth for its own sake. Tragic consequences resulted from King Daśaratha's open-ended promise as well as from Rāma's own adherence to it; but it is precisely this behavior, diffusely labeled *reverence for truth,* which is extolled as the foundation of life—a theme with a symphonic background in the whole of Vedic literature. Rāma's defense of keeping his father's vow lends credence to this theory. Like the ascetic Jābāli, the first priest of the kingdom (Vasiṣṭha) fruitlessly attempts to dissuade Rāma from undergoing voluntary exile. Rāma's response to the priest is a hymn in praise of truth: "Offerings.... asceticism and the Vedas have truth as their foundation; therefore truth before all. Alone it supports the world, alone it supports the family;..." (II,109)[16]

The supremacy and priority of truth before all other virtues receives only ambiguous confirmation in the classic, however, because of the authoritative role of "holy Vasiṣṭha" as first priest. While Vālmīki does not contest the prominent role of truth in Brahminic or Hindu thought, neither does he make it identical with Rāma's strict observance of his father's problematic pledge to Kaikeyī. Instead, the author seems to favor Vaṣiṣṭha's opposite position. Since the only refutation of the priest's stance is Rāma's, and since Vālmīki disagrees with Rāma on several issues, it is an open question whether the epic's author(s) would summarize the totality of their ethical statements in terms of truth and keeping promises. Instead, other topics predominate.

2. *Paragon of virtues.* Whatever his defects, Rāma was a model of virtue even in the earliest narratives. In later accretions like those in Book I his virtue seems to approach divinization. In the words of his father, King Daśaratha, Rāma heroically "makes people subject to him by his virtues, the Twice born [the religiously instructed top three *varṇas*] by his liberality, his Spiritual Preceptors by his obedience and his enemies by the power of his bow. Goodness, munificence, asceticism, renunciation, purity, integrity, prudence and submission to his Gurus are all the attributes of Rāghava [Rāma]" (II,12). At its very beginning, in a language borrowed from a common source shared by Brahmins and Buddhists or influenced directly by Buddhists, the Vālmīkian author affirms that Rāma is endowed with "heroic qualities, versed in all the duties of life, grateful, truthful, firm

in his vows, an actor of many parts, benevolent to all beings, learned, eloquent, handsome, patient, slow to anger, free from envy, and when excited to anger [he] can strike terror into the hearts of celestial beings" (I,1).

> Equal to Brahmā, the Protector of his people, pleasing to look upon, supporting the universe, the destroyer of those who contravene the moral code, the inspirer of virtue, the giver of spiritual grace to his devotees and to those who duly observe sacrificial rites and are charitable, conversant with the essence of the Vedic philosophy; adept in the science of warfare, incapable of cowardice, acquainted with the laws of this world as also of the other worlds...Equal to Vishnu in valour... in generosity like Kuvera [god of wealth]; in truthfulness the personification of virtue (I,1).

Before the conclusion of this seemingly later and *bhakti* or devotionally inspired overture, Rāma's benevolence is recorded four times together with his "devotion to the welfare of every living being," "his universal good will," "love of truth, and humility" (I,3 and see II,35). Measured by frequency of occurrence in these and other passages, two qualities (emulated by both Hindus and Buddhists) are sketched most trenchantly: benevolence and protection of every living being.[17]

3. *Not Thanatos, but life-affirmation.* Thanatos, the instinctual desire for death and self-destruction is, for some, an enemy more treacherous than the most egotistical cravings for pleasure, life, or self-affirmation. It sometimes disguises itself as a solitary flight from egoism *á deux* or from collective egoism. Labeled sado-masochism in its psychological dimension, Thanatos was regarded by Nietzsche, Schweitzer, and others as the curse of civilization. For Nietzsche its world and life-denying aspects found expression in the language of sin, guilt, and ascetic priests, Brahmins included. Is the teaching of the popular *Ry* Thanatos or life-affirmation?

It is from the *Ry's* omissions about sinfulness and *moksha* (liberation from this life of egoity) as well as from its instruction about the "ends" of life and the relationship of men and women that we can glean its ethos most directly. Although popular classics like the *Ry* do not tend to reduce sin (*pāpa*, *āgas*, *enas*, *kilbiṣa* [violation of social norms]) to mere ignorance (*avidyā*) in the reputed fashion of Brahminic and philosophical literatures, there is no general analogue in the epic for a state of depravity or of "original sin," nor is special attention paid to the power or pervasiveness of sin. In that regard, the contrast with some Christian literatures and ethical presuppositions is striking. Further, *moksha* gets no mention at all.[18] The hope for happiness in a heavenly after-life prevails over sparse and dubious references to *saṃsāra* (the wheel of reincarnation). Sītā believes that her marriage to Rāma will continue in heaven, for example (II,29). Heavens filled with gods and individual human beings also prevail in the basic plot of the other major epic, the *Mbh*, although some will insist that from the view of the whole of Hindu literature such heavens were not literal or permanent alternatives to *moksha*. This insistence presupposes the belief that there can be an integral view of all of Hindu literature, of course.

Not four, but three ends (*purushārthas*) of life are legitimate in this world, and their moral suitability is not confined to a developmental spectrum in which the first three can be eventually discarded. All three are necessary morally: *dharma* (virtue, morality, or duty), *kāma* (as pleasure and love), and *artha* (wealth). All three are not merely permitted, but commanded. In fact, it is when any one of them is neglected that trouble sets in. As Rāma proclaims: "He who divides his time judiciously between duty, pleasure, and the legitimate acquisition of wealth and honours his responsibilities in these things is truly a king....but he who neglects his duty, his true interests and legitimate pleasures is like one who sleeps on top of a tree and does not wake up till he has fallen" (IV,38).[19]

Two apparent contradictions emerge, one about *artha* (wealth) and the dangerous power which it brings or stands for, and the other about *kāma*, which sometimes means lust instead of pleasure and sexual love. The following pages summarize the classic's teaching as to how these two goals should and should not be pursued.

In an unrefuted discourse about wealth, Lakṣmaṇa sings its praises to Rāma, a theme sung frequently in popular classics. He condemns a path of *dharma* which would proceed without *artha* as weak and powerless. "The wealthy man is brave, wise, powerful and above all a man of worth" (VI,83). In isolation *dharma* is "meaningless" or non-existent. Conversely, the wealthy person acquires moral qualities, "Wealth is the creator of joy, pleasure, pride, anger, and inner and outer control!" (VI,83).

Is wealth, then, superior to virtue? Those whose religious assumptions cannot tolerate a plurality of moral opinions or outright contradictions in the epic are allowed several hermeneutical options. Among them are 1) rejection of the text (Lakṣmaṇa's hymn) as interpolated or spurious; 2) reading it as a stylistically Kierkegaardian declaration (i.e., one which is not the final position of its composer and which really depicts wealth as a temptation); 3) deciphering the discourse as poetical license stressing wealth's importance by overstatement; 4) accepting it as essential to the epic's total view that *dharma* without *artha* is an unlikely accomplishment. While nothing worthwhile is immune to abuse, it is as difficult to reach *dharma* without some form of *artha* as it is (transposing a metaphor) to pass through the eye of a needle.[20]

If one chooses to develop the last of these hermeneutical alternatives, one must assume that the epic really presents a total and integral position. Granted that presupposition, this interpretation contends that perhaps over two millennia before the Communist Manifesto, the doctrine arose that the poor are not blessed after all. That is, they are not blessed for their poverty, though they may be for their power to overcome it. The poor are neither physically blessed nor likely to become blessed even in spirit or in morals. Marx's Manifesto would some day argue in a similar vein not for poverty but for its opposite. Marx did not demand the abolition of property, but as he put it, of "the personal appropriation by an unjust, "bourgeois system of property" where one-tenth own everything and nine-tenths own nothing.[21] Similarly, the epic equated lack of wealth with a powerlessness which is more conducive to *ressentiment* and vice than to virtue. As one-line humor would eventually phrase it, wealth and power are not everything, but they are primary—the humor occasioned by the malaise within some religious beliefs about any place for wealth at all (in theoretical aspiration only).

In the above exegesis morality becomes boldly affirmative of this world's values. *Moksha* is out of the picture. Conjoined with *artha*, good moral character (*dharma*) is no mere means to another existence but is itself the end of life. As Khan concludes :

"The critics who believe that the Hindu moral thought has inherent weakness because it makes morality superficial, are invited to look into the *Rāmāyaṇa*, the National Manual of Ethics, where Dharma is the supreme goal of life and moral life is the primary object of human beings."[22] The poem teaches that pursuit of any one of life's goals by itself is destructive. But omission of one is equally harmful. The quest for wealth alone, with disregard for a morality which includes the interests of others, is gross manipulation. Kaikeyī's ambition brought suffering or death to her husband, to Rāma and Sītā and to everyone in range. On the other hand, a search for virtue which would disdain the significance of power and material productivity invites disastrous consequences. Poverty and powerlessness in the social structure are systemically related to countless and sometimes over-compensating forms of violence, disease, and mental and moral deterioration. Further, when poverty is spiritually idolized and when, as a result, some religious leaders or their imitators live from the labor of others and from religious practice itself, it is both donors and recipients who become victimized.

The same results can be predicted for *kāma* (as love and pleasure).[23] Sought by itself, it occasions the cruelty inflicted on Rāma by his father or on Sītā by her abductor, Rāvaṇa.[24] *Kāma* in the *Ry* operates as the source of pandemonium in so many and such key instances that one could make a case that the editors who had an upper or final hand in the epic's construction either were ascetical and *kāma*-denying or oscillated like so-called "typical Hindus" "between ardent sensuality and asceticism."[25] But given the idyllic conditions of married forest ascetics in the epic, including the connubial bliss of Rāma and Sītā,[26] it is no surprise to read: "Of the four conditions (stages or *āśramas*) of men, that of the head of the family is the highest and most exalted, according to the interpreters of the law" (II,106), just as in *Manu* it was the most excellent stage of life.[27]

Married status in the *Ry* is not a mere debt or duty to the human race. It is inseparable from *kāma* (as pleasure and sexual love). Far from reducing marital life to a chore to be fulfilled and forgotten or to be eluded by wiser and more fortunate ascetics, the epic depicts it in strains which herald or harmonize with the extensive literature of erotic Indian poetry and love songs, some of which betray a *Sitz im Leben* or matrix of social debate which cries for further form and socio-historical investigations. In the Vālmīki text the interests of those who defended the marital stage prevailed over the ascetical. Rāma insists that devotion to Sītā "invades my entire being and my love is wholly centered on her" (IV.1). "It were possible to bear the love I feel for her, if the spring with its flowers and trees did not increase my torment" (IV,1). "This fire of spring is consuming me. Nay, far from that lady of lovely eyelashes, beautiful looks, and gentle speech, I cannot survive O Saumitri !" (IV,1). Both Sītā and Rāma frequently protest their inability or unwillingness to live without one another (as in II,30; IV,1, and VI,83).

The force of the Vālmīkian affirmation of *kāma* cannot be comprehended without examining one or more of several passages in context, for example Rāma's lament after Sītā's abduction. After a twelve year union of deep and reciprocal love, Sītā had insisted on accompanying Rāma during his forest exile. Whatever the rigors of their existence as forest ascetics, they have little significance in comparison to their spousal happiness. Signaling the beauties of nature to Sītā, Rāma avows : "Bathing three times a day with thee in the river, living on honey, roots, and fruits in thy company, I do not regret Ayodhyā or the Kingdom" (II, 95). After Sītā's kidnapping, Rāma reveals to Lakṣmaṇa other feelings which seem to transcend marital "duty" and the bounds of a love reductively spiritual or Platonic. In competition with Solomon's Song, he cries: "With my separation from her as the coals and my thoughts of her as the shimmering flames, the fire of my love consumes my body day and night !" (VI, 5). In the following profession the imagery glows :

> O Lakṣmaṇa, remain here while I plunge into the sea ere I sleep so that the fire of my distress shall cease from tormenting me. It is enough that she and I sleep on the same earth. As dry land draws nourishment for its vegetation from marshy ground, so do I exist in the knowledge that Sītā still lives: O when shall I, having overcome mine enemies, behold her of graceful limbs, whose eyes resemble lotus petals, the equal of Śrī herself? When, gently raising her lotus-like face with its ravishing lips and teeth, shall I drink in her glances, as a sick man the nectar of immortality ? When will that playful maiden embrace me, her round

and quivering breasts like unto Tāla fruits pressed against my body, like sovereignty united with prosperity ?" (VI, 5).

In what has to this date been called classical Hinduism, married life and love are stepping-stones to forest asceticism, mind-culture, and final *moksha* (liberation) from *kāma.* But through the lives of Rāma and Sītā, insofar as they are normative, the forest exile is merely a penalty and interlude. It is not a goal or final stage, but a mere means to an unimpeded married love which is to continue both on earth and in heaven. "If death overtakes me, I shall be happy with thee," declares Sītā, "according to the instruction of the venerable brahmins" (II, 29).

One could more easily weave an ascetical theory that the multiple confirmations of the importance of *kāma* and marriage are spurious or later additions, were it not for the plot's reduction of the ascetical sojourn to an intermediate phase in the life of a couple who remain married householders (VII,42). In addition, the thesis that *kāma,* along with *dharma,* was not primary in the original epic must account for the fact that in the documents now extant and long expressing (as well as affecting) popular culture the ascendancy of *kāma* is manifest.

Together with *artha* and *dharma, kāma* is an indispensable member of a triad never nullified by *moksha.* The power of *kāma* was feared only when it reigned alone (as in VI, 113). In the ethics of the *Ry,* the affirmation of wealth, power, erotic love, of moral character in general; and of courage and benevolence in particular, is a far cry from the moralities of either the *Ups* or *Manu.* Its continuity with the moral elements in the *Vedas* is plainly visible. Given, therefore, the extraordinary dominance of the *Ry* in Indian culture, one might jump to the conclusion that Hindu morality has been severely misrepresented and that the picture of a passive, asocial, and life-denying morality demands review.

Which stream more fully captures basic Hindu beliefs, the Vālmīkian or the Brahminic ? The persuasive power of minorities like the Brahmins is not to be underestimated, particularly when they exercise the kind of literary and economic control described in *Manu* and the kind of religious and social authority recounted below. Even Khan, whose praises for the poem are among the loudest, and who calls Vālmīki the "Father of Hindu moral thought...." feels that its sublime moral concepts and traditions "got lost in the metaphysical wrangling of the Vedāntic philosophy and in the sacrificial smoke of the Mīmāṁsakas."[28] Until it is shown which sections represent ascetical, Brahminic, or possibly Buddhist notions, to say that the epic presents the general Hindu moral ethos more faithfully than the *Ups*, *Manu*, the *Gītā*, or the philosophical systems is a conjecture which lacks adequate verification. It falters in the face of objections that life-affirmation has simply coexisted with the more ultimate ethos of *moksha* in the psyches of the Indian people or that even in modern social reform an other-worldly tone prevails.

A more certain conclusion is that in theory if not in historical praxis the *Ry* furnishes evidence of a moral pluralism within which a this-worldly ethics competes for a voice. Whether the voice has been the one most historically representative remains to be settled. But the Rāmāyaṇic ethos (as professed ideals, if not surely as actual performance) remains an alternative moral option from which Hindus and others may continue to choose to learn. In the Vālmīkian classic, the goal of morality is not the rejection of this life, nor its extinction, nor absorption into a spiritual and universal consciousness, nor even transformation. It is continuation of life. The symbol of heaven expresses not Thanatos, but the wish and hope for life's perpetuation.

D. Systemic influences on individuals. What is left in our examination of Rāmāyaṇic ethics is the project of surveying the attitudes and actual dynamics which existed in the relationship of societal structures and individuals. The latter will be scrutinized in the light of three roles assigned to them: 1) women as objects, 2) members of castes, and 3) agents and objects of violence.

1) *Women.* From the perspective of modern emancipatory ideas, the women (and in a consequent symbiotic sense the men) of the *Ry* were hardly liberated. Sītā, who was dearer to Rāma than his own life, was still his plaything rather than her own person. Moreover, whatever the reader learns about women in the epics is distilled through the experiences of the poet, Vālmīki, and other bards who were men, not women. As a result, there are no primary witnesses about how the women of the *Ry* experienced their love-life, or life in general. What remains is the male, Vālmīkian opinion about society's ideals for women. Further, textual ambiguity about the kind of finale attributed to the Rāma-Sītā relationship (at least in the Vālmīkian version,

if not others) makes it difficult to separate social fact from moral aspiration.

In social fact women were subjected to discrimination in public, marital, and family relationships, facts already documented by contemporary scholars of Indian epics and supported and summarized in Appendix I below. As for *Vālmīki's ethical aspirations* for women, it is difficult to surmise with any precision when the *Vālmiki-Rāmāyaṇa* expresses ethical approval or disapproval of the historical facts. For example, one can only conjecture uncertainly that the epic's plot means to condemn the polygamous marriage of Rāma's father, King Daśaratha, as the root of later evils. But there are a few junctures at which censures of Rāma's treatment of Sītā take on didactic and normative tones, because they go unrebutted. In fact, the case can be drawn that the author's favorite character and oracular vehicle on issues is not Rāma but Sītā,[29] and that the pivotal thrust of the narrative is a prophetic pronouncement against Sītā's repudiation by Rāma. Indian society eventually transferred the source of Sītā's rejection from Rāma to the cruelty of social custom;[30] but in the *Vālmīki-Rāmāyaṇa* Rāma is not faultless. Accusations against him go unanswered. He is described as "apprehensive of public rumors" and "torn within himself." After Sītā's rescue, Rāma informs her that his arduous war against Laṅkā "was not undertaken wholly" at her request or for her sake, but to avenge the affront to his family (II,117). Crediting social suspicion of her fidelity, Rāma testifies that his "attachment" to Sītā is terminated and that she is free to marry elsewhere. As stated previously, she protests that physical force could not have controlled her will. "If despite the proofs of love that I gave thee whilst I lived with thee, I am still a stranger to thee, O Proud Prince, my loss is irrevocable." "But thou, O Lion among Men, by giving way to wrath and by thus passing premature judgment on a woman, has acted like a worthless man." "Thou has had no reverence for the joining of our hands in my girlhood and mine affectionate nature, all these things hast thou cast behind thee !" (VI,118).

In these and other demonstrations, Sītā's character contrasts with the passivity of the feminine mystic. She requested and passed an ordeal by fire, thus receiving public and divine vindication. Rāma then proclaimed that he had been certain of her innocence, but had tested her to keep the people from saying that he was controlled by lust (VI,120).

Further Vālmīkian censure of sexual subordination may be read from the quality of the Rāma-Sītā love perduring in the plot's final action. A happy love applauded or a shrinking and tragic relationship lamented might both be means of deploring the social subjection of women. In Vālmīki's account, Rāma and Sītā enjoyed "every kind of felicity" (VII,42), at least penultimately. In the verses and dramatizations of Kālidāsa, Bhavabhūti, Kamban, Tulasīdās, and others, as well as in the *Vālmīki-Rāmāyaṇa*'s opening synopsis of the plot (I,1), Rāma and Sītā live "happily ever after." But in Vālmīki's "final" or supplemental book (whose authenticity has been questioned), Rāma *again* yields to public opinion and to the belief that honor in this situation is more important than life. Overcome with sorrow, he exiles Sītā, who in turn echoes the lamentations of tragic love, Vālmīki himself depicted as her protector. Years later, Rāma acknowledges twin sons born from Sītā and begs pardon for the second repudiation which had been occasioned by "fear of the people." In the redaction used in Shastri's translation, Sītā descends into the earth in a scenario of glorious deification. Rāma's sadness assuaged by Brahmā himself, he suffers further pain and separation from Lakṣmaṇa and "ascends to Heaven" (VII,110). In some accounts, Sītā's and Rāma's transition to heaven are not without death—in fact they die of grief.[31] For Tulasīdās, Sītā is both subject and, as woman, also source of bereavement. In both Vālmīkian developments, it is possible to make two generalizations about the meaning of the finale. First, with or without death, there is passage to a life comparable to this one and full of happiness. Secondly, previous to their new status, their lives ended sorrowfully and tragically.

Restricting our observations to the *Vālmīki-Rāmāyaṇa,* we can formulate the hypothesis that the epic was not intent on exploring the drama of Thanatos in general or on exploring what de Rougement called the life-denying, abstract, and depersonalizing elements of tragic "*amour*" or *Love in the Western World* in particular—at least at a conscious level. The evil drawn on the epic's canvas is more generic. It is the totality of sorrows, separations, and deaths which eventually overcome all human beings. Hindu stress on karmic compensation for one's deeds (in this life or a previous one) may have expressed one attempt to define or give meaning to that sum of suffering. As for the epic at hand, in tune with Aristotle's analysis of the cathartic function of Greek tragedy, identification with the suffering Rāma and Sītā would hopefully make life somehow more bearable. Moreover, in the light of Sītā's unanswered protests, the poem's communication is more directly ethical. It is not merely that life is sad, a judgment of fact. A normative judgment is also added. Life is sad partly because of institutionalized societal attitudes, like prejudice against the strength and fidelity of women. In addition, the unanswered disapprobations and later apology of Rāma indicate his share of responsibility for the consequences of this prejudice.[32]

To discover the origins of a movement for women's liberation in such ancient materials would be crossing into the land of revisionistic projection. This danger admitted, it seems that a salient, if not primary, declaration of the *Vālmīki-Rāmāyaṇa* is its outcry against sexual discrimination. If so, fuel is there provided for the pragmatic theory that the qualities of the male-female relationship affect the entire gestalt of a social, moral system, including its values, priorities, norms, and the characters it holds up for imitation. This much is certain. Sexual discrimination was condemned by the epic's author(s); and, to whatever degree the epic's purported popularity and authority reflect widespread agreement in aspiration or practice, it was also censured by large segments of Indian society, however ineffectually for the future.

2) *Caste.* Allusions to the factual existence of four *varṇas* (classes) are few, terse, and clear (I,1). As is the case in most Hindu literature, including the writings of Gandhi, derogatory evaluations of the *varṇas* are lacking. In the *Ry*'s plot and dialogue both, some phrases manifest positive approval (I,1 and IV,4). Further, the *varṇa* is not merely defended for its efficiency in distributing functions in social life where not all persons share identical talents, or where, in Pauline imagery, hands cannot perform the operations of feet. In the *Ry* the *varṇa* system was also like a *jāti* or caste system, in the sense that it comprised more than nominal classifications. Divisions actually discriminatory are mirrored in customs affecting a) religious practice, b) marriage and mobility, and c) economic power.

a) When the religious practice of mortifications, legally reserved to the three upper *varṇas* or classes, was performed by the *śūdra*, *Śambūka*, it resulted in his decapitation by Rāma. The latter is congratulated by the gods for preventing the *śūdra* from attaining heaven (VII, 75-76).

b) Marriage was limited to one's caste, at least in theory. In other words, it was endogamous, the exception being that only men, not women, could marry down the social ladder. In such cases, moreover, inheritance was blocked.[33] "None were born of mixed castes..." (I,6) and, as Sharma indicates, "heredity was actually the main principle in determining the varṇa of an individual."[34]

c) Economic benefits among castes were not equal. "The brahmanas were considered the worthiest recipients of gifts and 'acceptance of gifts' remained the principal means of livelihood."[35] This practice is in accord with the *Mbh*'s records of land grants to Brahmins and of their custody of the royal treasury. Max Weber, D. D. Kosambi, and others would later focus on this phenomenon as one replete with social implications. The worst economic and marital immobility was experienced by the outcastes, a group which already existed during the epic's period of composition. Although the authenticity of the chapter in the original *Ry* has been questioned, "Caṇḍālas" "of dark complexion" (I, 58) are said to be outcastes or untouchables.[36]

Moving from alleged fact to judgment, the only passage which might be taken as a condemnation of caste discrimination concerns the Brahmin, Jābāli, who speaks derogatorily of the practices of other Brahmins. In a discourse intended to discourage Rāma from accepting exile as an ascetic, Jābāli "uttered these words contrary to dharma: O Rāmacandra [Rāma], these scriptural injunctions were laid down by learned men, skilled inducing others to give, and finding other means of obtaining wealth, thus subjugating the simple-minded. Their doctrine is: 'Sacrifice, give in charity, consecrate yourselves, undergo austerities and become ascetics' " (II,108). A conclusion that this pronouncement was Vālmīki's underhanded way of attacking the brahminic caste or their parasitical economical system, would, for lack of critical information about the text, be largely speculative. However, according to Vora, the story of the

Brahmin, Trijatā, in the first book of the epic echoes the Brahminic greed detailed in other classic sources.[37]

To attack Brahminic covetousness is not yet to assail the Brahmins' existence as a class (*varṇa*) or even caste-like (*jāti*) exploitation and inequities in general. Vālmīki's remonstrance against sexual discrimination, therefore, is not matched with an equally sure counterpart in regard to caste inequality and immobility.[38]

3) *Violence.* Violence, in the sense of force which requires justification, is not merely military or directly homicidal. In a wider and deeper sense, the subject of violence has already been confronted in the *Ry*'s statements about women, castes, and the power of public opinion and custom. Societal structures and attitudes oppress or bring harm (*himsā*) in a variety of ways. For one, they can bear the seeds of death, like those which brought death-inflicting grief to King Daśaratha, Rāma, and Sītā. War itself does not emerge from nowhere. Its germs incubate within inequitable societal systems and destructive social mores as well as within individual or collective greed. It is doubtful, nonetheless, that the *Ry* is meant to stress the attitudinal connection between Rāvaṇa's lust and the abduction and war which it seemed to occasion. War in the *Ry* (like battles in other epics or apocalyptic tales and myths) is symbolic of the struggle between the forces of good and evil, thus striving to satisfy the thirst for rationality and meaning in life. Rāma's foes are less clearly men than they are mythical titans, demons, or totemic figures resurrected from an archetypal past or a Jungian collective unconscious. Consequently, the prospect of reconstructing a moral theory about warfare or homicide from the *Ry* is dim from the start. Individual comments about moral ends and means in war may have no literal meaning apart from their intent to entertain or from the general belief or hope that evil is overcome by good. But the comments may be instructive, just as slips of the tongue or blocked memories can sometimes assist speakers to determine what they really wished to say.

Rāma's overt motivations for killing are the rescue of Sītā, the preservation of royal honor and of the caste system, punishment for incest (IV, 17-18), and the protection of hermits in the forest. On the last score he is challenged by Sītā. The basic premise of her argument does not involve unqualified *ahimsā* (nonviolence), but the opinion that war will become Rāma's moral (caste) duty only after he clearly resumes the duties of the warrior *varṇa* or class. For the present, as a forest ascetic, his obligation is to avoid violence. Given the last word in the conversation, Rāma feels bound by both his caste *dharma* and by his promise to protect the ascetics: "Even had I not promised them anything, O Vaidehi [Sītā], it is my bounden duty to protect the sages; how much more so now!" (III,10).

Ascetical interpolation or not, Sītā's previous dialogue may delineate boundaries for violence which apply universally, to other than ascetics. "O Warrior! the world looks askance on those who strike without cause." "Murderous thoughts, inspired by desire for gain, are born of the handling of weapons" (III, 9). Similarly universalizable are two other conditions tied into the epic's major battle. The war at Laṅkā is a kind of "ultima ratio" or last recourse, and the enemy is portrayed as wholly and hopelessly villainous.

When Sītā and the sages speak of the corrosive effect of violence on ascetics who perpetrate it, one has to recall the air-tight divisions claimed for *varṇa* stratification in order to understand why the same effects would not follow for members of other castes, warriors included. "As contact with fire works change in a piece of wood, so the carrying of arms works alteration in the mind of him who carries them" (III, 9). The hermits whom Rāma was to defend admitted that while they could destroy the forest demons by the power of their austerities, they were "loath to lose the fruits of their penances" (III,10). An interesting, if unprovable hypothesis, is that the author of these remarks was intentionally or inadvertently expressing a tension of viewpoints about violence, wondering if its effects would harm only ascetical agents or everyone. Supposition of composite authorship could render this theory more plausible.

In the end, and in a rationale not unlike that utilized in the *Gītā* (whose primary message concerned action rather than war), Rāma's caste duty as a warrior prevails over lingering doubts. Subsequent narration speaks of additional warfare without condemnation. Whatever Rāma's decision may be felt to disclose about the epic's stance toward the value of life and the significance of death, the picture might be broadened by future investigation of "religiously" motivated suicides in the Vālmīkian classic. Śabarī, for instance, a servant of "highsouled ascetics" immolated herself, with Rāma's approval, to join "her spiritual preceptors" (III, 74).

The final didactic testimony about violence is given by Sītā. Contrary to Rāma's option for violence, Sītā's address, already seen in another context, appeals to strict *ahimsā,* either literally or in spirit: "A superior being does not render evil for evil, this is a maxim one should observe. ...One should never harm the wicked or the good or even criminals meriting death. A noble soul will ever exercise compassion even towards those who enjoy injuring others or those of cruel deeds...." (VI,115).

Are both violence and its contrary, *ahimsā,* taught in the epic? If even Gandhian idealism would some day propose both choices at different levels, why not here? An alternate, if less likely, resolution of the dilemma can be built on the assumption that the *Ry*'s author(s) deliberately chose to demonstrate their oscillation on the issue. Like some would-be pacifists on the contemporary scene who have vacillated between nonviolent strategies and the deployment of demolitions, the Vālmīkian contributors could not make up their minds. A less speculative generalization can sum up the quandary: in the measure to which the *Vālmīki-Rāmāyaṇa* divulges ancient and popular beliefs, a strong and definite tendency to nonviolence was one of them. No straight "just-war theory" here.

E. *Ethical Validation.* The issue of how the epic appealed to sources of moral verification is the last metaethical concern of the present chapter. Long awarded the status of *smriti* (recollection or tradition), the *Ry* claimed for itself and its moral teaching (at least in later additions) a "supernatural" authority equal to that of scriptural *śrutis*, the *Vedas* (VII,98,111). In the role of supreme Deity, Brahmā states that the entire classic is both true and divine (VII,98). Reading it insures philosophical wisdom, other types of success within one's caste (I,1), or even a share in the epic's salvific effects. Recitation removes sins and guarantees good fortune, progeny, peace, and longevity (I,1). "This narrative," including the *Uttara Kāṇḍa* or supplemental book about the deaths or transitions of Rāma and Sītā, "has the approval of Brahma Himself" (VII,111). Assertions like these, even if they are subsequent additions (see Appendix I, A, e) seem bound to have augmented the *Ry*'s popularity over the more cumbersome *Mbh* as well as other materials which competed for public attention. But the point at issue here is not the epic's consequent popularity or impact, but the definitely religious and authoritative quality of its ethical validation. An even more intense appeal to transcendent moral governance and divine command will evolve in the increasing divinization of Rāma among the people.[39]

Divine jurisdiction in morals is shared by human beings. Rāma's moral conduct is grounded on the authority of his guru in the sight of the gods (II,109). To King Daśaratha's chief priest, Vasiṣṭha, is ascribed the role of "spiritual preceptor" (II, 82). He asserts a special prerogative in moral teachings which Vālmīki seems to approve. In his entreaty with Rāma to take his father's throne, Vasiṣṭha states:

> From birth, the spiritual instructors of a man are his Guru, his Sire and his mother ! O Kakutstha...the father gives man his life,...the Guru instructs him in wisdom and therefore is considered the superior [over the warrior !] I was thy father's Spiritual Preceptor and am thine,...in obeying me, thou wilt not leave this path of the virtuous. II,3; (see also IV, 18).

While this proclamation prescinds from the classically thorny and seemingly circular criteria whereby fallible human beings affirm/bestow vicariously divine and infallible authority on fellow human beings without a basis in direct "religious" experience, it clearly asserts that in the *Ry*, authority, whether human or divine, is a formidably powerful current within the epistemological fountains of moral judgment.

Yet there are other elements in the epic which appear definitely non-authoritative and humanly limited. When Lakṣmaṇa sought to inspire Rāma with the courage to kill Rāvaṇa, he revealed the uncertainty present in the moral discrimination of consequences: "O Thou Best of Men, after due consideration, discriminate between that which is good and that which is evil; persons of right wisdom are ever cognizant of what is right or wrong. Owing to the element of uncertainty, one cannot at once distinguish the advantage or disadvantage of a deed, but if one fails to act the desired result will not take place" (III,66).

Whether this discernment operates by non-inferential insight or intuition is not clear, but some texts point in that direction. According to Khan's translation, Rāma proclaims that the

"Dharma of the good is subtle and is very difficult to understand by an ordinary person. Yet it is within the heart of every person. It is the soul of all things which discerns the good and evil" (IV,18).[40] Possibly "the soul of all things" could be equated with *rita*, the ancient Vedic analogue for *lex naturalis* or Chinese *tao*: a kind of innate and generically normative cosmic order. If Khan's interpretation is correct, there may be allusion here both to cosmic moral order and to the human intuition which perceives it, thus contradicting the later opinions of some Mahāyāna Buddhist and Advaitic philosophers that the good exists merely in human subjects (or more exactly, only in the one absolute Reality), and not in a separate cosmic order. As a reality in things, good in the *Ry* is capable of being "intuited." Like Plato, Vālmīki felt that "good" is "supreme, the substance of all things and the ultimate object of life...."[41]

While non-inferential cognition of moral good is merely plausibly existent in the epic the presence of consequential or rational inference is certain. Rāma reasons to just taxes and wages, for example, by signaling the unsatisfactory effects which befall kings who levy harsh taxes or employers who hold back on wages (II,100). Truth-telling is defended consequentially : "Men fear a liar as one does a venomous serpent, truth is said to be the root of all in this world..." (II,109). Anger is wrong, concludes Rāma's ally, Hanumān (V, 55), because of the undiscriminating thought and actions to which it leads. Its fruits are devastating. To these passages may be appended many of those dealing with the karmic products of one's actions in the present life.

It does not follow that the epic's references to modest and rational ethical verifications bear *more* weight than its frequent allusions to divine or religious personages who command. In fact, comparatively speaking, Rāmāyaṇic strains of authority play so loudly that clever conductors might orchestrate them into moral authoritarianism. But in themselves neither authority nor reason seem sufficient.

Positions that ethical reason, by itself, is bankrupt, without the support of religion, charisma, or emotive value-feeling are shared by those who infer that rational wills cannot move without legislation, propaganda, behavioral reinforcement, or various forms of control or force. The stances of both groups await clearer rebuttal than that provided by the *Ry*. In fact, it is not at all clear that the power of moral reason alone was thought to be persuasive, either in the *Ry* or in the long historical queues of those who have heard, seen, or read it. A Rāmāyaṇic scenario more morally moving than one of reasoned morality working alone or with authority consisted of ethical reasoning co-working on a Schelerian stage of attractive moral persons—a world stage where there is nothing so stirring for thinking hearts as the personal intuition (*Anschauung*) of other people truly moral. As Rāma declared, the discerning *dharma* of the good is rooted in the heart of every individual; but for growth it needs to interact with the sun and light of other good persons.

F. *Conclusion*. If the x-ray structuralist methods of Claude Lévi-Strauss and leaders in other fields could be combined with more sensitive tools of textual and historical criticism, they might well ground and extend the tentative conclusion now to be summarized. In brief, the *Ry* possesses all the philosophical bones of an ethical body of thought, taking positions on 1) universal morality as well as mores, 2) epistemological legitimation, 3) ethos, and 4) the moral character of institutions. Behind the Rāmāyaṇic system's non-deterministic exposition of *karma* and its universal norms (*morality over mores*) lies an intricate process of *ethical legitimation*, plausibly an intuitional and clearly a consequential approach interwoven with a rather sophisticated notion of the dialectic between the meanings of freedom and the self-determining habits called character. Notable in the epic's *ethos* are concrete models of truth and of a compassionate, altruistic benevolence towards all beings which does not ground itself on an Advaitic or mystical premise of identification. At the top of the ethos stands an affirmative acceptance and embrace of wealth, power, and the kind of sexual love which spirals into altruistic love for other people. These are no mere instruments to another goal or life, but also ends in themselves (when combined with moral character). Regrettably, life is sad, but not wholly in itself. It is individually and collectively tragic partly because of systemic and institutional factors like sexual discrimination and societal attitudes and customs. The poem does not extend this indictment to caste inequities or religio-moral authoritarianism, as one might hope. But its powerful inclination to reject violence can be seen as an embryonic condemnation of all the forms and systems of oppression which effect human waste, destruction, and alienation. Whether it is a later addition or not, one of Sītā's final teachings encapsulates the Rām¯yaṇic ideal for humanity succinctly. Immorality is already its own punishment. "Who is without fault ? A superior being does not render evil for evil." The superior persons respond not with hatred, but "will ever exercise compassion" (VI,115).

In studying the *Ry*, one is reassured that thorough descriptive and historical exposition of texts is an indispensable prerequistite for comparative religious ethics and for the bolder philosophical follow-ups which seem so imperative in its future. Without a careful eye for texts and facts and without an at least *prima facie* detachment from Hindu or other religious advocacies, one could miss the epic's unconventional but crucial messages. As an alternative to the positive but merely germinal ethics of the *Vedas*, the Upanishadic morality of asceticism and other-worldly liberation, Manu's ethics of control, and the *Gītā*'s *non-attached* action,—the *Ry*, like other popular Indian classics, paints a unique moral ethos. From its interwoven themes about *kāma* and human compassion, one might call it an ethic of *abbraciamento*, the humanistic embrace. It is an embrace of the *tri-varga* (three goals) of sexual pleasure and love (*kāma*), wealth and power (*artha*), and of virṭue, human love, and moral strength (*dharma*). A most unusual imperative becomes categorical : none of these values should be sought alone or in a distorted manner, but none should be by-passed. The hope is that in this life or in another they will all be attained by everyone. The epic's fifth century dramatist, Kālidāsa, captured this *Geist* when he wished that all persons in all lands might find their own good, happiness, and "taste all desire."

Although Gandhi dreamed that Rāma's royal *dharma* would become the ideal of India and died while uttering Rāma's name, it was the Nobel laureate and more universalistic Hindu reformer Rabindranath Tagore who most vividly (if unconsciously) reasserted the ancient epic's ethos amid the clamor of competing voices. Appalled by what he saw as Indian backwardness and poverty, which according to some Indian reformers was aggravated by the recrudescence of Brahminic world-denial,[42] Tagore's vision projected the Rāmāyaṇic renaissance of life-affirming action. In the Indian particular, the great poet may have trumpeted a human universal :

> This death must be pierced through—this mesh of fear, this rubbish of inert mass heaped mountain high, dead junk. Oh wake up you must on this glorious morning, in this stirring world, in this world of action.[43]

NOTES

1. Crawford, *Hindu Ethical Ideals*, pp. 19, 79, 104-05. Pending translations and commentaries based on critical editions, historical and critical study of its genres or forms, and further literary and historical insights about which sections and later interpolations are ascetical, Buddhistic, or Brahminic rather than of Vedic or popular inspiration, the present analysis focuses on the most recent and thorough English translation of the Sanskrit, *The Rāmāyaṇa of Vālmīki* by H. P. Shastri (3 Vols., 2d rev. ed.; London : Shanti Sadan, 1970) and the commentaries mentioned *passim.* William T. de Bary and associates at Columbia University Press, who were unaware of the Shastri translation's *revised* edition, called it "the best available prose translation" which is "fairly reliable as well as readable" (*Sources of Indian Tradition*, I, 73). Citations here must reflect Shastri's sporadically idiosyncratic style of punctuation and his lack of diacritical marks and verse enumerations. His translation should be compared with the first Sanskrit critical edition of J. M. Mehta, G. H. Bhatt, P. L. Vaidya *et al* (1960-71). See Appendix I, e for further information on that edition. In de Bary's *Sources of Indian Tradition* I, 521-24, he employs the transliteration of L. Renou's *Grammaire Sanscrite* (Paris : Adrien-Masoneuv, 1936) in a brief but more accessible Indic word list. As usual, the same transliteration system is used and extended here.
2. Shantikumar Nanvaram Vyas, *Indian in the Rāmāyaṇa Age: A Study of the Social and Cultural Conditions in Ancient India as Described in Vālmīki's Rāmāyaṇa* (Delhi : Atma Ram, 1967), p. 318.
3. Adya Rangacharya, *Drama in Sanskrit Literature* (2d. ed. rev.; Bombay: Popular Prakashan, 1967), p. 194 : see also p. 207.
4. Sukumar Sen, *History of Bengali Literature* (rev. ed.; New Delhi : Sahitya Akademi, 1971; Milton Singer, "The great tradition in a metropolitan center : Madras," in *Traditional India : Structure and Change*, ed., Milton Singer (Philadelphia : The American Folklore Society, 1959), pp. 141-82; Venkatarama Raghaven, "Hinduism," in *Historical Atlas*, ed. Isma'il Rāgī al Fārūqi, pp. 69-96.
5. Benjamin Khan, *The Concept of Dharma in Vālmīki Rāmāyaṇa* (Delhi : Munshi Ram Manohar Lal, 1965), p. 98. This volume constitutes the only monograph on the poem's moral teachings. It's descriptive method which is light on analytical structure focuses not directly on my set of questions, but rather on freedom, relativism and this-worldly goals. It is an important part of the study of the epic's history and teachings.
6. Singer, *Traditional India*, p. xii.

7. Norvin Hein, "The Rām Līlā." in *Traditional India*, Singer, ed. pp. 73-98.

8. The second disavowal is absent in later versions like those of Kālidāsa, Bhavabhūti, Kamban, and Tulasidās. In one of the accounts which does contain it, Rāma not only banishes Lakṣmaṇa but, like Sītā, dies of grief. In other versions, Rāma simply joins the gods after a long and just reign.

9. Here the books or *kāṇḍas* will be designated by Roman numerals rather than by their names. I=Bāla Kāṇḍa, II=Ayodhyā, III=Araṇya, IV=Kiṣkindhā, V=Sundara, VI=Yuddha or Laṅkā, and VII=Uttara. A sample of an abbreviated reference : I, 1=Bāla Kāṇḍa, Chap. 1.

10. Max Scheler, *Formalism in Ethics and non-formal Ethics of Values*, trans. by M. S. Frings and R. L. Funk (Evanston : Northwestern University Press, 1973), p. 574.

11. P. V. Kane, *The History of Dharmásāstra*; Vol. II, 1, pp. 3ff.

12. Were it not for explicit references by Rāma to faults committed in previous lives (like those in II, 39, 53), one might conclude that all generic allusions to earlier sins apply only to the present existence. Dismissing the references to former lives as later interpolations, Khan excludes the weltanschauung of *karma-samsāra* (moral compensation now and in rebirths) from the *Ry*, (*The Concept of Dharma*, p. 90).

13. Philip H. Ashby "The history of religions and the study of Hinduism", in *The History of Religion* (Chicago : Chicago University Press, 1967), p. 153 attempts to play down alleged Hindu pessimism, as do some Vedāntic reformers, but Vyas, *India*, p. 290 thinks that sentiments of fatalism pervade the *Ry*. Khan, *The Concept of Dharma*, p. 245 discerns not fatalism but human cooperation in the epic as well as in its sister-epic the *Mbh* XIII, XXXII, 13-15, *Yājñavalkya Smriti* I, 348, 350, and *Manu* VII, 205.

14. Vyas, *India*, p. 317.

15. *Ibid.*, p. 130.

16. The epic's emphases on truth can be seen also in IV, 34 and in Ramashraya Sḥarma, *A Socio-Political Study of the Vālmīki-Rāmāyaṇa*, (Delhi : Motilal Banarsidass, 1971), p. 390. In II, 21 Rāma lends obedience to one's father an equally prominent role. Or one might say that of all the *dharmas* taken as duties the latter achieves priority in conflict in its identification with truth.

17. This conclusion is supported in the work of Khan, *The Concept of Dharma*, pp. 129-31, who also gathers from the epic lists of about fifty virtues and fifty sins, pp. 186-90, 208-10. Sītā's praise of *ahimsā* or nonviolence deserves special notice in this story of both love and war (VI, 115).

18. *Ibid.*, pp. 5, 42 and Vyas, *India*, pp. 290-91.

19. Similar declarations are enunciated in II, 21, 100; III, 9 and VI, 63. De Bary, *Sources of Indian Tradition*, pp. 213-15, gathers other supportive passages from *Manu Smriti* 2.224, *Yājñavalkya Smriti* 2.2.21, Cāṇakya-Kauṭilya's *Artha Shāstra* 1, 7, Vātsyāyana's *Kāma Sūtra*, and Kālidāsa's *Raghuvaṃśa*. These are merely samples of a whole sea of similar passages in popular classics. Declarations like these apparently escaped the notice of the celebrated historian, Sushil Kumar De, who wrote that while the *trivarga* (three objects or goals) of *dharma*, *kāma*, and *artha* are axiomatic in the *Purāṇas* and Sanskrit literature, they are not yet established in the epics. See his

Ancient Indian Erotics and Erotic Literature (Calcutta : Firma K. L. Mukhopadhyay, 1969), p. 93.

20. Khan, *The Concept of Dharma*, p. 39, concludes : "As there is no counter criticism of artha as the goal of life, I am convinced that the *Rāmāyaṇa* aims at conceding a high place to material values."

21. Karl Marx and Friedrich Engels, "Manifesto of the Communist Party," in *The Marxists*, ed. C. Wright Mills (New York : Dell Publishing Co., Inc., 1962).

22. Khan, *The Concept of Dharma*, pp. 50, 95, and esp. 98.

23. Inordinate *kāma* is depicted in II, 53; III, 9; and VI, 83, 113, 120.

24. Ramashraya Sharma, *A Socio-Political Study*, pp. 155, 179, 273, 279, and Khan, *The Concept of Dharma*, p. 57.

25. Ludwik Sternbach, *A History of Indian Literature : Subhāṣita, Gnomic and Didactic Literature* (Wiesbaden : Otto Harrassowitz, 1974), p. 53.

26. While at one point Sītā pictures her future forest life with Rāmā as "free from desire for pleasure, traversing the honey-scented woodland" (II, 27), the pleasure which she hopes to enjoy anyway may not lack its Freudian connotations : "I shall bathe in their [the forest's lakes' and pools'] waters. In constant devotion to thee, O Large-Eyed Prince, I shall live in the height of felicity, and should we have to pass a hundred thousand years together, I would never, even for an instant, weary of it. I have no desire even for heaven...had I to live in heaven far from thee...." (II, 27). "When in the dense forest, I sleep beside thee on a grassy couch, soft as a woollen coverlet, what could be more pleasant to me ?" (II, 30). From Rāma's viewpoint also, the three daily ascetical baths are not envisioned as entirely painful rituals : "Here where the perfected beings, free from all taint, rich in asceticism and mortifications, their senses under control, perpetually stir the waters, thou too should enter with me, and as on the breast of a friend, O Lovely Sita, thou should trust thyself to the Mandakini River where blue and white lotuses float" (II, 95). Even taken as ascetical reconstructions, these verses are perhaps redolent of more than ascetical meanings (even more so in Shastri's earlier and unrevised translation).

27. *Manu* III, 78. That the stage (*āśrama*) of the married householder (*grihastha*) is not to be avoided can also be inferred from the religious necessity of having sons (see *Ry* II, 107).

28. Khan, *The Concept of Dharma*, p. 108.

29. In the Hindi version of Tulasīdās, widely renowned in northern India from the sixteenth century, women were not so favored. See U. M. Macfie, *The Ramayan of Tulsidas* (Edinburgh : T. and T. Clarks, 1930), pp. 197-207.

30. Vyas, *India*, p. 130.

31. *Ibid.*, pp. 13-22.

32. In the measure that Rāma is taken as a male symbol, therefore, the poem has evaluatively appraised the origins of male chauvinism in the following language : precipitous judgments, forgetfulness of love received and of the loved one's very person, a false sense of honor, and inordinate fear of public opinion (VI, 118). This social commentary is all the more remarkable in that male, priestly, and ascetical interpolators left it intact (see Shakambari

Jayal, *The Status of Women in the Epics* (Delhi : Motilal Banarsidass, 1966), pp. 227 and *passim.*

33. Dhairyabala P. Vora, *Evolution of Morals in the Epics* (Bombay : G. R. Bhatkal, Popular Book Depot, 1959), pp. 106-08 and S. Jayal, *The Status of Women*, pp. 308-09. Although *pratiloma* marriages (to women of upper castes) were not unknown in practice, the only marriages permitted (*anuloma*) were those with wives of equal or lower castes. Vora, *Evolution*, p. 107, points out that in the *Mbh* XIII, 165, 21 the marriage of a Brahmin to a *śūdra* was considered sinful.

34. Sharma, *A Socio-Political Study*, p. 15; see also Jayal, *ibid.*, pp. 308-10.

35. Sharma, *ibid.*, pp. 19 and 23; and confer *Ry* I, 6.

36. See Vora, *Evolution*, pp. 167-68, who also comments on the social and ethical monopolies of the two upper castes in both epics.

37. For example in *Gautama* and in the *Mbh* XII, 165, 28. See Vora, *ibid.*, pp. 250, 252.

38. In spite of his strenuous attack on discrimination, the tyranny of custom, and Brahminic thought, Khan, *The Concept of Dharma*, pp. 106-08, 131, views caste in the *Ry* as an "incentive for social morality."

39. This conclusion may be contrasted with Khan's position, *ibid.*, pp. 47-48, 119.

40. Khan's Sanskrit source reads :

Sūkṣamaḥ paramavijñyeyaḥ satāṁ dharmaḥ plavaṅgama,
Hṛdisthaḥ sarvabhūtānām ātmā veda śubhāśubham.

Shastri's translation reads : "even for the virtuous duty is subtle and not easy to grasp, the soul residing in the heart alone knows what is right or wrong."

41. Khan's reference, *The Concept of Dharma*, p. 119 to II, 21 on this point is not verifiable in Shastri's translation.

42. Sukumar Sen, *Bengali Literature*, p. 290.

43. As quoted in *ibid.*, p. 264.

Chapter VI

ETHICS IN THE *BHAGAVAD GĪTĀ*

Abstract. As the "single complete and compact scripture" or chief devotional book for Hindus, the *Gītā* has been attacked on Buddhistic grounds for its egoistic activism, a mystical kind of charge which can be answered with some ease, at least to the satisfaction of non-Buddhists. However, the well-known Schweitzerian allegation that the *Gītā*'s mystical and world-renouncing spirit of non-attachment obstructs or does not properly encourage active social ethics has engendered softer species of the same basic criticism. These merit careful attention because of the significance of the *Gītā* as an inter-cultural literary classic. The indictment of ethical quietism and the world-wide dialectic it perpetuates about the relation between mysticism and the morality is paradigmatically crucial for all traditions which admit the realms of the numinous or the mystical. It is similarly pivotal for the cross-cultural question: "why be moral ?" The *Gītā* provides a window into both discussions, because its main theme seems to address the mystical justification not merely of a specific war, but of human action as such, including moral activity. NOTES.

A. *Against moral quietism.* The *Gītā*'s traditional justification of action on the grounds of 1) *varṇadharma* or class duty is a rationale which is more easily grasped by Hindus than by others. At another level, which is comprehensible at more universally philosophical or metaphysical dimensions, the classic contends either that 2) seemingly immoral social action is right because it really flows from Brahman, and/or that 3) since Brahman alone is real, nobody is really killed. 4) the *Gītā* further includes the psychological type of reasoning that people can elude moral killing by not thinking of themselves as killers, death being inevitable for all sentient beings anyway. If the *Gītā*'s mystical justification for such activity—which for some readers seems rather to deemphasize action—is not taken merely 5) metaphorically or 6) pedagogically as an eventually dispensable teaching, it may also be explained from 7) the democratic / egalitarian perspective that *bhakti* (devotion), *karma* (as action), and *jñāna* (mystical knowledge) are to be chosen according to subjective abilities. To each his own, with equal results.

More forceful interpretations defend the primacy among equals of each of the three paths. Epistemologically they appeal to one or more of the following justifications: 8) postulated logical identifications of the three paths or 9) resort to divine authority, a leitmotif in the *Gitā*. 10) *Av* versions of bi-level truth beckon to a perspective or blik which seems both irrefutable and non-verifiable on finally rational grounds rather than on correspondence with direct personal experience.

What stands above these conflicting rationales, which either defend or deny moral quietism in the *Gitā*, is the fact that, objections notwithstanding, it promotes a specific mystical ethos or style of activity which can be called egoless and non-attached.

B. *The Gitā's humanistically constructive ethos*; *war*; *and caste.* The topic of non-attached social action entails the cross-cultural, age-old, and classical debate about the possibility of ethical altruism or disinterestedness. The *Gitā* offers perhaps the most ancient record and thorough reflection on the controversy. As indicated above, it resolves it at least partly on the basis of a human-divine, mystical immanence or identification. Plausibly, it assumes that a "moral point of view" cannot finally be justified against the objections of an honest ethical egotist like Thomas Hobbes, without recourse to some species of mystical or incomprehensibly interhuman identity. In the interpretation of Ninian Smart, such an identification would not have to be world-negating from an overall Hindu point of view. As for the *Gitā*'s alleged approval of caste discrimination, this chapter offers no explanation beyond the usual ones available through Gandhi and other reformers.

C. *Ethical validation by authority.* In reference to the classic's central position on mystical unity and selfless love, either for the Absolute or for other human beings, the question lingers: is this vision and way of life (*dharma*), apart from its humanistic appropriations or imitations, exclusively a gift, grace, or authoritative command? Can one predispose oneself for its reception?

D. *Conclusion and postscript.* Whatever the answer, as Raimundo Panikkar and Thomas Berry have affirmed, it need entail no infidelity to one's own cultural or religious background.[1] Taken either as religion or as altruistic morality, mysticism may supercede the overly neat distinction between life- and death-affirmations and be utilized as bases for either ethos.

Empathetic and humanistic outsiders wish to dialogue with believers in the teaching of the *Gītā* about its grounds for practical and cross-cultural detente and growth, if not for the pursuit of truth itself. For the former non-Hindu group, the social potential of the *Gītā's* mysticism which also claims to offer something beyond human morality, can concur with the life-affirming "passionate indifference" of Teilhard de Chardin and other Eastern and Western mystical stresses on moral love.

The conscious goal in this chapter, therefore, is by no means to discredit the *Gītā*'s intuitively mystical wellsprings. On the contrary, it is to illustrate that modern philosophical and analytically ethical attempts have failed to reduce all intuitions to a univocal notion or reality which can then be disqualified a *priori* because of other insights which are obviously illusory or misinterpreted by humans everywhere. It will be seen that the *Gītā*'s avowal of inner realization has not been disproved. This is not to say that the mystical or the esthetical has been restricted to social morality alone. But the *Gītā* does highlight a religious dynamics without which human suffering and the frailty of international detente may not be alleviated nor moral cooperation improved.

Although a most unexplored and direct window into interreligious dialogue includes ethical inquiry, the conventional search for merely formal ethical thought may fruitfully be turned upside down. As has been noted, the ethical pluralism of what most Hindus aspire to practice appears in one-dimensional focus without the help of popular literature (*kāvya*) and devotional writings. Among the latter, the long celebrated *Ry*'s staunchest competitor for the hearts and minds of Hindus, and of those who would learn from them, is the *Gītā*, "chief devotional book" for "most Hindus."[2] In terms of antiquity, its stature is comparable to the *Ry*'s, given general agreement that it was composed between the fifth and the fourth or second centuries B.C.E.[3] In respect to the *Gītā*'s authoritative position, it is ranked at the top of tradition (*smriti*) rather than as scripture (*śruti*). But the distinction may fade at the level of popular reception, because, like the *Ry*, the *Gītā* asserts its divine prerogative. In its tenth chapter, Rāma ranks as one of the manifestations (*avatārs*) of such authority (x.31).

Gandhi's teaching about Rāma as the symbol of good and

freedom[4] was at least accidentally confirmed in his dying words, "Hei, Rāma". While Gandhi was apparently more acutely conscious of the *Gitā* than he was of the *Ry*, in popular belief Rāma had become, no less than the *Gitā*'s main speaker, Krishna, a manifestation of god, Vishnu, and of the ultimate reality, Brahman. Accordingly, it is difficult to conclude with certainty that Krishna or the *Gitā* by themselves totally predominated Gandhi's thinking.[5] If his proclivity towards synthesis could appropriate teachings of Jainism, Buddhism, Christianity and other sources into Hinduism, it was not theoretically impossible for him to merge the messages of the mystical *Gitā* and the this-worldly *Ry*. One of the tasks at hand is to discern the extent to which the *Gitā* might lend itself to such a merger. In a separate enterprise one could inquire if Gandhian or other modern syntheses with *Ry* morality did, in fact, emerge.[6] The immediate point is that for Gandhi, the most visible modern Hindu, as for other nineteenth and twentieth century Hindu reformers, the *Gitā* has been paramount in Hindu consciousness. For the now retired land reformer and Gandhian coworker, Vinoba Bhāve, it rises as the epitome and cream of Hindu belief.[7] Typical of scholarly Indian and non-Indian convictions, both classical and contemporary, is Venkatarama Raghavan's insistence that the *Gitā* is the "single complete and compact scripture of Hinduism" in its full and final form.[8]

This praise has been joined with serious, if little noticed, criticism of the *Gitā*'s mysticism and eclecticism, to say nothing of Buddhistic critiques. Before its final recension in the Gupta period (fourth-seventh centuries C.E.), the *Gitā* had supposedly undergone a mystical process of "Brahmanization," but because it was brief enough for memorization, it may have been subjected to a minimum of Brahminic modifications. It does not follow, however, that it is largely the original *Gitā* which has been revered throughout Indian history. Gandhi's first impressions, for example, came through the English translation of Sir Edwin Arnold.[9] Other prominent translations and interpretations have been chiefly Vedāntic in Advaita style. These strictures notwithstanding, the present study both assumes and will *partly* support but then qualify Albert Schweitzer's theory that the original *Gitā* was in little need of Brahmanization, since it was already Brahmanic, cast mainly in the mystical mold of world, life, and action negation. Since these categories were not favored in Schweitzer's *weltanschauung*, the *Gītā* gained his dubious praise as the most read and "most idealized book in world literature."[10] Schweitzer's assault on Hinduism in general collides head-on with the *Gītā* in particular.[11]

As for the *Gītā*'s alleged eclecticism, in an earlier stage of his thought Kashi Nath Upadhyaya once contrasted it with the systematic, clear, and straightforward accounts of Buddhism. Avoiding the euphemisms of "catholic" and "pluralistic," he found the *Gītā* "mostly vacillating, scrappy, unsystematic and at places ambiguous."[12] Denying the *Gītā*'s incoherence, Eliot Deutsch admits that its synthetic attempts are tentative or, at best, incomplete.[13] The most severe volley on its supposed inconsistency was fired by Schweitzer. He became, perhaps, Hinduism's most severe critic when he contended that the *Gītā*'s ultimately mystical and action-denying worldview simply could not justify theistic devotion or any other kind of activity, moral action included, without drawing on the ethically disastrous rationale of quietism.[14] In the latter view, action as such always corrupts the actor. Theistic worship and other exertion might evade deleterious effects only on condition that the actor could act unobtrusively, "coolly," without attachment to the fruits of action.

Schweitzer felt that the invisible but malignant moral cancer within that condition was the justification of every imaginable evil. If one could sidestep the evil result of good works by sheer, pious disinterest or non-attachment, why could one not do the same with evil or selfish acts? The Brahminic contributors to the thought of the *Gītā* would be neither the first nor the last mystics to become entangled in this logical snare for mysticism everywhere, although one may speculate that moral pitfalls were never as ominous in reality as they were in the imaginations of their critics. Be that as it may, Schweitzer's argument proposes that whatever authoritative disclaimers the *Gītā* might offer, it was logically inconsistent to proclaim interior immunity from action as such without extending it to sinful behavior as well.[15]

The *Gītā*, therefore, is attacked because of two different suppositions about it. First, in spite of its rationale for activity, it is said to suffocate life-affirming action. Second, to avoid logical inconsistency, it has to support conduct which is immoral. Since these two indictments are paradigmatic of charges brought by Nietzsche, Marx, and other humanists against most ethical norms or systems which are religiously based, they are to be examined in fuller detail. A survey of both sides of the issues will lead to (A) critical and (B) constructive analyses of the *Gitā*'s principal moral ethos, relevant sources, and related positions about caste and violence and (C) its epistemic forms of moral validation.

A. *Moral Quietism.* Schweitzer's broadside denunciation of quietistic immorality does not lack apparent textual support. Preliminary to a scrutiny of relevant texts, a word about context is required. When the authors of the *Gitā* transmitted their messages, they eventually chose to insert them within the central story of the longest poem and epic ever transcribed, the *Mbh.* Since this epic's plot and genealogy are nightmarish in length and complexity and because its principal figures are often morally ambiguous,[16] it has not lent itself easily to popular dramatization in the manner of the equally or more ancient *Ry.* This does not mean that the *Mbh* is not didactic in the moral realm or that, as one of the two salient classical Indian epics, it is not worthy of ethical study such as that pioneered in Appendix I below.[17] But the most popularized moral teachings were enunciated in that section of the poem called the *Gitā.* Minimally, the reader needs to know that the *Gitā* is proclaimed as the divine teaching of Krishna, *avatār* (manifestation) of the divine Vishnu and Brahman, to Prince Arjuna.[18]

To war or not to war was Arjuna's question. His potential foe consisted not merely of fellow human beings, but of blood relatives. Krishna's responding barrage of pro-war arguments became so embarrassing to Gandhi and other modern proponents of non-violence that they have limited the *Mbh*'s battle and its moralization to an allegory about life or action in general, having no literal reference to war. While there is little evidence to uphold the *Gitā*'s bracketing or exclusion of physical conflict, Gandhi may have been programmed on target when he interpreted the *Gitā*'s main thesis to have dealt *not primarily* with war, but with *life and action as a whole*, a more extensive topic to which the *Gitā* continually returns. In this hypothesis, behind the legitimation of war lies the real issue: the justification of activity as such.

Several arguments are pivotal. They are also sometimes contradictory, thereby stimulating curiosity about the *Gitā*'s ability to convince logically.

1. *Caste duty*. The first and best known of the justifications for or denials of moral quietism in the *Gitā* holds that Arjuna's inborn caste duty (*svadharma*) prevails categorically in Kantian style over trans-caste or universal injunctions about non-violence.[19] "There exists no greater good for a Kshatriya [warrior] than a battle required by duty (ii.31). "A man obtains perfections by being devoted to his own proper action" (xviii.45). Interestingly, the deontological or dutiful appeal to caste *dharma* (as duty) shades into a second reasoning process which is, on the surface, a rationale for evil conduct. "Better one's own *dharma* than another's well performed. Better death in (the fulfillment of) one's own law, for another's law is dangerous" (iii.35). The rationale becomes more explicit in a parallel passage whose second sentence varies as follows: "One does not incur sin when doing the action prescribed by one's own nature" (xviii.47).[20] Whether the author (or human authors) is trying to vindicate the priority of war to preserve peace, caste *dharma*, activity in general, or all three, the defense of sinful performance appears even more patently: "One should not abandon his natural born action...even if it be faulty..." (xviii.48). Immaculate preservation from the stain of activity, even faulty and sinful deeds, is defended at two dimensions, one metaphysical, the second psychological or intentional.

Metaphysically speaking, in turn, second and third competing motifs are offered. 2. The second (at a lower or more expedient level of truth) is that Brahman alone is the slayer, Arjuna being a mere instrument (ix.33). 3. The third and prevailing theme is that neither Brahman nor human beings are the agents of death. No one is really killed, since only Brahman is real. "The soul [the primeval one] neither slays nor is slain" (ii.19).[21]

4. *The psychological rationale*. In the psychological or subjective realm (ii.27), even if death should have been real, it is inevitable, so that one can become a killer only by thinking of oneself as a killer. Conversely, one eludes homicide or the stain

of any other deed by imitating Brahman's non-attachment as a subject. "Actions do not stain Me;" says Krishna for Brahman, "for I have no longing for their fruits. He who knows me thus is not bound by actions" (iv.14). "Having no desires...performing actions with the body alone, he [any person] commits no sin" (iv.2).[22] "He who is not egotistic, whose intelligence is not affected though he slays these people, he slays not nor is he bound" (xviii.17). In *bhakti* (devotion) or non-attached action one "becomes Brahman" (xiv.26 and xviii.53), realizes one's real identity as Brahman, and "is not affected by sin, just as a lotus leaf is not affected by water" (v.10). These passages would puncture or even deflate the usual mystical assurances that being "beyond good and evil" in Upanishadic style is not, of course, accompanied by immoral conduct. But there are other mountain passes through which the *Gītā*'s contradiction of moral principles may be circumvented.

5. *Caricature by metaphor.* The shortest way out is to postulate that the *Gītā*'s literary form is not the genre of systematic philosophy. It is "poetic and mystical" imagery.[23] Literal interpretation distorts its main intent and meaning. One can say of John Wisdom's Indian illustration, "Her hat was the Taj Mahal," that it is a uniquely satisfactory way of representing what her hat was really like, surpassing photographs. Or, the literally absurd "he never had an unpublished thought" may sometimes function as an irreplaceable picture of writers who sacrifice vintage for quantity. Similarly poetic, yet faithful to reality, would be the *Gītā*'s doctrine that devotees who are non-attached to the activity of theistic worship are as unaffected by their actions, even sinful ones, as lotus leaves are unspoiled by water. According to one scenario, Brahmanic scribes of the *Gītā* might have felt pressed by the popularity of Bhagavata theism and Buddhism to accommodate their mysticism to populistic incursions. Their intention might have been the absorption of those movements into the landscape of the forest, where not interrelationship but oneness was the ultimate reality. No poetic by-products about sin would have been intended literally.

6. *Integration as developmental pedagogy.* A second escape from the *Gītā*'s apparent approval of improper behavior begins with the route of "progressive teaching.,"[24] but ends up utilizing Śaṅkara's radically more sophisticated genre of "two-dimensional

truth." The law of progressive teaching is axiomatic in many forms of education, moral and otherwise. Students of music may be taught simple rules of harmony until they are qualified to abandon them for better laws. Morally, Christian penitents too powerless to abandon sinful life-situations are left, at least tentatively, in subjective "good faith." For the weak who know better or whose "good faith" is not cognitively invincible, an objective "morality of compromise" is constructed, whereby they are advised that what for others is obligatory, is for them gravely inconvenient and therefore morally impossible, if not destructive and immoral. All the symphonic powers of existential theories may be orchestrated to support this "pastoral" or "good physician's" accommodation of moral principles to "human nature" or to the uniquely situational limitations and capabilities of every individual.

This tender dimension in the adaptation of moral precepts to existential ability may be balanced with the heroic. Because of their strength, the moral elite are called to ever ascending exercises of moral perfection. If their talents are ten rather than one, they are to multiply them proportionately. Elite and weak alike are invited to heed every opportunity (Pauline *kairos*) for growth. The point here, then, is not to assail the law of progressive teaching nor to submit its vulnerability for abuse to subtle ironies. Without it, educational theory for morality or anything else would sink into Procrustean dungeons. The present examination simply focuses on how pedagogical truth about *bhakti* in the *Gītā* is said to be based in reality. Once it is assumed that *bhakti* is a universally lower road to liberation than is mystical knowledge (*jñāna*), one must explicate the ground on which it is still appropriate to tread *bhakti*'s "lower" path. One rationale is in effect democratic, if not egalitarian, while a second and third must variously resort to the hypothesis of two-dimensional or "double" truth.

7. *The democratic explanation* bases itself on a subjectivistic and relativistic *blik* or perspective which leaves its own premises bracketed or unscrutinized. It reasons that the greater suitability of action for some persons and of contemplation for others is entirely relative to individual needs. If mystical knowledge is superior to devotion in the abstract, in the concrete the two are as incomparable as apples and April. As apples are not better

than April, nor *vice versa,* neither is *jñāna* better than *bhakti* or *karma* (action) nor *vice versa.* In the egalitarian theory, Ramakrishna's vindication of religious pluralism may be applied to the *yogas* or paths of *bhakti, karma,* and *jñāna* as well: "As one can ascend to the top of a house by means of a ladder or a bamboo or a staircase or a rope, so diverse are the ways and means to approach God, and every religion in the world shows one of these ways."[25]

8. *Logical identification of opposites: two-dimensional truth, version one.* Rather than relegate the preeminence of quietistic contemplation to the relativistic and specious land of sheer abstraction, a more forceful and daring theory holds that one or more of the three *yogas* is *simultaneously superior and equal* to the others. When G. K. Chesterton opined that an opponent's model of double truth was what killed that master of the law of non-contradiction, Thomas Aquinas, he held in mind a construction less challenging and sophisticated than one which can be extrapolated from suggestions made by Eliot Deutsch.

In this hypothesis, the *Gītā*'s correlation between mysticism and action is similar to that between the personal manifestation of supreme reality, Īśvara, and the non-personal aspect of the ultimate oneness of being, Brahman. In a non-analogical yet metaphorical manner not wholly unlike the Father's and Son's identification with the one divinity as codified by the Christian Athanasian Creed, Brahman and Īśvara are different from one another, yet each wholly identified with the *puruṣottama,* the unknowable and highest Spirit.[26] Metaphorically, *bhakti, karma,* and *jñāna* would resemble the three equal angles and areas of the equilateral triangle employed in Christian Trinitarian pedagogy. Each angle is equal with, yet different from the other. In logical symbols "A," "—A," and "A"^{2} are reconciled by positing an unknowable reality more ultimate than any of them and identical with each of them. In a Hegelian sort of synthesis it can be symbolized as "$A + -A + A^2$." The whole is identical with each of its components, a ne plus ultra or ultimate in logical oneupmanship. In other words, authentic *bhakti* and karmic action are either experienced or postulated as transformed and transcendental activities which are simultaneously action and non-action. In the metaphor of the pyramid, one can favor *bhakti* without compromising *jñāna* and *karma* (and *vice versa*).

As one climbs the side which is *bhakti*, one inevitably ascends *jñāna* and *karma* to the apex which embraces them all in their highest being. The consequent practical maxim would approximate one formulated by the Benedictine mystic and scholar, Patrick Cummins: "Take care of *bhakti*, and *jñāna* and *karma* will take care of themselves." *Av* begins the maxim with *jñāna*. The *Gītā* begins it with *karma*, however unsuccessfully, giving practical, if unsystematic, priority to all three at the same time.

The interpretation refracted by Cummins' kind of adage suggests the practical primacy of *bhakti* conjoined with *niṣkāma* (non-attachment). This exegesis leans on the theory that the *Gītā*'s primary goal entailed the assimilation of devotionalism into the Hindu synthesis. Its final appeal rests on the *Gītā*'s concluding praise of *bhakti* (xviii.58-71). To repeat, alternative interpretations might similarly identify the three paths in theory (c.5), but underline the operative preeminence not of *bhakti* but of *karma*, *jñāna*, or *jñāna* as *buddhiyoga* (yoga of the intellect; discipline of intelligence, as in ii.49-51, x.10, and xviii.57). The last course is one charted with complex intricacy by G. W. Kaveeshwar: a way of life exists (*buddhiyoga*) in which all other yogas merge, although practically speaking the noetic aspect prevails.[27]

What the two-level truth process shares in common with logical oneupmanship is that after one theme has been declared to absorb all others, it is then reconfirmed in its original identity. Whether mystics favor *bhakti*, *jñāna*, or *niṣkāma karma* they strenuously deny, of course, that their paradoxes exemplify logical oneupmanship, and insist that it is not logic but experience itself which assures them that there are contradictory experiences where logic does not hold. They could plead that Wittgenstein may have well expressed the alleged non-logical but experiential basis for absolute religious and ethical claims when he wrote that paradoxicality or "nonsensicality was their very essence. For all I wanted to do with them was just *to go beyond* the world and that is to say beyond significant language. . . . against the boundaries of language."[28] A circular controversy is thereby sparked when the mystics' critics rejoin that no experience which has been subjected either to reflection or communication can claim immunity from all vestiges of rational process. Ironically, the final verification of the critics' reason-filtering claim lies not in an experience of logic alone but also in one of fact. At any rate the *Gītā*'s wondrous identification and differentiation (simultaneously) of action and non-action jettisons common logic, for better or for worse. As a result, the bi-or tri-level truth hermeneutic is, like Zen's, an appeal either to trans-conceptual experience, authority, or both.

9. *Argument from divine authority.* It is the *double* appeal which emerges in fact. With divine *authority,* Krishna opts for conduct with detachment as his "decided and highest judgment" (xviii.6) and as an experience described in the first person (e.g., in iv.14 and xv.15). One might best reinforce the *Gītā*'s claim not by resorting to dialectical logic, but by signaling that the phenomenon of identifying opposites has continually arisen "in very ancient folklore, legend, and primitive myth and out of the feelings [non-inferential experience] of the race,."[29] The *Gītā*'s further appeals to human and divine authority are treated also in other contexts on p. 147.

10. *Two level truth : Av version two.* Other than the blatantly paradoxical form just described, the more simple resort to two-dimensional truth is the *Av* view that from the perspective of an ultimate Brahman who alone is real, quality-less (*nirguṇa*), and action-less devotion and moral activity are illusory or at least inferior. From the opposite but imperfect standpoint of devotees, immersed in ignorance (*avidyā*) or illusion (*māyā*), *bhakti* and *karma* are equal or superior to *jñāna.* Found more logical by Deutsch than the stark kind of contradiction illustrated triangularly above,[30] this theory frankly admits the inferiority of the human viewpoint.[31] In either hypothesis about two-dimensional truth, one meets bliks which are both impervious to merely logical rebuttal and incapable of affirmative proof to those who have not experienced them.

In view of all these diverse, if not contradictory, interpretations of the *Gītā*'s central message about moral quietism, one might conjecture, accordingly, that final decisions on how the *Gītā* justifies moral action will derive only from the matching of experiences—conscious, unconscious, or imagined—, *not* from arguments about logical coherence.

A critique. Two-dimensional lines of thought apply more effectively to the reconciliation of action and non-action than to the coexistence of goodness and immorality in a positive and concrete sense, because talk about the latter involves more than merely inner attitudes. To common-sensical minds, contrary *theoretical* mentalities about killing, for example, are more easily identified than their embodiments in the world of *concrete* action. Sympathizers with the *Gītā* who are baffled on this practical terrain might more profitably remain non-verbal or return to the "poetic" theory that the *Gītā*'s morally inconsistent approbation of sinful conduct is verbalized at a merely literal level. Relative to the teaching of the *Gītā* as a gestalt, the approval is irrelevant and out of tune. For the *Gītā*'s primary message is neither ethics nor metaethics, neither formal logic, nor systematic philosophy. It is simply the religious experience of the authentic self's unity with Brahman. Supportive of this exoneration from immoral, if not inconsistent, dialectics are several normative codifications of virtues and vices.[32]

Like many ancient, cryptic documents, particularly those replete with poetical imagery, the *Gītā* appears to juxtapose unrelated materials. For some it casts a Sphinx-like and mysterious shadow, as if it were guarding its treasures from those who would misuse them. Often obscure, it has lent itself, or at least has been submitted, to each of the foregoing resolutions of its apparent inconsistencies. Also, like other celebrated texts, its appeal as truth is not popularly measured by its logical perfection, but by the way it speaks to or resonates common experience. In this sense, its word is not circumscribed to a mere rationalization of activity. It proposes a definite mode or ethos of activity called non-attachment, originating from a spontaneous actor who is comparable with Taoism's non-flailing survivor of the ocean waves.

B. *The humanistically constructive Ethos in the quietistic project.* From comparative ethical and religious purviews, it is not surprising that the crux of the *Gītā*'s teaching refers to acting without attachment (*niṣkāma karma*) to the fruits of action in imitation of the divine.[33] The theme of "disinterest" or "non-attachment" is a common cross-cultural thread in many classical, perduring, and interrelated debates like those about mystical passivity, contemplation, the justification of action in another's interest, or love itself. It is at the heart of the paradox of the Confucian and Christian golden rules and of Kant's categorical imperative. From the Pauline "love seeks not its own interests" through recurring historical controversies magisterially outlined by Anders Nygren,[34] the disinterested aspect of Christian *agape* has proved to be an unrelenting source of conflict in religious and philosophical ethics. Likewise, the epitome of virtues in the Hindu Patanjali's and Buddhism's *brahmavihāras*,[35] *upekṣā* or detached equanimity, is as disconcerning as the Taoist leitmotif of *wu wei* (actionless action) to those who lack directly or analogically experiential glimpses of its reality. Compared by Aldous Huxley to the "holy indifference" of St Francis de Sales,[36] the *Gītā*'s non-attachment is a Wachian aperture or typological window[37] on the two most basic questions confronting every philosophy: the (religious) correlation between human beings and ultimate reality and the human interrelationships which ground activities called moral. All the prominent issues of religion and ethics relate finally to these two types of ontological and/or functional relationships, both of which are addressed within the topic of non-attachment.

Whatever one concludes about the *Gītā*'s manner of response, it cannot be avoided as the most ancient record of direct and thorough human testimony about non-attachment. People are to act, Arjuna is assured, but always without interest or purpose (*artha*) "in action done in this world, nor any with action not done" (iii.18). "Therefore, always perform the work that has to be done without attachment" (iii.19 and see iii.5 and 24). One should not be attached to that Vedic triad of goals which caps the teleological summit of Rāmāyaṇic morality, "duty, pleasure, and wealth" (xviii.34). Finally normative is ultimate reality itself: "I am equal to all beings, there is none hateful nor dear to Me. But those who worship Me with devotion, they are in Me and I am in them" (ix.29). Divine imitation rings with the sounds of virtues which have an almost Buddhistic tone of the essentially mental or "televolitional" blessed dispositions (*brahmavihāras*) : "He who has no ill-feeling to any being who is friendly and compassionate, without selfishness and egoism, who is the same in pain and pleasure and is patient...is dear to Me" (xii.13-14). A similarly subjective, passive, and negative quality is present, if less patently discernible, in the *Gītā*'s general category of virtues (as in xvi.1-4). If apparent approval of immoral conduct is defused by exegeses previously mentioned, the *Gītā* still insists that authentic disinterest renounces "good and evil" (xii.17).

Apologetes for the *Gītā*'s position on detachment have contrasted it with religious teaching which would enjoin humans to love one another simply for the sake of God, who alone is the true "formal object" of charity.[38] In the latter sort of love, one has been accused of using others as mere means for one's own self-perfection. The *Gītā*'s compassion, contrarily, entails the only genuine love, because it begins not with manipulation but identification. The undeluded "see all creatures including the self without exception in the Self and in Me" (iv.35 and see xii.28). The *Gītā*'s solution to the classic problems of justifying other-interest, love or morality itself lies in the metaphysical postulate of identity.[39] Without it there would seem to be "no exit" from the hopelessly objectifying and exploitative (*pour soi*) relationships described by Sartre.[40]

Although the principle of identity also functions in dualistic religions,[41] it has attained such visibility in the *Gītā* that it has been assailed as offensive to divine sovereignty and transcendence. The *Gītā*'s type of pantheism (coexisting with monistic and theistic strands) has also been labeled a weak, "identification of lovers" (Tillichian) alternative to more satisfactory intersubjective, polar, and interactive models of reality and as redolent of the most patently idolatrous paranoia.[42] In those passages in which devotion and action may reign supreme over knowledge,[43] the divinity clearly describes itself as the center of all life. Some of those who cannot accept the *Gītā*'s divine authority may compare it with other pious literature like Thomas á Kempis' *Imitation of Christ* and point out that human fantasizing in the first person about a divinity who is the center of the cosmos is the acme of imaginable ego trips.

A more constructive humanistic critique on their part might theorize that the aspirations of those who have spoken in the name of divinity through the ages have voiced lasting needs of the human heart, for example, the desires for love and recognition (*bhakti*), for realization of the alienated individual's systematic oneness with other humans and with nature (as in *Ātman*) for more intense levels of consciousness and happiness, or even for the freedom and joy of play (*līlā*), or living as an end in itself.[44] At any rate, however ethereal, heretical, or ego-maniacal as the *Gītā*'s brand of "other"-interest may seem to its critics, its form of disinterested love has been defended by its advocates as the only kind of love which is real.

To Upadhyaya, however, love and action in the *Gītā* are far from ethereal. Their presence is real in what he, at least previously, felt was an activistically unfortunate one. As Krishna proclaims : "I am the desire in all beings which is not incompatible with *dharma*..." (vii.11). Not "by mere renunciation does he [a man] attain perfection" (iii.4). "Perform thy alloted work, for action is superior to inaction;..." (iii.8). "Thou shouldst perform action also with regard for the maintenance of the world [social order]" (iii.20).[45] Contrasting the *Gītā*'s "activism" (*pravṛtti*) unfavorably with the more detached renunciation (*nivṛtti*) of Buddhism, Upadhyaya once held that in the *Gītā*'s so-called reconciliatory synthesis of action and contemplation, the ultimate preference went to duty and action.[46] Salvation becomes egalitarian for laity and recluses alike, attainable with equal or even greater ease by mere householders.[47] Thus the *Gītā*, "notwithstanding its compromising attitude, enthusiastically supports worldly life."[48] This endorsement is fortified, Upadhyaya concluded, by the *Gītā*'s unbuddhistic bolstering of caste and of Arjuna's engagement in war.[49]

Conjoined with its "activistic" capitulation to less pure and perfect ideals,[50] and its flaccid relaxation of moral discipline,[51] the *Gītā*, added Upadhyaya, "is not completely free from the conceit of the 'I,' though, paradoxically enough, it over and over again professes the same."[52] The comparison of action to ritual sacrifice does not yet prove its lack of selfishness.[53] As opposed to Buddhism's pure doctrine of the non-self (*anatta*), which is said to be empirically known, behind the *Gītā*'s merely metaphysical or postulated (sic) identification of every individual with the one true Brahman-*Ātman*[54] lurked the conceited ego.[55] In the *Gītā*'s description of final reality, the self fully and with eudaemonistic happiness realizes its oneness with the one Self of Brahman.[56] In Buddhism, on the other hand, one can say nothing about the self now or in *nirvāṇa* (one's final state). Although Buddhist *nirvāṇa* is said to be not entirely negative,[57] the Buddhist attitude toward it heralded the adage encapsulated by Wittgenstein : "Whereof one cannot speak, thereof one must be silent."[58]

In the above view, therefore, the *Gītā* was an egalitarian, activistic, and even egotistical attempt to outflank the immensely popular and selfless charismas of Buddhists. The *Gītā*'s *dharma* offered successfully popular competition, or else Brahmanic power made it so, for it influenced Buddhism,[59] prevailed over its demise in India, and withstood the onslaught of eleventh century (C.E.) Islam.[60] The *Gītā*'s alleged doctrine of selfless detachment and discipline are only superficially Buddhist. At root it allegedly germinates a self-concerned action to which Buddhism is utterly opposed. To borrow the metaphors of wedges and cracked dikes, the *Gītā*'s principles would remain forever open to increasing compromises with the ego.

Exactly opposite to the Buddhistic critique of Upadhyaya is that of Albert Schweitzer, whose metaethics of life-affirmation leads to the judgment that the *Gītā* is gravely deficient in social ethics. In Schweitzer's simplified, if not simplistic, system, a world of life-negation continues to exist whenever it refuses to become ethically and socially active.[61] Therefore, since the *Gītā*'s negative domain continued to exist, ethical stagnation must have been inevitable. Tokenistic references to the sharing of food (iii.13) or concern for the maintenance of the world's social order (iii.20) founder in the face of contrary data.

The backward logical form of Schweitzer's own syllogism betrays that an exclusive relationship was undemonstrated by him. Theoretical negativism is not yet proof of factual amorality. Moreover, inquiry into his primary charge of basic unconcern or negativism awaits more complete developments in the study of the *Gītā*'s forms and origins.[62] As for the *Gītā*'s sources, tentative judgments, like Sarvepalli Radhakrishnan's, move in Schweitzer's direction by stating that it formulated a living and ongoing synthesis of positive Bhāgavata theism and Vedic sacrifice with the negative aspects of the Sāṅkhya philosophical dualism, Upanishadic mysticism, and Yogic meditation.[63] In addition, the *Gītā* can be read to represent a negative spiritual reaction to the limitedly material orientation of Cārvāka philosophy (xvi.6-8).

Therefore, the *Gītā* can be envisioned as imitative of life-denying aspects of Buddhism.[64] While Upadhyaya's lengthy research into the *Gītā*'s sources[65] has pronounced its liaison with Buddhistic negativism more reactive than assimilative, one can instead experiment with the fruits of his inquiry as corroborative of Schweitzer's counterthesis (the *Gītā*'s negativism), once it is viewed in the light of a Schweitzerian rather than a Buddhistic *weltanschauung*. But even if one sways back from Schweitzer's counterposition to the thesis of Upadhyaya, one certainly hears no ringing affirmation of *kāma*, *artha*, or *dharma* in the manner of the *Ry*. When all present tentative analyses are said and done, the *Gītā* may be taken at its literal word. Its ethos is not sheer Upanishadic mysticism, śāstric power, or Rāmāyaṇic emphasis on wealth, love and morality. With the *Gītā*, the pluralistic ethics of Hinduism increases and multiplies by one more option, a moral ethos and humanistic project of non-attached action. If it is not appropriated fully as a relentless Kierkegaardian "suspension of moral goals" in favor of mystical religion, it offers a minimal non-dualistic challenge to every ethical project, especially pragmatism : morality may make no sense without some form of ontological or at least psychological interhuman and ecological identification.[66]

War. Upadhyaya constructs his case that the *Gītā* upholds both war and the caste system to further his charges of activism and egotism. However, his contention that these institutions are unbuddhistic persuades more cogently than his parallel thesis against the *Gītā*'s activism. Its pro-war and pro-caste positions do not of themselves demonstrate a worldly and an activist spirit. As seen above, the *Gītā*'s main pro-war arguments (ii.11-59) relate to the warrior's caste duty and to the belief that in battle human beings are neither really slain nor slayers, both death and life being finally unreal, or at least inevitable. (In the earliest *Mbh* versions the war ends happily if not justly in that all the leading warriors on both sides were killed but joined one another in heaven because of their great valor.) Subsidiary to the *Gītā*'s mystical justifications are its recrimination of Arjuna's "defective pity" (ii.7) and Krishna's appeal to Arjuna's honor and fame as a warrior (ii.35). But the leading thrust of this whole dialogue is neither war (action) nor detachment taken singly, but both together (ii.38). True, in spite of affirmative, though unemphatic, references to *ahimsā*,[67] the *Gītā*'s non-Jaina and unbuddhistic assent to violence, as an institution in tension with individual rights, cannot be eschewed. But violence is not Krishna's primary teaching. What is directly propounded is neither war not action as such, but a manner of war and action, a paradoxical style of non-attached action, a soldierly quality hardly attractive to generals or other kinds of leaders who are activistically intent on this-worldly victories and successes.

Caste. The *Gītā*'s backing of the caste system, on the other hand, reveals assent to a worldly institution, yet not in any sense of defending this-worldly moral rights of individuals or of socially protecting them from relationships which corrupt both victims and perpetrators. Caste is socially desirable (i.41-43) and divinely approved. "The four caste system was created by Me [the divinity]" (iv.13). Whereas lofty qualities like wisdom, generosity, and courage are specified for the Brahmins and Kshatriyas, no lower caste virtues are listed or idealized except work for the Vaishyas and service for the *śūdras* (xviii.41-44). Like women (*sic*), lower castes can reach the highest goal through devotion to the divinity (ix.32), but for them the *dharmas* of the upper castes are dangerous or even sinful (iii.35 and xvii.47).

The *Gītā*'s endorsement of caste accordingly militates against contemporary ideas of social equality on two scores. First, it enjoins work and service with potentially inequitable consequences for certain groups. Secondly, by omission, it neglects *sādhāraṇa* or general *dharma*, by encasing some virtues within the duties of specific castes.[68] To the extent that an active social ethic must be based on a universal morality rather than caste or in-group mores, the *Gītā*'s stand on caste, therefore, deprives it of a sound foundation.

Future studies of other factors affecting the *Gītā*'s status as morals rather than mores would take into account the dialectic between cognitive *jñāna* and a possibly more volitional *bhakti* and *karma*. They would also measure the *Gītā*'s approval of Sāṅkhya thought on freedom and deterministic elements and its stance on the origin of sin. In different ways Deutsch, Upadhyaya, and de Smet finally opt for a kind of freedom of will in the face of karmic (ix.28 and xviii.60) and other determinations in the *Gītā* like desire, wrath, and greed or passion (iii.36).[69] Beyond these and further indications in particular passages (e.g., "do as thou choosest" [xviii.63]), one must decide whether or not the *Gītā* as a whole is written in authoritative or hortative genres which presuppose some kind of personal choice (volitionally).

C. *Ethical Validation.* While reflective reference to ethical validation by reason is scant (*apohana*, xv.15), the *Gītā*'s chapter on war (chap. ii) provides a concrete illustration of its reliance on rational argumentations, numerously evident as seen above in section A. In that rational process, however, inductive appeal to empirical effects like reputation subsides in the wake of deductive inference from metaphysical postulates. The latter, in turn, are rooted in appeals to authority, the experience of intuition, or epistemic combinations thereof.

Vedic authority in the *Gītā* is occasionally subordinated to devotion (xi.53-55) or to mystical knowledge (xi.42-43 and 53), which effects a bliss exceeding the transitory happiness of Vedic heavens (ix. 20-21). In tension with those devotional and also Brahminic provisos are declarations in which the divinity both sanctions the commands of the *śāstra* and identifies itself with the *Vedas*. "Therefore let the scripture [*śāstra*] be thy authority in determining what should and should not be done. Knowing what is declared by the ruler of the scriptures [law ?], thou shouldst do action in this world" (xvi.24). Brahman's oneness with the *Vedas* is a source of knowledge which is interior to the human heart. "I am seated in the hearts of all : from Me (come) memory, wisdom, and argument. I am that which is to be known by the *Vedas* : I am the author of the Vedānta [*Ups*], and I am also the knower of the *Vedas*" (xv.15). The *Gītā*'s esoteric wisdom is both divinely proclaimed (xviii.63) and rationally examined (*ibid.*), yet it is inseparable from devotional faith (iv.39 and xii.2) and a "seeing of all beings in Brahman (vi.20, 29),[70] which is really the "eye of knowledge" (xiii.34), intuition,[71] an inside-out experience of the supreme Self, seeing itself equally in all beings (xiii.27 and 30). "The highest Spirit in this body is said to be the witness [*upadraṣṭṛ*], the consenter [*anumantṛ*], the supporter [*bhartṛ*], the experiencer [*bhoktṛ*], the great Lord, the supreme Self" (xiii.22).

In sum, obedience to divine authority (xviii.73), the *Vedas*, and the example of the ancients (iii.20; iv.15) merge into internal imitation (xii.29) and intuitive self-realization as the ultimate, stained-glass/mosaic-like authentication and guide for action of any kind. This insight, however, is not yet the equivalent of *multiple* intuitions into moral principles, that much larger claim which alienates so many against any form of intuitive recognition or feeling. Also, conspicuously absent is any appeal to *dharma* as an innate or natural order (Vedic *rita*) which is morally normative.[72]

D. *Conclusion.* If, apart from its brief and vague catalogue of virtues, the *Gītā* waives specific moral guidance not already offered in the *śāstra, Vedas*, and *Ups*, one need not conclude that, besides being morally asocial, the *Gītā* is radically amoral. Alternatively, and not entirely tautologically, one can posit that, except for incidental treatment, the *Gītā* does not talk morality, because it is not about morality. Instead, it is chiefly about *bhakti* and the incorporation of Bhāgavata theism into the Brahminic synthesis. Parenthetically, nevertheless, it prescribes a fundamental moral tone or ethos of *non-attached* action (*niṣkāma karma*), an attitude made possible by the subjection of what Swami Nikhilananda called objective ethics to the realization of the Self.[73] Duty stems from one's *karma, guṇas* (qualities), and caste. Further, by justifying conduct on the authority of mystical experience, the *Gītā* delegates the final interpretation of scriptural injunctions to those who claim that experience, an event of the most critical significance. Remaining Hindus would thereby be cornered into that classic, typological, religious "either-or," the choice between the voice of their own heart and the wisdom of other human beings humbly considered superior to their own. Inexorably and with infinite regress, the open question would linger for the adult conscience: according to what criteria or on whose authority may another's knowledge be considered more authoritative than one's own personal and unmatched experience of one's own life's situations ? The question seems to fade away only if one's delegation of one's conscience to another human being is based on one's claim to inward or revelatory experience of the divine.

In view of these and other factors, there are those who cannot subscribe to the *Gītā*'s worldview or other positions. However, even for them it stands ethically didactic in the way it sharpens two basic questions to a razor's edge. One is epistemic; the other substantive. The epistemological issue reads : unless one rejects *a priori* the moral wisdom of other human beings, how can such knowledge be contextually appropriated with due autonomy and dignity ? The substantive question remains : can morality as at least partly other-centered[74] make sense without some form of intercosmic or intersubjective identification or real relationship? If not, under what conditions can this necessary realization of unity avoid the indolent moral ennui often associated with it or attributed to it?

Putting aside any *ontological* speculation about unity, an outsider to Hindu belief may choose to internalize functionally the *Gītā*'s ethos of moral composure or non-attached action merely as the most fitting *operational* (pragmatic?) response to life, one not dominantly oriented to ends or steered by laws,[75] but inwardly propelled from a natural energy (*bhakti-jñāna* in Hindu religious language) which in English could be called the spirit of humanistic love. In other words, the *Gītā*'s *niṣkāma karma* is not plausibly reducible to a morality of style without substance or form without content. Like *ahimsā* or other forms of moral ethos, non-attached action, with the emphasis coequal on the non-attachment and the action, might never happen without some force from within a person, be it Brahman-*Ātman* or even a Promethean *Geist* or driving human spirit less than divine.

By way of interpretative postscript I shall add two personal comments and express them in more appropriate use of the first person. First, Austin Creel has informed me that his extensive research shows, contra Schweitzer, that the *Gītā* is so self-evidently supportive of dharmic action that the whole question of moral quietism faced earlier in this chapter is, in my own words, "a straw man." Our disagreement may stem largely from Derrett's practical distinction: intense kerygma favoring non-attached *active* response to caste duty and custom (*sadācāra*) is so strongly emphasized in the *Gītā*, as it is in *dharmaśāstra* in general, that it occasioned a reaction precisely opposite to that intended: historical inertia or, in my language, *non-attached* action instead of non-attached *action*. Although this question of historical fact cannot be settled at a textual level, it seems impossible to waive the *Gītā*'s Upanishadic, Brahminic, negative, and quietistic passages, Creel's otherwise crucial insights and eminent scholarship notwithstanding. Supporting and even overstating my own position is D. C. Mathur's developed thesis that historically Indians have interpreted the *Gītā*'s detached action passively and fatalistically (p. 44) and that social reformers still need to revise or reinterpret its concept of *karma* or action radically.[76] As I have pointed out and shall repeat again, to ground a social ethic the mysticism of the *Ups* and the *Gītā* will have to take on new historical forms. Yet these could be logically "orthodox" alternatives faithful to the tradition of Hindu mystical morality.

Second, Schweitzer's position which is so diametrical to Creel's needs to be cross-examined with the following question: in the context of the *Gītā*'s primarily mystical *Geist* or ethos, it seems quite logical to ask what greater meaning to human life than to lighten the appalling sum of its suffering in any way, spiritually, but also materially (an inversion of the British utilitarian principle)? True, the final karmic pain (*duḥkha*) of every human or sentient being is the unending wheel of reincarnated lives (*saṁsāra*). It follows that the apex of the *Gītā*'s mystically altruistic morality—to speak in "dualistic" ethical language—concerns the extinction of craving attachment to egoity. Increasingly, as one nears liberation (*moksha*), the primary gift (*dāna*) flowing from the compassionate individual is loving concern for the other's relief from life as it is individualistically experienced.

But plans for social welfare and morality, are not thereby omitted. In fact, they may require amplification in bewildering times when the mystical life appears increasingly out of reach, as does the lessening of that most radical of all suffering, attached egoism. All the stronger, then, is the drive for plans involving socio-economic equity and development, similar to those initiated and carried out by great Hindu reformers. Even if such programs remain also instrumental toward the final esthetical/mystical realization of life, beauty, or liberation (*moksha* transcending mere vision), their impetus has been provided.

In sum, I have tried to lay out the interpretative stances of the *Gītā*'s critics in objective detail. But as an empathetic outsider to Hindu experience, I conclude that these critics have not disproved the possibility of a social ethic flowing from the *Gītā*'s mystical and religious approach. This more activistic interpretation is not, I think, a logical revision of Hinduism, especially that Hinduism which includes both populist and elitist dimensions. Rather it lies within the traditional bounds of Hindu and other potentially humanistic mysticisms. Further the case for *Gītā*-inspired social cooperation has been partly strengthened by positive realizations which spontaneously spring into socially moral cooperation and reform, intra- and inter-culturally. This type of morality is also evinced in the cross-cultural search for meditative response and in the age-old collective experience of hunger for "transcendental" wisdom. Lastly, the argument has been supported by the belief of some, like Sri Aurobindo Ghose or Teilhard de Chardin that mysticism will culminate the final stage of human evolution.

Like other mystics, Hindus have frequently created practical accommodations for others. Given the human condition, a mystically based social morality should admit its need not only for authoritative religious and legal sanctions, but also for popular, charismatic and esthetical appeal, like that in Hindu poetry and drama. Above all, however, a vision seen through the window of the *Gītā* beckons everyone to an inner mystical realization of oneness, an either humanistic or religious awareness whose dynamics inspire and resurrect moral cooperation from the tomb of dead aspirations into living practice.

NOTES

1. See Thomas Berry, "A Multi-Cultural World," in Wm. T. de Bary, ed., *Approaches to the Oriental Classics* (New York : Columbia University Press, 1959), pp. 11-23; and Raimundo Panikkar, "Christians and So-Called Non-Christians," *Cross Currents* 22, 3 (Summer-Fall, 1972), 281-308.

2. Franklin Edgerton, trans., *The Bhagavad Gita* (2nd printing, 1 vol.; Cambridge, Massachusetts; Harvard University Press, 1974), p. 105. The *Bhagavad Gītā*'s full and exact title is "the mystic doctrines (*upaniṣads*) sung (or proclaimed) by the Blessed One Krishna" (*ibid.*, p. 106). Henceforth, for brevity, this classic will be called the Gītā, although there are many *gītās* or songs. In an unpublished version of his 1974 AAR paper, "A Socio-Analytic Critique of the *Bhagavad Gītā*," Gerald J. Larson related the modern upsurge of the *Gītā*'s Indian popularity due to Western influences and its use as a symbol by Indian nationalists. This paper is now available as "The *Bhagavad Gītā* as Cross-Cultural Process," *Journal of the American Academy of Religion* 43, 4 (December 1975), 651-70.

3. As for the relative dates of the *Ṛg* and the *Gītā* Moriz Winternitz placed the *Vālmīki-Rāmāyaṇa* in the third century B.C.E. See his *A History of Indian Literature*, trans. S. Ketkar (Calcutta : The University of Calcutta, 1959), I, 516-17. On the *Gītā*'s dates see Kashi Nath Upadhyaya, *Early Buddhism and the Bhagavad Gītā* (Delhi : Motilal Banarsidass, 1971), p. 28 and Eliot Deutsch (translation and essays), *The Bhagavad Gītā* (New York : Holt, Rinehart, and Winston), p. 6. Although Edgerton's definitive translation has been consulted constantly, Deutsch's version is the source of all quotations in this chapter for its clarity as well as its combined use of Sanskrit and English terms in its notes.

4. See Raghavan N. Iyer, *The Moral and Political Thought of Mahatma Gandhi* (New York : Oxford University Press, 1973), p. 74.

5. Benoy Gopal Ray, *Gandhian Ethics* (Ahmedabad : Navajivan Publishing House, 1950), p. 15.

6. Inquiry into this possible synthesis should examine Gandhi's subordination of contemplation to action and of *moksha* (spiritual liberation) to *dharma* (as social morality). See Iyer, *Moral Thought of Gandhi*, pp. 67, 76, and 158.

7. Vinoba Bhāve, *Talks on the Gītā* (New York : The Macmillan Company, 1960), p. 16.

8. Raghavan refers to the coexistence of the three paths to perfection : *bhakti* (devotion), *jñāna* (knowledge), and *karma*. See his article "Hinduism," in *Historical Atlas*, ed. Isma'il Rāgi al Fārūqi, p. 84.

9. See Larson's "The *Bhagavad Gītā*" and Edgerton, *The Bhagavad Gītā*, pp. 106-07. The latter (p. xiv) defends the unity of the *Gītā* (and single authorship ?) against views of Winternitz and Rudolf Otto.

10. Albert Schweitzer, *Indian Thought*, p. 195.

11. See William F. Goodwin, "Mysticism and Ethics," 25-41. Goodwin nominates Schweitzer for Hinduism's most thorough and penetrating critic and feels that Radhakrishnan failed to prove the continuity between this-worldly *dharma* and world-negating *moksha*. Edgerton agrees that the *Gītā* is negative, insofar as it is pessimistic about the present life. But he denies that it is pro-ascetical. See his *The Bhagavad Gītā*, pp. 131 and 159.

12. Upadhyaya, *Buddhism*, p. 197.

13. Deutsch, *The Bhagavad Gītā*, p. 160 and Edgerton, *The Bhagavad Gītā*, pp. 108-90.

14. See Schweitzer, *Indian Thought*, pp. 191, 195, and 251.

15. See *ibid.*, 195; Upadhyaya, *Buddhism*, pp. 422, 463-64; and Max Weber, *The Religion of India*, pp. 189-90; and a quite curious illustration of Schweitzer's fears by Sally Wang, "Can Man Go Beyond Ethics ? The System of Padmasambhava," *Journal of Religious Ethics*, 3, 1 (Spring 1975), 141-55.

16. Characters are described morally by C. V. Narasimhan, *The Mahābhārata* (New York : Columbia University Press, 1965), pp. xxi-xxiv.

17. Ethical work has been pioneered in S. Jayal's *The Status of Women*; D. P. Vora's *Evolution of Morals*; ethical selections in S. Radhakrishnan and Charles A. Moore, eds., *A Source Book in Indian Philosophy*, pp. 164-71; and in Appendix I below.

18. A helpful summation and genealogical diagrams may be consulted in J. A. B. van Buitenen, trans. and ed., *The Mahābhārata*, Vol. I (Chicago : The University of Chicago Press, 1973) xiii-xxii, and 1-16.

19. See Schweitzer, *Indian Thought*, p. 188; Upadhyaya, *Buddhism*, p. 149; and Edgerton, *The Bhagavad Gītā*, p. 162.

20. Compare with iii. 8, 19 and iv. 36.

21. Compare with Katha Upanishad I.2.10. Verbatim and other quotations from the *Ups* are collated in Edgerton, *The Bhagavad Gītā*, p. 199 and in Upadhyaya, *Buddhism*, pp. 110-14.

22. According to Deutsch (*The Bhagavad Gītā*, p. 147, n. 7), *kilbiṣa* (sin or guilt) like *pāpa* refers to a violation of social norms.

23. Upadhyaya, *Buddhism*, p. 197. See also Edgerton, *The Bhagavad Gītā*, pp. 106, 182; and on the rhetorical paradox of mystics, W. T. Stace,

Mysticism and Philosophy (London: Macmillan & Co. Ltd., 1961), pp. 253-57. Stace also details other theories about mystical paradoxes or logical contradictions, e.g., double location, ambiguity, and misdescription (incorrect interpretation of experience).

24. See Deutsch, *The Bhagavad Gītā*, pp. 20-22.

25. As quoted in Huston Smith's *The Religions of Man* (New York : Harper and Row, 1958), p. 77.

26. See Deutsch, *The Bhagavad Gītā*, pp. 170-72 and contrast with the more exclusively theistic interpretation of Edgerton's *The Bhagavad Gītā*, pp. 154, 173.

27. Edgerton, *ibid.*, p. 174. On the ultimate merging of yogas, compare Upadhyaya, *Buddhism*, p. 471 and Edgerton, *The Bhagavad Gītā*, p. 174, whose practical stress is on *bhakti*, with G. W. Kaveeshwar, *The Ethics of the Gītā* (Delhi: Motilal Banarsidass, 1971), pp. 270, 274, 277, 289, 294, and 296. Part of the last volume's complexity may stem from the fact that it was "laboriously prepared" (p. iv) from an original edition in Marathi. Disregarding *bhakti* and *karma* in the *Gīta*'s alleged synthesis without explanation, Kaveeshwar's prevailing practical emphasis on contemplation (e.g., pp. 17 and 43), especially at life's close (p. 288), relegates action, even as non-attached, to a subordinate role. Kaveeshwar's opposition to B. Tilak's pro-action reading relies heavily on the assumption that the *Gītā*'s unity of composition and theme precludes the existence of more than one practical motif. Also at play in his hermeneutical method is the prominence of the *Gītā* as a literal part of the *Mbh*'s central story. Taken in no aspect as a literary device used to launch the teachings of the *Gītā*, the dialogue between Krishna and Arjuna and historical conjectures about Arjuna's psychological state of mind in terms of the epic as a whole are used to predetermine the *Gītā*'s main theme. What results is the conclusion that *jñāna*, as opposed to confusion (*moha*), predominates over *bhakti* or *niṣkāma karma* (pp. 45 and 47). The same hermeneutical premises function in Kaveeshwar's comments on *varṇas* (pp. 223-31) and moral validation (see note 71 below).

28. Ludwig Wittgenstein, "A Lecture on Ethics," in *Ethics : Selections from Classical and Contemporary Writers* (New York : Holt , Rinehart and Winston, Inc., 3d ed., 1974), pp. 414-15.

29. Stace, *Mysticism*, p. 215. Lévi-Strauss reputedly included in the very essence of myth the functional, meaning-giving reconciliation of factual opposites. But he did not claim that the tension of these opposites was also logically resolved.

30. Deutsch, *The Bhagavad Gītā*, p. 174.

31. Contrast Śaṅkara's views on illusoriness in George Thibaut, trans., *The Vedānta Sūtras of Bādarāyaṇa with the Commentary by Śaṅkara* (2 Vols., New York : Dover Publications, Inc., 1962), (abbreviated here as *VS*), I, 243 and II, 401 ff.

32. The Blessed One said :

1. Fearlessness, purification of essence,
   Steadfastness in the discipline of knowledge,
   Generosity, control, and religious worship,
   Study of the Holy Word, austerities, uprightness.

2. Harmlessness, truth, no anger,
Abandonment, serenity, no backbiting,
Compassion towards creatures, no greedy desire,
Gentleness, modesty, no fickleness,
3. Majesty, patience, fortitude, purity,
No injuriousness, no excessive pride,
Are (the qualities) of him that to the divine lot
Is born, son of Bharata.
18. Egotism, force, pride,
Desire, and wrath they have taken to,
Me in their own and others' bodies
Hating, these envious men.

Referring to his translation above, Edgerton's last analysis of this catalogue is that beyond two other primary vices, wrath and greed, desire [not ignorance] is the root of all evil" (*Bhagavad Gītā*, p. 184).

33. See Upadhyaya, *Buddhism*, p. 146 and Deutsch, *The Bhagavad Gītā*, pp. 168-69.

34. In *Agape and Eros*.

35. Also in *Yoga-Sūtra* I, 33. See Surama Dasgupta's *Development of Moral Philosophy*, p. 131.

36. Huxley's introduction to *The Song of God : Bhagavad-Gītā*, trans. by Swami Prabhavananda and Christopher Isherwood (New York : The New American Library, Inc., 1951), p. 20.

37. See Joachim Wach, *Types of Religious Experience, Christian and Non-Christian* (Chicago : University of Chicago Press, 1957).

38. "What we love in our neighbor is God alone." "Non enim diligimus per caritatem in proximo nisi Deum : ...." See Thomas Aquinas, *Summa Theologica*, II-II, q. 103, a. 3 ad 2. See *ibid.*, q. 27, a. 3.

39. See Edgerton, *The Bhagavad Gītā*, p. 185.

40. Admitting the tentativeness of his views on egoism and disinterestedness, Sartre found it necessary to promise a future ethical study of the issue in his conclusion to *Being and Nothingness*, trans., H. E. Barnes (New York : Washington Square Press, 1966), pp. 796-98. This study is said to exist vicariously in Sartre's life companion, Simone de Beauvoir's *The Ethics of Ambiguity*, trans., by B. Frechtman (Secaucus, New Jersey : The Citadel Press, 1948).

41. As in V. de Montcheuil, "*Le ressentiment d'apres Max Scheler*. 147-48.

42. On the Tillichian "identification of lovers" weakness see Paul Ramsey, "Jean-Paul Sartre : Sex in Being," in *Nine Modern Moralists* (Englewood Cliffs, New Jersey : Prentice-Hall, Inc., 1962), pp. 71-109.

43. X.8-11, xi. 44, 54-55, and xviii. 65.

44. See William A. Sadler, *Existence and Love* (New York : Charles Scribner's Sons, 1969), pp. 212-21.

45. See also iv. 15-20.

46. Upadhyaya, *Buddhism*, p. 478. Edgerton (*The Bhagavad Gītā*, p. 160) agrees to the extent that the *Gītā* is definitely opposed to the quietistic life. N. V. Banerjee calls the *Gītā* predominantly activistic" in his *The Spirit of Indian Philosophy*, p. 43.

47. Upadhyaya, *ibid.*, pp. 363, 478, 486, 497, and 539.
48. *Ibid.*, p. 498.
49. *Ibid.*, pp. 498 ff.
50. *Ibid.*, pp. 482 and 539.
51. *Ibid.*, p. 461.
52. *Ibid.*, p. 331.
53. See Richard de Smet, "Towards an Indian View of the Person," in *Contemporary Indian Philosophy*, Series II, ed. Margaret Chatterjee (London: George Allen and Unwin, 1974), p. 67.
54. If the unity is traced to experience, it is a case of misinterpretation. Upadhyaya, *ibid.*, p. 354.
55. *Ibid.*, p. 331.
56. *Ibid.*, p. 349.
57. Upadhyaya, *ibid.*, p. 342.
58. *Tractatus Logico-Philosophicus* (London: Kegan, Paul, Trench Trubner & Co., 1923), p. 189.
59. While de Smet ("Indian View of the Person" pp. 68-69) measures the *Gītā*'s impact on Mahāyāna Buddhism's Bodhisattva, Surama Dasgupta (*Development of Moral Philosophy*, p. 103) agrees with her historian husband, Surendra Nath Dasgupta, that the *Gītā* preceded any form of Buddhism.
60. Schweitzer, *Indian Thought*, pp. 191 and 196.
61. *Ibid.*, p. 251.
62. That is, studies of the caliber of Sternbach's and Derrett's. See Jan Gonda, ed., *A History of Indian Literature*, Vol. IV : *Dharmaśāstra and Juridical Literature* and Vol. IV : *Subhāṣita, Gnomic and Didactic Literature*, by Ludwik Sternbach (Wiesbaden : Otto Harrassowitz, 1973 and 1974).
63. See Radhakrishnan and Moore, *A Source Book*, p. 101. Edgerton (*The Bhagavad Gītā*, p. 171) thinks that the *Gītā* also opposed Sāṅkhya followers in the action it attributes to them. The *Gītā*'s ethics can be compared with Sāṅkhya ethics through I. C. Sharma's *Ethical Philosophies*, pp. 190-99.
64. Samples of ideas reminiscent of Buddhism and/or its Sāṅkhya progenitor can be found in references to desire and hatred (vii.27), the welfare of all (xii.4 and v.25), a world of unhappiness or suffering (ix.33) and the cessation thereof (vi.23), a "moderate path of ascetical rigor (vi.16-17), *nirvāṇa* (see Edgerton, *The Bhagavad Gītā*, p. 125, etc.) On *nirvāṇa* in the *Gītā* ii.72, xiv.20 and Crawford, *Hindu Ethical Ideals*, pp. 114-15; it may be compared with *moksha* in T. M. P. Mahadevan's "Social, Ethical, and Spiritual Values in Indian Philosophy," in *The Indian Mind*, pp. 158-60.
65. Upadhyaya, *Buddhism*, pp. 60-150.
66. De Smet's attempts to show that identification in the *Gītā* is really personalistic may resonate with the reader's experience more than mine. See de Smet's "Indian View of the Person," especially his conclusion on p. 73. References to my alternate approach which may assimilate the principle of identity are in note 72 below as well as in previous references.
67. X.5, xii.7, xvi.2, and xvii.14.
68. On *sādhāraṇa dharma* or general *dharma* in the *Ṛy*, confer P. V. Kane, *Dharmaśāstra* and chapter five above. On the *Gītā*'s apparent approval of caste, see Crawford, *The Evolution of Hindu Ethical Ideals*, p. 121.

69. See Deutsch, *The Bhagavad Gita*, pp. 181-88; Upadhyaya, *Buddhism*, p. 586; de Smet, "An Indian View of the Person," p. 68; and Edgerton, *The Bhagavad Gītā*, p. 184.

70. Upadhyaya, *ibid.*, p. 164.

71. Edgerton, *The Bhagavad Gītā*, p. 193. In *The Ethics of Gītā*, G. W. Kaveeshwar minimizes the role of insight and instead conjectures a greater relative stress on inferential logic (as in iii.24 and xviii.25) than this chapter's focus on validation by authority would allow. Kaveeshwar does recognize scriptural authority, however, as the "normal rule of conduct" (p. 236). His use of hermeneutical presuppositions not accepted here is referred to above in note 27. N. K. Devaraja also accepts ethical reasoning from consequences without connecting its multiple conclusions to the grounds of the fundamental mystical insights. See his *The Mind and Spirit of India* (Delhi : Motilal Banarsidass, 1967) and *Hinduism and Christianity* (New York : Asia Publishing House, 1969).

72. See Austin B. Creel, "The Reexamination of Dharma in Hindu Ethics, *Philosophy East and West*, 25,2 (April 1975), 170. For a survey of *dharma* and *li*, a whole issue of this journal may be consulted 22,2 (April 1972). Humanistic and reconstructively "neo-pragmatic" attempts to synthesize these origins of moral knowledge can be consulted in articles of mine previously mentioned or in my "Muslim and Christian Ethics," *Cross Currents*, 22,4 (Winter 1973), esp. 392-94.

73. Swami Nikhilananda, "Hindu Ethics", in Ruth Nanda Anshen, ed., *Moral Principles of Action* (New York: Harper and Brothers, 1952), p. 616. From another perspective M. Rangacharya states that the *Gītā*'s main interest is ethical. See his *The Hindu Philosophy of Conduct* (*Lectures on the Bhagavadgītā*), 2 vols., (Madras : The Educational Publishing Co., 1st ed., 1914; 4th ed. 1957).

74. In addition to issues of the *Journal of Religious Ethics* recently focused on this question, see David Little and Sumner B. Twiss, "Basic Terms in the Study of Religious Ethics," in Gene Outka and John P. Reeder, ed., *Religion and Morality* (Garden City, New York : Anchor Press/Doubleday, 1973), pp. 57-58.

75. These exclusions received their most lucid clarification in H. Richard Neibuhr's noted *The Responsible Self* (New York : Harper and Row, 1963).

76. D. C. Mathur, "The Concept of Action in the *Bhagavad Gītā*," *Philosophy and Phenomenological Research*, 35,1 (September 1974), 34-43.

CHAPTER VII

ETHICS IN OTHER POPULAR CLASSICS, POETRY, AND DRAMA

Abstract. A popular, Vedic, social, and life-affirmative ethics parallel to Brahminism was focused on the *tri-varga* or three goals of wealth, pleasure/love, and moral *dharma*. This morality did not oppose but coalesced with mystical traditions, even if the latter did not reciprocate. Aside from the epics, which have required special attention in chapter five and Appendix I, ten popular figures or works are singled out here for future ethical studies. Due to this project's necessarily programmatic introduction to such a wide body of literature, the usual descriptive inquiries are left implicit. Instead, the ten literary samples are surveyed in a provisional chronological order. In regard to ethical grounds and validation, popular literature reflected a basically harmonious ocean of earthly and heavenly life which could be navigated less with authoritative guidance or karmic threats than with commonsensical analyses of the consequences of conduct. The aspiring life-affirmative ethos of populist tradition was not avaricious, though it enjoined prudential cleverness in respect to wealth and fortune in general. This spirit was neither hedonistic nor narcissistic in its passionate assent to romantic, familial, and more universally compassionate loves. The familiar Indian motifs of non-violence, non-attached sharing, and truthfulness indicate that popular Hinduism and Brahminic mysticism shared themes which might co-inspire a mystical, humanistic ethics for the future. Other phenomena like caste and sexual discriminations gave way to the prevailing, unauthoritarian mood of an earthy, unsentimental ability to learn from collective and repeated moral experience. NOTES.

Introduction. A tendency to reduce religions and cultures to both the altruistic and vested interests of their intellectual and professional power elites is met in studies of Hinduism as well as other religions. It is well known that Hindu ethics has been often identified with what Schweitzer alleged to be (paraphrased): "Brahminic and philosophical life-and world-denying mysticism which has lacked social concern." Pro-Hindu denials of this chorge often highlight a developmental model with the clarification that Hindus are taught to embrace wealth, pleasure, love, and the world in the married stage of life, and then to transcend them in later, higher ascetical stages. According to this picture, the pinnacle of life's four goals is *moksha*, the liberated and detached realization of one's identity as Brahman, which terminates an otherwise endless cycle of reincarnations. Moral concern for this-worldly happiness and relationships is endowed with only provisional status.

An alternate approach to the criticism that Hinduism lacks a social ethic refuses to accept the idea that it has been simply reduced to Brahminism, let alone, even smaller philosophical systems like *Av*. This viewpoint is openly empathetic and considers itself more authentically phenomenological than academic in-groups which arrogate the multi-layered term "phenomenological" to their own restricted methods, claiming to be "phenomenologically scientific" in spite of their own latent cultural or religious assumptions. The empathetic perspective insists that there has existed for millennia a belief system, inspired by both Hindu and "secular" sources, concerned with the goal of human happiness, both here and in a heavenly kind of existence. *Artha* (wealth), *kāma* (pleasure and love), and *dharma* (as the moral aspect of religious teachings) reigned as the three central goals of life. Their prevalence is traceable to the *Vedas* of the people. In this outlook, Hinduism, far from being "reduced," was actually in constant dialogue with so-called separate "secular" values, as were other living religions. The *Vedas* and later popular literary records of those values have been ignored by many, especially during the last century's popularity of non-dualistic Vedānta philosophy. However, since Indians have remained largely a-literate like most peoples, it is to the classical audial and visual sources to which they have been most directly exposed that a fuller exposé of Hindu ethics must now turn, as it did in chapter five.

Before taking up this chapter's rationale for its broad, yet very limited, Sanskrit selections, the author recognizes first those scholars and readers who are already quite aware of the existence of these classics, not to mention those of Hindi, Bengali, and other Indian literatures. These persons are also cognizant of the fact that Hindu mystics have sometimes tried to embrace, integrate, or lend popular, life-affirming themes their effectively motivating religious foundations. Readers should also be forewarned of the chapter's programmatic and limitedly informative or descriptive method, necessitated by the present state of ethical interest in these classics. This initial contribution must content itself with encouraging other scholars and students to book-length, ethically interpretative commentaries and analyses. In the interim, in spite of these strictures, it seems vital to inform, convince, or remind many who are interested in comparative religion, philosophy, and ethics that they cannot neglect or deemphasize the crucial role of Hindu popular classics as well as other cultural popular classics.[1] Finally, the Hindu life-affirmative ethos is one not always or necessarily (logically) opposed to the dynamics of Hindu mysticism. Conversely, one could argue non-apologetically or even agnostically, as the author has done previously, that far from being a social ethic's necessary enemy, either religious or humanistic mysticism, together with emotive charisma and esthetical attraction, may in practice function as a necessary, integral part of the only effectively motivating factors through which social morality may wake up from dormant dreams to living practice.

Rationale for selections. Beyond systematic treatises (*śāstras*), scriptures (*śruti*), and traditional writings (*smṛiti*) like the *Ry* and the *Gītā*, whose religious and authoritative functions resembled the *śrutis*', there is an enormous ocean of popular Indian prose, poetry, and written drama which was eventually composed as a form of formal art (*kāvya*).[2] Ethically didactic as well as esthetic, *kāvya* comprises a large collection of extant literature about moralities either correlated with or coexistent with Hinduism. An ethical overview of popular classics in India, even if it leaves aside *kāvya* of Buddhistic inspirations, would seem to be so titanic a task that arbitrary selection of texts is unavoidable. This danger is diminished by several facts. For example, most early Sanskrit writings have been lost. Second, according to Indian historians, later literary creativity mummified into rigid conventionality so rapidly that new or regenerative ideas, moral or otherwise, flowered only rarely after the eighth century C.E. Third, dramatic plots were confined almost exclusively to variations of the *Mbh*'s (400 B.C.E.—400 C.E.) sister-epic, the *Ry* (300 B.C.E.—200 C.E.). Last, although drama taught morality, it painted it less with the brush of analytical norms, rationales, and didactic passages than with the broadest, simpler etchings of repetitive stories and vivid characters. The modern trends to biographical ethics of virtues and model characters, like those following Iris Murdoch or Max Scheler, can uncover rich resources in Indian as well as other cultures.

With the assistance of the standard histories and indices of Sanskrit and some other classical Indian literatures, it is possible, therefore, to single out ten literary figures or works which were both popularly known and morally significant without claiming apodictically that their impact was the most representative. As the historian, Moriz Winternitz observed, Indian literature intended to teach morality, not chronology. At present, therefore, cautious scholarship must avoid definitive assertions about chronological specifications and single authorship. Nevertheless, commonly conjectured date-spans and names provide a referential apparatus which is both convenient and reflective of tentative scholarly opinions. The provisionally chronological order in which works and authors are surveyed here is based on this body of scholarship. They include: 1) *The Kural* of Tiruvalluvar, 2) Vātsyāyana's *The Kāmasūtra*, 3) Cāṇakya-Kauṭilya's *Arthaśāstra*, 4) *The Pañcatantra*, 5) Kālidāsa, 6) *Mṛcchakatika* (*The Little Clay Cart*), 7) Bhavabhūti, 8) *The Bhāgavata Purāṇa*, 9) *The Gīta-Govinda*, and 10) Vidyāpati's *Love Songs*.

While some of the above works are more accurately described as devotional or systematic (*śāstras*) than as artistic *kāvya*, they participate in *kāvya*'s concreteness and widespread familiarity. In two referents, *The Bhāgavata Purāṇa* and *The Gīta-Govinda*, the devotional genre predominates. In others, like *The Kāmasūtra* and *The Arthaśāstra*, *prima facie* concerns relate to technical practicalities about politics, wealth, and sexual love-making. But in all of these selections, there emerges an ethos similar to that of the queen of all popular Indian literature and drama, the *Ṛy*. Far from advocating other-worldliness and pessimism,[3] this moral mood endorses the ethical pursuit of wealth, power, and the various loves of sexual partners, family, and friends.[4] In Sanskrit as well as in the third century *Hāla Sātavāhana* collection of Prakrit literature, not to mention the ancient, simpler poetry of Amaru, the love which is most predominant is romantic love.[5] However, it never vaporizes into the abstract and sometimes sado-masochistic "amour" which infected "love in the Western world" as depicted by de Rougement.[6] The historian, Sushil Kumar De, expresses its existential character in an appropriately poetical vein. Love is not idealized into a dying world of dreams, nor is it philosophized out of existence. It does not vaporize into the troubador's idolatry of an abstract maiden or feminized virtue for whom he would rather die than live (Beatrice, Madonna, Lady Poverty ?). Lastly, it is not diffused into spiritual mysticism or nature worship. For De, authentically humanistic romantic love does not beat about the bush. Like Molière De was quick to discern the dishonest or repressed loves which disguise themselves in spiritual metaphors or other linguistic codes. It should be admitted that truly romantic love becomes ecstatic, however humbly and limitedly, precisely in its earthiness. A cleavage of its physical and spiritual dimensions destroys both.[7]

Prescinding from its life-and sex-affirming content, the most characteristic feature of *kāvya*'s method of ethical thought might be its prudential, commonsensical, and quasi-utilitarian calculations of the consequences of conduct—appeal to authority settled in low profile. Perhaps in future research, diverse configurations and forms may bare themselves to the x-ray cameras of structuralist explorations.[8] In any event, from a view at the surface, and perhaps also in depth, the leitmotif of *kāvya* is not Manichean or Puritan flight from sexual love. It is rather its pursuit, and a consequent, spiralling embrace of further circles of life and being. Since life affirming *kāvya* is not abstractly "secular," but is tinged only with the dimmest dichotomies between the sacred and the profane, it is not surprising that A. K. Warder could proffer a historian's conclusion about Indian religion as well as culture : "Fundamentally Indian religion is not ascetical and hostile to the world."[9] Already skeletally apparent in the *Ṛy*'s earliest redactions, the ethos of *kāma* was not repressed, but was fleshed out by Indian *kāvya* as a whole. Completely overturned are reductionistic attempts by some to identify pluralistic Hindu morality with Brahminism or with non-dualistic (*Av*) asceticism and mysticism. Even within the latter, the ethos of *kāma* has been allowed a developmental function.

Before proceeding to documentary support for the above position, one must consider the authenticity of *kāvya*'s representativeness and respond to the allegation that it was the ruling class who subsidized and composed it.[10] Most known poets (*kavis*) were Brahmins. Consequently, even if drama was "the *Veda* of the people, the whole people," was it a *Veda* which was really *by* the people and *for* the people ? The question applies directly, of course, only to later and Brahminized versions of popular literature. Restated, it still inquires in that more limited ambit if the other-worldly dimension of Hinduism would have remained so influential, had it not been for the supposed control of the Brahminic power elite in literary and other areas ? While solid answers to these queries now remain tantalizingly out of reach, it is quite possible that an anti-dialectical process took place: that is, that the ruling classes, like systematic ethical philosophers in many cultures, might have been limited in their freedom to construct or reconstruct traditions or to move people in traditional directions (a conjecture bolstered by historical inertia). Brahminic opportunities for articulation might have been circumscribed by boundaries of what were already widely accepted opinions among the people about ideal moral values and norms. In other words, in the past as well as the present, the popular role in the elitist-populist dialectic cannot be forgotten. In either instance, the present assumption simply repeats Gerardus van der Leeuw's near platitude that the only way to know the so-called "essence" of Hinduism is by way of its pluralistic cultural forms or manifestations. Otherwise, putting it metaphorically, one may peel away the onion without ever finding its core. Among these manifestations, *kāvya,* and a few other popular classics below, to whatever degree they genuinely stemmed from the people, rank among the foremost.[11]

1. *The Kural* of Tiruvalluvar (between first-sixth centuries, C.E.).

One of the earliest sets of moral aphorisms exists not in Sanskrit, but in Tamil. It has been called the Tamil Veda, the *Kural,* the *Muppāl,* or the maxims of the poet, Tiruvalluvar (Valluvar, second century C.E. ?). Esteemed by Schweitzer as the "ideal of simple ethical humanity" and as "lofty wisdom,"[12] the collection of the *Kural* sums up the ethical *dharma* of the classical period of Tamil literature.[13] It also deals with the practical details of politics and love. Prescriptions under *dharma* (as righteousness) feature the householder's or marital stage of life, offspring, the husband's primacy, and energetic efforts in the face of *karma* (as the law of moral compensation). Injuring others by speech, envy, or fornication is contrasted with uprightness, forgiveness, *ahimsā* (non-violence),[14] and a form of the golden rule found in many cultures : "When a man hath felt a pain for himself, let him take care that he inflicteth it not on others" (*Kural*, No. 316).

But the *Kural*'s primary themes touch on the rational form of the process of moral consciousness and on the substantive matter of giving. Destructive conduct like gambling, also a pet object of Vedic and later Indian criticism, can be avoided by learning from its effects. Similarly, the consequences of poverty are not a blessing, but a curse (Nos. 751, 1045). Greed is a worse curse; the "feelings of I and mine" being "nought but vanity and pride" (No. 346). It is giving and sharing which makes the world go round. Without it

> the whole world would have no more meaning than a dance of marionettes (No. 1058). Though it leads unto heaven, receiving is bad: and though heaven should be denied to the giver, even then the giving of alms would be the highest virtue. It is only the high-born man that giveth without ever really saying *I have not.* Bitterer verily than the beggar's bread is the hoarded meal of the miser eating alone. Nothing is bitterer than death, but even death is sweet when one hath not the wherewithal to give to those who appeal for help (Nos. 222-23 and 229-30).

Conjoined with these charming, *Veda*-like praises of sharing one's wealth is an invitation to a sustained outpouring of one's wider resources, if not one's very self: "Behold the men that alter not in their affection for their old friends: even enemies will look upon them with tenderness" (No. 810).

2. Vātsyāyana's *The Kāmasūtra* (fourth century C.E.).

In contrast to the *Kural*'s specific ethical norms, other portraits of moral instruction were penciled in only the lightest shades, two of which were Vātsyāyana's *Kāmasūtra* and Cāṇakya-Kauṭilya's *Arthaśāstra.* In his summary and analysis of the former treatise, which deals not with love or friendship in general, but with erotic love in particular, Sushil K. De makes two deductions: 1) the *Kāmasūtra* discloses the existence of a floating mass of previous tradition on erotica; 2) it overshadows later imitations.[15] Taken literally, the tradition symbolized by this classic rests on three presuppositions which attract attention. First, since erotic satisfaction is said to be as necessary as food, repression might bring insanity or death.[16] Second, sexual enjoyment is situated in a context wider than erotica. It is merely a segment of the man-about-town's (*Nāgaraka's*) fine living in general, supposedly subordinated to *dharma*. Yet everything is as fair in love as in war. Third, the fulfillment of social and religious *dharma* in marriage is not the sole object of sexual union. Another legitimate end is pleasure itself. Correspondingly, "prostitutes" are to be treated with consideration and respect. In De's evaluation, "from remote antiquity Indian opinion never made a confusion between love and marriage."[17] Beyond its tension on that score with the *dharma* codes, the *Kāmasūtra* records an ancient and widespread conviction that *kāma* is not merely an instrumental value, but one that can be cherished and enjoyed in itself. Should this thesis become actually accepted as more humanistically rewarding than its opposite in contemporary debates and consciousness, it could then be argued that until recent times healthy aspects of sexual attitudes and practice had undergone a long period of chauvinistic or other retrogressions and decline from an era of esteem as portrayed in the *Kāmasūtra*.

3. Cāṇakya-Kauṭilya's *Arthaśāstra* (fourth century B.C.E. or much later).[18]

Comparable regard for the direct pursuit of *artha* or wealth is exhibited in this celebrated treatise. In an introduction to his critical edition (the first) of the *Cāṇakya Nīti Text Tradition* Vol. II, I, Ludwik Sternbach, like the historian Moriz Winternitz rigorously insists that he knows not when or where these collections of unconnected Sanskrit aphorisms were composed.[19] However, in his summary and partial translation of the epigrams on *rāja-nīti* (government) which, like Israelite wisdom literature, gradually came to address morality as well as polity, Sternbach does admit that next to the heroines of the epics and *Purāṇas* (discussed below), the most familiar and nearly universally respected name "was that of Cāṇakya."[20] Judgments outside India which transformed that respect to notoriety were unwarranted, in the opinion of M. Krishna Rao. Unlike Niccolo Machiavelli's supposed attribution of absolute authority to the state, Cāṇakya's laws, in Rao's reasoning, derive neither from the state nor the people, but from *śruti*. Contrary to a "Machiavellian" justification of base means for the common good, Cāṇakya condemned such means, including unrighteous war and its methods.[21] If Machiavelli considered human beings as fundamentally worthless, fearful, and covetous, and if, on that account, conventional morality and laws were "realistically" construed as inefficient, the same pattern is said to be imperceptible in Cāṇakya.

Nevertheless, Rao's version of Cāṇakya is qualified by at least a few aphorisms which suggest a moral atmosphere not unlike that of Machiavelli's *Discourses or the Prince*. The latter's "Safer to be feared than loved, if one of the two has to be wanting".... For men are generally "ungrateful, voluble, dissemblers, anxious to avoid danger, and covetous of gain....,[22] can be compared with Cāṇakya's pronouncement on royal punishment (*daṇḍa*) and the attitudes of subjects. Manu is echoed that "by threat of punishment the whole world is kept in check; through fear of punishment the universe enjoys blessings." "...dealings with kings should be cautious : kings may be destructive." A similarly Machiavellian tone rings in the axiom : "Rules that are ruthless, a teacher without knowledge, a wife with a temper, and relatives who have no affection should be abandoned."[23]

The comparative metaphor "Machiavellian tone" connotes moral disapproval only to the extent that one rejects the Machiavellian system, thinking it espouses evils beyond acceptable moral compromise. Similarly, one might have difficulty with Machiavelli's implication that equally ultimate values may coexist in irreconcilable conflict, and that the final contradictions of moral dilemmas are rooted in the whole of reality, rather than in human hearts and minds alone.[24] To cope with such a *Weltauschauung*, one would almost need a Dionysian mythical symbol like the Indian god of destruction, Śiva, who is also a symbol of growth. But the points at issue here are more simple than either approval or condemnation of such worldviews. First, in regard to the moral stances of both Machiavelli and Cāṇakya, those of the Indian figure, in particular, invite more direct ethical analysis than they have been given. Cāṇakya paradoxically advises the Indian *rāja*, regardless of his means, to rule by *dharma* and to protect religions.[25] Second, the dominance of consequentialistic reasoning is striking in both sources. In Cāṇakya, if caste and non-violence (*ahimsā*) are defended, or if the householder's stage of life is shielded against Buddhist and Jaina oppositions, his final moral validations do not depend on authority, but on a calculation of effects, which is an autonomously rational act.[26]

4. *The Pañcatantra* (fourth-fifth centuries C.E.).[27]

This moral rationality is even more obvious in the quasi-utilitarian emphases of the *Pañcatantra*, later amplified and remodeled in the fourteenth century *Hitopadeśa*. These collections record folk stories and wisdom on *nīti*, the wise conduct of life. Often they present animal fables and maxims within larger framing stories. Their frequently didactic identification of human roles and mentalities with various animals is characteristic of the so-called savage, meaning universal, mind's unfailing intelligence.[28] The persistence of animal symbolizations from primitive tribes through Aesop to contemporary cinematic and athletic industries may reveal some of the most basic functions of human consciousness. If one remains skeptical of the theory that all animal tales, including those of the *Pañcatantra*, originated in Greece, one is then open to the hypothesis that whatever the *Pañcatantra*'s moral teachings, it speaks in a language less Grecian than cosmopolitan, less archaic than ageless.[29]

On the surface, the *Pañcatantra* presents stories and sayings which favor the outwitting of roguery, and practical intelligence rather than virtue. However, in the Aristotelian sense of prudence (both mental and moral), concern for security, prosperity, and friendship has an ethical as well as an intellectual dimension. From this viewpoint the tales of the *Pañcatantra* are eminently ethical. Imprudence does not thrive on a cognitive island but stems from the moral "neglect of the three things worth living for—virtue, money, and love" (Ryder trans., p. 101). While some proverbs recognize determinative mechanisms in *karma* (as fate) and *samsāra* (the wheel of reincarnation, pp. 78, 203-04, and 291) others are polemically anti-fatalistic (pp. 129-31) and insist that consequences, once felt, should furnish moral instruction for later :

> How did Raven [Rāvana] fail to feel
> That 'tis wrong, a wife to steal?
> How did Rama fail to see
> Golden deer could never be (p. 184)?

Whereas some sayings favor the retribution of evil (p. 345), others extol self-sacrifice and generosity (pp. 121, 189, and 292-93) or analogues of the golden rule : "The moral law is briefly told: To help your neighbor—this is good : To injure him is devilhood" (p. 276).

In spite of the presence of other familiar Hindu moral themes dealing with *ahimsā*, female subordination, and caste (that is, castes (*jātis*) and the four *varṇas* or classes alike in their discriminatory aspects, pp. 114, 276, 290, and 293), the prevailing mood promotes an earthy, moral, rational, and unsentimental ability to learn from repeated experience, for example from poverty at one extreme and greed at the other. Poverty is evil, because it preoccupies, obstructs, corrupts, and disables virtue and giving :

Conduct, patience, purity,
Manners, loving-kindness, birth
After money disappears,
Cease to have the slightest worth.

But greed is an equal and more persistent foe :

The hair grows old with aging years;
The teeth grow old, the eyes and ears.
But while the aging seasons speed,
One thing is young forever—greed
(pp. 367, 394 and see 373).[30]

5. Kālidāsa (fifth century C.E.)

According to S. K. De "the three great Sanskrit dramas" are Kālidāsa's *Abhijñāna-Śākuntala*, Bhavabhūti's *Uttararāma-carita* (*Rāma's Later History*), and Śūdraka's *Mṛcchakaṭika* (*The Little Clay Cart*). Besides the *Śākuntala*, two other plays are attributed to Kālidāsa, the *Vikramorvaśiya* (*The Hero and the Nymph*) and the Rāmāyaṇic *Mālavikāgnimitra*, named after its hero and heroine. All plays of Kālidāsa echo the popular Indian motif that spousal love remains passionate and happy while merging with the wider loves of ideals, art, nature, and family.[31] In the *Vikramorvaśiya*, a less romantic and more simplified version of the *Śākuntala*, the husband, Purūravas, sings of his love as a father and of his affection for all human beings:

Child of thy mother [Urvaśī], O come to me !
Let me feel my son ! The touch of his own child
They say, thrills all the father; let me know it.
Gladden me as the moonbeam melts the moonstone;
May every man find his own good,
And every man be merry of his mind,
And all men in all lands taste all desire.[32]

Kālidāsa's *Śākuntala*, named "the masterpiece of the Indian theatre," not only effects a similar integration of romantic and familial love, but also explores the classical subject of love purified by suffering. But purification does not mean Platonization. A full analysis of the core story in the *Mbh*, omitted here because it requires a disproportionately lengthy and independent treatment, and of Kālidāsa's dramatization, would verify that Śakuntalā remains both a distinct heroine on her own as well as her husband's "second self." Her personage is consonant with what S. N. Dasgupta called the authentic Indian optimism that this life "tends to happiness."[33]

6. *Mṛcchakaṭika* (*The Little Clay Cart*, fifth — seventh centuries C.E. ?).

Assigned to Śūdraka, this drama is a realistic portrayal of the familiar topic of the courageous, generous, dignified, and self-sacrificing courtesan or prostitute, here named Vasantasenā. Henry Wells inferred that "generosity in every sense is the moral of this highly moral comedy, for all Indian plays of consequence are in one way or another works of edification as well as amusement, spiritual as well as aesthetic..." and that this work "represents a colossal affirmation of the value of human living."[34] The love between the heroine, Vasantasenā, and her lover Cārudatta, kindles other virtues, especially generosity in the heroine. On Cārudatta's part, this same love is pictured as somehow coexisting strongly and purely with his love for his wife and son. Toward the end, his son's toy cart is filled by the departing Vasantasenā with jewels, symbols of her self-sacrificing liberality.

7. Bhavabhūti (eighth century C.E.).

Mature conjugal and familial love united with love of life in general is again encountered in the dramas of Bhavabhūti, reputedly the last of the great Sanskrit dramatists.[35] In two productions representing the Indian stage's "major efforts" to dramatize the *Ry*,[36] the *Mahāviracarita* and the *Uttararāmacarita* (*Rāma's Later History*),[37] Bhavabhūti takes elaborate pains to insure that the enduringly romantic, marital love of Rāma and Sītā (the core epic's major moral model of life-affirming compassion) does not result in aborted tragedy. Unlike a few widespread versions of the epic, Bhavabhūti's drama remains faithful to the core (*Ur*) and Vālmīkian picture of a love which continues in this life and in heaven. While Bhavabhūti's third famous play, the *Mālatimādhava*, extols happily enduring love with ardor and pathos, the *Uttararāmacarita* highlights compassion (*karuṇā*) as its primary virtue, with the glorification of the family as its basic message.[38] Although it is the latter work's power of expression which is supposedly unparalleled in Sanskrit literature, it is the former play which expresses that theme most succinctly. The love between wives and husbands is the potential epitome of human relationships, friendships, and life itself.[39] Fears within some religions that such a relationship may approach egoism *à deux* sometimes remain unbalanced in forgetting that solitary egoism is also a potential pitfall and that one usually manages life in dyads and larger groups. Further, if one thinks that Indian *kāvya* protests too much the treasure of conjugal union, one may also infer that there must have been elements in Indian society which necessitated that protest (a point both verified and illustrated by the negative yet beautiful poems of the Buddhist-like Bhartrihari (seventh century C.E.?)[40]

8. *The Bhāgavata Purāṇa* (ninth-tenth centuries C.E.).

Usually conceived as un-Brahminic and plebeian in origin, the *Purāṇas* were constructed or reconstructed for the purpose of assimilating specific, popular cults to Brahminism and are, to that extent, of Brahminic rather than popular origin. In the possible one-dimensional, Marxian judgment of D. D. Kosambi, the *Purāṇas* popularized *bhakti* (devotion) for the purpose of filling basic social and economic needs in feudal ideology. *Bhakti* functioned better than other types of religion in holding society and state together.[41] One could build a similar case that the philosopher Śaṅkara's elaborate system of two-level truth fulfilled at least unconsciously the same function in assimilating both popular and Buddhistic cults (see chapter eight).

The most widely known and influential of all *Purāṇas*, the *Bhāgavata Purāṇa*[42] was composed in a religious genre distinct from those of dramas or romantic poetry. Although it inspired devotional poetry among the neo-Vaishṇava sects, its main moral interest probably consists in its unselfconscious acceptance of love-making as naturally good and capable of religious symbolism. In the figure of Krishna, intercourse becomes symbolic of Vishnu's union with the soul.[43] While this investigation of ethics in popular Indian literature reaches only a survey's provisional conclusion that the *Bhāgavata Purāṇa* is merely of secondary importance morally, it does not intend to preclude future ethical analyses of its contents any more than it has in the instances of the dramatist, Bhāsa, the outstanding poetry of Bhartrihari, or the *Mbh* (see Appendix I). In fact, the studies of P. V. Kane intricately demonstrate that while *bhakti* may be the *Bhāgavata Purāṇa*'s central theme (including wifely devotion to husbands),[44] allusions to karmic retribution, *ahimsā*, and especially giving (*dāna*) are not lacking.[45] In connection with *dāna*, a proto-socialistic aphorism about property appears : "...men have ownership over only that much as would fill their belly; he who thinks as his own more than that is a thief and deserves punishment (as such)."[46]

9. *The Gīta-Govinda* (twelfth century C.E.).

This *gīta* (song) deserves brief mention, not for its detailed comments about moral matters, since these are missing, but for its direct and simple affirmation of an ethos. Jayadeva's *Gīta-Govinda* has been called the end of the best erotic and religious poetry and of Sanskrit poetry in general.[47] Govinda is one of the several names for the *avatār* (divine manifestation), Krishna. Other names are Hari, Rāma, etc. In the devout and sensuous *Gīta-Govinda*, Jayadeva sings of love in the service of religion. Praise of *kāma* is said to honor Krishna. The converse is also predicated. Morally, nothing new is proposed about the meaning of love, but its inclusion as a part of life itself is reemphasized in the strongest terms.

10. Vidyāpati's *Love Songs* (fifteenth century C.E.).

The *Love Songs of Vidyāpati*, composed in Maithili, indicate that sexual love is a phenomenon not limited to the biological order.[48] Further, it emerges as a vital need for women as well as men. As was the case with the *Gīta-Govinda*, the primary ethical significance of Vidyāpati's songs is the simple persistent, dramatic, and commonplace testimony, contra Bhartrihari (or a dimension of him) and some writers about Brahminic tradition, that this life and world are not to be scorned in the name of religion.

Conclusion. These vignettes of *kāvya* and other popular classics, ranging from the earliest centuries of the common era until the fifteenth century, have spotlighted Indian themes still celebrated in and beyond India today and have partly documented this chapter's several opening assumptions. For readers whose interests are of a more general literary and humanistic type, they support the coexistence of a life-affirmative ethos within a pluralistic Hindu morality. For scholars and others with more specific historical, literary, or ethical concerns, their moral breadth and quality invite further ethical studies of both classical and contemporary popular literatures, poems, and dramas,[49] projects which may follow up the varied types of references and citations offered for those with pluralistic and diversified concerns. Like the greatest written and dramatized Indian classic of all, the *Ry*, which the author has dealt with in chapter five and elsewhere,[50] Indian literary traditions are part of an ongoing process which runs in tension with some currents of isolated Brahminism and Advaita Vedānta (*Av*) (especially some of its Western interpretations). Indian popular literature provides a challenge to the alleged representative monopoly of those currents.

As in the *Ry*, systemically present, if not systematically exposed, one finds in popular classics nearly all the ethical wisdom or ideas commonly identified with the body of *dharma* and thought called Hinduism in general: the four classes, stages and the three (rather than four) goals of life,—also characteristic virtues like *ahimsā*, non-attachment, compassion, and truthfulness. But coexisting with belief in karmic retribution in present and future lives or births is an emphasis on human happiness both here and hereafter. Concomitantly, other less Brahminic and more this-worldly virtues share the limelight: responsible care for wealth, self-earned wealth, that is, prudence, fidelity in friendships, the sharing of food and wealth, and the fostering of conjugal and familial friendships. Peoples' classics present a this-worldly ethics which verifies both its principles and its exceptions without outside help. In its common-sense appeal to the consequences of actions, it shows human intelligence logically daring to come to grips with ethical problems rather than passing on decisions to chosen or accepted delegates. It displays human love's revolutionary refusal to be robbed of its limited but honest dignity in the face of fear or power, however spiritually conceived or contrived.

Finally, the Hindu life-affirmative ethos is one not always or necessarily opposed to the dynamics of Hindu mysticism or mystical philosophy. Conversely, one could argue that far from being a social ethic's natural enemy, religious and/or humanistic mysticisms together with charismatic and esthetically emotive appeal, may be practically indispensable as one of the action-inspiring motivations through which social morality may arise from the tombs of dead ideals to living practice. It seems that even in the most authoritarian modern regimes, leaders or party leaders cannot make effective progress without charismatic appeals verging on human personality "cult". While this phenomenon does not prove the universal truth of "cult" or "religion," it does evince a universal need for it or for a humanistic substitute.

NOTES

1. For these readers, the numerous references or notes on variously available texts and translations extend options which may curtail travel to libraries and thus offer the chapter's most helpful service. Diverse kinds of readers, according to their linguistic and other needs and discretion, will wish to refer to only some of these notes.

2. A helpful overview on literary and dramatic forms, including biography and the novel, is offered by A. K. Warder, *Indian Kāvya Literature* (Delhi : Motilal Banarsidass, 1972), Vol. I, 122-99. On the comic and erotic notion of the thirteenth-seventeenth century Sanskrit monologue play (*bhāṇa*), see Sushil Kumar De's *Aspects of Sanskrit Literature* (Calcutta : Firma K. L. Mukhopadhyay, 1959), p. 2. The Sanskrit transliteration system employed here continues to imitate and extend that used in Wm. T. de Bary, *Indian Tradition*, Vol. I, 521-24. Taken as popular classics, the two epics, the *Ry* and the *Mbh* are treated in chapter five and Appendix I.

3. See Warder, *Indian Kāvya*, p. 29 and J. P. Rao Rayapati, *Early American Interest in Vedanta : Pre-Emersonian Interest in Vedic Literature and Vedantic Philosophy* (New York : Asia Publishing House, 1973). Rayapati hopes to "blast the myth that Hindu thought is essentially pessimistic and other worldly..." (p. viii).

4. De's *Indian Erotics*, p. 7 contrasts this endorsement with the Buddhist view of life as he sees it. Since the ambivalent popular poems of Bhartrihari seem more negatively Buddhistic than Hindu, they are ommited in this study, in spite of their great beauty and display of the love-affirming tension in Indian life.

5. See *ibid.*, pp. 14 and 21-27.

6. Some of the "Western" neglect of conjugal love is supposedly rooted in preoccupation with courtly love where the gallant knight preferred to die for his lady than to know her or live with her. See Denis de Rougement, *Love in the Western World* (rev. ed.; New York : Pantheon Books, Inc., 1956).

7. *Indian Erotics*, p. 36.

8. "Deep" processes, for instance, like the dialectical ones which Lévi-Strauss discerns or constructs in his analysis of the Oedipus myth, may also pulsate beneath Indian myths, epics, and dramatic plots and characters. But whatever profound economic, linguistic, psychological, or conceptual

determinisms may operate under moral surfaces, the obvious themes should not be neglected. Sometimes people talk precisely about what they claim to. Lévi-Strauss' "The Structural Study of Myth," made available in *The Structuralists from Marx to Lévi-Strauss*, eds. Richard T. and Fernande DeGeorge (Garden City, New York : Anchor Books, 1972), p. 194, sorts out patterns in the Oedipus myth in support of his thesis that (unconscious ?) mythical logic "is as rigorous as that of modern science."

9. See Warder, *Indian Kāvya*, p. 29.

10. *Ibid.*, pp. 204 and 217.

11. Giles Gunn's elaborate essay on the need for literary criticism in the study of religions can be applied to Indian *kāvya*. With an eye to critics rather than their materials, Gunn feels that literary and cultural situations are "great elaborate fights about moral issues." See "Threading the Eye of the Needle : The Place of the Literary Critic in Religious Studies," *Journal of the American Academy of Religion* 43 (June 1975), 180.—The metaphor of peeling the onion is one which I believe I recalled from a most helpful essay by Michael Pye, "Comparative Hermeneutics in Religion," in *The Cardinal Meaning : Essays in Comparative Hermeneutics : Buddhism and Christianity*, ed. by M. Pye and R. Morgan (The Hague and Paris : Mouton, 1973), pp. 9-58. To this competent comparativist I owe not only ideas but an apology for the tone of my review of his anthology, a tone really directed at the market policies abused by some modern publishers (see *Journal of Chinese Philosophy* 2 (1974), 95-97). The review overstated my lack of grasping the rationale for Pye's selections. Although my problem stands, it could have been stated more constructively and concretely without falling with haste into the widening, competitive academic trap of abstract, negative, and often crushing criticisms.

12. Schweitzer, *Indian Thought*, p. 203.

13. An English translation by V. V. S. Aiyar is entitled *The Kural or The Maxims of Tiruvalluvar* (3d ed.; Madras : The Jupiter Press, 1952. References here proceed by verse rather than page. For background see X. S. Thani Nayagam, *The Tamil Culture and Civilizati n : Readings : The Classical Period* (New York : Asia Publishing House, 1970), pp. 98-99 and 102-03. On the *Kural*'s influence see V. Kanakasabhai, *The Tamils, Eighteen Hundred Years Ago* (2d ed.; Madras : The South India Saiva Siddhanta Works Publishing Society Limited, Tinnevelly, 1956).

14. The *Kural*'s penchant for *ahimsā* (nos. 314 and 321) should be compared with its defense of capital punishment (No. 550).

15. Imitations are listed in De, *Indian Erotics*, p. 105. On the *Kāmasūtrā*'s sources and editions see *ibid.*, pp. 94-95. English translation : *Vātsyāyana Kāma Sūtra : The Hindu Ritual of Love* (New York : Castle Books, 1963).

16. De, *Indian Erotics*, p. 96, traces this claim to *Kāmsūtra* 1.2.46.

17. *Ibid.*, pp. 95, 98, 100, and 103.

18. English translations : 1) Selections from books 1,2,7, and 8 by T. N. Ramaswamy, *Essentials of Indian Statecraft : Kautilya's Arthasastra for Contemporary Readers* (Bombay : Asia Publishing House, 1962); 2) R. Shamasastry; *Kautilya's Arthasastra* (7th ed., Mysore : S. Srinivas, 1961 [originally 1915]- 3) Critical translation, notes, and commentary by R. P. Kangle, *The Kau-*

tiliya Arthaśāstra (3 Vols.; Bombay : University of Bombay, 1960 and 1963). In this most promising of English translations, the commentary (Vol. III, p. 101) adheres to the traditionally conjectured date, fourth century B.C.E.; 4) Selections in S. Radhakrishnan and Charles A. Moore, eds., *Indian Philosophy*, pp. 193-223. Mukhopadhyaya publishers in Calcutta list *Kautilya on Love and Morals* by P. C. Chunder.

19. Published at Hoshiarpur : Vishveshvaranand Vedic Research Institute, 1970, p. vi. See also Ludwik Sternbach, *Subhāṣita*, pp. 44-46.

20. *Cāṇakya-Rāja-Nīti : Maxims on Rāja-Nīti* ed. with critical apparatus by Ludwick Sternbach (Madras: The Adyar Library and Research Center 1963) pp. 2,6 24-40 and 43.

21. M. V. Krishna Rao, *Studies in Kautilya* (2d ed.; Delhi : Munshi Ram Manohar Lal, 1958) pp. 89-108 146-47, and 173.

22. *The Prince* No. 17 Luigi Ricci trans. (New York : The New American Library, 1952) p. 90. In *The Discourses* III, 21 the concept of "safer" is refined to one of more efficient obedience. See ed. by Bernard Crick and trans. by Leslie J. Walker (Baltimore : Penguin Books, 1970) p. 463.

23. Sternbach *Cāṇakya-Rāja-Nīti* Nos. 100, 271, and 153 respectively (pp. 29, 40, and 32). Compare with Manu VII.20-22.

24. Defense of the moral caliber of Machiavelli's worldview can be found in Isaiah Berlin, "The Question of Machiavelli," *The New York Review of Books*, pp. 20-32, esp. pp. 24 and 30 (date recent, misplaced) and in Bernard Crick's introduction to *The Discourses*, pp. 61-69.

25. Sternbach, *Cāṇakya-Rāja-Nīti*, pp. 20-24.

26. See Rao, *Studies in Kautilya*, pp. 23, 45, 231, 234, and 247-48.

27. *The Pañcatantra*, trans. by Arthur W. Ryder (Bombay : Jaico Publishing House, 1949). Problematic dates offered by Winternitz, *Indian Literature*, Vol. III,I, 12 : and by S. N. Dasgupta, *A History of Sanskrit Literature, Classical Period* (Calcutta: University of Calcutta, 1947), p. 88.

28. The so-called "savage" mind's preoccupation with animal stories and totemic identifications "is logical in the same sense and the same fashion as ours." Claude Lévi-Strauss, *The Savage Mind* (Chicago : The University of Chicago Press, 1962), p. 268. And see note 8 above.

29. Some of these tales were absorbed into the Buddhist Jātaka stories. See Dasgupta, *A History of Sanskrit Literature*, pp. 86, and 697-98; and Krishna Chaitanya, *A New History of Sanskrit Literature* (New Delhi and New York : Asia Publishing House, 1962), p. 366.

30. As A. K. Warder notes in *Indian Kāvya*, p. 217, more than dramas based on such heroines as Śakuntalā of the *Mbh*, it was the plays woven out of the Rāmāyaṇic and other legends which became the *Vedas* of the people and the early subjects of central dramatization. Thirteen plays of potentially comparable origin, omitted here, may rank with the earliest dramas and were discovered as recently as 1912. They appear to have been penned by one person, and have been conjecturally attributed to a fourth century Brahmin and devotee of Vishnu named Bhāsa. Analysis of the life-affirming plays of Bhāsa about ongoing spousal love and joy is deferred in this volume until their historical origin is more fully verified; also for reasons of space. Commentaries on their positive themes can be found in Winternitz-Jhā, *A History*

of Indian Literature, Vol. III,I, 187; and Dasgupta, *ibid*; also in N. B. Purohit, trans., *The Pratimā of Bhāsa* (Baroda : The Allied Stores, 1957), pp. 2 and 25. In Addition to English translations of Bhāsa's plays by A. C. Woolner and Purohit, see "The Vision of Vāsavadatta," in *Six Sanskrit Plays*, ed. Henry W. Wells (London : Asia Publishing House, 1964). pp. 1-42. Wells uses the A. C. Woolner and L. Sarup translation and his collection also comprises plays attributed to Śūdraka, Kālidāsa, Bhavabhūti and Harsha (the Buddhistic *Nāgānanda*). Chronological details are provided in Dasgupta's *History of Sanskrit Literature*, pp. xlvii and 709.

31. The life-affirmative interpretation is elaborated by S. K. De., *Indian Erotics*, p. 64. In the H. Kohn translation of Winternitz, *A History of Indian Literature*, Vol. III,I. 36-41, there is reference to many works wrongly assigned to Kālidāsa and to the two great epics of Kālidāsa : the *Raghuvamsa* and the *Kumārasambhava*. Contrast with Winternitz-Jhā, *A History of Indian Literature*, Vol. III,I, 47. Translations of Kālidāsa's *Śākuntala* by A.H. Edgren and of his *Vikramorvasīya* by Sri Aurobindo Ghose in Wells, *Six Sanskrit Plays*. On the spiralling of conjugal love, see *ibid.*, p. 96. Another translation of *Shakuntalā* : Arthur W. Ryder, *Shakuntalā and Other Writings* (New York: E. P. Dutton and Co., 1959).

32. Wells, *ibid.*, pp. 341 and 347.

33.. S. N. Dasgupta, *A History of Sanskrit Literature*, p. xlvii; an opinion shared by A. K. Warder, *Indian Kāvya*, p. 29. On other themes like Kālidāsa's *varṇāśrama* (classes and stages of life) ideals see Dasgupta, *ibid.*, p. xxx.

34. Wells, *Six Sanskrit Plays*, p. 41. See also De, *Indian Erotics*, pp. 76-82 For alternative translations of *The Little Clay Cart* and *Shakuntalā* see Wm. T. de Bary and A. T. Embree, ed., *A Guide to Oriental Classics* (2d ed.; New York and London : Columbia University Press, 1975), pp. 113-14, 117-18.

35. Confer Chaitanya, *A New History of Sanskrit Literature*, p. 342.

36. See Wells, *Six Sanskrit Plays*, p. 351.

37. Trans., C. N. Joshi in Wells, *ibid.*, pp. 358-432. S. K. Belvalkar's translation in the Harvard Oriental Series appeared in 1915.

38. See R. D. Karmarkar, *Bhavabhūti* (Charivar : Karnatak University, 1963), p. 64 and Wells, *ibid.*, p. 354.

39. Translated in De, *ibid.*, p. 70. If the play is taken to be backgrounded religiously with Hindu beliefs, the text in question, spoken by a Buddhist nun heroine (a common figure), recalls the coexistence of the two religions in the Indian milieu for several centuries.

40. Starkly in contrast with the ancient Indian poet Amaru's exclusive treatment of love in its playful moods and as isolated from the rest of life, romantic love (*śṛṅgāra*) comes to epitomize the basic problem of life in the gatherings of poetry ascribed to Bhartrihari. These aphoristic and didactic verses, usually placed within the century preceding Bhavabhūti, vascillate in a reputedly typical Hindu manner between intense sensuality and asceticism. Wm. T. de Bary agrees with this judgment to the extent that the poetry conjures up a people both worldly and world-renouncing, deeply attracted to both sensual beauty and emancipation from it. See de Bary's foreword in Barbara Stoler Miller, trans., *Bhartrihari : Poems* (New York : Columbia University Press, 1967). Her translation is based on D. D. Kosambi's critical edition

(Bombay : Singh Jain Series, No. 23, 1948).

41. See D. D. Kosambi, *Myth and Reality : Studies in the Formation of Indian Culture* (Bombay : Popular Prakashan, 1962), pp. 31-37.

42. See Purnendu Sinha, *A Study of the Bhāgavata Purāṇa*, 1 Vol., (2d ed.; Madras : The Theosophical Publishing House, 1950)., p. ix. Sinha marks book ten as the *Bhāgavata*'s most characteristic and popular section. As for dates, P. V. Kane sees no reliable evidence of composition earlier than the ninth or tenth centuries, C.E., but extends the ambit back to the fifth century : *History of Dharmaśāstra*, Vol. V, I, 399. Other English translations : 1) A. C. Prabhupada, *Śrīmad-Bhāgavatam* (10 Vols.; New York and Bombay : The Bhakti-vedanta Book Trust, 1972); 2) J. M. Sangal *The Srimad-Bhagavatam of Krishna-Dwaipayana Vyasa* (Calcutta : Oriental Publishing Co., 1951); and 3) H. P. Poddar, *The Bhagavata* (Gorakhpur : Gita Press, 1952).

43. See G. W. Archer's introduction, p. 18, to Deben Bhattacharya's translation, *Love Songs of Vidyāpati* (Delhi : Orient Paperbacks, 1963).

44. "Devotion to husband is the one great religion. . . ." P. N. Sinha, *A Study of the Bhāgavata Purāṇa*, p. 417.

45. Kane, *History of Dharmaśāstra*, Vol. V, II , pp. 933, 944-46, and 936 respectively.

46. Kane's translation, *ibid.*, p. 950, n. in English and Sanskrit.

47. Dasgupta, *A History of Sanskrit Literature*, p. 396.

48. English translation as in note 43 above. Dated by G. W. Archer between 1380 and 1406, *ibid.*, p. 24. Or see *The Songs of Vidyāpati*, ed. Subhadra Jhā (Banares : Motilal Banarsidass, 1954).

49. The reader may wish to pursue the contents of other, if perhaps less known, works in the standard histories of Indian and Sanskrit literatures: for example, those of the tenth century Rājaśekhara and Kṛṣṇamisra (pro-Advaita).

50. On the *Ṛy* see note 2 above and Chapter five.

Chapter VIII

ETHICS IN THE PHILOSOPHERS AND REFORMERS: ŚAṄKARA AND GANDHI AS TYPES

Abstract. The basic assumption underlying this chapter does not preclude the possibility of Hindu or other mystical experience any more than it defends it. Nor, contra Albert Schweitzer, does it rule out mysticism's theoretical potential for grounding an effective, social, this-life- and world-affirming morality. With a methodology which is historically agnostic and which tries to remove hidden presuppositions behind its phenomenological dimension, it focuses on the Hindu philosopher Śaṅkara (c. 788-829 C.E.) as a paradigmatic interpreter of Hindu mysticism and morality. In so doing, this study will single out *three kinds of previous versions or critiques of Śaṅkara's seemingly life-denying amorality* : 1) *hard,* 2) *moderate, and* 3) *soft.* It will then offer 4) *the author's alternative direct exegesis of Śaṅkara's own writings,* one which happens to arrive at an unintended synthesis of the former types of analyses. While this contribution does not strive to discredit the versions of Śaṅkara or others about the coexistence of "absolute" and "relative" truth, it does point to amoral conclusions which follow from Śaṅkara's non-dualistic worldview (in logical fact, but not from necessity).

After *a glance* (5*a*) at the supposedly antithetical and more *humanistically moral ramifications of Rāmānuja's teaching and of modern prophetic reformers* (5*b*), the chapter will conclude that within the whole gestalt and context of both ancient and perduring Vedic and popular Hindu traditions, Hindu mysticism may be reinterpreted more pluralistically. It can provide a potentially positive basis for social and life-affirming ethical humanism, one which stands beyond a merely developmental moral stage, which some mystics and philosophers tolerate on the journey toward final mystical and renunciatory liberation and realization (*moksha*). Readers may then decide if this interpretation revisionistically violates or remains within the wider circle of historical (including mystical) Hindu convictions. They may also evaluate the extent to which this analysis is analogously helpful to those for whom "mystical" experience derives from humanism alone or from other Hindu (e.g. *bhakti*) or non-Hindu religious claims. NOTES.

A grasp of why "Hindu ethics" has been restrictively equated with its Upanishadic, Brahminic, and philosophical versions (points of view or *darśanas*)[1] is inseparable from a broad comprehension of the paradigmatic Śaṅkara's monistic (or rather non-dualistic) philosophy (*Av*). His viewpoint contends that in an ultimate sense only Brahman is real. All else is finite and relatively existent (*māyā*). Subsequently, the immediate objective of this chapter can be undertaken : to analyze the interpretations of Śaṅkara's teachings and of its ramifications for ethics. By default, social ethics would seem to be relegated to a subordinate and unenthusiastic concern for the traditional moral codes (*dharmaśāstras*).[2]

Preliminary understanding of the background and meaning of the rise of Śaṅkara's elaborate teachings requires one to place this eighth century philosopher in the ambit of the "decline" of Buddhism and the resurgence of devotional Hindu cults and sects. Lal Mani Joshi's compendium of the elements involved in the deterioration of Indian Buddhism underlines the thesis that the ideals of Buddhist ethics had grown less attractive, not necessarily as aspirations but in actual practice.[3] Practical decay explains in part a Buddhist demise which had become clearly visible by c.700 C.E. The people were apparently irritated or confused by fierce intra-Buddhistic, sectarian disputes, by monastic wealth and greed, and by lack of discipline in which verbal profession outstripped actual performance. Additional extrinsic factors inimical to Buddhism were also at play. These included sporadic persecutions, withdrawals of royal support and protection, and direct Brahminic hostility. Moreover, the Brahminic religion's adherence to ritual, castes, and stages of life was supposedly more culturally Indian than Buddhism's relatively casteless, ritual-less, more universal features which would thrive in other cultures.

But perhaps the most compelling key to the disintegration of Buddhism in India is the hypothesis that rather than *disappear*, Buddhism *reappeared* in an eclectic Hinduism literarily enshrined in the writings of Śaṅkara, his followers, and his adapters.[4] Either by natural syncretistic growth or by planned eclectic assimilation, Hinduism absorbed both Buddhism and the many Indian sects devoted to various deities by placing Buddha[5] and the theistic gods, Vishnu, Śiva, his consort Śakti or Devī, etc., within a pantheon roofed by the open concept of an impersonal Brahman. Vedântic Brahminism might not have attracted or re-attracted the masses without giving significant status to those popular figures and to the devotion (*bhakti*) which they inspired.[6] To bestow simultaneously the dignity of supreme deity in many directions, it would be vital to refine a system like Śaṅkara's, one in which the deific function and reality of each could be both affirmed and denied. A system of thought was needed, in other words, in which gods and the Buddha could be affirmed in some relative or lower sense of existence and denied in an ultimate sense. Although future detractors might label this kind of thought structure double-truth or Orwellian double-think, the apparent contradictoriness could be attributed not to a fault of logic but to the "radical finitude of human sensory perception," to a "superimposition" of the unreal on the real. This itself was finally a kind of ignorance (*avidyā*).

1. *The hard critique.* The hard critic eyes Śaṅkara's role in the process of the absorption of Buddhism and popular religions into Brahminism as follows. It was not limited to the immediately and widely influential monasteries which he modeled after the Buddhist communities and from which ten contemporary sects trace their lineage. Neither was his role restricted to alleged anti-Buddhist expeditions and propaganda.[7] Rather, it also included religious and philosophical borrowings from Nāgārjuna (Buddhist) and from Mādhyamika (proto-Mahāyāna) Buddhism—like *māyā* and Buddhistic perceptions of non-dualism or a paradoxical "non-dual duality of worldview." Śaṅkara's synthesis of these and other Buddhistic elements with Vedānta was an embrace which became for Buddhism a kiss of death. As for Vedāntic Brahminism, it reached in Śaṅkara an evolutionary development (if not Buddhistic mutation) into what many would thereafter restrictively define as "Hinduism."

Just as Mahāyāna Buddhism had conjecturally lost identity and popularity because it imitated theistic Hindu traditions without creative ingenuity, Theravāda Buddhism had shared in the same loss, but with Brahminism as the agent. For the genius of effective cooption and promotion entails the incorporation of the competitor's more marketable features without neutralizing the distinctiveness of one's own. In this kind of adaptation, Brahmanism succeeded where Buddhism had failed, but not without overcoming a momentous obstacle to its powers of planned, eclectic synthesis.

The elements to be harmonized faced one another in stark polarity. Theravāda Buddhism's atheism was as diametrically opposed to Hindu theistic and polytheistic beliefs as its doctrine of non-self (*anatta*—not widely accepted at the popular level) was contrary to the Vedāntic realization that each person's true "self" is Brahman. Moreover, the assertion of other Mahāyāna Buddhists that consciousness alone was real was poles apart from the simple Indian conviction that individuals who relish their food, for instance, are enjoying more than the experience of their own subjectivity, whatever their disclaimers.[8] Somehow, one would have to manage simultaneous assent to these sets of contradictory propositions, say, by maintaining that "being" and "consciousness" are neither themselves nor their opposites, but transcend them. Śaṅkara declined to credit Buddhist intellectuals for their own insistence on such a reconciliation of antitheses, but it is a feat for which he himself has received lavish plaudits. Combined with his split-level ("upstairs-downstairs") model of a) higher truths set above b) lower, propaedeutic, and ultimately illusory truths, Śaṅkara's methodological power to combine could seemingly harmonize all discords.[9]

Ironically, however, Śaṅkara maintained that there were indeed some theses and antitheses incapable of synthesis—not within Brahminism, but within Buddhism. For him three of Buddhism's major schools (*Sarvāstitva*, *Vijñānamātra*, and *Śūnyavāda*) held positions about the reality of being and consciousness which were irreconcilable. "Buddha," wrote Śaṅkara,

> by propounding the three mutually contradictory systems teaching respectively the reality of the external world, the reality of ideas only, and general nothingness, has himself made it clear either that he was a man given to make incoherent assertions, or else that hatred of all beings induced him to propound absurd doctrines by accepting which they would become thoroughly confused. ...Buddha's doctrine has to be entirely disregarded by all those who have regard for their own happiness.[10]

Not discernibly ecumenical in their tone, these remarks were uttered by the same Śaṅkara who, shortly below, will insist that nobody has the right to contest alleged ultimate claims of other individuals, like the claim of Brahman-knowledge. As a result Śaṅkara's judgment of Buddha has led some hard critics to respond that he projected his own incoherent syntheses on to Buddha. Others have inferred not only that Śaṅkara was ignorant of original Buddhism, but that his eagerness for the renaissance of Brahminism, through accommodation to features of popular and Buddhist religions, was not a lucid exemplification of Hindu non-attachment or *disinterested* action, but rather of a driving, if not a vested *interest.* Speaking of the Brahminic revival in general, Max Weber recorded an observation which he thought was crucial for the understanding of every religion, particularly those in which selected groups would earn their bread by religious practice itself: "the driving motive of the Brahmans in this reception and accommodation process was in part quite grossly material. They wished to protect the many prebends and incidental fees which were available if one accepted the service of these ineradicable folk deities."[11] In the absence of historical records or Marxian views which explain all phenomena economically, one would be hard pressed to provide satisfactorily scientific proof that Weber's important censure may be applied to Śaṅkara in person as well as to Brahmins in general. But as for the latter, general allegations do exist —even in the "early" versions of the *Mbh*—of enormous, tax-free land grants, of Brahminic power and prestige gained in legal and feudalistic familial services, and of Brahminic custody of the royal treasury.

2. *The moderate critique.* A less ambitious judgment would by-pass Śaṅkara's personal motives or unconscious interests in the restoration of Brahminism. Instead it would simply state that up to the present century his *darśana* or synthesis has been consistently utilized by leaders of subsequent religious generations. With a preoccupation not clearly or consistently exceeding monetary or political inspiration Śaṅkara's *followers* strove to integrate the many popular circles of Indian religions and mores into Brahminism's own single ambit. Although many Brahmins, let alone members of other classes, were not actually converted to the new or renewed asceticism and mysticism of Śaṅkara, they were inspired by it in the way that masses are often attracted by the life styles of intelligentsias or other power elites.[12] From the ethical perspective, in other words, in spite of the continuing popularity of so-called "secular" or popular Hindu values and morality, Śaṅkara's school had created or occasioned a passive atmosphere which was not conducive to social ethics in the Western sense, whatever the latter's own shortcomings.

3. *The soft or sympathetic critique.* Without claiming the infal-

libility of the cynic's power for total generalization, one may observe that these wondrous assimilative processes, whereby a multiplicity of religions can be incorporated into one, are not unique to the history of Hinduism and have manifested themselves in the histories of other major traditions. Unless one statically relegates religions to their original phenomena, one cannot deny that they discover within their own traditions developmental seeds or values capable of intra-traditional growth.[13] Prescinding from theoretical justifiability, in point of fact religious and philosophical structures have consistently arisen in many lands and times to accommodate the most disparate beliefs under the same roof. Whatever the causes, these incorporations have undeniably served economic, political, and other social amalgamations. The point presently intended is that they may be designated as intra-traditional developments, whether they were conservative, reformative, or even revolutionary. Sometimes the unions required consolidations, other times break-ups preliminary to regrouping.

The soft critical innuendo that Śaṅkara's thought too was not purely religious in its growth but wholly or largely epiphenomenal or reflective of other socio-economic forces already at work is an inference which requires more scientific proof or rebuttal. The circle of testimonies would have to include Śaṅkara's own self-justification, which defended his religious and not consciously economic motives through the ultimate unchallengeability of alleged inner experience: "For how can one man contest the fact of another [person] possessing the knowledge of Brahman—vouched for by his heart's conviction—and at the same time continuing to enjoy bodily existence?"[14] This insistence on the irrefutability of religious experience brings up, of course, the classic question of its verifiability for others and the extent to which maxims of verification might be relevant, for example: "By their fruits you shall know these intuitions." At any rate, Śaṅkara, like his followers, claimed the authentic absorption of disparate devotions into what they said was the traditional core of Hinduism, namely, non-dualistic Vedānta.

Śaṅkara's final enthronement of *Av* as Hinduism's principal or ultimate point of view is found mainly in his commentaries on the *Ups*, the *Gītā*, and on the *Vedānta* or *Brahma Sūtras* (aphorisms) of Vyāsa (Bādarāyaṇa).[15] In his commentary on the latter in particular, Śaṅkara's split-level ontology of ultimate and relative truth proposed non-egalitarian and double standards of ethics which were not thought to be discriminatory for arbitrary reasons. Instead his commentary beckons the reader to the apparently incontestable fact that some individuals simply lack the capabilities of others. Not everyone can presently live "beyond good and evil" in a final liberation (*moksha*) from the dualistic illusion that they are different from Brahman. Although not their last, the best hope of some is restricted to producing the *karma* (as moral compensation) which will effect better rebirths.[16] For these less "equal" and less fortunate individuals who require higher, this-worldly rebirths, ethical deeds serve a more directly preparatory function than they do in the case of those ready for *moksha*. In Eliot Deutsch's theorization, the liberated individual (*jīvanmukta*) realizes his non-dualistic identification with Brahman in the concomitant awareness that ultimately Brahman is categorically one and lacks personal or theistic qualities or attributes (*Nirguṇa Brahman*). Liberation in this case does not originate in moral deeds but in the matrix, or at least context of mind-culture (*jñāna-yoga*). One could even say that abstention from immorality lacks a positive soteriological function and that "all obligation is an erroneous imagination."[17] In practice, nonetheless, immoral deeds presuppose egoity (*ahaṁkāra*) which is based on an individualistic conception of the self, the opposite of which would entail a kind of love.[18] Thus, almost begrudgingly, an altruistic morality is given backdoor entry after all. But the good (*śreyaḥ*) does not include the pleasant (*preyaḥ*), let alone *artha* (wealth) or *kāma* (as pleasure or love).[19]

Still, according to interpreters like Venkatarama Raghavan, this other-worldly rejection of *kāma* or *śreyaḥ* does not preclude a social ethic. Raghavan opines that Śaṅkara's own life's position as an ardent religious devotee is a sign that those already liberated "in this body" may continue, like Brahman, to "work for the welfare of humanity."[20] In Mysore Hiriyanna's opinion, this kind of love is universal, spontaneously virtuous, and most solidly grounded, because it is based on the trans-egoistic principle of identification of everyone with the one *Ātman* (Self)-Brahman.[21] Cromwell Crawford concurs in that a life of contemplation (*jñāna*) for Śaṅkara was "a complete expansion of the inner life" and encompassed a life of moral willing free from "moralistic individualism."[22]

4. *An alternative critique.* In contrast with Deutsch's exegesis about moral works or deeds, this much seems directly obvious from a reading of Śaṅkara's own commentary. Śaṅkara admits that all works, even non-attached good works, cease at *moksha*,[23] (where knowledge and will are one).[24] In addition, ritual sacrifices and virtues like calmness and subjection of the senses "are to be looked upon as remote—indirect—means" to knowledge.[25] For the present, in a sense surpassing the *sola fides* (faith alone) of Martin Luther or later Mahāyāna Buddhism, moral acts and norms seem to be merely permitted rather than enjoined. Works are at very best normative in an ethos of non-attachment and whatever passive, psychological, and social atmosphere about activity is consequently created or inferred. True knowledge will prevent the fruits of actions from clinging to an individual even "should he perform works during his whole life. ..."[26]

If one chooses to insist that Śaṅkara's mysticism does or must lead to social, this-worldly passivity, one may also refer to his personal style of life as well as to his writings. For Śaṅkara personally promoted the innovative conviction that one might omit the first three stages of life, including the married householder's and earning stage and the works it embodied. In clearest counterpoint with the epics and with other Vedic and popular praise for the householder's stage, Śaṅkara's exegesis is revolutionary : "as thus the four *āśramas* [stages] are equally taught by scripture,they are to be gone through equally either in the way of option (between them) or in the way of comprehension (of all of them)."[27]

Eyed through some Indian evaluations about a land which grew permanently burdened with Jaina and Hindu ascetics (*sadhus*, *sannyāsin*, and *yogis*) and with Buddhist monastics subsisting on the labor of lay men and women, Śaṅkara's magisterial ability to confirm the solely ascetical life-style must have had the widest social and economic implications. Brahminic, Buddhist, and Jaina codes all carefully specified the ordinary person's responsibilities for monetary care of religious *virtuousi*, to borrow Weber's appellation. Nevertheless, if it fell to laity to finance the lives and careers of this vast array of priests and ascetics, Śaṅkara felt sure that the laity's subsidy would not lack compensation. For the *Ups* declared, in his words, that somehow "the fruit of meditations in which the priest is the agent goes to the Sacrificer."[28] If this doctrine met no archcombatant or Lutheran reformer as did the Roman teaching on indulgences, perhaps lay submission to it occurred because Śaṅkara's (heterodox?) divergence from classical belief and practice was *quantitative* rather than qualitative. In short, perhaps most Hindus accepted non-dualistic, passive moral mysticism as the true core not only of Upanishadic Brahminism (perduring in *Manu* and the *Gītā*), but of historical Hinduism as a whole, including its Vedic and popular dimensions.

Alternatively, the bolder conjecture states that in general Śaṅkara's doctrines stood against the wider Vedic and ongoing popular traditions in a *qualitative* way. His teachings about works, the married and earning stage of life, and the this-worldly goals of life-affirmation (*artha*, *kāma*, and *dharma*) varied substantively from the wider umbrella called Hinduism. It thereby triggered the most far-reaching ramifications for Hindu morality. For all of his eclectic genius, the moral by-products of Śaṅkara's views were in historical fact, if not from logical necessity, opposite to the world-affirming social moralities of the *Vedas*, epics, and popular culture in general.[29] In this factual sense, they were revolutionary. They left a prevailing psychological mood even in their two-way dialectic with the so-called "secular" and popular moralities. The further extent and concrete details of this impact awaits measurement in other studies. These would include not only popular literature above all, but also the labyrinthine, mystical words of Śaṅkara and his school. The latter may still conceal more than they will processively reveal in the future (that is, possibly some form of positive ethics).[30]

In lesser contrast with the wider tradition, but not without its own social and moral implications for anyone who would respect Śaṅkara's authority in the future, was his teaching about the four classes or *varṇas*, especially the lowest class, the *śūdras*. Adamantly and vividly, Śaṅkara upheld the tradition that the latter were incapable of either studying the *Vedas* or knowing Brahman:

> There is, moreover, an express prohibition (of the Śūdras studying the Veda). "His tongue is to be slit if he pronounces it; his body is to be cut through if he preserves it."[31]

5a. *Rāmānuja's qualified non-dualism* (*Viśiṣṭādvaita*). Within a few centuries after Śaṅkara, a number of Vedāntists and their followers, led by Rāmānuja (1046-1137 C.E.) a) tried to qualify and popularize Śaṅkara's doctrines of unqualified non-dualism and b) practically reemphasized devotion (*bhakti*). They spoke of Brahman with qualities or attributes (*saguṇa*-Brahman), who could be an object of worship. Why? Possibly because devotion was increasingly useful after the "demoralizing" Muslim invasions. It was a culturally and politically unifying force which could better integrate folk religions than could Śaṅkara's synthesis.[32]

A phenomenal factor frequently ignored is that followers of Śaṅkara and Rāmānuja fought strenuously with one another.[33] Depending on one's point of view, eventually a Vedāntic, existential coalition or syncretism, or else a planned, eclectic synthesis, would pull these forces and ideas together in dialectical if not complementary relationships. But first there was a battle. Whether it really centered on truth, power, economics, other socio-cultural elements, or mixtures, the point here is that Rāmānuja's devotional and more popular version of non-dualistic Vedānta embodied the following *moral* implications.

Rāmānuja's *saguṇa* Brahman (Brahman with attributes or virtues) was morally normative for everyone (of every caste!): compassionate, just, and generous. Yet, ultimately, since Brahman-*Ātman* remained the true subject, agent, and ground of all moral activity and love, as a principle of trans-egoistic identification, the tradition of *non-attached* action (*niṣkāma karma*) stands out as the ideal ethos of moral conduct. Conjointly, caste (*varṇa*) and stage-of-life (*āśrama*) duties (still extant!) are, as previously, to be performed for duty's sake, in continuity with the teaching of the *Gītā*. Rāmānuja also retained Śaṅkara's ethical assumption that *karma* (as moral action) stands as a mere prelude to knowledge (*jñāna yoga*). Therefore, Rāmānuja's virtues may be perceived as a total ethos of moral passivity: "calm, subdued, patient, satisfied, and collected."[34]

While the reader may interpret or reinterpret Rāmānuja's moral teachings as interpersonally I-Thou (à la Martin Buber or H. R. Niebuhr) and within the reach of everyone, for most people even this kind of devotional and preparatory moral asceticism was too difficult. For them Rāmānuja's technique of instant self-surrender (*prapatti*) was introduced.[35] It resembled the soon-to-follow, fideistic, simple profession of belief in and salvific recitation of Amida Buddha's name in Japanese Mahāyāna Buddhism (Shinran Shōnin's [1173-1262 C.E.] *Jōdo Shinshu* [True Pure Land of Bliss Sect]). The preliminary self-control required for true devotion (*bhakti*) and knowledge (*jñāna*) had become too much. Instantaneous, devotional self-surrender, not to mention the attainability of Brahma(n)-realization by all castes, rendered Rāmānuja's teachings more popular. Like the followers of Śaṅkara and of the dualistic Vedāntist, Madhva (1197-1276 C.E.), future reformers would have to take Rāmānuja's impact into account.

A hard critique might infer that Śaṅkara attracted both the masses and modern reformers simply because of the dazzling (if widely uncomprehended), intellectual intricacy of his system —a common cross-cultural phenomenon in religion and philosophy of awe turning into belief. Similarly, it might conclude that the less intellectual but more charismatic Rāmānuja relied on "cheap grace" or easier salvation. Bracketing these conjectures, the present thesis is simply that the thought of Rāmānuja, like that of Śaṅkara, was and is susceptible to passive moral interpretations. The question then lingers: does either leader satisfactorily represent a coalition of pluralistic Hindu ethics or exhaust its mystical wellsprings?

5b. *The modern, prophetic, and charismatic revitalization of Hindu morality.* With a dash of poetical license Max Scheler once argued that as an attempt to justify applied morality the origin of philosophical ethics "is always connected with processes of disintegration in an existing ethos. Of course, such a 'scientific' ethics has no value *beyond* the intuitive evidence of its ethos. ...It only formulates the predominant and traditional opinions about moral values. It cannot subject them to criticism, because they are its factual basis."[36]

From Scheler's rather fragmented view on this issue, therefore, one could surmise that the continuing absence of philosophical, analytical ethics in the Vedāntic and other Indian philosophical systems is simply a correlated tribute to the ability of the people's ethics to survive on its own. Speaking comparatively, some have contended that in China and Japan Mahāyāna Buddhism has provided only a way of *seeing* or experiencing life, relegating moral ways of *doing* to the capable guidance of Confucianism, folk religions, Shinto, or the *samurai*, warrior code of absolute loyalty (*Bushidō*). In parallel, one could build a case that applied Hindu morality was already so capably administered by the law codes (*dharmaśāstras*), epics, and other popular classics and oral traditions that the philosophical systems could simply bypass the ethical task entirely. Like well-fed and protected social, Western liberals, the Indian philosophers need not have feared either deemphasis or downright detraction of moral law and order, because morals were already adequately secured in the *śāstras*, rituals, dramas, and hearts of the people. Therefore, the philosophers' residual, silent attitudes about ethics or metaethical justifications cannot be taken for their most comprehensive or final word. That is, they require further interpretation along the lines of modern neo-Vedāntists and reformers. In other words, the philosopher mystics harbored implicit, positive, moral opinions after all, but felt no need to express or develop them. These opinions lie buried in their writings, ready for historical excavation, explication, or reconstruction and development. Some continue in the conviction, however, that no such excavation or development would be successful. Philosophical, analytical ethics was put into limbo, for morality was simply left to popular laws and customs.

The problem with this upbeat hermeneutic relates to its hidden stamina for tolerating and even accepting the ways in which morals had been and were being recently realized in practice, an endurance beyond the tolerance of modern Indian reformers like Aurobindo Ghose, R. Tagore, M. K. Gandhi, or Vinoba Bhave. Not that the reformers came to place their humanitarian hopes in the analytical justification of ethical norms or in popular, consequentialistic argumentation about which actions are more morally rational. The record of moral reasoning's isolated power to move the self or others is almost as discouraging as David Hume portrayed it. It seems that society must rather rely on the suasive powers of reinforcing rewards and punishments, rhetoric, propaganda, and more explicit means of force; institutional, legal, military, or even dictatorial. Living in India and other third or "fourth" world countries, to say nothing of the inner cities of the first two worlds, tempts one to believe that provisional dictatorships, right or left, are the only hope to get people on their feet and moving in moral cooperation, if not with some moral altruism. Further, the familiar rejoinder that appeals to moral reason have never had a fair trial seems unhelpful. This allegation dissolves into the limitedly academic question as to whether the factual weakness of reason stems from the finitude of human ears or from the faintness or confusion of reason's voice. Or, at least it so dissolves unless the populace can be (reasonably?) convinced that clarification of moral language and reason would produce a stunning array of successfully negotiated conflicts of interest.

But if Hindu reformers ever conceived of ethics in such limitedly rationalistic, metaethical, or utilitarian fashions, they might well have despaired of its outcome, given the morally immobile human condition which perdures to the present. Alternately, reformist hopes rather tended, in Indian as well as other cultures, in the direction of morals prophetically instigated, charismatically impelled, and legislatively enforced by various strategies, like civil rights' laws, however physically non-violent. In general, therefore, the reformers' prophetic stance would bolster the view that Indian social morals had and has been in a state of deterioration, and that if Indian philosophers thought that codes and customs were in little need of rational clarification or of more emotive and esthetical inspiration, they were regrettably mistaken.

While the targets of reformist denunciations were customary, political, and economic institutions, their immediate objectives did not entail the construction of a new ethical system. Neither did they involve the enunciation of new middle axioms or norms which would almost magically untangle or negotiate all conflicts of interest. Instead, the reformers sounded a prophetic, charismatic, and esthetical call to action through ritual, drama, and poetry. For instance, Sukumar Sen, in describing Nobel Laureate Rabindranath Tagore's (1861-1941) pain at his country's "shameful backwardness ... placid stupidity and profound unreason" records the following stirring lines from Tagore's *Naivedya*—poetry quoted above which may be applied cross-culturally:

> This death must be pierced through—this mesh of fear, this rubbish of inert mass heaped mountain high, dead junk. Oh! wake up you must on this glorious morning, in this stirring world of action.[37]

Postscript. M. K. Gandhi. Paradigm for Intra-cultural Social Reform (1869-1948).

Among Hindu visionaries and social reformers, M. K. Gandhi, in spite of all the greatness of his dream and his deeds, seemed separated from the breadth of his culture's tradition. On the other hand, the esthetically oriented Rabindranath Tagore seemed at one with it. A few concluding words about Tagore at the end of this section will highlight Gandhi's relationship to previous tradition in general. Contrary to the expectations possibly raised by the chapter's title, Gandhi has not been given equal attention in this volume with Śaṅkara, simply because others like Iyer and Erikson have already treated Gandhi so thoroughly. Yet as the chapter title attempts to signify, Gandhi is equally important as a paradigmatic figure for other religions and cultures (see note 40).

Perhaps the most fascinating aspect about Gandhi as a social leader of the masses is that he was fundamentally a mystic. He was also more representative of populist moral aspirations than the philosophers. Gandhi claimed the twofold realization or belief that 1) God is spiritual truth and non-attached love (*satyāgraha*) whose antithesis is hatred expressed in *himsā* (violence) and symbolized by Rāvaṇa (the demonic within people) instead of Rāma; 2) God's theistic, overcoming, and world-concerned activity is normative for human beings; hatred and violence must be increasingly minimized by loving and non-violent resistance. In promoting national and cultural autonomy from British rule through such resistance Gandhi's leadership prepared the way for national liberation and independence.

Further, in terms of eradicating racial oppression, Gandhi's traumatic experience and struggle with South African racial discrimination towards all dark skinned peoples (including Indians) catapulted him into pioneer battles for civil rights, especially for outcastes and untouchables. To such destitute masses Gandhi became credible by his voluntary non-possession, labor, and identification with the poor. Lastly, in his passion for Indian unity between Hindus, Muslims, and others, it seemed to some as if he might compromise traditional Hinduism beyond recognition. His synthesis of Western Christian and political ideas with Buddhism, Jainism, a type of Vedānta, and Hindu devotionalism—*bhakti* Vaishnavism or devotion to Vishnu as well as to Rāma—did little to alleviate the fears of those who mistrusted the direction of his charismatic power and leadership. It was such uneasiness about cultural and religious compromise which led to Gandhi's assassination by a fellow Hindu in 1948, a martyrdom which only enhanced his leadership toward human equality by largely non-violent means and helped to inspire similar leadership—at least until the assassination of Martin Luther King and concomitant world trends back to *military* resistance.

With regard to Gandhi's directly moral teachings, the comparative philosopher, P. T. Raju, has observed that Gandhi regarded universal "*dharma* [the welfare of the whole world] as the highest human value, *an end in itself* [emphasis added] to which even *moksha* is secondary during life on earth."[38] *Dharma's* primary virtues, including courage, could be cultivated by the most unliberated of human beings. Such persons could and would become what they believed themselves to be—self-fulfilling prophecy.[39]

If the charismatic pen is mightier than sword or gun, Gandhi's direct and indirect worldwide influence must have caused his opponents considerable alarm. The quantity of his writings, when completely published, will fill over eighty large volumes. However, Raghavan N. Iyer is eager to correct the dominant impression that Gandhi's impact was mainly devotional and charismatic. Instead, argues Iyer, it was political and highly moral. In his exhaustively thorough research into Gandhi's moral and political thought, Iyer emphasizes that the origin of Gandhi's formation was not only the *Gitā*. It also comprised earlier and contemporary Hindu reformers like Aurobindo Ghose and other sources mentioned above. The non-dualistic *Ups*, Manu, Śaṅkara, and the theistic *Ry* also contributed to his development.[40] Gandhi's dying words expressed the devotional-moral worldview of *bhakti* : "Hei [oh] Rāma."

In the *Gitā*'s devotional spirit, Gandhi felt that morality was grounded in the human heart rather than in an isolated intellect. The autonomy and supremacy of individual conscience over civil authority was, therefore, guarded religiously. However, Gandhi expected unquestioning obedience to duty as portrayed in the *Gitā*. Detached service to humanity for its own sake and treating every individual as an end rather than an instrument were idealized in categorical Kantian fashion. Accordingly, critics, like Tagore accused Gandhi of enslaving human conscience to duty as *Gandhi* saw it—disciplined, blind obedience.

Unlike Kant, Gandhi thought of no one as inherently depraved or morally helpless or dependent on reason alone. Nevertheless, he eventually became disillusioned with the inertia and non-obedience of undisciplined, "unmonasticized" masses. In spite of Gandhi's appeal to the powerful sanction of karmic compensation, in spite of his surprising relativistic willingness to compromise on the use of psychological force (propaganda), physical violence, and even war, Gandhi's rule of qualified non-violence was short-lived. It survived only among a small minority who were willing to accept it as a given absolute rather than on debatable empirical and tactical grounds. The same phenomenon occurred when *ahimsā* was given inter-cultural transplants by Martin Luther King and others. Abstracting from the oppressor's perduring unwillingness to cooperate reliably with oppressed groups' non-violent strategies, perhaps other factors would have to appear before sufficient numbers could be persuaded about *ahimsā* to make it an ideal which worked—factors like strengthened and more open lines of communication by mass media, a greater recognition of the need not only for discipline but for the charismatic and esthetical dimensions of life, or perhaps simply a more developed stage of evolution within humanity as a whole. Add to these factors the removal of in-built oppressive elements, like gross economic inequity, which in themselves are daily declarations of war.

Like Kant, Gandhi strongly contended that ends were colored or discolored by means. The use of violence would inevitably subvert and replace the noblest of ends. Two questions which Gandhi left for posterity, therefore, were : 1) could not *ahimsā* in turn be so absolutized as to preempt and invert every other human goal (transcendentalizing them out of existence); and 2) could the disciplined, monasticized elitism of Gandhian leaders neglect the fuller, esthetical wellsprings of the Indian tradition ? In point of fact, notwithstanding Gandhi's heroism, genius, emotive charisma, and his dispositive contribution to modern civil rights in India and elsewhere—a movement which swept from racism to sexism and numerous other exploitations of minority groups—the great souled (*Mahātma*) leader fell far short of his own goals. This failure occurred even though he had great disciples like the land reformer and distributor Vinoba Bhave. Although Gandhi's eclectic genius had blended a thousand Indian and foreign sources into an orchestrated program of devotional action and mystical contemplation, it had overlooked the populist and esthetical traditions without which the heart stands still. True, Gandhi had asserted that the *Rāmāyaṇa* of Tulasīdās was the greatest book in literature and that with the *Gītā* it was his infallible guide of conduct. But he had taken both books in their limitedly devotional rather than their fuller, esthetical dimension, especially the *Rāmāyaṇa*'s.

Rabindranath Tagore. To the contrary, the mystic and poet, Tagore seemed to bypass entirely Vedāntic other-worldliness for a direct and unambiguous interest in human beings as such, especially lower castes, widows, children, and the poor. His devotionalistic theism clashed more loudly than Gandhi's with the teachings of Śaṅkara and *Av.* God as Truth is known through the insight of love rather than reason. Religious elitism is intolerable. Priests are to earn their living.[41] For Tagore the earliest Indian ascetics

> lived in an atmosphere of purity but not of Puritanism, of the simple life but not the life of self-mortification. [Unlike Gandhi] They never advocated celibacy and they had constant intercommunication with other people who lived the life of worldly interest. ... It was never a [Upanishadic] philosophy of renunciation of a negative character, but arealization completely comprehensive.[42]

In the illustrious poet Kālidāsa's day, the forest colonies did not consist of "ascetics fiercely in love with a lingering suicide, but men of serene sanity who sought to realize the spiritual meaning of their life."[43] Denying that poverty had spiritual merit, Tagore refused to glorify or "imagine any special value in poverty when it is a mere negation."[44] Without the householders' world-building wisdom, discipline "is not true discipline, but merely the meaningless following of custom, which is only a disguise for stupidity."[45] or for spiritual egoism. Afraid of Gandhi's nationalism, Tagore moved out of the pioneer reformer, Ram Mohan Roy's (1772-1883) theistic, nationalistic *Brahmosamaj* to become a poet of universal human feelings. Tagore was the first Asian to receive the Nobel Prize in literature

—for *Gitāñjali, Song Offerings*. It is precisely through Tagore's esthetical sensitivity that he has presented modern Hindus and the world with a still available mystical-social alternative to Gandhi's.

Tagore's esthetical, mystical summons to the "stirring world and morning of action and sharing" is concrete testimony that Vedic and popular Hindu imagery can be used to depict a mystical-moral world-view which is intuitively and movingly affirmative of life and morality. In this sense, Tagore is more representative of the entirety of Hindu traditions than either the philosophers or previous reformers, including the great Śaṅkara and the great-souled Gandhi themselves. In the final analysis, how Tagore's words move to action is conceptually indescribable apart from his own poetic lines, where beauty is its own summons to gratitude for life and to moral response. Tagore's stirring flower of Hindu tradition appeared from the people's soil rather than cosmic, mystical space. With the imagery of the embrace, kiss, heart, love, canker of deception, stars, feminine in the core of creation, streams, waves, etc., Tagore speaks most movingly of the suffering of love and the joy of life. Notes 46-48 indicate how I had intended to quote these most beautiful lines as an integral part of this volume and project and in the promotion of Tagore himself. But due to the complex and, for me, most demanding economic and other limitations imposed on this thirty-one line collage by the publishers of the texts in question, I am unable to fulfill what scholarship would request.

Conclusion. Arriving at this chapter's final query, does Hindu mysticism, or its Śaṅkarite and neo-Vedāntic versions (both indigenous and Western) necessarily slow down active empathy toward a social ethic of committed decisions and humanistic interaction? The answer is sadly affirmative, even if the life-affirmative stage of life is allowed (merely) a developmental, expedient, or instrumental position on the path to mystical realization. But if traditional Vedic and Hindu values like non-violence, compassion and sharing can simultaneously be sought as ends as well as means, Hindu mysticism, like the life-and world-affirming ethos of "passionate indifference" of Pierre Teilhard de Chardin, need not beget an atmosphere non-conducive to the evolving growth of a cosmos which, for some mystics, is non-dualistically a divine-human milieu.

Put positively, from either a supposedly pure, phenomenological *weltanschauung*, or even an agnostic perspective, there is both Hindu and cross-cultural evidence to demonstrate that Hindu and other non-attachment and contemplation does not always obstruct but often leads on in the journey towards practical compassion—an ethos which embraces both the spiritual and material well-being of others.[49] A mysticism which does not disincarnate the spiritual from the material, nor the ethical from its emotive and esthetical wellsprings, can in part jump over the thorny problem of reasoning from facts and complex consequences to normative values and "oughts." The source of this leap lies in either religious or even limitedly humanistic convictions that all human beings are somehow one with one another and the cosmos—like the Hindu conviction that all are one Self in Brahman.

As for Hindu mysticism in particular, the documentary support for this hope lies in further study, not of isolated philosophical systems alone, but of the pluralistic gestalt of Hindu traditions divulged in a broad range of popular and esthetical literature (*kāvya*), so familiar to the Indian people and many scholars. This gestalt includes, among many others, the ten sources surveyed in chapter seven from the *Kural* to the *Love Songs of Vidyāpati*. There, alleged manisfestations (*avatārs*) of the divine, like Rāma, Sītā, and Krishna, became increasingly inseparable from human goals and values : *artha* (wealth), *kāma* (as pleasure and love), and *dharma* (as moral justice, love, and active service). In the historical populist-elitist dialectic, some *mystics* separated religion from social morality and rendered the exchange competitive rather than complementary and harmonious. But the *converse* did not occur, at least not quite. *The people's ideals* joined human life and action much more frequently with the esthetical in its most comprehensive sense, reaching beyond vision to every experience. For all that even agnostics may know, this esthetics might include not only human manifestations of life and beauty, but Life, Beauty, and conscious Bliss itself (as the Absolute). If, in the face of human finitude and seemingly meaningless suffering for many, the agnostic cannot move himself or herself to believe in this dream or even to live one's life as a wager in favor of it, perhaps it may still be respected as a *wish*. If it is futile, it does not compromise human intelligence.

If it is a dream to come true, then perhaps the Almighty will mercifully accept it as a token or a "widow's mite" of faith. If faith or religious realization is a gift, perhaps it is less evenly distributed in its strength than in its aspect as human integrity. Merely pretended belief or religious experience would seem to be more of a religious obstacle than a help, especially if by some wild chance eternal life depended more on openness and honesty than on religious gifts not distributed (at least equally) to every person.

To stress, therefore, what the author hopes is already obvious to many, the evidence for the traditional Hindu correlation between humanism and mysticism lies far less in the isolated works of Śaṅkara than in the entire ocean of the people's poems, rituals, and dramas. The author's previous verification of this ethical claim can be spot-checked in the popular works surveyed in chapters five and seven or in nearly any large sample of comprehensive, Hindu literature and drama beyond the smaller Brahminic and Vedāntic circles.[50] In that wider traditional milieu the mystical "word," is theoretically capable of helping to galvanize both indigenous and intercultural social visions and moralities about which some people have not yet dared to dream.[51]

NOTES

1. Some readers may wish to review the phenomenon that *Av* of Śaṅkara and others is only one of six major *darśanas* (points of view, literally, but systematic ones). These thrived particularly between 500-750 C.E. The other *darśanas* may be grouped as *Nyāya-Vaiśeṣika*, *Sāṅkhya-Yoga*, and *Pūrva Mīmāṃsā* (*Early Inquiries*). All are said to be faithful to the *Vedas* (orthodox or *āstika*) and somehow complementary to one another. The unfortunately neglected *Cārvāka* philosophy was, like Buddhism and Jainism, called unorthodox (*nāstika*), because it admittedly rejected Vedic authority and remained materialistic and categorically atheistic. As happened in other religions, these elitist *darśanas* waned in influence between the sixteenth and nineteenth centuries, but within the last century *Av* in particular has regained varying influences on reformers, on the general Indian mood, and on Western philosophers who have been eager to project their own monistic and transcendentalist tendencies. Like the ancient *Ups* and the original *Uttara Mīmāṃsā* or *Vedānta* or *Brahma-Sūtras* of Badarāyaṇa (555 of them attempting to summarize the *Ups*), the six main *darśanas* (developing the *Brahma-sūtras*) did not wholly ignore the potentially this-worldly virtues of non-violence, giving, and compassion. Moreover, they entailed varied dependencies on human authority,

ethical reasoning, and intuition. The most helpful summary of their moral content in terms of primary sources exists in Crawford, *The Evolution of Hindu Ethical Ideals.* The increasingly sparse ethical content of these systems may be partly responsible for the fact that there is little interest in analytical ethics or metaethics in India today: see N. K. Devaraja in *Hinduism and Christianity.* But lack of ethical analysis is not the same as lack of moral statements. The largely aliterate Indian people would have to hear of the *darśanas* indirectly through recitation or dramatization. Thus, their exposure to *Av* must have been limited to some degree. So also would be their own moral feedback to the system, especially given the authoritative posture assumed by Brahmins. —While this chapter will conclude that the *moral* teaching of the most celebrated Vedāntist, Śaṅkara, (also the most famous philosopher of India in general) stood in lowest profile, it does not contend that traditional Hindu mysticism is incapable of grounding or partly inspiring a life-affirming social ethic— as in the interpretations of modern reformers like Aurobindo Ghose, M. K. Gandhi, Vinoba Bhave, and especially Rabindranath Tagore.—A bibliography, complementary to Crawford's most recent of all Hindu ethical volumes, and which extends to philosophers, Vedāntists, and reformers may be found in S. Radhakrishnan and Charles A. Moore, ed., *A Sourcebook in Indian Philosophy*, pp. 646-69. On the ethics of reformers one must add several important sources, like Robert A. McDermott's comprehensive studies in *Cross Currents* 22,1 (Winter 1972), 2-115.

2. On the Vedāntic acceptance of the *dharmaśāstras* or law codes see Eliot Deutsch, *Advaita Vedānta : A Philosophical Reconstruction* (Honolulu : East-West Center Press, 1969), p. 100 n. 1. One may add to his highly selective bibliography of philosophical works his own *A Source Book in Advaita Vedānta*, ed. with J. A. B. van Buitenen (Honolulu : East-West Center Press, 1971); K. C. Bhattacharya, *Search for the Absolute in Neo-Vedānta* (Honolulu : University of Hawaii Press, 1975); S. Bhattacharya et al, *The Encyclopedia of Indian Philosophies*, Vol. I (Delhi : Motilal Banarsidass, 1970); and Karl H. Potter, *Presuppositions of India's Philosophies* (Englewood Cliffs, New Jersey : Prentice-Hall, Inc., 1968). In his empathetically phenomenological *The Comparative Study of Religions* (New York and London : Columbia University Press, 1958), Joachim Wach seemed to extend the priority of metaphysics over epistemology from Vedānta to the whole of Hinduism. See p. 20 and passim.

3. See Lal Mani Joshi, *Studies in the Buddhistic Culture of India* (Delhi-Patna-Varanasi : Motilal Banarsidass, 1967), pp. 286-97.

4. Raimundo Panikkar distinguishes planned eclecticism (identified in the present corpus with "synthesis") from after-the-fact, existential syncretism. Either process, of course, may be authentically or at least sincerely pursued, and also abused. See Panikkar's "Some Notes on Syncretism and Eclecticism Related to the Growth of Human Consciousness," in *Religious Syncretism in Antiquity*, ed. Birger A. Pearson (Missoula, Montana : Scholars Press, 1975), pp. 47-62; references to some of Panikkar's other works as well as his comparison of the Christian and Hindu religions can be located in "Christians and So-Called 'Non-Christians,'" 281-308.

5. *Bhāgavata Purāṇa* X.20.22.

6. See Milton Singer, *The Great Tradition in a Metropolitan Center : Madras,*

pp. 151, 155, and 176. Within the context of the still popular cults of devotion (*bhakti*) popularized through rituals, recitations, dramas, films, and other mass media, Singer notes that "these urban Brahmans" are still taking "an increasing interest in popular religious culture, traditionally designed for lower castes, women, and children" (p. 176).

7. Joshi, *Studies*, pp. 396-97.

8. Śaṅkara, *Śārīraka-Bhāṣya*; George Thibaut, trans., *The Vedānta Sūtras of Bādarāyaṇa with Commentary by Ścṅkara* (=*VS*), The Sacred Books of The East, Vols. 34, 37 (Oxford : The Clarendon Press, 1890, 1896), II,2.28. Like Rāmānuja's commentary, Śaṅkara's was reprinted by Dover in 1962. According to Eliot Deutsch, *Advaita Vedānta*, p. 96, Śaṅkara's non-dualism does not extend Hegel's or Berkeley's idealism. The phenomenal world of names and forms (*nāma-rūpa*) is "realistically" known and philosophically necessary. Whereas knowledge of this world is "ultimately false," restricted to only a finite "portion of human experience (*ibid.*, p. 97), still, in present existence, the dualistic separation of "subject and object in all noetic experience" is "an undeniable fact of experience" (*ibid.*, p. 96). Further, according to T. M. P. Mahadevan, "Contemporary Relevance of the Insights of Advaita," in Chatterjee, ed., *Contemporary Indian Philosophy*, p. 115, even Śaṅkara's statements about finite reality's final illusoriness do not approach nihilism. That is, they do not negate, but re-interpret the world, equating its reality with Brahman. In spite of the provisional acceptance of the reality of relative existence, the moral life in Vedānta remained a mere means towards liberation, as in the *Vedantasara : or the Essence of Vedanta of Sadānnda* trans. Swami Nikhilananda.

9. The lower knowledge of the phenomenal world (*aparāvidyā*) must be accepted until one experiences the knowledge of reality of Brahman (*parāvidyā*). See Deutsch, *Advaita Vedānta*, p. 81.

10. *VS*, II.2.32.

11. See Max Weber, *The Religion of India*, p. 297; see also p. 299. Daniel Ingalls adds that "an enormous number of land grants [tax free to Brahmins] are revealed by the inscriptions." See his "The Brahman Tradition" in Singer, *Traditional India*, p. 6. Brahmins served as priests for the ruling class (*kshatriyas*) and the well-to-do. Ministers of kings everywhere were "Brahman scholars who wed much of their wealth and prestige to their intellectual accomplishments in the Sastric tradition" *ibid.*, p. 7.

12. See Ingalls, *ibid.*, p.8; and Singer's introduction, *ibid.*, pp. xi and xiv. Already possessing official custody of the general or great Hindu tradition, the Brahmins would assimilate (in Robert Redfield's diagram of small circles within a large one) the "many local and popular traditions," Singer, *ibid.*, p. xv.

13. Panikkar, *Some Notes on Syncretism*, pp. 56-62.

14. *VS* IV.1.15.

15. The *Brahma Sūtras*' first codification or formulation of the Vedānta system selected passages of the *Ups* which could be turned in monistic, mystical, and world-denying directions. These *sūtras* furnish literary records of a tradition (500-200 B.C.E.?) which unites the ethos of the *Ups* to that of *Av*. They are often identified with the philosophical system (the sixth major *darśana* called the *Uttara Mīmāṃsā* (*Latter Inquiries*).

16. For Deutsch, *Advaita Vedānta*, p. 68, Śaṅkara's explanation of rebirth and *karma* means conjointly the law of moral causation and *samsāra* and is undemonstrable by any of the six *pramāṇas* (valid means of knowledge) recognised by the *Av* system; see *ibid.*, p. 77 and *VS* III.4.26. It must be added that these self-validating sources of knowledge differ from the inside-out ultimate realization of *moksha*. However, the alleged existence of *moksha* alone is not contradicted or sublated ("subrated") by other knowledge or experience" *ibid.*, p. 86. Why? Because, short of that experience, the *pramāṇas* do remain pragmatically valid. They include perception (*pratyakṣa*), inference (*anūmāna*), illustrative analogy (*sāmānyatodṛṣṭānumāna*), and testimony (*śābda*). The testimony of the *śrutis'* authority (scriptural authority), which is derived from spiritual experience, is accepted only for "those truths that transcend reason and the senses" *ibid.*, p. 75.

17. *VS* II.3.48.

18. Deutsch, *Advaita Vedānta*, p. 102, n.3.

19. *Ibid.*, p. 101.

20. Raghavan, *Hinduism*, p. 85.

21. Hiriyanna, *Outlines of Indian Philosophy*, p. 381.

22. Crawford, *The Evolution of Hindu Ethical Ideals*, p. 183.

23. *VS* IV.1.14 and II.3.48.

24. Crawford, *The Evolution of Hindu Ethical Ideals*, p. 185.

25. *VS* III.4.27.

26. *Ibid.*, III.4.14. Also "man's goal is effected through knowledge alone; (see *ibid.*, III.4.26) without religion or morality." See also II.3.48.

27. *VS* III.4.49.

28. *VS* III. 4.46.

29. "That so many Indian intellectuals and academicians have adopted such an interpretive philosophy [two levels-of-truth] is surely one important reason why modern Indian philosophy has failed to develop a significant tradition of social criticism" Gerald Larson, "The *trimūrti* of *dharma* in Indian thought: paradox or contradiction?," *Philosophy East and West* 22, 2 (April 1972), 152. This same issue carries 1) Austin Creel's argument that *sadācāra* (as custom and obedience) was the prevailing and really amoral grounds of "ethical" activity: "*Dharma* as an ethical category relating to freedom and responsibility," 156-68; and 2) Arthur C. Danto's supportive conjecture that through its own control of *dharma* "the Brahman caste retains its monopoly on sacrifice by extending the franchise to...other castes, especially the *Kṣatriya* [ruling class]," "Role and rule in Oriental Thought," 217. Perhaps this alleged Brahminic obstacle to genuine morality, whether wholly or only partially effective, was why, like other reformers, "Rammohan Roy insisted that moral doctrines be kept beyond the reach of 'metaphysical perversion' and within the reach of the understanding of all people learned and unlearned" according to Roland W. Scott, *Social Ethics in Modern Hinduism* (Calcutta: YMCA Publishing House, 1953), p. 45. An example of Vedāntic control of popular literature is the *Yogavāsiṣṭha* version of the people's *Ry*; see B. L. Atreya *The Yogavāsiṣṭha* pp. 1-3.

30. See Panikkar, "The Silence of the Word," *Cross Currents* 24/2-3 (Summer-Fall 1974), 154-163. One may further defend the position that

Śaṅkara, at a potentially more "deep" structure of his "words," holds a revolutionary interpretation which is paradoxically Hindu in the more comprehensive sense, that is, not totally quietistic, because of his overwhelming productivity of scholarly "works."

31. *VS* I.3.38. In spite of the modern illegality of such caste discrimination, its actual continuance may partly explain the continuing resurgence of a more social version of neo-Buddhism led by the Untouchable, Bhimrao Ambedkar, since 1956 (nearly four million adherents by 1971—largely from the Untouchables).

32. See Kosambi, *Myth and Reality*, p. 10. The author is highly critical of the "reluctance to admit the primitive roots of Indian religious philosophy" as a partial reaction to India's colonial experience (p. 10).

33. *Ibid.*, pp. 15-16.

34. Crawford, *The Evolution of Hindu Ethical Ideals*, p. 193, refers after this phrase to *Brahma Sūtra* 3.4.27. The entire section of the present corpus on Rāmānuja summarizes Crawford's treatment, *ibid.*, pp. 187-95; Crawford's compendium in turn derives directly from Rāmānuja's *Śrī-bhāṣya*; George Thibaut, trans., *The Vedānta Sūtras with the Commentary of Rāmānuja*, The Sacred Books of the East, Vol. 48 (Oxford: The Clarendon Press, 1904).

35. Crawford, *ibid.*, pp. 200-01.

36. Max Scheler, *Formalism in Ethics*, p. 308.

37. Tagore, *Naivedya* (*Offerings*), as in Sen's *History of Bengali Literature*, p. 264. While for Sen cultural progress was menaced by the recrudescence of Brahminic orthodoxy, others have felt that orthodox tradition (meaning Vedāntic tradition) is finally being galvanized into a humanitarian spirit.

38. P. T. Raju, *The Philosophical Traditions of India* (London : George Allen & Unwin Ltd., 1971), p. 67. Remarks of this philosopher are especially important for their lack of a provincial attitude. As Burke has pointed out in his *The Reluctant Vision*, the major disease of the philosophy of religion is that it is almost exclusively "Western." Raju is one of the very few philosophers who has transcended the parochial mentality.

39. *Ibid.*, pp. 70-71.

40. Iyer's ethical and bibliographical study, *The Moral and Political Thought of Mahatma Gandhi* is unsurpassed. Within the massive secondary literature about Gandhi, see especially Sibnarayan Ray, ed., *Gandhi, India and the World* (Philadelphia; Temple University Press, 1970); Benoy Gopal Ray, *Gandhian Ethics* (Ahmedabad : Navajivan Publishing House, 1950); S. Chand, *Mahatma Gandhi, A Descriptive Bibliography* (Delhi, 1968); and M. K. Gandhi's own *Autobiography, The Story of My Experiments with Truth*, trans. Mahadev Desai (Washington, D.C. : Public Affairs Press, 1948). The present chapter has also taken into account psychological accomplishments or qualities largely projected on to Gandhi, I believe, in Erik H. Erikson's *Gandhi's Truth* (New York : W.W. Norton & Company, Inc., 1969), esp. pp. 428-40.

41. Tagore, *Gitanjali and Fruit-Gathering* (New York : The Macmillan Co., 1916), 8, 9, and 64. Other selections and translations from Tagore are listed in de Bary, *A Guide to Oriental Classics*, pp. 137-38.

42. Tagore, *The Religion of Man* (rpt.; Boston : Beacon Press, 1961), p. 167.

43. *Ibid.*, p. 168.

44. *Ibid.*, p. 179.

45. *Ibid.*, p. 201.

46. *Fruit-Gathering LXVI.*

47. *Ibid.*, LIII.

48. *Ibid.*, LXI.

49. Thomas Berry supports the optimistic judgment of this conclusion through his analysis of the socially symbolic idea of "journey" in "Contemporary Spirituality: The Journey of the Human Community," *Cross Currents* 24, 2/3 (Summer-Fall 1974), 172-83.

50. See chapters five and seven above.

51. See note 30 above. In the spirit of Merleau-Ponty, Philip H. Ashby concludes that the cross-cultural transfer-value of Hinduism to humanists and non-Hindu types of believers can be encountered, felt, and utilized, even when they are not (experientially or culturally) shared. See his *Study of Hinduism*, p. 148. Since the completion of my book negative appraisals of Gandhi's long-range effectiveness have appeared in Ved Mehta, *Mahatma Gandhi and His Apostles* (New York: The Viking Press, 1976) and V. S. Naipaul, *India : A Wounded Civilization* (New York : Knopf, 1977). Whatever Gandhi's inconsistencies and failures may be, I would still credit him as a futuristic symbol of people who learn pleasurable lifestyles whereby they can replenish the planet with as much energy as they have consumed—omitting, even in developing countries, the primitive, wasteful phases of the technological era. A new appreciation of R. Tagore's worth appears in William Cenkner, *The Hindu Personality in Education* (New Delhi : Manohar, 1976). After reading these books I am content to let stand my previous remarks about these two eminent persons.

CHAPTER IX

A COMPARATIVE ETHICAL SUMMARY OF PLURALISTIC HINDU TRADITIONS :

EPILOGUE : RELATIVISM AND MOTIVATION IN ETHICAL JUDGMENTS

Originally "Hindu" was an outsider's term intended to embrace a wide diversity of devotional, popular, and mystical phenomena on the Indian sub-continent. Now, it functionally describes and happens to match the actual and perduring *Av* attempt to incorporate many religions and their cultures into one *Av* synthesis. Since the time of Śaṅkara, at least, it seems clear that neo-Brahminic "Hinduism" can be traced through the later layers of both epics, the *Gītā*, Manu, and the *Vedānta Sūtras* back to the ascetical-mystical teachings of the *Ups*. Likewise it has roots in Buddhism and in non-Aryan, pre-Vedic beliefs in the primacy of the ascetical and the meditative as means for liberating individuals from the wheel of rebirths.

In an inversion of terminology, this ascetical-philosophical tradition has portrayed itself as both Brahminic and Vedic, perhaps because of populistic pressures. But it is not Brahminic in the more ancient Vedic sense of priestly. Instead it is more philosophically monastic.The neo-Brahminic philosophers would later rediscover the practical advantage of retaining or regaining "priestly" control over popular ritual. However, their more ultimate concerns were opposed to the religious sacrifice of animals, the violence (*himsā*) entailed, related devotional and theistic ritual and belief as a whole, and the Vedic Brahmins' preoccupation with progeny.While in this volume the prevailing usages of the appellation "Brahmin" and "neo-Brahmins" have been respected until now, it has been suggested that "neo-Brahminism" really began not with the *Brahma Sūtras*, Śaṅkara, or in later times, but long before, with the philosophical composers of the *Ups*. These writings depict static photographs of a highly mobile and adaptable organism which opposed and by-passed teachings of the earlier *Vedas* and Brahmins—their verbal insistence on their "Vedic orthodoxy" notwithstanding.

Furthermore, this current more clearly approximated Buddhism than Vedic Brahminism, both in general and in its moral implications. The historical origins of Upanishadic Brahmins derived, like Buddhism, not from the Aryan *Vedas*, but from the pre-Vedic views and practices of the ascetics, variously known as *munis*, *yatis*, or *śramaṇas*. Noticing the etymological similarity of *śramaṇas* (*śrama* means "exertion") to the third and fourth ascetical *āśramas*—from which all four stages of life took their name—one concludes that, unlike the notion of caste, the ascetical stage was not Vedic. It was anti-Vedic. This antagonism was already evidenced in the *Rv* itself (viii.39). Unlike the *Vedas*, the records of the *śramaṇas* were highly non-theistic, non-devotional, and centered on the cycle of rebirth, culminating in mysterious liberation (*moksha*) rather than in an on-going human existence in heaven. The this-worldly denial of neo-Brahminism is a thread which, in its historical interaction, has remained highly distinguishable from Vedic and popular tradition. It is only the latter which mirrors and develops Vedic life-affirmation and which will be generally identified with the Vedic in the following synopsis of issues compiled from foregoing comparative descriptions. Support for the ensuing generalizations about five questions in descriptive ethics may be verified either in previous individual chapters or in appendix two's comparative diagram of topical parallels and contrasts.

A. *The Vedic and Popular Tradition.*

1. *Morality, not mores*; 2) *grounded in a chiefly "cooperative" moral worldview.* Coalescing the questions of morality and its grounds, one may first recall that the Vedic sense of sin in an ethical context appears only in dim pastels. First, it lacks depictions of inner human visciousness or depravity or of an original *state* of sin. Second, its attention to sinful *actions* gives way to any emphasis, almost entirely positive, on good actions, virtues, and character.

Dealing not merely with in-group or class mores, but with universal virtues, the Vedic moral tradition was based primarily on a worldview which was not mystical, but "cooperative."

The non-Vedic notion of cyclic rebirths and karmic retribution is entirely absent in the *Rv*. Although it had a subsequent impact on the popular justification of moral conduct (why be moral?), *karma* was never separated from a simultaneous and more salient belief in heavenly rewards and reunions for respecting the cosmic *rita* or later the moral *dharma*—the harmony of all individuals' common interests. This belief prevailed from the earliest core (*Ur*) plots of both epics to the teachings of R. Tagore. Other-regard triggers a natural self-compensation which is implicitly self-regarding. One need not hate oneself to love another. In later popular trends, if not that of the *Rv*, an old and mythic theme began its second spring; while the moral point of view was primarily cooperative, secondarily it entailed self-sacrificial altruism. While the latter world-view was not analyzed for its intuitive or emotional groundings, its embodiments were frequently symbolized by feminine and emotively appealing figures. They were also portrayed with great esthetical beauty—as in the stirring loves of Sītā, Sāvitrī, and Vasantasenā, the heroine of *The Little Clay Cart*.

3. *Other ethical validations: the prevalence of common sense over appeal to authority*. The sheer authority of elites and popular customs received short shrift in the portrayal of popular ideals. While the *Ry* attested to the tyranny of custom as a regrettable fact, in terms of moral aspiration, the authority of either popular customs or elitist precepts was drowned out in a search for the consequences of moral acts collectively perceived. There were exceptions, of course: mesmerizing and discriminatory conventions about classes; Brahminized, authoritative layers of the epics; and the *Mbh* core plot's toleration of Brahminic struggles for economic and political control. But, in general, from the *Rv* through the *Kural*, *Pañcatantra*, dramas, and devotional literature, the only authoritative competitors with common moral reasoning were popular divinities who happened to personify the same moral ideals. Moreover, an intricate, consequentialistic type of moral reasoning to necessary exceptions became interwoven even with the later, and probably Brahminic, versions of *Mbh* XII and XIII.

Nevertheless, Vedic demonstration by consequence was not an isolated act of logic. In Vedic and popular traditions there are many signs that moral language was intended not only to convince but to persuade. Although neither Rigvedic poetry nor later, esthetical dramas evinced reflective thought about "cognitive intuition" or moral "value-feeling," they presupposed hearers and viewers who could be emotively moved by the rhetorical epithet or esthetically enlivened by symbolic (animal) and human characterizations. Like the earliest Rigvedic divinities, Rāma, Krishna, and others were later divinized as divine model persons who reacted "interpersonally" with their devotees.

4. *Central ethos : life affirmation.* In the *Rv*'s life-celebrating "Hymn to Dawn" there shines an ethos which knows neither *moksha* nor *nirvāṇa*. Lacking the ascetical word *āśrama*, the *Rv* frowned on an asceticism which would bypass or diminish marriage and the raising of children. The Rigvedic preoccupations with *artha*, *kāma*, and an embryonic *dharma* flowered in the life-affirmative core plots and characters of the epics, especially the *Ry*, which never spoke of *moksha* and which looked upon Rāma and Sītā's somewhat ascetical exile in the forest precisely as an exile, an unfortunate episode which was made instrumental for their royal restoration and their earthly and/or heavenly happiness. While the *Ry*'s didactic affirmations about non-violence and compassion may depict neo-Brahminic, and ultimately, Buddhistic influences, the themes of giving and generosity never lost their original Rigvedic luster. They came alive in the most popular characters of Indian stories, poetry, and drama. For the non-advaitic, devotional, and theistic R. Tagore, if not for Gandhi, Brahman could be reached through a life focused on love rather than contemplation. Reversed was the Advaitic maxim : take care of contemplation and love will take care of itself. While Tagore eschewed poverty and qualified asceticism, this great and popular poet sounded the ancient Vedic call to dawn—to wake up to the stirring world of social and moral action.

To such an ethos, those imbued in the *Av* tradition might respond that the *Vedas* and popular literature captured only part of the total atmosphere to which the people were always exposed. The *Vedas* and the *Ry* were never intended to portray the ascetical and mystical aspects of life. Instead, this kerygma was already amply taken care of by pre-Vedic and Upanishadic ascetics and their neo-Brahminic philosophical successors.

As a result, in this line of thought, Hindu life was never so compartmentalized that Vedic life-affirmation could evolve autonomously.

While partial interaction seems historically plausible, this pro-ascetical argumentation for the inevitability of synthesis may or may not succeed in logical theorizing. Success depends on one's opening premises. It is analogous to the political liberal's thesis that all socialists and capitalists will inexorably amalgamate into a new breed—a conjecture which many in the latter two groups would strenuously deny. As they see it, in the most valid synthesis either socialism or capitalism will come out on top, appropriating its counterpart's perspective and declarations into its own definitional control and language. Similarly, many neo-Vedāntists envision popular, life-affirmative, and social concern only developmentally and instrumentally. In this model, if the Vedic tradition has been historically undeniable, it is finally to pass away.

Conversely, Hindu social reformers might theorize that the *Av* tradition could be reconstructed, so as to ground and inspire social and ethical reform, sought as an end as well as a means, without surrendering its own belief that the phenomenal world is transient. In this world-affirming synthesis, it is really the Vedic and popular tradition which will overcome, as least as far as visible human existence is concerned. The epilogue will respond to this debate about *logical* possibilities in respect to its cross-cultural value. Meanwhile, the *historical* question cannot be ignored. Which spirit has psychologically dominated the Indian scene as it perdures today? Did the Vedic tradition make room for *Av* or did *Av* coopt popular morality and devotion? Or have both survived in equal tension? To address this query, the present summary of Vedic ethos must proceed to its investigation about how ethos was concretized.

5. *What were the basic Vedic attitudes about the interrelationships between individuals, societal conventions, and institutional structures*? Although the *Rv* in no way promoted human slavery in the fashion of the ancient code of Hammurabi (1728-1686 B.C.E.; extant document later), it condemned neither racial nor sexual slavery. Subsequently, in the *Ry*, sexual inequalities were severely censured, but class inequities went unchallenged. However, until modern times, dreams of caste, racial, and even

sexual equalities must not have developed beyond the state of dormant aspirations, given the vigor with which injustices were cited and assailed by modern Hindu reformers. In brief, the positive Vedic ethos has never really been translated into social programs as envisioned by Hindu reformers or some non-Hindu cultures. Never unequivocally condemned in Vedic tradition, *himsā* or violence conquered, even after the heyday of Gandhi. The latter qualified physical *ahimsā* frequently and was condemned by R. Tagore for his strategies of psychological force and blind obedience.

For all its interculturally paradigmatic appreciation of the emotive and the esthetical, until today the Vedic tradition has not been fully tried on its homeground. Why? The ensuing examination of the Upanishadic and neo-Brahminic tradition will disclose part of the answer. Most modern and contemporary Hindu social humanists arose from and adhered to the *Av* current. In general, *Av* proponents have so contained the centers of power that their non-Vedic views could not help but obstruct or condition Vedic ideals—for better or for worse.

B. *The Upanishadic and Neo-Brahminic tradition.*

1. *Mores, with morality in low profile*; 2) *grounded in a mystical, non-dualistic life-view of rebirths and moksha.* Prescinding from theoretical reconstructions of *Av* non-dualism which might build social altruism more directly and inspire it more energetically, in historical fact social altruism, like devotionalism, was given only an ephemeral and secondary reality in a world of bi-level truth. Immoral deeds did presuppose an erroneous dualism, individualism, and consequent egoism (*ahaṃkāra*) whose logical converse would be a type of love. But additional historical records have to be summarized to discern if and how this love came to life.

3. *Other sources of moral validation : the priority of Brahminic authority.* Loving and moral behavior like compassion and non-violence were positively incited—as in the *Ups*, Manu, and *Gitā*—by recourse to *śruti,* what was heard inwardly from divine authority (not external revelation). Further, at least with the sages, divine authority was identical with the voices of those who avered that they had realized or approached Brahman-realization/*moksha*. Therefore, from a phenomenal or outside

viewpoint, neo-Brahminic authority prevailed over the divine authority which it claimed to represent. In addition there are more explicit declarations in the *Ups*, Manu, and Śaṅkara's *VS* that neo-Brahminic authority was the last moral recourse. It was the neo-Brahmins who held on to the powers of defining reality and of specifying human conduct, especially through legal codes and unchallenged class conventions, as in Manu. Although some historians contend that Manu was little heeded and feebly enforced, there is other evidence, as in the *Gītā*, that the authority of caste mores or *varṇadharma* was thought to be supreme over one's own fallible conscience. According to Tagore, even Gandhi's elevation of conscience above civil authority left his disciples in a stance of blind obedience to Gandhi's belief in the infallibility of *ahimsā* and therefore of Gandhi himself.

4. *Central historical ethos : the mystical routinization of social humanism*. Amidst professions of compassion and non-violence founded on the identity of all beings with the one *Ātman*-Brahman, the pivotal spirit of the *Ups* quickly swung to ascetical self-restraint, the fourth ascetical-mystical goal of *moksha*, and an ultimate denial of all this-worldly human values, including morality itself. True, in Manu one discerns a nearly distinct ethos of power and caste contentment. All-powerful Brahmins defined the very meaning of life as well as its rules. But in the synthesis of the *Gītā*, which attempted to incorporate theistic devotion and moral action within the neo-Brahminic tradition, the notion of *niṣkāma karma* or non-attached *action* subsided in an ethos of *non-attached* action. When the ethos of control was splintered by indigenous confusions and imperialistic foreign oppressions, what stood out as the nearly singular ethos of the whole neo-Brahminic tradition was not an effective morality. Rather it was the spirit of amoral non-attachment. Morality was relegated to the *śāstras* and *sadācāra*, caste codes and customs. And thereby it was entirely routinized. In the following section this judgment will undergo further scrutiny in the light of legal attitudes about the individual.

5. *Basic neo-Brahminic attitudes about individuals and societal structures*. Constructively taken, the all-embracing, if not personally intrusive, laws of Manu, were similar to the intricate code of Hammurabi and the elaborate casuistries of Jewish, Christian,

and Muslim laws. That is, positively speaking, they mirrored a concern for concrete and unambiguous social decisions. Theoretically, law and order were to be firm. The *Ups* had already taught giving, compassion, and self-restraint. Negatively, Manu's proscriptions, addressed to all classes, embraced the last seven commands of the Jewish decalogue as well as Buddhistic or Jaina injunctions against alcohol, abortion, and violence in general. While Upanishadic *ahimsā* was considerably qualified, as it was in the *Gītā* and the *Mbh*, the speculatively universal caliber of morality appeared in ten virtues prescribed for all classes (*sādhāraṇadharma* or general *dharma*). These virtues were theoretically universal and moral, even if they were limitedly negative, ascetical, and "dianoetical" or cognitive in practical content.

Two related legal areas deserve special mention, the individual's sexual and caste rights. First, whatever rights women had held in the Vedic period continued to decline, as in other cultures, in societal disdain for women, in polygamy, and in literal norms to worship one's husband—in Manu, but especially in the *Mbh*, Books XII and XIII. Second, caste discrimination was practiced at economic, legal, and punitive levels. Class differences were divinely legitimated both in the *Ups* and Manu. In the *Gītā*, too, the differences amounted to discrimination. For Śaṅkara, *śūdras* were to be dismembered if they pronounced or read the *Vedas* which were reserved for higher classes.

Turning to the *āśramas* (stages of life), until Śaṅkara all four stages had been honored in a schema which paid individual and sometimes competing respect to each stage, including the earning and familial period of life. This developmental model was again highlighted in twentieth century *Av*. But for centuries Śaṅkara had lent his considerable authority to the omission of all but the ascetical stages. In such a setting, the problem of economic support could be relegated to land and tax grants and to stipends from lay devotees. In contrast, the quasi-Vedāntist Gandhi seemed to derive his charismatic power from his stark, voluntary life of poverty and his self-sacrificial social action against class discrimination and religious unity, a cause for which he was finally assassinated in 1948. More boldly still, R. Tagore not only fought caste, but insisted that Brahmins should again work for a living. Lastly, his universalist opposition to nationalism, even that of Gandhi's variety, brought him closer to a potentially cross-cultural ethic.

But Tagore's listeners and readers were locked in by a morality which had been promulgated through class *dharma* and conventions. With its stress on non-attachment to ritual and moral deeds, the Upanishadic ethic had, in practical effect, abandoned morality to authoritative conventions and codes, a phenomenon described above as the mystical routinization of social humanism. In other words, however large a role neo-Brahmins had played in composing the legal codes, the people's conduct was steered away from inward motivation to authoritative force. This dead-end course resulted in ineffectual codes, unquestioning obedience, the mushrooming deployment of sanctions, and, according to some, the deterioration of human initiative and motivational strength.

Armed with the *Gītā*'s slogan of non-attached action and with the charisma of his own person, even Gandhi became disillusioned with peoples who were unresponsive to that ethos. Perhaps part of their passivity arose from their having lived under legal regimes whose major solution to every problem was authoritative law rather than moral motivation. At present, the conservative solution to motivation is similarly simple: contemporary civil law in India only awaits translation into the language or thought patterns of authoritative *dharma* and *sadācāra*. Interior morality, after all, functions with great difficulty for both the wealthy and the poor, as well as for both oppressors and the oppressed. In *Av*, morality is a transient phenomenon anyway, being subservient to *moksha-dharma* or neo-Brahminic moral mysticism.

However, from humanistic worldviews, especially non-mystical ones, recourse to force and authority alone is an unthinkable retrogression to cultural childhood. Hindus, they say, must search together with Muslims, neo -Buddhists, and others within their own pluralistic cultures for the heritage which will motivate them to help themselves freely, both materially and morally. As has been indicated before, one may inquire if the Vedic tradition does not contain the ethical, esthetical, and possibly religious seeds for another "second spring" of moral humanism. In turn, Hindu mystics need not instrumentalize their worldview as a mere means to humanism. But, in so-called phenomenal existence, they could bolster the motivation of their devotees or sympathizers by signalling that non-dualism does not have to end in non-action. Rather, it can help to cultivate the esthetical sense of morality and ground it in an effective compassion for every suffering, however material or trivial.

Epilogue. Ethical Relativism and Motivation in Ethical Judgments

Cross-cultural ethical relativism. Given Western influences on Gandhi and other reformers as well as the pitfalls of cultural imperialism, some observers have wondered if Western ideas about privacy and equality can or should be transplanted to Indian soil. By necessity, people have learned to live there with only minimal space and have accepted the multiple strictures which crowded community living engenders. This problem of cultural relativism must be raised, whatever one's own preconceptions about the potentially universal contributions of more nutritional food, space, and privacy towards a more humanizing, interacting community of give and take (*Gemeinschaft*) as opposed to impersonal collective living (*Gesellschaft*). Even when social humanists repeat that change does not necessitate obstructive, accelerated, or total change—let alone outside interventions —they must still justify their premise that the masses of India are really suffering from their own Indian, experiential point of view. Likewise, proof is required to demonstrate that Indians should agree with those who believe that toleration of this suffering must be exposed as destructively immoral.

The justification for changing to a more social ethic involves a judgment on the condition or contentment of others, whether this evaluation is rendered by a native or by an outsider. This problem is met in India or in any culture. The right to recommend a moral norm for another person is as thorny an analytical issue as the justification of morality itself. Going little beyond the brief analyses and assumptions stated in chapter one about the pragmatic necessity and intuition of the ethical, the following justification of social reform brings up mainly a point of *fact* and only secondarily a matter of *conjecture.*

The *fact* is the cross-cultural actuality of moral norms, including the golden rule. As for Hinduism in particular, it is variously intrinsic to Vedic, popular, and even neo-Brahminic traditions to prescribe moral action guides for social betterment.

Wherever people believe in a golden rule of treating others as they would wish to be treated, the fact that they prescribe rules and reforms as beneficial for themselves leads them to offer the same to others. Actually they have already begun such a process intra-culturally, yet interpersonally. Consequently, one naturally expects Indians or natives of any such tradition not to resent outside judgments which are meant to be helpful and not culturally imperialistic. No humanistic or religious adherents to the golden rule can escape the logic of deciding *if* their neighbours are suffering or are in need.

As for my own observations about whether Indians and other "less developed" peoples are really suffering —and prescinding from intra or inter-national origins of this suffering—I think that the answer lies not merely in reading printed statistics about early deaths, disease, starvations, and caloric intake. Otherwise, one meets endless arguments about quality as opposed to quantity or length of life. The solution lies rather in a more varied and concrete, existential experience of Indian bodies, movements, faces, expressions, and feelings. In spite of elegant beauty in their character, *Gemeinschaft*, sharing, thrift, joy, and esthetical taste—random samples of Indian cultural highpoints which are frequently lacking in the most affluent societies—I would finally appeal to a spontaneous, single insight or "value-feeling" which occurs when these and other suffering peoples are not merely read about but looked directly in the eye. On that occasion the powerful absolutizing of cultural relativism and "non-intervention" becomes much more uncomfortable. A hollow sound rings in maxims like: "Leave them alone; they love their poverty" or "Don't move a thing or you'll destroy the whole system."

The above declaration about moral intuition necessitates the following matter of conjecture. 1) Ethical analysts have underlined the apparent arbitrariness and arrogance of all intuition cavalierly; 2) without due warrant they have jumped from the factual contradictions of secondary and multiple "intuitions" to the impossibility of a single insight into goodness in general; 3) they have mixed obviously contrived or deluded intuitions into one bag with interculturally alleged insights about moral goodness as such; and 4) they have not adequately distinguished the pursuit of personal intuition in one's own life from the imposition of it on others. In Hindu and other traditions, moral insight does not usually function in an isolated and dangerous vacuum without verification from collective experiences of consequences: By their fruits you shall know these intuitions. As a result, in spite of nagging doubts about unfailing or divine-like accuracy, I favor the postulation of a fundamental moral insight (*synderesis*) or "value-feeling" which can go wrong, but which can and should be continually tested against factual consequences. I do not presuppose that any intuition or "recognition" arises suddenly, out of nowhere, or always from conscious effort. On the contrary, even unconsciously generated recognition is variously preceded by multiple experiences and inductions. In this way—in a single a-logical recognition—I "feel" that Indian peoples really suffer and for their own sakes (in other-regard or love) ought to be helped to better themselves. The destructive or beneficial effects of the assistance offered can and should be used to measure the validity of this feeling, and *vice versa*. But without some such feeling, it seems that one is logically exiled to the island of cross-cultural ethical relativism and the culturally compartmentalized worldview it presupposes. Any exchange becomes impossible in moral wisdom and motivation.

Speaking paradigmatically, Hindu alternatives are the world's alternatives. The same choices face most cultures and religious traditions. For those who choose not to surrender moral humanism to authoritative or programmed conventions, the common question is not merely how does one discern what is right or wrong, but how does one move oneself to embrace freely what is right or good ? As for contemporary Hinduism, if the Upanishadic and neo-Brahminic tradition of moral quietism should go on to drown out the Vedic, life-affirmative and esthetical bases of social humanism, I would not predict the survival of free movement to moral action. Logically, the same prognosis could be projected to every major ethical tradition around the globe. In research completed on other traditions, I have concluded that the Upanishadic and Vedic polar currents are typically cross-cultural. When it comes to ethical motivation, every major culture's symbol system, avowedly religious or not, faces at least two options : 1) despair of the existing human condition with a concomitant relegation of morality to the authoritative sanctions of cultural, civil, or legal force; 2) full attention to moral and social humanism, either in collaboration or tension with mystical, religious, or other "counter-cultural" forces. The second option presumes that if "counter-cultural" powers like the neo-Brahminic tradition have not previously joined in the support of social ethics, they will in the future either encourage or at least not oppose it. Even a practically neutral stance of non-opposition could be insufficient for the construction of a social morality, depending on the size and power of the "neutral" tradition. In spite of that necessary qualification, the concluding two sections will now argue against the first option of moral despair and favor the second alternative of moral and social humanism.

Option one. Despair of the human condition. The most convincing position against this attitude would first have to review cross-cultural data about successful moral endeavors. Second, it would probably not be formulated by an individual with a disdainful self-image or low self-esteem, -respect, or -love. Third, how people accept a logic against moral despair depends on the measure in which they have been influenced by others with low self-esteem in the socially concentric circles of life. I have written elsewhere of the acculturation towards self-hatred which Christians, in particular, have undergone, relentless pressures stemming from Manicheanism to modern Puritanism ("Muslim and Christian Ethics"). More than many Hindus, Christians would be historically disposed to accept the conviction that human beings are innately depraved, wicked, or totally helpless in a moral sense. Christians might be the least inclined to accept the thesis of Eric Fromm and other psychologists that the greatest enemy of individuals and societies is not self-love but the lack of it, expressed in sado-masochistic behavior and founded on a low self-image which is projected onto others.

There is little doubt that a negative self-image will become a self-fulfilling prophecy about one's future life, whatever the real capabilities of one's moral character. Conversely, it is equally reasonable to expect that a positive self-esteem will also function as a self-fulfilling prophecy about one's moral future. Paradoxically, a more positive estimate of human potential does not deny that people are factually immersed in the mire of egocentric self-pity, quietistic passivity, or addiction to suffocating guilt-feelings—all expressions of *thanatos*, the instinct for pursuing death. But positive life-affirmation holds out the hope that the mire of *thanatos* is not intrinsic to the human condition. The pure or golden lotus can blossom in its midst—to borrow a most popular East Asian symbol.

Admittedly, the predication of new moral responsibility for the future implies at least minimal responsibility for one's past. It also suggests that people may continue to reject their own better judgment. But, from a Hindu perspective, these failures stem from the lack of emotive and esthetical education to living knowledge as opposed to purely conceptual convictions. These "sins" are not signs of intrinsic human depravity, perversity or malice.

It follows, in my opinion, that sin-consciousness does not enhance sensitivity to moral responsibility. Instead, it obstructs it. True, no moral growth can be cultivated without the admission of previous errors, a kind of confession to oneself and often to others. But it is equally apparent that "to err is human ." Further, the forgiveness of oneself and others is the first and indispensable step for correcting a previous "missing the mark" (the old Hebrew meaning of sin). Immersion in regret and sorrow without amendment is a centripetal, ulcerous movement which is destructive and inefficacious for the self and others. At any rate, whether lack of self-love emanates from a "malicious" will or ignorance or various combinations, I see it as the primal source for despair towards humanity and one's own moral life. This despondence seems to contradict the historical roots of Jewish, Christian, and other expressions of the golden rule. To love one's neighbor presupposes love of self, admitting, of course, that the two loves interact circularly. The question then becomes : how to cultivate a healthy self-love ?

The neo-Brahminic, mystical belief that each self or *ātman* is identical with the one *Ātman*-Brahman in the fullness of divine goodness can lend support both to self-love and to hope in the goodness of others. In addition, the absence of "original sin," as well as the low profile of volitional sin in popular Hindu traditions and its almost total absence in neo-Brahminism, invites a whole new look at the question of whether "sin" is a necessary postulate or consequence of a moral point of view.

In many traditions peoples believe that no one can sin in heavenly existence. Heaven is the climax of enduring wisdom, freedom, and liberation. Some have believed that both Jesus and his mother remained all the more free for their immaculate sinlessness. These beliefs seem to imply that "sin" is rooted in a lack of wisdom and freedom rather than in malice. They coincide with the motif of the divine physician who looks upon sin as a sickness. The most important, if still unrealized, factor in the deep symbols of the lotus or the immaculate conception may lie in their application to every person instead of a select few. Be this as it may, the point at hand is that even these defenders of a moral stance who feel that the potential for sin must be real at some point in time are left with a variety of options as to how corrupt or lovable people really are. In large part, this diversity stems from the unavoidably subjective dimension of the issue. To appropriate a popular maxim: what you project or see in yourself and others is what you get. Naturally, expectations which are too high can backfire in individual and social disillusionment and inactivity. But, if moral expectations are not kept at a minimum height, there is equal danger. Christians have called this expectation "hope." "Non-religious" humanists may call it trust in the capabilities of other human beings.

At any rate, to the extent that sin can be placed in lower profile, both religious believers and other humanists may experiment with the Socratic idea that people can be educated to goodness, that sinfulness is, at least, not *chiefly* volitional. This hope coincides with the conviction that humanity's real enemy is not flesh and blood but chaotic, if not demonic, powers beyond. Through moral education these forces can be subjected to some human control with or without, as people variously insist, the help of God.

Option two. Moral and social humanism. Just as education is both an individual and social venture, in morality as well as in other areas, it is also more comprehensive than a restricted rational process. The history of Hindu ethics confirms the early Greek and Confucian philosophical positions that the emotive and the esthetical play indispensable roles in any communication about morality which provides effective motivation. If this inspiration is conceived of not individualistically, but socially, in terms of whole peoples, some existing social and individual obstacles come to mind.

A social obstacle. One instance of a social impediment arises in partly democratic or free republics which, in the name of the liberty of the individual, do not restrict the liberty of corporations from unduly infringing on the liberty of individuals. Let corporations symbolize societal structures in general. The promotion of culture can be taken from the populace of individuals and placed in the hands of corporations. This phenomenon may be concretely illustrated by focusing not on the arts in general, but on the entertaining arts in particular. If they are left only to the exploitation principle of "how little can be sold for the greatest profit," then it seems unlikely that cultural levels will rise above their present heights or depths. On the other hand, a new, if small, beachhead might be established to the extent that the performing arts would be lifted from the control of power elites which operate chiefly or entirely out of the exploitation principle. The transfer of the economic control of the arts back to the people might be realized through private, governmental, or mixed subsidies. But this support would need the company of effective legislation against virtually unlimited and, therefore propagandizing advertising.

Lastly, cultural education in the arts would also necessitate reasonable ceilings on profits acquired in artistic production, distribution and performance. Like producers and distributors, performing artists in the media of stage, film, sound, or sports arenas are forced by existing economic systems to accumulate every available profit in the present. This situation happens in the measure that subsequent productions or performances remain financial risks. Gradually performers will price themselves out of existence for most direct viewers or live audiences. It remains to be seen if the only thorough-going alternatives to this unfortunate dilemma is the partial or total economic socialization of the arts and all the bureaucratic problems that socialization brings in its wake.

Leaving creative explorations of that issue to specialists in contemporary economics, the thesis at hand is simply that the cultivation of the esthetical cannot proceed satisfactorily when it is impeded either by socialistic totalitarianism or by the exploitation principle of "the least for the greatest profit." In the arts, this principle is transposed into "the lowest quality of art for the greatest profit." Yet without great art, a giant portion of civilization and enjoyment is lost not only in terms of its own values, but in terms of its nearly indispensable service towards ethical motivation.

The practical, moral necessity of art has been vigorously confirmed by writers for The People's Republic of China. Previously, if less moralistically, it was assumed throughout the whole history of Confucianism. The Vedic and popular appreciation of life, beauty, and art has been thwarted from attaining or remaining in full blossom on Indian soil. However, throughout Asia the persistent populistic turning to emotional and esthetical arts and literature rather than to professionally philosophical treatises divulges a lesson in motivation which has cross-cultural significance.

An individual obstacle. If anyone is more than historically or literally intrigued with the phenomenon that social morality springs from the emotively esthetical as well as the rational, and if one wishes to imitate or utilize actuating, charismatic and esthetical qualities, one will not succeed with scientific information alone. Mere study about replicative conditions will not do the job by itself. What is needed further is personally experienced grasps of what it means either to hustle, to be moved, or to impel oneself to morality and to love. Some psychologists have contended that no child or person can be brought to love without having experienced the primal conditions of being loved, accepted, confirmed, cared for, sustained, or forgiven.

Some religious thinkers have appended comparable beliefs from their various non-theistic or theological points of view. To abridge the Johannine maxim, they proclaim that we should "love God and our fellow human beings, because God first loved us, because God is love" (1 John 4:11, 16, 19). This proclamation has been taken to mean that the real fountain of being moral or loving is the gift of having been loved—divinely, humanly, or both. In the thinking of some religionists, like Rudolph Otto or perhaps Joachim Wach, one should extend the charismatic source of moral actuation not only to the esthetical in the widest sense, but also to the numinous dimension which that embraces. At any rate, not by reasoned consequences alone do people live—nor without them—but also by love and beauty, and for some, by the experience of the holy or of grace.

Yet, even with this help, individual resistance endures. As some disconsolate connoisseurs can testify, massive exposures to great art, literature, and films do not of themselves generate moral activity, whether it is called cooperative, mystical, or altruistic. Intimate disciples of the greatest religious and humanistic leaders have added to that witness. Therefore, prescinding from situations where human energies are physically or psychologically impaired, unborn, or dead, the free step from the charismatic and the esthetical into moral movement and love is not a leap without labor. Yet, it relates less to reason or even to a descriptive comprehension of the preconditions for love and beauty, than it does to one's own cumulative personal experience, either first-order or imaginatively reconstructed.

In brief, the communication of the meaning of the concretely esthetical or charismatic lies beyond description noetically conceived. The understanding of why a statue of the Buddha, Moses, or the Pieta, a verse from Tu Fu, Bhartrihari, or Dante, or loving persons like Gandhi or Jesus impel persons to the moral corresponds to how one personally appropriates the experience of the statue, poetry, novel, or person. It goes without saying that such an unavoidably personal project or life-task requires an assessment which lies beyond the scope of this volume. Part of the enigma of moral charisma and movement remains inexorably, existentially "my truth", one's own personal question, and something practical learned only in the doing. On the other hand, every individual needs assistance for his or her autobiographical self-assessment of personal moral resources and capabilities. While this aid may arrive out of professional religious, moral, or psychological counselling, it occurs more naturally as a gift from caring friends and acquaintances, the people with whom one has really shared life.

The recommendation that gifts of wisdom from others should be accepted presupposes the anthropological view that no person has a monopoly on wisdom. As populist traditions signify, everyone can learn from nearly everyone, so pluralistic and diversely perceived is the treasury of collective wisdom. So radically basic for the communication of ethical motivation is this premise that if finally emerges as the foundation block of populistic morality. Consequently, this volume ends in accepting and rearticulating the Hindu and intercultural populistic principle that moral wisdom is not the prerogative of professional philosophers or other elites, but the domain of every human being. "Lover of wisdom" (philosopher) is a title which every person has the right to freely accept or reject. Populist traditions would recommend acceptance. I agree. Whenever popular rejection of this title has been recommended by power elites—often because of the "depraved" human condition—their interests have been self-centered, vested, and elitist in the derogatory sense, not really aristocratic at all. In those instances, they have abandoned the complementary paradigm of human collaboration for the competitive models of masses against elites, and of persons in general interacting like competing wolves.

The democratic and ultimately more aristocratic ("best-powered") rejection of competition for cooperation presupposes that people can excel in their diversity. The question of equality is in this sense irrelevant. As star differs from star in grandeur or flowers vary in non-competitive beauty, populist wisdom and goodness extends this imagery to every human being. To revive a biblical and Rigvedic metaphor for "sin," those who would reserve truth, moral goodness, and non-ego-centric love to a chosen few have missed the "straight" path for the "crooked". In the name of "everyman" or so-called "common" people, their leadership must be challenged.

CHAPTER X

AN INTRODUCTION TO ETHICAL THOUGHT IN MAHĀYĀNA BUDDHIST TEXTS

Abstract. In contrast to *Advaita Vedānta* the Vedic ethos of this-worldly love and compassion reappears in Mahāyāna Buddhism's Bodhisattvas who function as stirring models of compassion as well as moral wisdom. "Western" readers have interpreted D. T. Suzuki and other eminent Buddhist scholars to mean that both Mahāyāna Buddhism and its worldview are categorically amoral. The ethical hypothesis assumed in this chapter is that even if normative texts appear with relative infrequency or lack of emphasis, their very presence evinces a Mahāyāna-moral function, whatever Mahāyāna Buddhism's integral relationships with Hindu, Confucian, and folk or local religions throughout East Asia and South Asia. The chapter's introduction will clarify the meaning of this hypothesis. The ensuing five sections will describe I. A Method toward a Solution of the Problem; II. Mahāyāna Buddhism in the Light of Early Buddhist Ethics, Common and Theravādan; III. The Historical Origin of Mahāyāna Buddhism; IV. Criteria for Textual Selections; and V. Samples of Mahāyāna Texts with Moral Implications. Due to the tentative nature of the findings and their need for further analytical scrutiny, the chapter will conclude with the briefest answers to this volume's usual questions about morality, worldview and other validations, ethos and social structures, but it illustrates how they can extend beyond Hindu traditions. NOTES.

In spite of the Mahāyāna Buddhist (henceforth MB) bodhisattva's apparent function as a model of both moral wisdom and compassion, readers have generally interpreted D. T. Suzuki and other eminent Buddhist scholars to mean that MB is categorically amoral.[1] The ethical hypothesis defended in this chapter about a Mahāyāna moral function is either ignored or taken for granted and needs to be explicated in an era newly sensitive to the issue of international human rights. While the author's presently limited humanistic approach betrays his lack of Buddhist experience (at least beyond the penultimate experience of paradox and contradiction), it may help to bridge further dialogue between conventional social humanisms and the divergent, but perhaps complementary, Buddhist ways of seeing and living human life.

INTRODUCTION

Moral behavior can be *directly* specified through sets of action-guides, virtues, and models for imitation. Or it can be delineated *indirectly*, but still powerfully, by a worldview or "way of seeing" life, like inwardly realized and not objectivized views depicted in some Mahāyāna texts. For brevity's sake, the first mode of specification will be referred to as a *moral system*. The second will be called a *worldview*, ontology, or moral anthropology. As for moral systems, they are not necessarily woven together with explicit philosophical threads or with logical consistency. More simply, they may comprise a minimal network of implicit prescriptions which relate to human life and relationships. On the other hand, explicitly systemic worldviews may state concrete norms, without stressing them. Still, they may exert a strong normative impact on human conduct.

A *Weltanschauung's* correlation with behavior is moral, first of all, because it is prescriptively proposed as a way of viewing or of experiencing which one *ought* to embrace. A "way of seeing" is in itself an action-guide. Secondly, after a given outlook on life is accepted, it can automatically trigger specific forms of moral conduct. For instance, to envision all life and nature exclusively as instrumental for increasing production and consumption is like locking an airplane into a flight pattern. All kinds of particular actions follow in program, even without human consciousness.

Or, elaborating the Copernican metaphor, to realize life self-centeredly is to predispose decisions favoring the self at the expense of others in concrete value conflicts. Dualistic self-centeredness sets behavior into an inexorably centripetal course. Religious or humanistic reformers, for example, may preach forms of altruistic love and service eloquently, but for their own ego-needs or admiration, at the potential cost of others. With egotistical motivation, teachers of social reform can turn proclamations of freedom for others into self-serving demagoguery. Their maxim becomes a paradoxical : "Silence, I want to talk about freedom." In sum, once locked into orbit, egotistical and other worldviews can predetermine all subsequent action with little or no stress on specific action-guides.

In short, while worldviews may lack or fail to underline explicit behavioral norms, rarely would moral systems lack an ultimately prescriptive worldview. Even personal or idiosyncratic systems are rooted in ways of seeing or experiencing, consciously or unconsciously, with or without reflective awareness. In this essay, Mahāyāna texts which indirectly imply a normative worldview will be referred to only briefly, without repeating numerous summaries of Mahāyāna ontology already available. But texts which directly reveal moral systems will be examined more specifically through several samples.

I. *Method toward a Solution of the Problem*

Religious and ethical humanisms can begin dialogues with an alleged Mahāyāna ethics by outlining the method or procedure of its questions and assumptions. Is Mahāyāna Buddhism (henceforth MB) exclusively or primarily a way of *seeing*? Do some MB schools propose ways of *acting* latently, overtly, or in both manners ? Were MB schools moral originally, or did they become so developmentally ? As I indicated at the beginning, the prevailing opinion in the West seems to be that of the two great living forms of Buddhism, Theravāda Buddhism (henceforth TB) and MB, only TB asserted ethical norms explicitly. While MB does not openly deny TB precepts, it assumedly bypasses them, leaving ethics to Hinduism, Confucianism, or other formal and popular Asian traditions. Accordingly, modern literature on Theravāda ethics is not lacking. Earlier volumes by W. Bohn, Caroline Rhys Davids, and Louis de la Vallée-Poussin have led to more recent works by S. Tachibana, H. Saddhatissa, and Winston King and to abundant periodical literature.[2] But there is a lacuna in modern MB ethical analyses, perhaps a total gap. This would support the contention that MB "seeing" lacks normative implications, because it is not the viewing of an objective or dualistic, outside world. Rather it is an inward, centrifugal realization which is beyond dualism and (for some) its opposite, non-dualism. In either case, subject and object are not two but one. In MB, morality is supposedly irrelevant.

The religious and humanistic objections that worldviews without ethics are incomplete and immoral are countered with the rejoinder that MB has relegated the transitory world of human relations to Hindu *dharma*, TB *dharma*, or Confucian *jen* and *li*; that is, to other ethical systems. Both Chinese and Japanese have experienced relatively little or no tension in living the three teachings (*san chiao*) of Buddhism, Confucianism, and Taoism (or samurai ethics—Budhidō or the way of the warrior —and Shinto for the Japanese). Therefore, MB has supplied only ontology, while other traditions teach morality—to the same peoples.

The present inquiry begins with a contrary presupposition. The more plausible opening assumption is that after centuries of coexistence, if not originally, MB teachings and other traditions did not remain compartmentalized. Instead, probabilities favored their intermingling in living and interrelated human acceptance, the moral dimension included. Of course, this theory must be bolstered with fact, through subsequent samples of a widespread presence of MB moral texts. My second assumption holds that until more seasoned critical textual analyses prove otherwise, it is unwarranted to read all moral allusions as later accretions.[3] My third postulate is that even those who lack MB experiences of enlightenment can partly assess what is a distinctively MB input. Such assessment assumes that human experience does not lack some commonalities and the possibility of detached empathy (*epoche*) and analogous experiences.[4] My fourth and final presupposition contends that textual evidence is one necessary part of a larger historical and scientific process. While only the latter, total network of both historical and empirical methods can offer satisfactory answers about the causal impact or representative validity of textual claims, literary study is one preliminary and vital part of the wider enterprise. In some aspects, textual analysis demands less empathy than ambitious empirical inquiries at more concretely cultural and structural levels. The latter studies more clearly demand empathy with cultures in which one ought to have lived for years, if not for a lifetime. This prerequisite is particularly salient when MB is observed by outsiders less as a transcendental truth or universal ethical movement than as particular historical and cultural manifestations at given times and places (a needed but more specialized focus than the present programmatic overview).

With these assumptions grounding a rationale for cross-cultural MB textual investigation, the following thesis will be pursued: MB texts evince moral implications not only as an implicitly normative and programmed way of seeing life, but with explicit action guides. The first of two further background sections will compare MB thought with Buddhism in general.

II. *MB in the Light of Early Buddhist Ethics, Common and Theravādin*

The ancient physical necessity and cultivated ability to memorize and utilize oral instead of written traditions is a stumbling block to the contemporary, "linear" mind. It is difficult to realize that earlier peoples, especially the formal keepers and chanters of canonical and popular traditions, *sūtras*, or stories, had trained their memories to accurate retention of enormous quantities of materials (phenomena now textually and archaeologically verifiable). Naturally this practice has impeded critical methods of modern historical research which rely heavily on written documentation. The phenomenon of exclusively oral sources, therefore, must be dealt with in the history of Buddhism as well as in those of other traditions. If Jesus wrote only in dust, the historical Buddha (c. 563-483 B.C.E.) seems to have surpassed him in his disregard for the written word. Possibly this neglect was related to the Buddha's rejection of Hindu doctrinal writings, rituals, and religious authority. At any rate, extant documents do not seem to have been codified in script by either Theravādins or Mahāyānists before c. 70-80 B.C.E., four centuries after the Buddha's death.[5] Enlightenment was perhaps to be found not in searching the *sūtras* or *sūtras* alone, but in one's heart. While textual and historical studies point to the probable preexistence of some textual passages in the form of oral communications as early as 340 B.C.E.,[6] the earliest written texts from which one can attempt to infer what the historical Buddha taught are traceable only to the first centuries B.C.E. and C.E. By this period doctrinal disagreements had finally helped to inspire written codification.

If Edward Conze's well-known hypothesis is correct, that Buddhist "documents as we have them, date back no farther than the Christian era," then the ensuing speculation is relevant for Buddhist ontology and moral teachings alike. But it would still seem to call for clearer verification. Some historians and philologists see Iranian, Greek, Zoroastrian, and even Christian influences on Buddhist symbols which were not similarly present in previous Asian life; for example, the importance of the theme of light, images of the Buddha, halos, alleged Trinitarian symbols, and the prediction of the Maitreya Buddha who, like Jesus in his second coming, is to arrive in this world in a future historical period.

Prescinding from such speculation and from other possible geographical, physical, and cultural influences on Buddhist teaching, Theravādins and Mahāyānists both have claimed that their respective written canons stem directly from the historical Buddha. In fact, some Mahāyānists are not concerned about historical derivations, on the grounds that enlightenment is found not through scriptures, but inwardly. In their opinion, verification of authentic Buddhist teachings does not need an historical basis.[7] Where Mahāyāna teachings diverge from Theravāda, some Mahāyānists would argue the accuracy of their own views experientially rather than historically. For experiential outsiders, however, the divergences must be compared historically. In either case, since these two forms of Buddhism claim equal antiquity and "orthodoxy" and since they are not in agreement on some key points, an initial sketch of MB thought relevant to morality can begin by referring to ethical elements which seem common to both paths. If the outline also describes high profile features in TB, it will prepare those less familiar with Buddhism for clearer observations of MB emphases or divergences from TB ethics.

Initial allusion to moral commonalities is significant from two points of view about history and doctrines. For those who are concerned with historical continuity as a criterion of authenticity or truth, it is the teachings reflected in both paths which are more capable of being traced to the historical Buddha and consequently to the so-called essence of Buddhist teaching. Others, who envisage Buddhism more developmentally or experientially, focus their attention not merely on what the *Buddha* taught but on what *Buddhists* have taught; each of them being at least potential Buddhas or manifestations of the one Buddha-nature. Their legitimation of this quest may be expressed metaphorically in terms of peeling the onion. The onion-peeler who probes for its essence or core will find no core. In fact, he may miss noticing the onion itself in the process.

Even from this developmental perspective, nevertheless, the search for common ethical elements in the two paths is fruitful for Buddhist dialogue within Buddhism and with other religious and human traditions. It may also base practical, intercultural, or international agreements which would work more effectively or durably than present accords or detente. Not that the discovery of common moral norms and values of itself offers adequate validation of their truth. Forty million Marxists, Frenchmen, or humanists of any background can be wrong. Arguments from numerical or historical consensus, taken as arguments from authority as such, possess only a limited weight. But commonality provides more than an appeal to the *authority* of consensus. It functions primarily as a utilitarian indicator of collective experience and of what works transculturally. The quest for common Buddhist moral teachings is a small, but vital, part of the humanistic quest for a minimal common denominator ethic of human survival and cooperation on this planet of swiftly depleting resources. From Buddhist points of view their teachings are part of the karmic reduction of suffering and of reaching better rebirths or final enlightenment. In the present context, the search for common Buddhist convictions is an integral part of grasping MB ethics by those who lack Buddhist experience.

A. *Common Buddhist Moral Teaching.* With the problematic exception of some Mahāyānists, general Buddhist doctrines directly pertinent to ethics include the 1) fourfold noble truth and the eightfold path, 2) ten Buddhist commandments, 3) virtues like liberality (giving, *dāna*) and the "four unlimited virtues" *brahmavihāras* of compassionate equanimity, and 4) value emphases such as caste equality.

1. *The fourfold noble truth and the eightfold path.* The world-view proposed in the Buddha's fourfold noble truth is that i) existence itself is suffering (*duḥkha*); ii) suffering is caused by craving or desire (*taṇhā*) especially for individual selfhood; iii) desire and suffering are relieved by an existential awakening

or enlightenment (*nirvāṇa*) to "non-self" or egolessness (*anātman*, Skt; *anatta*, Pali). In other words, they disappear in the realization that the "self" is not dual in relation to other beings (non- or trans-dualism) and that the perception of the independent existence of any being is illusory or at least, for some, unknowable. (The depth of this conviction at the popular level remains problematic). The last factor in the fourfold noble truth, which concerns the means for attaining enlightenment, is iv) the practice of the eightfold path which involves qualities of correct seeing, but also entails correct doing (*sīla*).[8] For Buddhism in any form, life, seen as a problem, is the relief of suffering. Different interpretations, however, will evolve about whether the relief comes through autonomous wisdom and "self"-intuition, gradually or suddenly, or by faith and help from bodhisattvas (enlightened beings on the verge of realizing *nirvāṇa* or Buddha-nature, with its endless synonyms). Thus, MB in particular will bracket the fourfold truth only in emphasis.

2. *The ten commandments*. Correct behavior or *sīla* for both laity and monks (the *saṅgha*) prohibits killing, stealing, lying, adultery, and the use of intoxicants. These precepts were contained already in Hindu ethics, as well as in other traditions. Thus, it is by no means clear that they divulge the specificity of Buddhist ethics. Chinese Buddhists will later correlate them with the five Confucian norms of *jên* (human-heartedness), *i* (justice), *li* (propriety), *chun-tzu*, *te*, and *hsin* (gentlemanliness, moral character, and trust)—also with *chih* (wisdom). While one may question the perfect correspondence of these Buddhist precepts and Confucian norms, it was very important for some Chinese Buddhists to insist on it. Their ultimate goal was to reassure the Confucian dynasties and literati that far from excluding the Confucian ethical relationships, especially filial piety (*hsiao*), Buddhism universalized them. Thus, at least in later Chinese versions, the five Buddhist precepts became Sinicized or more emphatically moralized, as Michihata Ryōshū and Kenneth K. S. Ch'en have insisted.[9] This ethical emphasis concurs with Winston King's belief that from the TB point of view, including that of its monastic elite, the five Buddhist precepts "may be inwardized into attitudes and further extended by more positive ethical qualities...,"[10] like the four Hindu and Buddhist unlimited virtues of compassionate equanimity.

In either simplified or extended ethical dimensions, Theravādins believed that the first five precepts were externally binding on everyone. But only the saint could really observe them.[11] The same moral pessimism/humility will appear again in Pure Land Mahāyāna thought, which will appeal to salvation from outside the self.

Beyond the five precepts, some early TB and MB redactions of commands for everyone also refer to covetousness, slander, wrong views, hatred, insult, and idle talk. These versions, usually grouped mnemonically in tens, are called *daśa-sīla* (ten precepts) or *daśākusala*, the "ten not-right" or evil deeds (Chinese: *Shih-e*; Japanese: *Jūaku*). Although the thoroughly detailed correlations by Soothill and Hodous of Hindu, TB, and MB commandments seem to hint that the more interiorized and sophisticated commands are of exclusively MB origin, this implication is corrected by Winston King and S. Tachibana.[12] From humanistically social and activistic viewpoints, all of these norms may seem self-centered or negative unless they are surveyed in the wider context of Buddhist virtues and values.

3. *Virtues*. Besides the precepts, there are other common Buddhist qualities considered crucial for the path to better rebirths or enlightenment. They consist of giving or liberality (*dāna-sīla*; sharing without clinging) and the four unlimited virtues (*brahmavihāras*) of *maitrī* or benevolence (Pali: *metta*), *karuṇā* or compassion (*karunā*), *muditā* or sympathetic joy, and, above all, *upekṣā* or equanimity (*upekkhā*).[13] While compassion will vie with or complement equanimity, neither of these or the other cardinal virtues pretend to exhaust the Buddhist capacity for describing the path toward enlightenment. Further, as is the case in other systems, mere lists of commands and virtues do not unveil the entirety of Buddhist morality nor do they yet unfold its specific ethos or dynamic. One must look more closely at value emphases, especially as portrayed in moral models.

4. *Value emphases*. Comparable value emphases exist in both the TB and MB paths in that five offenses are judged especially grave. They prohibit killing one's mother, father, an Arhat (*arahant*), a Buddha, or harming the community of monks (*saṅgha*). MB versions expand the five grave sins to include the killing of a bodhisattva or a nun, sacrilege, slander, and wrong

views about teachings, including the karmic or natural moral effects of good and bad deeds.[14] In addition to the virtues of compassionate equanimity, therefore, one begins to discern a more concretely expressed Buddhistic ethos of non-injury (*ahimsā*), whatever its affinities with Jainism. Another central value phenomenon not generally highlighted in the milieu of Buddhist moral ethos is the fact that the Buddha's rejection of Indian caste discrimination implied revolutionary consequences for morality and human rights and perhaps for the Indian expulsion of such Buddhism until the twentieth century. If Buddhist monks eventually came to control temple slaves and tenant farmers, as Kenneth Ch'en contends, performance need not be wholly identified with professed ideals, nor alleged spiritual elitism with the expressed hope of universal enlightenment or salvation. Statements attributed to the historical Buddha insist that personal dignity is not related to birth, but to conduct.[15] Omitted here is a potential debate that the *saṅgha* at least sometimes functioned as a spiritual caste, a cross-cultural problem in religious leadership.

Another value not to be forgotten is that while in TB practice and in some MB teachings there is no place for an autonomous morality in which individuals think and decide for themselves (especially laity), the Buddha reputedly rejected an ethic based on heteronomous authority. Instead he urged his followers to be lamps and refuges to themselves.[16] The heritage of this tradition was to live on in dynamic tension with countercurrents and reappear not only in TB but in MB Ch'an (Zen) and elsewhere. In humanistic terms and at first glance, therefore, common Buddhist morality does not seem to offer moral precepts, virtues, or value emphases inferior to other religious and human traditions. This point will be repeated in a later context of Buddhist moral models.

B. *Theravāda Moral Ethos.* For a clearer look at MB moral texts, the next step is the delineation of the moral ethos claimed to be specifically Theravādin. Since contemporary scholars have already examined TB ethical texts in some detail, observations and documentation can, in the MB focus of this essay, rely largely on theirs. By contrast, a subsequent survey of MB ethics will have to proceed directly to primary scriptures and classics. Even in such an initial and programmatic survey such as this there is no alternative, because no study of MB moral texts yet exists.

Commandments in TB ethics might be more appropriately described as counsels, inasmuch as they are reputedly not received by peoples in an authoritative fashion. In spite of the intricacy of TB canonical texts and commentaries, the authority of magisterial interpretation is at least ideally disavowed. It is said that the *saṅgha* does not command, but merely signals actions which lead away from or toward better rebirths and enlightenment.[17] Be that as it may, perhaps it is in TB virtues rather than in its commandments where the particular specificity of TB ethics will attract recognition.

Virtues considered notably characteristic of TB ethics comprise, from an outside view, a somewhat positive yet passive gestalt of self-restraint, temperance, contentment, patience, purity, celibacy, humility, toleration, reverence, gratitude, righteousness, and benevolence. S. Tachibana's pioneering and lengthy collation of these virtues seems to disclose the configuration of a passive moral ethos.[18] But as indicated previously, an ethos can be manifested less in virtues and values held to be basic than in evils which are judged most radical.

The fundamental TB evils are hatred, ignorance (rather *moha* or delusion), and covetousness. Prevailing scholarly conjectures place ignorance clearly at the roots of Theravāda immorality. As in Brahminic Hinduism, morality refers more to enlightenment or mind culture than to volition, more to wisdom than to good in itself or for others. If the regulation of one's social relations is ultimately oriented to the eradication of ignorance and the attainment of "personal" enlightenment, then some would contend that Theravāda morality is no morality at all, but a form of philosophical egoism, subjectively amoral. Both Caroline Rhys Davids and Louis de la Vallée-Poussin have called Theravāda ethics deliberately eudaemonistic or egoistic.[19] Not that egoistic morality is necessarily selfish in practice, particularly in a non-dualistic ambit; but behavior is prescribed in terms of the effects it will have on the "self" rather than on others.[20] Anger is bad because of what it does to the person who is angry. Helping others is good because it helps the self.[21]

This kind of consequentialist rationale for morality operates smoothly, especially in an allegedly atheistic tradition like TB.

But it works only insofar as persons continue to see the good of others as identical or coherent with the good of the self. TB's moral dysfunctions are additionally minimized to the extent that concrete value conflicts can be resolved by authoritative appeals to canonical or interpretative sources. (Paradoxically, authoritative interpretations arose even about the Buddha's teachings on the primacy of autonomous decision over external authority). When an authoritative ethic functions this efficiently, precodified or externally imposed solutions cannot escape the perils of arbitrary, legalistic, and harmful judgments. This Procrustean hazard is not unknown in the annals of other religious and human casuistries. The temptation of legalism has been attractive everywhere, perhaps because it is explicit, specific, and efficiently tailored to eliminate the burden of personal decision-making. Better to surrender the weight of liberty to the Grand Inquisitor. At the theoretical level legalistic action-guides also remove the arduous metaethical labor of justifying altruism and of analyzing the epistemological grounds of conflicting value claims. As a result, dialogue with Theravāda ethics cannot begin directly at an analytical or metaethical level in contemporary European or American fashions.

In mentioning the topic of metaethical validation of moral claims, it should be underlined that TB verification of values ends up grounding itself not only on autonomous intuition or decision and authority, but also on an experience of karmic (*kammic*) effects on the self (the "chain of causation" or "of dependent origination").[22] The *Dhammapada* encapsulates the thought in axioms like the following: "Hatreds never cease by hatred in this world; by love alone they cease." This is an ancient law. The others know not that in this quarrel we perish; those of them who realize it have their quarrels calmed thereby.[23] In practice, therefore, consequentialist moral logic overrides the theoretical and not clearly popular belief in non-self (*anatta*).

To qualify metaethical judgments about philosophical egoism like those of Rhys Davids and Vallée-Poussin, it is not entirely evident that Theravāda ethics are as amoral as it would first appear, much less utilitarian in the derogatory sense of the term. The thesis that TB sin is basically wrong-viewing rather than bad will must compete with the fact that of the three roots of evil (hatred, ignorance, and covetousness), the last root, covetousness, functions concretely, if not in theory, as the final ground of all evils. This is not to preclude debate over the possibly cognitive meaning of covetousness, nor to retract what has been conjectured above about the possibility of freedom without the coexistence of sin as perversity. At any rate, the TB stress on covetousness is evinced in the unique need to employ (volitionally or not) over seventy terms to express the basic pervasiveness of covetousness in human life.[24] Examples of this language include attached craving or desire (*taṇhā*), greed, and avarice. One may conclude that in practice the source of desire is only problematically reducible to ignorance (*avidyā*) and amorality.

Nonetheless, dialectically opposite to the vice of willed covetousness, there remains the Theravāda accentuation of detached, contemplative equanimity rather than compassion which is productive for others. This feature would seem to support an outside humanistic judgment that TB morality would operate egoistically, and thereby dysfunctionally, in cultural systems where there is no adequate authority to insure a proper sharing of social goods and solutions of conflicts over values and rights. But, as indicated above, if such characterization is to avoid caricature, it must be balanced with the fact that Theravādan, non-dualistic equanimity entails non-attachment also to the "self" and to mine-thine distinctions.[25] The ideal recluse's contemplative or "televolitional" wish to radiate effective moral goodwill to his community may not be irremediably removed from a dynamic which could put that goodwill into action. This distance may be bridged above all when, like modern TB monks, the Arhat or recluse feels incapable of final enlightenment (*nirvāṇa*; *nibbāna*). He is then motivated to practice penultimate and social works like educational or medical aid. Further, the eminence of TB "self"-love as a prerequisite for mature love of others implies an instruction comparable to whatever wisdom exists in some contemporary psychological theories about the necessity of authentic self-love replacing thanatos or the instinct for self-destruction. The same comparison may be drawn with strands of Confucian, Jewish, and Christian traditions.[26]

Apart from ideals about caste equality and moral autonomy (to be further examined below), there is little in the material content of TB ethics that had not already appeared in Brahminic ethics, although the case is convincingly argued that there were both Buddhist and Jain influences on Brahminism. This generalization about similarity also applies to TB's different yet parallel claim that enlightenment means the inward realization that each individual being is really the one Hindu Brahman-Ātman. The picture begins to emerge, then, of a negative ethos stemming from idealized qualities which, as Winston King expressed it, are less dissimilar to *nibbāna* than are their opposites. This negativity is highlighted especially by the prevalence of detached equanimity.[27] In the TB symbol system, this virtue is conjoined with the image of the monk (*bhikku*) who finally becomes an Arhat and is assured of enduring *nibbāna* at death. That goal could be attained by no laity and by increasingly fewer monks without many rebirths. Thus, the ethos of non-discriminating love or equanimity, however unegoistical in itself, seemed distant and unreachable to Mahāyānists. For them, the Arhat, a figure of invisibly helpful equanimity, stood in stark contrast to an allegedly forgotten symbol of original Buddhism, the compassionate bodhisattva (enlightened being).

Compared with other religious and ethical models who have permanently or indefinitely departed to their various paradises, the bodhisattva is a striking personage who delays his or her own enlightenment to help all other beings obtain the same *nirvāṇa*, either in this life or in another birth. Textual inquiry will indicate that this image is displayed as a moral ideal and altruistic model for many, if not all, Mahāyānists. The bodhisattva's purpose in life was not to die for others but to live for them, again and again. In Greek terminology, thanatos yielded to eros or life-affirmation. Textual description will also verify that key altruistic virtues and norms, not entirely invisible in TB ethics, take on a new form and prominence in MB.

III. *The Historical Origin of MB*

If all readers could grant the "orthodoxy" or complementary significance of MB as Buddhist truth, they could immediately set up criteria for MB ethical textual selections. But since MB's historicity and importance is still challenged by some, especially its nearly theistic deification of the Buddha, if not bodhisattvas, they insist on reviewing MB's historical origin.

Theravādins would admit that according to their own *sūtras*, like the *Dhammāpada*, the Buddha gave his monks the mandate to wander out of compassion for the good and welfare of gods and men.[28] But Mahāyānists counter that although the TB Arhat wished enlightenment for others, he was satisfied with his own.[29] MB points to the historical Buddha's compassionate willingness to remain to teach his followers after his own enlightenment. It looks to his altruistic *life* rather than to his more self-focused *teachings*. Consequently, Mahāyānists have felt that Theravādins neglect an important and creative dimension of original Buddhism, the bodhisattvas. The latter, like the historical Buddha, are to live virtuously the six perfections or *pāramitās* not only for themselves, but for others.[30] This compassionate dimension more neatly parallels the early (pre-TB and pre-MB) or pre-canonical, social interpretations of the Ashokan inscriptions.[31] For insights into early Buddhism the stone engraved inscriptions of Ashoka are invaluable. As the third Mauryan emperor in India (c. 268-233 or 304-236 B.C.E.), this warrior king turned partly against war and caste and toward a layman's moral interpretation of Buddhist dharma (Maskī Rock Edict). Ashoka is important, first of all, for aiding present historical reconstructions of so-called archaic or pre-canonical Buddhism, i.e. the state of Buddhism predating divisions which later survived mainly as MB and TB (other divisions having grown dormant). Ashoka is significant secondly for his most ancient codifications, still observable in Nepal and India today and clearly legible. Thirdly, his notable moral contribution is that he evinces the early moralization of Buddhist teaching. His fourteen rock, five pillar, and one cave inscriptions and edicts literally carve out a program of social thrift, welfare, distribution of wealth, and non-injury to life (Pillar Edict VIII). In the context of his times, his respect for slaves and women also deserve consideration (Rock Edicts XI and XII). Virtues especially prominent for Ashoka were compassion for the suffering, liberality, gentleness, and religious toleration (Rock Edict XIII and Pillar Edict VII). *Dharma* entails "few sins and many good deeds, of kindness, liberality, truthfulness, and purity" (Pillar Edict II). As a whole, it must be pointed out that bodhisattvas are absent and functionally replaced by the motivations of karma and the world to come (Pillar Edict III). But the remnants of the Ashokan version of early Buddhism seem more reflective of MB aspirations than less socially conscious Buddhist ideals.

Turning from pre-canonical Buddhism to MB *sūtras*, the historical Buddha (Śākyamuni or Gautama) fades from prominence. Through his declarations to his disciples, he becomes the legitimator of another Buddha, among whose many manifestations and names are Nyorai, Tathāgata, and Amida (Amitāyus, Amitābha) Buddha. Amida Buddha is a transcendent "being" whose historical existence is of relatively little or no importance. The account of his life is vital only insofar as it records his compassionate vows or promises. While he was still a bodhisattva, he pledged to help all beings to birth in his Buddha-land of pure bliss (Western Paradise) and to eventual enlightenment. It was precisely in this expression of compassion that he became enlightened as the transcendent Amida Buddha who would remain beyond time and save others through the intercession and help of Avalokiteśvara and other bodhisattvas.[32]

In early MB texts relatively few beings are to become bodhisattvas. But after birth in a Buddha-land and an indefinitely (sic) long period of bliss (which might function popularly like a Christian heaven), all beings will finally obtain enlightenment. Some bodhisattvas, however, delay their own full and permanent destiny and return to this life to help other beings toward the same goal.

In some later MB thought like that of Shinran (1173-1262 C.E.), not just some beings, but all beings, are to return as bodhisattvas in countless rebirths for the sake of others. For Shinran, the compassionate faith attained in this life brings such joy that it almost seems to be more prominent than *nirvāṇa* itself.

Among the many Buddhas or manifestations of Buddhahood, Amida Buddha increasingly emerges in China and Japan as the pivotal figure (a trend which the Buddhist leader, Nichiren, tried to oppose in Japan). Devotion to Amida by the people, conjoined with a faith-full and prayerful reliance on his help, approaches the kind of theistic and soteriological relationship which some Christians claim to have had with Jesus. Amida's land, the Pure Land of Bliss, becomes the central heaven. For some scholars, this worldview will take on less literal than metaphysical and symbolic functions. At either level, Amida Buddha and his heaven will answer to the transitoriness of life and offer eschatological models of perfection (bodhisattvas) whose virtues or *pāramitās* display moral compassion as the supreme Buddhist ethos.

In sum, the historical Buddha, Śākyamuni, assumes a growing mythological appearance from the time of the *Lotus Sūtra* (1st-2d centuries C.E.) and another transcendental Buddha, Amida, of whom Śākyamuni was but one manifestation, becomes salient. His pure land of happiness is already described in Pure Land and other *sūtras* (specified in note 32). He stands as an object of devotion and a source of salvation. In Pure Land MB, faith will rank high above the works of morality. Yet bodhisattvas, who forego enlightenment endlessly for others, appear to offer the paradigm of a thoroughly altruistic and morally concerned ethic both for present and future lives. If D. T. Suzuki was correct, for some Mahāyānists even the historical Buddha begins to resemble a bodhisattva, for he is never at ease in *nirvāṇa* and is ready to reappear in the world when necessary, "the sufferer of others' suffering."[33]

The bodhisattva, and all that he may now or later symbolize morally, including a potential, if not actual, basis for a social ethic, seems to emerge suddenly, like a meteor in the sky of Buddhist history. It will be helpful for some readers, therefore, to diagram how some Mahāyānists authenticate the bodhisattvas' doctrinal position and authority on historical and textual grounds,[34] granting the merely "expedient" or pedagogical nature of such justification for others.

Contemporary Mahāyānists reject the paradigm of MB as a later and perhaps spurious development of TB. This recalls how Christian reformers have protested that their form of Christianity is not a development of Roman Catholicism, but a return to essential aspects of an earlier religion which Catholicism, like TB, had come to neglect. In a simple diagram the MB model may be expressed as follows:

The Historical Buddha

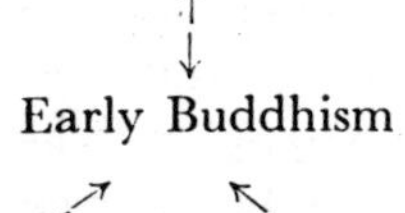

Early Buddhism

Mahāyāna traditions (all-inclusive)	Only some Theravāda traditions (and these not all-inclusive)[35]

In MB history, therefore, MB thought and *sūtras* not only equal TB but surpass it in both antiquity and authenticity.

Edward Conze spells out the details of this highly simplified schema with attention to the traditional count of eighteen schools of Buddhism within its first five centuries. MB fragmented into further schools or trends as it crossed from India through China and especially into Japan. Prescinding from the *Avataṁsaka* or *Hua-yen* schools,[36] those which survived and influenced Chinese and Japanese cultures in particular are 1) Pure Land, 2) Ch'an (Zen), and 3) T'ien-t'ai (which stemmed from Chih-i's [538-597 C.E.] interpretation of the *Lotus Sūtra* and evolved into Japanese Tendai and, later, Nichiren Buddhism). The present omission of Vajrayāna or Tantric MB (Japanese Shingon) will be explained below. The complexity of these three schools alone, not to mention their sub-species, and the massive quantity of their *sūtras* and commentaries is so overwhelming that criteria must be sought for estimating which schools and texts can be meaningfully representative of MB thought.[37]

IV. *Criteria for Textual Selections*

The first and most obvious criterion is the practical, if historically elusive one : which schools are alive? This question does not ignore schools, sects, or texts which are not prominent in the living center of MB today, Japan. The historical and potential value of Tāntric MB illustrates a special case in point. Neither can it avoid minimal allusion to the Indian and Chinese origins of and impact on Japanese MB. But because of the overt suppression of MB in Tibet and the People's Republic of China and because of long decline in India and increasing Hindu appropriation (a tide only partly and recently reversed), the criterion of "aliveness" legitimates an attempt to isolate MB schools and texts which thrive more vigorously in Japan than they do in other countries. Lastly, this kind of question brackets missionary footholds of Buddhism around the globe.

A. *Representativeness*. Abstracting, then, from esoteric Vajrayāna (*Chen-yen Tsung* or *Shingon*)[38] living MB teachings in China, but especially in Japan, can be representatively surveyed through an examination of texts utilized by the sects of three active and influential schools: Pure Land (especially Jōdo Shinshu or Shinran's True Pure Land Sect); Zen; and Nichiren (named after its founder, 1222-1282 C.E.)[39] Statistics alone, of course, can only suggest, not document, historical impact. This matter awaits confirmation, not only from more refined statistical methods and cooperation, but also from historical and social analyses. With these reservations it can be noted that the Japanese Agency for Cultural Affairs published the following data in 1972, noting also that "adherents" is ambivalent enough to allow for cross-overs and highly tenuous membership: Pure Land: 20, 941, 532; Zen 10, 150, 010; and Nichiren 31, 887, 015.[40] Since the Nichiren numbers partly include adherents of twentieth century "new religions" which are not purely Buddhist but syncretistic (including over sixteen million Japanese members of the missionary Sōka Gakkai), the above outline is not a precise indication of Nichiren strength. A judgment accounting for syncretism as well as scholarly and practical Buddhist activity at home and abroad would position Pure Land and Zen MB as the most simply representative forms of living Buddhism. Thus, it is within these schools and their subgroups where representative MB moral texts can be most efficiently located. The practicality of this rationale is confirmed in that Nichiren Buddhism focuses wholly on the *Lotus* and *Diamond* scriptures, both of which are utilized in Pure Land and Zen. In conclusion, an introduction to MB ethical writings can be conveniently studied in two categories: Pure Land and Zen.

Later, it will be illustrated how a full account of influential moral texts would also include popular poetry, stories, plays, and films in addition to formal literature. While the examination of all these materials is an undertaking too vast to be encompassed in one essay, further remarks in the corpus and notes will offer a programmatic beginning for future moral analyses. The size of the full project indicates why this study may reasonably conclude with brief illustrations from the following samples. Formal literature: *The Dimond Sūtra*, *The Lotus Sūtra*, Shinran's *Letters*, and Dogen's *Diamond*. Popular samples: the most famous Japanese *Nō* play, *Matsukaze* and the samurai drama (with Confucian and Buddhist allusions), *Chūsingura* (*The Tale of the Forty-seven Ronin*). A grasp of the impact of MB ethics in popular Japanese classics will necessitate reference to its previous and (surprisingly) continuing significance in Chinese classics.

B. *The Role of Popular Classics.* Second to extant representativeness among criteria for MB textual selections is its corollary criterion: should one turn to popular as well as to formal or canonical literature ? While historical records may remain permanently unsatisfactory about the extent to which literate leaders spread the messages of the longer *sūtras* and commentaries to a-literate masses, the popularity and impact of recitations, poetry, fables, and simple or ornate theater may be more easily documented.

The addition of this criterion of more directly observable popularity directs one back to Chinese Buddhist classics as well as the Japanese. Curiously, for example, Confucian appropriations of popular fables and beliefs in novels like the fourteenth century *Water Margin* was attacked by Mao Tse-tung's press as late as 1976.[41] But the same regime finds it convenient to praise Buddhist novels like the sixteenth century *Journey to the West*[42] —this, in spite of the formal suppression of Buddhism.[43] In the Buddhist novel, *The Dream of the Red Chamber*,[44] praised as the literary pinnacle of all Chinese novels, Chinese Marxists have found a model of detached anti-feudalism. Thus, an incorporation of popular literature in textual selections shows that Chinese Buddhism may not run only underground, if at all, but also in open popular channels.

A key objection against the inclusion of popular literature in any religious history is the allegation that it generally represents pre-religious or secular trends which were either separate or inimical to religions. But a closer inspection of Chinese poetry and novels or of Japanese *Nō* theater, *Kabuki*, and films, to say nothing of novels which they sometimes retell, like *The Tale of Genji*,[45] may establish that indigenously religious and moral themes were often quite popular in themselves. This attraction existed before they were absorbed within more formal traditions, as in Buddhism, or coopted by moral or humanistic programs, as in Chinese Marxism.

Formal and elitist traditions commonly appear in complementary as well as in dialectical relationships with popular beliefs. The low qualitative common denominator of cultural taste which sometimes exists or is read into popularity en masse is only sporadically present. In some of these cases, the popularization of the vulgar (like in *The Water Margin* or allegedly in some Japanese theater and film) springs from economic or religious elites more often than it emanates spontaneously from the masses. With caution, consequently, the popularity of peoples' classics may serve as a second criterion for "textual" selection.

C. *Latent Ethical Convictions.* A third factor in literary choices (in a list which cannot yet claim to be exhaustive) can be stated more briefly. Do not MB authors, like Victorian, Jansenistic, and Puritan literary artists, sometimes "protest too much" or too briefly about the tales of this-worldly love and life which they depict in such vivid and lingering beauty ? Listeners or readers are then left with the task of distinguishing overt judgments from covert, or at least unconscious, moral sympathies, especially in past eras and present situations where various species of censorship have been rigid and sometimes punitive. In addition to the first two criteria of indirect representativeness and direct popularity, a third one, literary analysis, must ally itself (at either ordinary or professional levels) with psychological, sociological, political, and other perspectives.

Bearing in mind previous sections about I) the difference between normative worldviews and explicit moral systems, II) the common early moral teachings of Buddhism contrasted with TB ethics, III) MB versions of past history, and IV) the above criteria for choosing samples of moral texts, six samples of formal literature and two popular masterpieces will now be scanned for moral content. This brief, concluding section cannot yet prove, but strongly suggests that MB texts in general divulge both a partly moral way of seeing and systemic codes of behavior.

V. *Samples of MB Texts with Moral Implications*

The subsequent isolation of formal literature in Pure Land Buddhism deals with 1) *The Diamond Sūtra*, 2) *The Lotus Sūtra*, and 3) Shinran's *Letters*.

1. *The Diamond Sūtra* (*Vajracchedikā Prajñāpāramitā*). As a fourth century C.E. compendium of the earliest Indian MB wisdom (*prajñā*) literature about perfection (*pāramitā*), the brevity of this *sūtra*, if not the synthesis of its themes, kept it memorizable and popular in Pure Land, Ch'an (Zen) and T'ien'tai (later Nichiren) Buddhism. While each MB school utilized some *sūtras* as favorites, like *The Larger Sūtra of Eternal Life* or *The Meditation Sūtra* in Pure Land Buddhism,[46] the latter school is less exclusive in its concurrent use of Lotus and *Prajñā* literature

like *The Diamond Sūtra.* This *sūtra*'s model of human conduct summarizes wisdom ideas traceable to its larger textual predecessors c. 100 B.C.E.,[47] notably the bodhisattva who "unsupported gives a gift" whose merit is not easy to measure.[48] It is the giving of the six *pāramitās*. The fact that these perfections are sought not only for "one's own benefit but for others"[49] is what D. T. Suzuki called one of the original ideas which TB lost sight of.[50] As elsewhere, the six *pāramitās* here cover the moral dimensions of 1) giving one's whole self, *dāna*, 2) morality (*sīla*) or all Buddhist precepts conducive to the moral welfare of self and others, and 3) humility (a feeling of limitation and sinfulness). They also entail a contemplative emphasis on striving, meditation, and intuitive wisdom.[51] The first two perfections could conceivably lead the bodhisattva to relieve not only the suffering of life itself (by teaching the way to enlightenment), but, however secondarily, also to alleviate suffering in any form, no matter how minute or physical. Here lies an ancient basis for a potential social ethic. Yet belief in an *invisible* extension of good karma or merit to others may interweave with it dialectically.

In *The Diamond Sūtra* the bodhisattvas are clearly ethical as well as contemplative models. They "are gifted with good conduct, gifted with virtuous qualities, gifted with wisdom, ..."[52] However, these sparse references do not demonstrate that a moral model overshadows the primacy of right seeing or realization. The same qualification is to be applied to the following work, although not as strongly.

2. *The Lotus Sūtra* (*Saddharmapuṇḍarika*), 1st-2d centuries C.E.[53] Popular for its mysterious Indian origins, its concrete descriptions and parallels, and its synthesized variety of sources, this text has attracted universal MB attention. As it has been already noted, it has served as the key text of T'ien'tai, Tendai, and Nichiren Buddhism. Chapter IV tells the parable of a prodigal son which extols moral frugality and compassion.[54] Chapter XXIV praises the virtues of the compassionate bodhisattva, Avalokiteśvara. With its references to Amida Buddha, universal salvation, and compassionate equanimity, this *sūtra* links the bodhisattva's role as moral model to both early and multiple schools of Buddhism. Chapter three on skillful means (*upāya-kauśalya*) is highly popular in this *sūtra* and remains a major theme for many Buddhists.

3. *The Letters of Shinran.*[55] While the cult of Amida Buddha had its genesis in northwest India, use of the Pure Land *Sūtras* and actual belief in Amida's land of bliss is more patently traced to China (with Hui-yuan, c. 350 C.E.). It is commonly stated that by the time of Shinran's True Pure Land Sect (*Jōdo Shinshu*), the sympathetic and unjudging Amida will have been increasingly portrayed as one who loves and saves not only all men but also women, however sinful. Since all human beings possess a sinful nature, the sole condition for salvation is faith alone rather than moral merit. Yet, for the first time in history, Buddhist monks are to marry as a sign of their sharing the burdens of ordinary peoples. Similarly, common moral precepts are to be obeyed. Nonetheless, with the fifteenth century St Rennyo (called the second founder of *Shinshu*), morality is theoretically lowered to a second level of truth.[56]

Apart from the interpretations of followers like Rennyo, Shinran's major commentary on the Pure Land *sūtras* has been edited and translated into English by the Eastern Buddhist Society as *The Kyōgyōshinshō*. (*The Collection of Passages Expounding The True Teaching, Living Faith, And Realization of the Pure Land*) by Shinran Shōnin (1173-1262 C.E.). Important above all for the editors' glossary as well as its companion volume on *Collected Writings on Shin Buddhism* by D. T. Suzuki, this edition of *The Kyōgyōshinshō* shows that for all Shinran's stress on Amida's eighteenth vow which evokes faith, there are ample codifications of virtues and sins.[57] The same may be posited of the widely read, thirteenth century *Tannishō* which lists the ten evil courses of action and five deadly sins.[58] But it is in the songs and, particularly, in *The Private Letters of Shinran Shonin*—where moral discipline and virtues are most esteemed.[59] Here Shinran explicitly denies that morality can be bypassed and condemns those who use his teaching to justify evil deeds. "How could it be permitted of us...to behave as we will, steal, or kill others ?"[60]

Turning from the moral implications of Pure Land Buddhism to the formal literature of Zen Buddhism, the outside observer must admit the language of this second central form of living Japanese MB seems to be even more amoral than Pure Land's. But, these appearances are belied by the ability of some Zennists to lead social or academically productive lives in the present. The ensuing comments on part of Dogen's (1200-1253 C.E.)[61]

Shōbōgenzō are offered not as proof but as an illustration that there is an abundance of moral language in Zen writings. However low the profile of Zen respect for the written word, Zen literature has been utilized regularly and ritually by religious and laity alike. Its considerable library includes, first of all, the *sūtras* called *Diamond, Laṅkāvatāra, Avataṁsaka, Vimalakīrti*, and the *Platform Sūtra of the Sixth Patriarch* (1st-5th centuries C.E.).[62] Reserving the crucial study of Rinzai Zen to future enterprises, the subsequent observations apply primarily to Sōtō Zen. At the contemporary pole of both Zen sects, Zen literature comprises preceptive ceremonials and the trans-cultural writings of Nishida Kitarō, Abe Masao, Nishitani Keiji, Hisamatsu Shin'ichi, and, in part, D. T. Suzuki. All of these authors have had a great deal to express about the inexpressibility of Zen enlightenment and its way of life. This phenomenon is not uncommon in many religions by those taken up with the otherness or transcendence of God or the absolute.

4. *Kyojukaimon*. In the middle period, Zen texts embraced the many precepts enumerated in the thirteenth century Keizan Zenji's *Kyojukaimon* (*Giving and Receiving the Teaching of the Precepts*).[63] Tracing the precepts to the historical Buddha, with reference to greed, anger, delusion, and pride, Keizan wrote: "From Zazen the Precepts arise eternally, whether they are the five, the eight, the Great Precepts of the Bodhisattvas, the Precepts of the priesthood...or the Highest Law. ..."[64]

5. *Shōbōgenzō*. The central Zen work of the middle period for ethics is Dogen's *Shōbōgenzō*. The most complete English translation (thirty-five chapters) of the Shōbōgenzō's ninety-two chapters has been published by Kosen Nishiyama and John Stevens as *Shōbōgenzō* (*The Eye and Treasury of the True Law*). A full translation has been promised by autumn 1977.[65] English translations of chapters 1, 5, 6, 18, 29, and 35 by Norman Waddell and Abe Masao have also been produced recently in *The Eastern Buddhist* (New Series). The latter translations ground the remaining observations of this paragraph. The *Zazenji* (*zazen* or meditative practice, chap. 10) speaks not only of thinking beyond good and evil, but also of the unity of contemplative realization and practice.[66] The *Bendōwa* (chap. 35) introduces Dogen's work as a whole, treating *zazen*, precepts, and compassion.[67]

In the Nishiyama-Stevens translation, chap. 2 accentuates *dāna*, chap. 15 Kannon or Avalokiteśvara as the bodhisattva of compassion,[68] and chap. 33 renunciation of the world and acceptance of the precepts.[69]

Masunaga Reihō's partial English translation of the repetitive *Shōbōgenzō Zuimonki* or *A Primer of Sōtō Zen* expounds at length about the primacy of *zazen*,[70] but also about repentance, benefits to others, precepts, poverty, and perseverance in spiritual and material aid to others even after enlightenment.[71] Like Chinese Buddhists, the author "Buddhizes" and extends Confucian filial piety toward all beings.[72] Dialectically he further moralizes Buddhist *dharma*.

In her English translation of the *Shōbōgenzō* section called *Shushōgi*, Jiyu Kennett renders the "three commands as : "Cease from evil. Do only good. Do good for others." She continues:

> The following ten precepts should be accepted next:
> (1) Do not kill. (2) Do not steal. (3) Do not covet. (4) Do not say that which is untrue. (5) Do not sell the wine of delusion. (6) Do not speak against others. (7) Do not be proud of yourself and devalue others. (8) Do not be mean in giving either Dharma or wealth [sic]. (9) Do not be angry. (10) Do not debase the Three Treasures.[73]

Later Dogen insists that true wisdom means willingness to save "all living beings before one has actually saved oneself" by charity, tenderness, benevolence, and sympathy."[74]

6. *Sōtō Ceremonies*. Added to this translation is Kennett's inclusion of the official ceremonial handbook for Sōtō Zen in Japan.[75] This includes prayers for peace and the overcoming of evil by good, the veneration of Buddhas and bodhisattvas, honoring the precepts, and promising to keep them at the ritual heart of ordinations, marriages, and funerals.[76]

A final decision about whether morality is purely ceremonial and instrumental or also integral and identical with Zen Buddhism awaits further investigations, especially of the *Shōbōgenzō*'s most explicitly moral section, the *Shoakumakusa*, not yet published in English. The following comments on this section are gratefully based on an unpublished translation by my generous friend, Hayashi Takashi, who like other philosophical translators of the *Shōbōgenzō*, finds some words too ambivalent for accurate translation. Without help from specialists in many languages, generalists could not focus energies on wider comparative work. In other conversations and correspondence, Hayashi has relayed a startling picture of Japanese, yet universalizable, sadness and delicate gratitude for the gift of life. Like the great Nishida Kitarō,[77] he inspires one to realize the converse of Joachim Wach's maxim: "*wer kennt eine Religion, kennt keine Religion*"—whoever knows one culture well (like Zen) knows the humanity of every culture.

In commenting on the text "Do not various evils [evilness]," (*Sho-aku*), Dogen states that good/evil are conditioned by human perception of the order of things (*dharma*). When you are taught or read (in *sūtras*) about enlightenment, you must also hear the commands against various evils. If you do not hear in this way then you are not being told "the right doctrines of Buddhism but the evil doctrines of Satan." Talk about avoiding evildoing is "a manifestation of the supreme enlightenment." Whereas evils are nothing but *Maku-sa* (that is, nothing substantial, causal, or harmful to the Buddha-nature at the transcendental level), you should not talk about this consciously. Admittedly, Dogen's context is the elaboration of nondualistic MB ontology. Yet it does not deny morality. Rather, it identifies with it. It identifies the ethical with the dynamic and unborn Absolute Buddha-nature (*śūnyatā* or emptiness), a nature which is not externally imposed but spontaneously realized from the inside-out. Morality is grounded in and geared primarily toward the enlightenment of self and others about the Buddha-nature of every being.

From a humanistically active moral point of view, the above theme may or may not lend itself as the basis for a social ethic, depending, doubtlessly, on the condition and intention of listeners and readers. Future and more thorough penetrations of Zen literature and teaching should take into account the function of the bodhisattva in both the writing and hearing of *sūtras* and other literature utilized in Zen MB. If the readers of D. T. Suzuki and S. Hisamatsu come to understand that Zen offers no ethical principles, they must also recall Suzuki's judgment that from "our world point of view...the great Compassionate Heart is the ultimate principle on which our moral life depends."[78]

Morality in popular literature. Reluctantly relegating *The Tales of Genji*, *The Manyōshū*, the plays of Chikamatsu, and other literature to future enterprises, this study of moral texts concludes with two samples from Japanese theater: 1) *Matsukaze* and 2) *Chūsingura.*

1. *Matsukaze* (by Kan'ami, 1333-1384).[79] As a drama, this most popular of Japanese *Nō* plays on Buddhist themes does not signal its message primarily in literary genres. Rather it is conveyed in the music, choreography, and conventional, surrealistic style and symbolism typified by the motionless *Nō* masks of the performers. *Matsukaze* is named after its principal character, the ghost of a girl who had lost her love, Yukihira, while she was still alive. Her emotional heartbreak over his death is conveyed with a mood of delicate and haunting loneliness. Buddhist references to Amida and to the sad misery of life are apparent not only in its theatrical form but in its literary style for those who merely read it. The avowed dreary, passing uselessness of human existence and attachment is contrasted with the loveliness of the moon above, a symbol of Buddhist enlightenment in its multiple reflections on the ocean. The pain of Matsukaze's sad love did not end with death or teach her the value of non-attachment in a workable manner. The drama ends with Matsukaze's declaration of helplessness in her ongoing love for Yukihira, with prayers for rest from her passion.

Here one finds sentiments which may have universal as well as Buddhist dimensions. Far less than formal literature does this celebrated play directly reveal moral notions beyond detachment. Indirectly, its brevity, as well as its popularity, intimate that some Japanese Buddhists are in fact emotionally torn by the transient or illusory frailty of life and of love. A positive moral ethos might attempt to appeal to the this-worldly, affirmative side of Matsukaze's spirit.

2. *Chūsingura* : *The Treasury of Royal Retainers.*[80] Alternatively, a Pure Land Buddhist ethos might renounce this life and still uphold a kind of humanistic and moral life-affirmation, if it should refer strongly to extended after-life in hells and in Amida's Pure Land of bliss. This theme is woven into the Kabuki puppet drama, *Chūsingura.* The play's central theme of absolute samurai loyalty to one's master has been labelled both Confucian and Bushidō, the latter referring to the Japanese samurai ethic of loyalty, vendetta, and *seppuku* (ritual disembowelment and symbolic emptying of one's whole self). While the literal practice

of this code reached its climax in feudal times and in dangers wherein its utility might be more easily comprehended, a factor beyond political and sociological utility must be noted. Strong Buddhist belief in immediate entry into the Pure Land of bliss may have bolstered other possible motivations for such a difficult form of living and dying—(motives like fame, the death-wish, sincere courage and loyalty, etc.). The samurai ethos is still reflective of Japanese mentalities in attenuated forms, nationally or industrially, if the popularity of *Chūsingura* and similar dramas in theater and film constitute acceptable evidence. The point here is that the play is intertwined with a positive Pure Land ethos on which outsiders, if not Buddhists, could build or negotiate a social ethic.

Conclusion. A conclusion drawn from mere samples cannot be scientific. But it can be suggestive. The conclusion implied by the above illustrations is twofold. First, a thoroughgoing inquiry into formal and popular MB literature would dispel the over-simplification that MB is amoral or life-denying. If, from an outside view, MB's emphasis is dominantly mystical or other-worldly, its teachings do not deny the need for moral relationships, especially in the prominent figure of Amida and his compassionate bodhisattvas. Secondly, there are enough references to precepts, virtues, and moral models to suggest that MB involves a moral perspective not merely as a worldview, but directly as a system. In either case ongoing research may uncover the phenomenon that MB morality contains no precepts and values which cannot be found in alternate or even stronger forms in other major ethical traditions. On the other hand, it may more profoundly realize that a new moral gestalt or ethos ensouls this ethics with a unique and still unappreciated dynamic, one symbolized by bodhisattvas, who go on living for others and surrender not to death, and by savior Buddhas with extended hands.

> The Buddha sent them forth with these words: Go...out of compassion for the world, for the good, for the gain, and for the welfare of gods and men.[81] It is apparent that the ethical application of the doctrine of nirvāna is nought else than the Golden Rule [not coming from mere external authority, but flowing from]...the oneness of things...; when the cursed

barrier of Egoism is broken down, there remains nothing that can prevent us from loving others as ourselves.[82]

Conclusion. Taken not only as a controlling ethos but also as a worldview which justifies universal moral action (not merely local mores), the cosmos of a transcendental Buddha and of life-giving bodhisattvas is reached variously, according to different Buddhist claims, by faith alone, by an inner mystical experience, or by its implicit rational/intuitive appeal to the often harmoniously cooperative consequences which follow a life of humanistic compassion. Both cooperative and altruistic moral anthropologies coexist and sometimes interact with a mystical worldview. Taken both as moral justification and inspiration, esthetical feeling evolves to new heights in Japanese MB, reminiscent of those reached by the Hindu, R. Tagore. Individuals gain or regain a new respect in their identification with the universal and the transcendental and, for some, in the conviction that there are earthly and heavenly lives for each individual which are of practically indefinite duration—a functional eternal heaven. For humanists, early Buddhism's condemnation of caste and its promotion of moral autonomy rise again and again as cross-cultural challenges to the absence of human rights in other concerns and in other cultures.

While these final observations might be schematized as a comparative addition to the topical parallels or concordance of themes offered in Appendix II, the seminally textual character of this chapter's findings precludes such an addition as premature. Further conversation is needed as to whether moral life is a finally dispensable scaffold for faith, wisdom, or enlightenment or is rather a symbolic non-distinct embodiment of those ideals. If the latter and similar ideas are further verified in Buddhism, Confucianism, and other major religious and humanistic traditions, then the factual claims needed to ground international human rights, responsibilities, and law might make the case for social ethics more attractive, if not yet self-evident.

NOTES

1. Out of a composite of generously and patiently offered interviews with Buddhist scholars, especially those affiliated with the Eastern Buddhist Society and with the Universities of Otani, Kyoto, Hawaii, and Temple,

I began to build the initial premise. Of the six Buddhist perfections (*pāramitās*) or ego-denying virtues which include wisdom (*prajñā*), it is precisely intuitive wisdom which absorbs and transcends all the other perfections. This wisdom entailed non-attached *dāna* or immaterial giving which is also concrete and material. See Kenneth K. S. Ch'en, *The Chinese Transformation of Buddhism* (Princeton: Princeton University Press, 1973). p. 294. While my first guidance had been received from friends and colleagues like Surama Dasgupta, Bernard Phillips, Richard DeMartino, Charles Wei-hsun Fu, Alfred Bloom, Robert Bobilin, and the gracious help of Morris Augustine, I am particularly indebted to opening interviews at Kyoto, which Dr. Augustine arranged, with Bandō Shōjun and Abe Masao. Subsequent conversations, textual guidance, book-loans, and corrective correspondence were provided by Professors Nishitani Keiji, Takeuchi Yoshinori, Kenneth Inada, Nakamura Hajime, Kajiyama Yuichi, Hattori Masaki, Doi Mashatoshi, Sunthorn Na-Rangsi, Winston King, James Smurl, and H. S. H. Princess Poon Pismai Diskul, President of the World Fellowship of Buddhists. While these specialists cannot be held responsible for the errors or final conclusions of a groping comparative ethicist like myself, my debts to them and other Temple University colleagues and students are considerable.

It was from Abe Masao that I first learned the clear proposition that all Buddhist virtues and morality flow from within, with naturalness (*jinen*). See (among his several dozen articles in English and Japanese) "Man and Nature in Christianity and Buddhism," *Japanese Religions* 7, 1 (July 1971), 1-10. At a second stage I surmised, however, that the five Buddhist precepts and the ten grave sins have appeared consistently in Buddhist formal and popular classics. Thirdly, John Blofeld brought to my attention his insistence that the compassionate Buddhist relief of ignorance refers primarily to ignorance about enlightenment. Yet, like Ch'en, he too admitted that this sympathy extends to the lessening of sufferings of any being, however material.

In spite of these three competing yet integral factors, I see that D. T. Suzuki and others are consistently interpreted by so-called Westerners or "outsiders" (of Buddhist experience) to mean that Mahāyāna Buddhism is categorically amoral. Some of the qualifications of this thesis attributed to Suzuki can be located in his "Eastern Ethical and Social Practice," in *Readings in Eastern Religious Thought*, Vol. III, *Chinese and Japanese Religions*, ed. by A. M. Frazier (Philadelphia : The Westminster Press, 1969, p. 157 and in Suzuki's *Outlines of Mahayana Buddhism* (New York : Schocken Books, 1963), pp. 53-54.

In sum, outside interpretations of scholars like Suzuki (whom some have entitled bodhisattva), generated the central question of this essay : can Mahāyāna Buddhism, with its symbol of the sympathetic bodhisattva, function morally and socially in intercultural and international dialogues and accords, if not within Buddhism itself? The paradigmatic value of the study arises, in other words, not only from preliminary questions, which constitute a methodological exercise in comparative ethics, but also from the potential practical and truth value of the principal question itself. Further investigations should, like Winston King's analysis, take into account many other crucial distinctions within MB and especially TB, such as the differences and correlations between monastic and lay Buddhism. This and many other specialized linguistic, historical, etc. inquiries must occur before initial overviews such as this one can be sharpened and perfected. In my opinion the works of interdisciplinary generalists and specialists must build upon one another and transcend defensive feelings that one task intrudes upon the other.—The reader may judge the species of a single transliteration in terms of its reference to TB (usually Pali) or MB sources (generally Sanskrit). In dual transliterations, the Sanskrit comes first.

2. Earlier studies of Theravāda Buddhist ethics, which relied primarily on the collaborations of the Pali Text Society, lacked the aid of more recent bibliographical and other contributions provided by the annual *Bibliographies of Asian Studies* (Universities of Illinois and Michigan), the Eastern Buddhist Society, e.g., Hanayama Shinsho, *Bibliography on Buddhism* ed. by the Commemoration Committee (Tokyo : Hokuseito Press, 1961); Jean M. Lalou et al, *Bibliographie Bouddique,* which surveys Buddhist publications around the world from 1928-58, (Paris : Maisonneuvre, 1934-61); or *Buddhist Text Information,* ed. by Richard Gard (New York : The Advanced Studies of World Religions, begun in 1974). Those pioneering works on Theravāda morality were constructed by Caroline A. F. Rhys Davids, trans., *Manual of Psychological Ethics* (*Dhammasangaṇi*) (London : Pali Text Society, 1885); W. Bohn, *Die Psychologie und Ethik des Buddhismus* (München und Wiesbaden, 1921); Louis de la Vallée-Poussin, *La Morale Bouddique* (Paris : Nouvelle Librairie Nationale, 1927); and S. Tachibana, *The Ethics of Buddhism* (London : Oxford University Press, 1926). Most recent volumes on Theravāda morality include H. Saddhatissa, *Buddhist Ethics : Essence of Buddhism* (New York : George Braziller, 1970); Winston King, *In the Hope of Nibbana : An Essay on Theravada Buddhist Ethics* (LaSalle, Illinois : Open Court, 1964); and Siddi Butr-Indr, *The Social Philosophy of Buddhism* (Bangkok : Mahamakut Buddhist University, 1973). Aside from moral allusions in well known introductions to and anthologies of Pali literature like those of Christmas Humphreys, H. C. Warren, Wm. T. de Bary and others, Buddhist morality in a limitedly Indian context is treated in Surama Dasgupta, *Development of Moral Philosophy in India* and I. C. Sharma, *Ethical Philosophies of India,* pp. 147-69. In addition to later references to some of the abundant periodical literature on Theravāda ethics, see *The Wheel Publications* (Kandy-Ceylon : Buddhist Publication Society); Thomas T. Love, "Therevāda Buddhism : Ethical Theory and Practice," *JBR* 33, 4, 303-13; and Bardwell Smith, "Toward a Buddhist Anthropology: The Problem of the Secular, " *Journal of the American Academy of Religion* 34, 3 (September 1966), 203-16, on the relation of *nibbāna* to social ethics. Other current periodical literature studies Theravāda Buddhist moral thought about international law, war, race, Marxism, and capitalism.

3. Documentation and rationales for the antiquity and continuity of MB are elaborated by Edward Conze, *Buddhist Thought in India* (London : George Allen and Unwin, 1962); Takakusu Junjirō, *The Essentials of Buddhist Philosophy,* ed. by Wing Tsit Chan and Charles A. Moore (3d ed.; Honolulu : Office Applicance Co., Ltd., 1956); St. Shayer, "Pre-canonical Buddhism," *Archivi Orientali,* 7 (1935), 121-37; and A. K. Warder, *Indian Buddhism* (Delhi: Motilal Banarsidass, 1970), p. 353.

4. In "Intuition," *The Encyclopedia of Philosophy,* Vol. III (New York and

London : Macmillan Publ. Co., Inc., 1967), 204-12, Richard Rorty identifies the multiple usages of the term, intuition, and assumes the prevalent analytical view that alleged non-inferential experiences and intuitions, including the mystical, are cognitive neither of "outside objects" nor of the certitude and content of subjective experience. In this perspective, cognition begins only with interpretation, communication, and the concomitant subjection to possible inferential error. Therefore, commonality of experience and intuition does not seem possible or necessary for interpretative communications. These can be checked by their coherence and alliance with "facts." In short, my third assumption of an at least inferential *epoche* seems to provide a minimal, workable basis for intercultural and interpersonal moral understanding.

5. Takakusu, *The Essentials of Buddhist Philosophy*, p. 49.

6. Conze, *Buddhist Thought*, p. 31.

7. Bearing in mind the conflicting heuristic ideas about essential non-development and historical development of religions, see the helpful essay of Michael Pye, "Comparative Hermeneutics in Religion," in *The Cardinal Meaning : Essays in Comparative Hermeneutics : Buddhism and Christianity*, ed. by M. Pye and Robert Morgan (The Hague and Paris : Mouton, 1973), pp. 9-58. Pye traces three different European trends of interpreting Buddhism: the Anglo-German, Russian, and Franco-Belgian.

8. The four truths and eight paths are recorded in *The Book of the Kindred Sayings* (*Saṃyutta Nikāya*), trans. by F. L. Woodward (London : Pali Text Society, 1930), Vol. V, 520-29. See also the Buddhist laity's *Sigālovāda Suttanta* in *The Long Dialogues of the Buddha* (*Dīgha Nikāya*), trans. by C. A. F. Rhys Davids (London : Pali Text Society, 1951), Vol. III, 173-79. With reference to the contents of these materials, David Bastow points out ("Buddhist Ethics" *Religious Studies* 52 (December 1969, 195-206) that the Buddha's morality of a middle path claims no originality, but rather uses ethics as a common ground for conversations with Brahmins and householders. Suggesting a comparison between the five Buddhist precepts and Hindu commands he refers to *Chāndōgya Upanishad* 5.10.9. For these and similar primary preferences see *The Thirteen Principal Upanishads*, 2d revised trans. by Robert E. Hume.

9. Ch'en's, *Chinese Transformation of Buddhism* contends that Buddhism in China was Sinicized and further moralized. He leans heavily on the several works of Michihata Ryōshū, especially, *Tōdai bukkyōshi no kenkyū* 357-76; *Bukkyo to Jukyō-rinri* 133-54; and *Chūgoku bukkyōshi no kenkyū* 262-65 (Kyoto, 1957, 1968, and 1970). English titles would be respectively : *Studies in the History of T'ang Buddhism*; *Buddhist and Confucian Ethics*; *Studies in the History of Chinese Buddhism*.

10. King, *Nibbana*, p. 29.

11. *Ibid.*, p. 77.

12. The extension of TB precepts by King, *ibid.*, pp. 29-30 and by Tachibana, *The Ethics of Buddhism*, pp. 86, 141-44 contrasts with more restricted, preceptive implications in the schemas of Wm. E. Soothill and Lewis Hodous, *A Dictionary of Chinese Buddhist Terms* (London : Kegan, Paul, Trench, Trubner, and Co. Ltd., 1938), 50a-51a.

13. The four ethical virtues or *brahmavihāras* (blessed, divine, or unlimited

dispositions) are mentioned in what some consider to be pre-Buddhistic sources, for example, Patañjali's *Yogasūtra* 1.33 ("*maitrikaruṇāmuditopekṣānām*. . . ." See *The Yoga Sutra of Patanjali* in *Sacred Books of the Hindus*, trans. by B. D. Basu (Allahabad : Panini Office, 1924). Confer also the Buddhist *Dīgha Nikāya* III. 1, 224 and IV.76, 28 Engl. trans. ref. above in note 8). These virtues are translated as *metta* (Pali), loving-kindness, *karuṇā*, compassion, *muditā*, sympathetic joy, and *upekkhā* (equanimity). The assumption by King, *Nibbana*, pp. 139, 149-75 and Saddhatissa, *Buddhist Ethics*, pp. 182-83 that all four virtues are subsumed under primarily nibbanic (contemplative), if other-reaching, equanimity is countered by Sunthorn Na-rangsi's opinion (see note 1, above) that the latter is only one among four equals. It is also qualified by King's final reconstructive idea (*Buddhist Ethics*, pp. 169, 276) that with the bodhisattva ideal all four virtues together offer greater motivation for social service. From the viewpoint of two volumes, taken by themselves, Conze's *Buddhist Thought*, pp. 80, 217-18, 276 note I, 6, 279 and Lal Mani Joshi's *Studies in the Buddhistic Culture of India* (Delhi-Patna-Varanasi : Motilal Banarsidass 1967), pp. 115-16 show an evolution from contemplative well-wishing to a more visible compassion, especially in MB. Hence, the conjoined reference in this essay to these four cardinal virtues as "compassionate equanimity".

The social ramifications of this composite notion may be contrasted with translations and commentaries in *The Wheel Publications* (Kandy-Ceylon : Buddhist Publication Society, 1976, 1964, and 1971 respectively) on the *Brahmavihāras*, *metta*, and *muditā*. See publication Nos. 6 by Nyanaponika Thera, 7 by Nananoli Thera, and 170, essays by Nyanaponika Thera, N. Jackson, C. F. Knight, and L. R. Oates. Although these publications generally lack critical apparatus, they specify several canonical references, among others, to *muditā* in *Anguttara Nikāya* V, 342; to *metta* in *ibid.*, *Suttakanipāta* 60, *Majjima Nikāya* 21, 128, *Anguttara Nikāya*, *Pañcakanipāta* 16, *Saṁyutta Nikāya* XX, 3 [add V, 115], and *Sutta-nipāta*, 143-52.

14. Soothill and Hodous, *Dictionary*, 128a.

15. *Sutta Nipāta*, 136. No brahman or outcaste is such "by birth. By deeds an outcaste he, by deeds a brahman he !" English trans. by E. Hare, *Woven Cadences of Early Buddhists* (London : Oxford University Press, n.d., preface in 1944), p. 24. See also No. 142.

16. "Therefore...be ye lamps unto yourselves. Be ye a refuge to yourselves. Betake yourselves to no external refuge" (*Dīgha Nikāya* II, 110, trans. as *Dialogues of the Buddha* II, by C. A. F. Rhys Davids (London : Pali Text Society, Luzac & Co. Ltd., 1951), p. 108. If as King holds, in *Nibbana*, p. 196, the laity depend on authoritative interpretations of the *saṅgha*, then the practice of thinking for oneself becomes a modified ideal. This procedure may be partly explained by a-literal capabilities and the massiveness, cost, and lack of indexing in Theravāda scriptures.

17. King, *Nibbana*, pp. 30, 72, 74, 133ff., 199.

18. Tachibana, *The Ethics of Buddhism*, devotes entire chapters to each of these virtues. The historical passivity of TB virtues reviewed above in note 13 is developed by King's (*Nibbana*, pp. 152, 183) take-off on C. A. F. Rhys Davids concept of hope in the effective radiation of sheer good will or

"televolition." King also expounds on the dangers of *dāna* (giving), *ibid.*, p. 54, which alone constitutes a mere rebirth ethic in tension with the more ultimate and ideal nibbanic ethic.

19. See Rhys Davids, *Manual*, pp. lxxxiii-v, xciv; and Vallée-Poussin, *La Moral Bouddique*, p. 28.

20. King, *Nibbana*, pp. 42, 53 and *The Dhammapada*, trans. by Nārada Thera (London : John Murray, 1954), chap. 1:3-21 and *passim*.

21. To help others is to help oneself. See Tachibana, *The Ethics of Buddhism*, pp. 150-52. Later continuity of kammic or consequentialist moral reasoning can be seen in Buddhaghoṣa's *The Path of Purification* (*Viśuddhimagga : Bhadantācariya Buddaghoṣa*), trans. by Bhikku Ñaṇamoli (Colombo, Ceylon : R. Semage, 1956), I.1: 23-23 (p. 9).

22. The mosaic-like aspect of ethical validation is summarized by Tachibana, *ibid.*, pp. 197-98.

23. *The Dhammapada* I, 5-6. Kammic morality, which in popular practice took for granted the existence of some kind of self, is also widely documented in lay literature like the *Sigālovāda Sutta* and the popular *Jātaka Tales* of Buddha's previous lives. See the *Jatakas or Stories of the Buddha's Former Births*, e.g. Vol. I, ed. by E. B. Cowell (London and Boston : Pali Text Society, Routledge, Kegan & Paul Ltd., 1895). These often totemic or at least animal-centered stories illustrated canonical *sūttas* or *gāthās*. Some of them appeared in Greece and elsewhere as early as the fifth century B.C.E. They illustrate violence, cunning, and a low opinion of women. Theistically and preceptively oriented, they also deal with giving, love, and the distribution of property, without a clear condemnation of class discrimination.

24. Tachibana, *The Ethics of Buddhism*, pp. 53-55., lists all seventy terms.

25. The phrasing of this concept, whose original source I cannot recall, may be inferred from Saddhatissa's treatment of desire or *taṇhā* and the self, *Buddhist Ethics*, pp. 38-43.

26. In these perspectives, not self-love, but self-hatred (thanatos) appears as life's basic obstacle. As the great Confucian, Mencius, maintained against Mo-Tzu, other-love must be grounded realistically on centrifugal family love and piety. Similarly, in the TB system, love and liberality would be vulnerable to covetous self-seeking, unless a detached self-concern would precede attempts at *metta* or loving kindness. In practice TB monks, who have relinquished the probability of *nibbāna* during their present birth, are paradoxically and highly involved in moral education and in medical and social help to others. For theoretical and practical observations on the viability of TB social philosophy today see Butr-Indr, *The Social Philosophy of Buddhism* and Donald Swearer, *Buddhism in Transition* (Philadelphia : Westminster Press, 1970).

27. See King, *Nibbana*, p. 89.

28. *Vinaya Piṭaka* 1.21 as quoted in Tachibana, *The Ethics of Buddhism*, p. 12; English trans. in *Sacred Books of the East*, Vol. 13, 112-13 (Oxford, Clarendon Press, 1882). Reprint : (New York : Dover Publications, 1961).

29. In TB the bodhisattva is not yet the suffering servant who lives for others, a function reserved to distinctively Mahāyānist convictions. See Shinran's *The Kyōgyōshinshō* (*The Collection of Passages Expounding the True*

Teaching, Living, Faith and Realization of the Pure Land), trans. by D. T. Suzuki and edited by the Eastern Buddhist Society (Kyoto; Shinshu Ōtaniwa, 1973), pp. 227, No. 73, and 274, No. 123.

30. Perhaps the earliest extant version of the six perfections or *pāramitās* can be located in the *Prajñāpāramitā Sūtras*, e.g. in Edward Conze, trans., *The Perfection of Wisdom in Eight Thousand Lines and its Verse Summary* (Bolinas : Four Seasons Fd., 1973), p. 17.

31. Early or pre-canonical Buddhism is also referred to as "archaic." See *The Edicts of Ashoka*, ed. and trans. by N. A. Nikam and Richard McKeon (Chicago : University of Chicago Press, 1958).

32. In the *Lotus Sūtra* (Chap. 25), popular from India through Japan, the bodhisattva Avalokiteśvara, strikingly appears as a model of the six *pāramitās* or perfections. These comprise detached equanimity and compassion for sinners and the suffering. In China he is portrayed with the symbolic extension of a thousand hands towards all sufferers. There he also takes on the female form of Kuan-yin. In Japan he is called Kannon, a transcendental and future Buddha. In spite of the Chinese feminization of Avalokiteśvara, the women of the *Lotus Sūtra* do not enter heaven. See *Saddharma-puṇḍarīka, The Lotus of the True Law*, trans. from the Sanskrit by H. Kern, *Sacred Books of the East*, Vol. XXI, ed. by Max Muller (New York : Dover Ed., 1963). Avalokiteśvara, who is "virtue itself" and "worthy of adoration" stands beside Amida Buddha (Chap. 8) in the Pure Land of bliss, mythologically or theistically, according to one's conviction. An abridged but better trans. from the Chinese by W. E. Soothill was published as *The Lotus of the Wonderful Law* (Oxford : Clarendon Press, 1930). Chinese translations had begun to appear by the third century C.E. Wing Tsit Chan called this syncretic (one vehicle of salvation) *sūtra* the most universally influential of all MB *sūtras*. See his "The Lotus Sutra," in *Approaches to Oriental Classics*, ed. by Wm. T. de Bary (New York and London : Columbia University Press, 1959), pp. 153-65. His judgment should be measured against the popularity of the wisdom literature which paralleled the Lotus tradition. The continuity of wisdom literature with the short *Diamond* and *Heart sūtras* is reviewed in *A Guide to Oriental Classics*, 2d ed. by Wm. T. de Bary and Ainslee T. Embree (New York : Columbia University Press, 1975), pp. 98-101.

In the concurrent three Pure Land *sūtras*, Amida and his universal salvation in the Pure Land or Western Paradise becomes more dominant. Avalokiteśvara's role as Amida's helper and human escort supplements faith in Amida's name, expressed as Namu Amida Butsu or Nembutsu in Japanese. In China, seventh-thirteenth centuries, Amida replaced the eschatological manifestation of Buddha, Maitreya. Pure Land *sūtras* consist of the large and small *sūtras* of eternal life (*Sukhāvati Vyūha*), second-third centuries C.E., and of the *Meditation Sūtra on Amitayus* (Amida) (fourth century C.E.). English translations from the Sanskrit by E. B. Cowell et at (which omit later Chinese additions are published in *Sacred Books of the East*, Vol. 49, ed. by Max Muller (Oxford : Clarendon Press, 1890). Popularized in Chinese and Japanese Pure Land Buddhism, sections with morally oriented notions like filial piety and compassion appear in the *Larger Sūtra*. pp. 15-16, 25, 39-40, 54-55, 73 and in the *Meditation Sūtras*, pp. 167-68. Until later commentaries, like those of Japanese Jodo Shinshu (the true Pure Land sect), the three Pure Land *sūtras* were supplemented in Pure Land Buddhism chiefly by Nārgārjuna's (c. 150-250 C.E.) *Commentary on the Large Prajñāpāramitā* and the sixth century C.E. *The Awakening of Faith*, trans. by Y. S. Hakeda (New York : Columbia University Press 1967), which does not lack its own moral dimension.

33. Suffering and living one's virtues for both self and others is one of the original ideas of Buddhism, according to D. T. Suzuki in *Collected Writings on Shin Buddhism*, ed. by The Eastern Buddhist Society (Kyoto : Shinshu Ōtanika, 1973), p. 6.

34. As has been noted in TB texts, while the bodhisattva is not a suffering servant for others, he is mentioned, however much forgotten by contemporary Theravādans.

35. More elaborately the MB schema appears as follows : the historical Buddha's (563-483) enlightenment as the Buddha in 535 began the Buddhist era called Early Buddhism. This included the dialectical divisions of Mahāsānghikas (proto-Mahāyānists) and Sthaviras (Sthaviravādins or proto-Theravādans). Both conflicting streams remained one Buddhism until the separation which occurred c. 295 B.C.E. (or 140 years after the Buddha's enlightenment, 140 Buddhist Era [B.E.]). The larger, Mahāsānghika community and the Sthaviras (elders and monks) then began, in pursuit of accuracy, codifying texts (MB between 100 B.C.E. and 100 C.E.), Theravādans no earlier than 70 B.C.E. MB views itself as complete Buddhism and TB as incomplete.

36. *The Avataṁsaka or Gaṇḍavyūha Sūtra* (Garland, Wreath) textually grounded the Chinese *Hua Yen* (Flower or Garland School), which had been established by the seventh and eighth centuries C.E. This group claimed to synthesize the three major MB concepts of totality, emptiness (*śūnyata*) and mind only (*Yōgācāra*, store-consciousness), enlivening the last subjectivistic approach in particular. See the English trans. of Garma C. C. Chang, *The Buddhist Teaching of Totality* (University Park and London: The Pennsylvania State University Press, 1974). Store-consciousness was supposedly related to the partly Mahāyāna Vasubandhu's (c. 420-500 C.E.) *Abhidharma-Kośabhāṣya*, French trans. by Vallée-Poussin, 5 vols. (Bruxelles : Institute Belge des Hautes Etudes Chinoises, 1971), a point in need of further verification. Its teaching has been said to evince new attraction for some scholars because of the recent Énglish trans. by Wei Tat of Hsūan Tsung's *Ch'eng Wei Shih Lun, Doctrine of Pure Consciousness* (Hong Kong : The Ch'eng Wei Shih Publication Committee, 1973). For its moral allusions (mostly on self-discipline) see pp. 165-69, 413-75, 673-78, and 711-26.

37. Whereas the sheer mass of Buddhist texts was registered above in note 2, the intricacy of its divisions is detailed in Takakusu's *The Essentials of Buddhist Philosophy*. For other *sūtras* and popular literature omitted in these notes, see Ch'en, *The Chinese Transformation of Buddhism*, pp. 241-76, especially on the *Hua-yen* and *Vimalakīrti Sūtras*.

38. Vajrayāna, Mantrayāna, or Tantric MB later synthesized esoteric metaphysics, rituals, and popular teaching permeated with magic. See *A Complete Catalogue of the Tibetan Buddhist Canons. Tibetto daizōkyo sōmokoroku*, 2 vols., ed. by Ui, Suzuki, Kanakura, and Tado (Sendai : Tohoku Imperial

University, 1934). As Edward Conze has pointed out (*Buddhist Thought*, pp. 270-72), it is difficult to deal with the important school of Mantrayāna for various types of reasons. For one, a profound knowledge of early Hinduism and popular practice is vital. Another obstacle derives from Tantrayāna's esoteric and allegedly undecipherable language. Nevertheless, recent literary discoveries bring increasing notice. Among recent summaries and translations of its literature, theory, and especially its practice, see John Blofeld, *The Tantric Mysticism of Tibet* (New York : E. P. Dutton & Co., Inc., 1970). Confer also *The Hundred Thousand Songs of Milarepa*, trans. by Garma C. C. Chang (New York : Harper Colophon Books, 1962).

Until most recent times, this form of Buddhism thrived openly in Tibet, Mongolia, parts of Siberia, China (as *Chēn-yen Tsung*), and Japan. In its Japanese form, *Shingon* or the true word, it lacks neither popularity nor ethical teachings. See *Kūkai* or Kōbō Daishi, trans. by H. S. Hakeda (New York and London : Columbia University Press, 1972). Kūkai's (774-835 C.E.) doctrine does not seem a-moral in that it speaks of the five precepts (p. 168), the five cardinal virtues (similar to Confucian norms), p. 159), the ten precepts (pp. 16, 68, 94), and the ten evil deeds. However, Kūkai's successors have preserved his teaching unchanged and have restricted their goals to the refinement of intricate and elaborate rituals. Aside from ethical influence, *Shingon* may exert a more pervasive general impact throughout Japan even than Zen Buddhism, if the 1970 statistics of "adherents" and clergy can be taken as an accurate and final indication. They rank slightly higher than Zen's.

39. Previous to its modern offshoots, original Nichiren Buddhism traces its heritage through Japanese Tendai and the distinctively Chinese T'ien-tai, introduced by Chih-i (528-597 C.E.). Although its principal, if not exclusive, source, was originally Indian, the school underwent definite development. As recorded in note 32 above, its elaborate ontology of one vehicle of salvation led to the ethical ramifications of Avalokiteśvara's compassion and extension of universal salvation by faith. In integrating the three "bodies" of the Buddha (universal, eternal, and transformation bodies), Nichiren played down the position of the transcendental Amida Buddha. Instead he stressed the historical Buddha's transmission of the *Lotus Sūtra* and its ideal of suffering and self-sacrifice in the bodhisattva. Amida's sacrificial vow was extended to repetition by all sentient beings (see Suzuki, *Collected Writings*, p. 18). This spirit of sacrifice would be increasingly utilized for national goals. The correlation of the Lotus teaching and the ethics of modern Japanese religions has been investigated by Werner Kohler, *Die Lotus-Lehre und die Modernen Religionen* (Zurich : Atlantis Verlag,, 1962) Kohler notes the modern, syncretistic Nichiren preservation of four Tendai essentials. These include an ethical foundation for politics (p. 190).

40. Statistics from *Japanese Religion, A Survey by the Agency for Cultural Affairs* (Tokyo and Palo Alto : Kodansha International Ltd., 1972).

41. See Hsu Ying, "Why The Criticisms of the 'Water Margin' "? (Peking) *China Reconstructs*, April 1976, 31-33. Further comments and excerpts in C. T. Hsia, *The Classic Chinese Novel* (New York : Columbia University Press, 1968), pp. 75-114.

42. Chinese title : *Hsi yu chi*. See Hsia, *ibid.*, pp. 115-64.

43. Confer Holmes Welch, *Buddhism Under Mao* (Harvard University Press, 1972), p. 297.

44. Chinese title, *Hung-lou ming* (1972 C.E.). See Hsia, *The Chinese Novel*, pp. 245-321; also his edition of *Twentieth Century Chinese Stories*, with the assistance of J. S. M. Lau (New York : Columbia University Press, 1971), translation and commentary on nine stories. For ethical aspects of Chinese poetry see Burton Watson's *Early Chinese Literature* (New York : Columbia University Press, 1962) and *Chinese Lyricism, Shih Poetry From the Second to the Twelfth Century, with Translations* (New York : Columbia University Press, 1971).

45. Confer Donald Keene's translation and commentaries on *Twenty Plays of the Nō Theatre* (New York : Columbia University Press, 1970); Earle Ernst, *The Kabuki Theatre* (Honolulu : The University Press of Hawaii) : *Major Plays of Chikamatsu*, trans. by Donald Keene (New York : Columbia University Press, 1961); Murusake Shikibu, *The Tale of Genji*, 2 vols., trans. by Arthur Waley (New York : Random House/Modern Library, 1960; and *The Manyōshū, The Nippon Gakujutsu Shinkokai Translation of One Thousand Poems* (New York : Columbia University Press, 1969). Further recommendations for moral analysis may be gleaned from Sen'ichi Hisamatsu's *Biographical Dictionary of Japanese Literature* (Tokyo and New York : Kodansha International, 1976); "The Vocabulary of Japanese Literary Aesthetics," *Centre for East Asian Cultural Studies*, 1963; and "The Characteristics of Beauty in the Japanese Middle Ages," *Acta Asiatica*, Toho Gokkai, 1966.

46. See note 32 above.

47. See notes 48 below and Conze's, *The Perfection of Wisdom*, pp. 64, 69, 71.

48. *The Diamond Sutra*. Translated and explained by Edward Conze, *Buddhist Wisdom Books Containing the Diamond Sutra and the Heart Sutra* (New York : Harper Torchbook, 1972), pp. 26-27.

49. *Ibid.*

50. See note 33 above.

51. See Shinran's *Kyōgyōshinshō*, trans. by D. T. Suzuki; Eastern Buddhist glossaries on pp. 232, n. 86 and 244 n. 123. A further overview of Shin Buddhism can be located in Michael Solomon, "Charisma and Leadership in Shin Buddhism," *Journal of Asian Studies* (May 1974); Alfred Bloom, *Shinran's Gospel of Pure Grace* (Tucson : University of Arizona Press, 1965; and Yamamoto Kōshō, *An Introduction to Shin Buddhism* (Oyama-Ono-ku-Ubc City : The Karinbunko, 1963). In spite of English inaccuracies, one can see reflected here dialectical emancipatory and moral aspects of *Jédo Shinshu* (pp. 171-73, 176).

52. Conze, *Diamond Sutra*, p. 30.

53. See notes 32 and 39.

54. *Lotus Sutra*, IV. 101ff. Dover ed. pp. 99-106; also available in *The Buddhist Tradition in India, China and Japan*, ed. by Wm. T. de Bary (New York; Vintage Books, 1972), pp. 85-90.

55. *The Private Letters of Shinran Shoten*, trans. from the *Shinshu Shogyo Zensho* by Yamamoto Kōshō (Tokyo : The Okazakiya Shoten, n.d. (preface 1956).

56. See Bloom, *Shinran's Gospel*, p. 74 and *The Words of St Rennyo*, trans. by Yamamoto Kōshō (Oyama-Ono-ku-Ube City : The Karinbunko, 1968), p. 22. Rennyo's similarities to the Confucian ethos and relationships evokes the on-going interpenetration of Buddhist and Confucian ethics. This interaction had begun in the edicts of Prince Shotoku, through whom both traditions were effectively introduced into Japan. Robert N. Bellah, *Tokugawa Religion : The Values of Pre-Industrial Japan* (Boston : Beacon Press, 1970) exemplifies the kind of study which must follow up textual introductions like this essay on MB moral texts. Bellah refers to the impact on Japanese and Buddhist life of Confucian filial piety, thrift, Mencian unity between action and mysticism, and common daily life (pp. 68-69, 75, 154). Zen's relation to the economy (p. 107) is also discussed, along with the Shin approval of economic productivity for salvation, if sought for one's family or larger groups rather than the self alone. The Shin notion of or self-consciousness of one's sinfulness is seen to lead to a kind of individualism in moral and economic effort. Confucian *jen* in Japan becomes identified with Japanese loyalty and honesty (thanks in part to the influence of the Bushidō, Samurai code of loyalty).

The Confucian influence on the educational system (pp. 172-73) subsided, at least theoretically, with the secularization of the Japanese government, particularly after World War II. On response to my questions about possible Buddhist or Confucian residual influence in contemporary Japanese education Fujita Shoji, Fukuda Hiroshi and also Akira Goto of the Japanese National Institute for Educational Research and The Centre for East Asian Cultural Studies were most generously cooperative. At least through junior high school, moral teaching is conducted not only directly, but in social studies and in moral readers supplied by the Ministry of Education (untranslated). Courses in morality are officially described as inculcating respect for democracy peace, and national and international respect for humanity. Fujita and Fukuda wrote that there are thirty-two items concerning expected morality and attitudes in the primary schools' moral courses and thirteen in junior high. While teaching of family love has been overtly de-Confucianized, the Confucian influence may still live on, especially among older teachers. Lastly, they sent me a list of eight publications about materials used in addition to the moral, social studies of senior high school education. These reflect official national concern for the building of moral attitudes in the classroom. The Centre for East Asian Cultural Studies has recently proposed to publish a series called *Oriental Studies in Japan : Retrospect and Prospect*, 1963-72. It was to include a publication entitled "Pedagogy in Japan" with a bibliography of Japanese titles.

57. Confer Suzuki's translation of the *Kyōgyōshinshō*, pp. 13, 19, 20, 28, 65, 113. See also this volume's Eastern Buddhist Society's glossary, pp. 228 No. 78; 232-33, No. 86; 257-59, No. 164; 263, No. 180, and 278, No. 237. Confirmations of these moral allusions may be found in Soothill and Hodous, *Dictionary*, under commands, sins, evil courses of action, and perfections, 50a-51a.

58. *Tannisho, A Tract Deploring Heresies of Faith*, trans. by Kosho Ko-nyo Otani with D. T. Suzuki (Kyoto : Higashi Honganzi, 1962).

59. Yamamoto translation, *Private Letters,* no. 16 (p. 39).

60. *Ibid.*

61. Dogen, pupil of Eisai (1141-1159) and founder of Sōtō Zen (in contrast to the other major group of Eisai, Rinzai) was a Tendai monk who accepted sources from both TB and MB, rational self-perfection through meditation and ethical striving, and gradual enlightenment as opposed to sudden enlightenment through the use of koans or paradoxes meant to set the stage for enlightenment. Like the Pure Land and Nichiren groups, Dogen's Sōtō Zen Buddhism strove to teach a spiritual simplicity and enlightenment within the range of ordinary men. While Sōtō texts seem to be more accessible in English and capable of moral interpretations, the author thinks that he could demonstrate the paradoxical presence of moral language, even in such purportedly a-moral treatises as S. Hisamatsu's "Zen : Its Meaning for Modern Civilization," trans. by Richard De-martino and G. Tokiwa in *The Eastern Buddhist,* New Series I, 1, 22-47. This claim is made without conscious Buddhist experience, from an outside, this-worldly, or humanistic perspective which finds that Zen can identify itself with moral living, whereas the latter does not necessarily lead to Zen or to its own moral goals.

62. Scriptural references taken from D .T. Suzuki's *Manual of Zen Buddhism* and *Essays in Zen Buddhism, First Series* (both; New York: Grove Press, Inc., 1960 and 1961). While the latter volume deals with compassion and morality (pp. 89, 192-93), all these virtues and precepts may be taken merely as expedient means (*upāya*), dispensable pedagogical stages or scaffolds for a transcendental human development. One can doubt with justification if Suzuki's moral statements are to be understood in any further sense (e.g. his "Ethics and Zen Buddhism" in Anshen's *Moral Principles,* pp. 612, 615, his *Essays* I, p. 1, or his *An Introduction to Zen Buddhism* (New York : Grove Press, Inc., 1964), p. 64. Some Zen Buddhists or others who have demythologized the heaven and faith of Shin Buddhism probably take Suzuki's *upāya* literally as a scaffold, when applied to morality. But from a humanistic and moral point of view, I would think of him as an eminently moral humanist who never dualistically separated morality from wisdom. Meanwhile, non-Buddhists may profit from frequent Buddhist insistence that action flows from meditative wisdom rather than authority externally imposed. Whether Suzuki is seen as a Zen interpreter of Shin and Buddhism in general or a synthesizer of Zen and Shin, I would consider his teachings ultimately life-affirmative rather than denying, ones with which other cultures can dialogue and interact.

63. See Keizan Zenji's *Kyoju-Kaimon,* partly translated by Jiyu Kennett in *Selling Water by the River, A Manual of Zen Training* (New York : Vintage Books, 1972). This volume includes her translation of the *Shishoji* section of Dogen's *Shōbōgenzō,* as well as some Sōtō ceremonials.

64. *Ibid.,* p. 216.

65. Sendai, Japan : Daihokkaikaku Publishing Co., 1975. See also Yūhō Yokoi, *Zen Master Dōgen* (New York :John Weatherfield, Inc., 1976).

66. *The Eastern Buddhist,* VI, 73, 119, 127.

67. *Ibid.,* IV, 133, 148-49.

68. Nishiyama-Stevens trans., pp. 65-67.

69. *Ibid.*, pp. 137-38.
70. Honolulu : University Press of Hawaii, 1971, pp. 48-49.
71. *Ibid.*, pp. 68, 10, 18, 72, 34-59, and 103 respectively.
72. *Ibid.*, pp. 42, 60, 79.
73. Kennett, *Selling Water*, pp. 132-33.
74. *Ibid.*
75. See Kennett's bibliographical references to Sōtō ceremonials, pp. 121 ff.
76. *Ibid.*, pp. 240, 250-55, 278-82.
77. See beautiful excerpts of Nishida, trans. by Abe Masao in Wm. T. de Bary, *Sources of Japanese Tradition*, Vol. II (New York : Columbia University Press, 1958), pp. 350-65; and Kitaro's *A Study of Good*, trans. by V. H. Viglielmo (Gov. Printing Bureau, 1960). Among Nishida's other works are *Intelligibility and the Philosophy of Nothingness*, trans. R. Shinzinger (Tokyo: Naruzen, 1958) and *Fundamental Problems of Philosophy*, trans. David Dilworth (Tokyo : Sophia University, 1970. Nishida's *Art and Morality*, trans. D. Dilworth and Waldo Viglielmo (University Press of Hawaii, 1973) is of special significance in this chapter's context.
78. From "Ethics and Zen Buddhism" in Ashen's *Moral Principles*, pp. 612, 615.
79. Trans. by Royall Tayler in Keene, *Twenty Nō Plays*.
80. Trans. by Donald Keene (New York : Columbia University Press, 1971).
81. *Vinaya piṭaka* 1.21 as quoted in Tachibana, *The Ethics of Buddhism*, p. 12. For the original see *Sacred Books of the East*, Vol. XIII, pp. 112-13.
82. Suzuki, *Outlines*, pp. 53-54.

APPENDIX I

CRITICAL TEXTUAL MATTERS: A) THE RĀMĀYAṆA; B) THE MAHĀBHĀRATA: 1) BOOKS XII AND XIII AND 2) CORE (*UR*) PLOT AND CHARACTERS

A. *The Rāmāyaṇa*: *The Sanskrit Critical Edition and other Versions*; *Sexual Discrimination in Historical Fact*

This section of Appendix I summarizes or indicates further information and literature about 1) the epic's international impact, 2) its various forms of presentation in classical Sanskrit, 3) popular Hindi, 4) Bengali, 5) the *Vālmīki-Rāmāyaṇa*'s critical edition in Sanskirt, and 6) sexual discrimination factually alleged in the epic.

1. *International impact.* Illustrations and uncritical data of varied qualities dealing with the attention the epic commands in India, Sri Lanka/Ceylon, and Southeast Asia today can be gathered from *All India Ramayana Conference*.[1] Contributors trace Chinese translations of the epic to 251 C.E. and 471 C.E., seventh and fifteenth century presence in Indochina, a ninth century East Iranian version, seventh and ninth century manuscripts in Tibet, and influence stretching to Mongolia and "the banks of the Volga."

2. *Ancient versions.* The version of the *Ry* within its sister-epic, the *Mbh*, is called *Rāmopākhyāna*. Other accounts of the ancient Rāma legend are listed in Khan.[2] Rai Sen details the legend's inclusion in Buddhist *Jātakas* (Buddha's "previous birth" stories) and Jaina literature as well as ancient Hindu traditions.[3] Although Rangacharya contends that from the time of Ashoka (third century B.C.E.) Buddhism, and probably Jainism, purposely discouraged popular entertainments until the tenth century C.E. *bhakti* revival, he records the familiarity of the Rāma story to every individual.[4]

3. *Versions in Hindi* (*The Indian State language*) *and other modern Indian languages.* English translations of the sixteenth century

Tulasīdās *Ry* from Hindi and of Kamban's Tamil rendition, together with commentaries are available in Macfie, Hill, and Rajagopalachari.[5] Bibliographical data on other English translations of Tulasīdās' devotional account can be located in Hein[6] and in de Bary and Embree.[7] Dwivedi lists other familiar Hindi presentations ranging from the eighth to the twentieth centuries —for instance, those of the poets Svayambhu, Kabīr, Senāpati, and Maithili S. Gupta.[8]

Rām Lilā. The classically perduring and pervasive presence of the Hindi *Rām Lilā* play (referring literally to Rama's divine *sport* with creation) is excellently documented through the field experience of Hein.[9] In my own experience the traditional *Rām Lilā* was not only popular as part of an annual religious celebration and as a first-rate theatrical production in Delhi (October 1974), but was regarded worthy of Marxist re-presentation in New Delhi during the same period.

For comparisons of the *Ry* with Indian and also Greek epics see Jayal, Vora, Antoine, and Artola.[10] In a single paperback volume adaptable for use in undergraduate classes, Rajagopalachari, like Tulasīdās, rejects and omits the sad ending of Vālmīki's supplement (*Uttara Kāṇḍa*), while admitting that it expresses "the untold sufferings of women."[11] Another version easily available in paperback in the United States is Bapu's.[12] The condensed (paperback) English translation of R. C. Dutt remains quite practical and accessible for classroom use. If the reader does not mind its imitative and mnemonic rhyming scheme and traces of the Victorian era in which Dutt was educated, this translation has the advantage of being published together with Dutt's translation of the *Mbh* (in abridged form).[13]

4. *In Bengali literature* the Rāma tale is more celebrated than the *Mbh* or *Purāṇic* tales, and according to S. Sen "has always exerted the greatest influence in the formation of the Indian mind and morals," for example, through Kandalī, Sandarhev, Kṛittivāsa, D. L. Ray, or R. C. Dutt.[14] In his analysis of seven or more poetical versions of Bengali *Rys*, Rai Sen conjectures that the Brahminic quasi-cooption of Rāma's divinity was an attempt to compete with the popular (*Mahāyāna*) deification of Buddha.[15] Sen also suggests that the Bengali writer, Rāmānanda, utilized the work for Buddhistic purposes.[16] Taken either as epic, recited poetry, or drama, the *Ry* would be an intriguing subject

in terms of historical conjecture about textual revisions and appropriations for competing Buddhistic, Brahminic, and political purposes.

5. *The Sanskrit critical edition of the Vālmīki-Rāmāyaṇa.* This edition of the Baroda Oriental Institute furnishes critical notes, concordances, and other materials in English along with its Sanskrit text. In the introduction to its first volume, G. H. Bhatt claims general agreement that the epic's first and last volumes or books (*kāṇḍas* I and VII) are later additions, especially I, 1-4.[17] Vaidya believes that the original *Ry* consisted only of volumes two, three, and six.[18] Bhatt also grants the present lacuna in "higher criticism." "The text of the Epic has to be reconstructed *solely* on the evidence of the MSS, without bringing in the question of Higher Criticism at this stage. The Higher Criticism which is no doubt most important and interesting can be better applied to the Critical text prepared with the help of the MSS only."[19] Among seven principles used in constituting the critical edition, two are of special significance: 1) texts are accepted only if both Northern and Southern recensions agree; 2) "When a passage is omitted in any Version of N. or S., and if it is not necessary for the context, it should be dropped."[20] Under these one-dimensional criteria which exclude "higher" (=contextual?) criticism," the editors judge that a notable portion of the classic does not belong to the oldest core *Ry*. For example, of 3170 stanzas in *Ry* II, 1131 are rejected.

It must be added here with the strongest emphasis that although the editors have presented no conjectures on the dates of later additions, these supplements are not only variously ancient but are thereby representative of what generations have traditionally felt is the *Ry*. Obviously the question of its historical import cannot be solved by mere reconstruction of the original "Ur" or core, oral tradition. Ethical and other analysis of the *Ry*'s teaching, therefore, must work from accretions as well as the core or "critical edition(s)."

H. D. Sankalia thinks that the original *Ry* existed as early as 1000 B.C.E. and that most interpolations occurred between the second century B.C.E. and the third century C.E., some persisting to the tenth century.[21] He disagrees with P. L. Vaidya on the relative antiquity of the critical edition and the *Rāmopākhyāna* (one of the Rāma stories found in the *Mbh*).[22] Vaidya had reasoned that the *Rāmopākhyāna* was older. In either case the narrative entails only one repudiation of Sītā and a happy ending, but this does not mean that it is only these versions which became entwined, as Aurobindo Ghose would put it, with the consciousness of the Indian "race."[23]

This summary has to be concluded with the registration of two disappointments. The first is that according to Vaidya no manuscript of the *Ry* is older than 1020 C.E.—a matter of no surprise, given the earliest uses of paper in India around this period and the easy deterioration of other materials other than Ashokan pillars. The second is that the Shastri translation (even in the revised edition, part of which was chronologically subsequent to the critical edition) offers no critical notes or information about the sources which it employed—a gap which I hope will be filled in the near future.

6. *Sexual discrimination in the Ry factually alleged by the epic.* Segregation of women from public relationships during the epic period was manifest in forms of *purda*[24] and by their treatment like mere property who in turn were allowed the use but not the ownership of property itself.[25] Sītā was once offered to Bharata (by Rāma) like chattel (II, 19). In VI, 115 Sītā states that women function as mere slaves.[26] Reification as possessions may have been conjoined with the phenomenon of *satī* (*suttee* or widow immolation), a convenient effect of which did happen to relate to property settlements, although it is theorized that it did not become common until centuries after Vālmīki. In Vora's judgment *satī* became ascendant "only" after the ninth century C.E. until its prohibition in 1829.[27] I have seen earlier figures elsewhere.

The relationships of women with their families were ones of marked subordination. Designation of spouses was not individual but familial.[28] Those who believe that individual freedom is a fundamental right can admit that the familial system may have effected fewer dysfunctions against intelligent and satisfying match-makings than other social organizations. They may even grant that some systems confuse free choice with blind choice or confound the lack of a single programming factor such as the family with an alleged or consequent absence of all other societal determinants, economic, conventional, etc. But they would also maintain that explanations do not constitute justifications

According to Jayal, a key motivation for the familial specification of spouses was the preservation of racial purity.[29] A similar concept of biological instrumentality for women may also have been operative in the custom of *niyoga*, the widow's "permission" to produce progeny through a brother-in-law or nearest relative.

Spousal relationships were polygamous (VII, 8), without polyandry and unequal, if not idolatrous.[30] "For women who are anxious to fulfill their duty, the husband, whether he is endowed with good qualities or not, is a visible God to them, O Queen" (II, 62). The servility demanded of women is exemplified in a formula used at Sītā's wedding. Her father, King Janaka, addresses Rāma: "Here is my virtuous daughter, Sita, whom I bestow on thee; receive her and be happy; place her hand in thy hand; may she, faithful to her consort, be happy and follow him like a shadow !" (I, 73).

B. *The Mahābhārata*: 1) *Books XII and XIII and* 2) *Core UR Plot and Characters*

Literally a world apart from popular fables and morally common sensical proverbs is the extant Brahminic version of the celebrated *Mbh*, widely regarded as the *Ry*'s competitor for the title of India's chief or national epic.[31] Not that this galaxy of verse fails to include pockets of conventional wisdom or legends or the eventual inclusion of the devotional and highly popular *Gītā*. However, the popular stories are reputedly so encrusted with strata of Brahminic reconstruction as to make the epic, taken as a unified opus, no longer identifiable at first glance as *kāvya* of the people. With the *Purāṇas*, the *Mbh*'s books are judged by D. D. Kosambi to have "suffered a major revision" between 150-350 C.E.[32] "The *Mahābhārata* in particular was in the hands of Brahhmins belonging to the Bhṛgu clan, who inflated it to about its present bulk (though the process of inflation continued afterwards) before the Gupta age [fourth-seventh centuries C.E.] came to flower,"[33] While Kosambi's estimation doubtless awaits verification from scientific critiques of sources, forms, and composition, it is recorded here as a possible aid in explaining why the *Mbh* never achieved the popularity—either when recited or dramatized—ascribed to its earlier sister-epic, the *Ry*. From Kosambi's kind of viewpoint the *Mbh* is less reflective of common wisdom than it is of the pondered statements of the priestly caste and philosophers like the Sāṅkhya. In contrast with the *Ry*, itself not preserved from priestly revisions, the *Mbh* achieved dramatic form only in the tenth century C.E.,[34] whereas by the fifteenth century the *Ry* alone was capturing dramatists' attention.

Although the present survey of the epic's later books seems to contradict the above observations by viewing them in the context of popular classics, it intends to avoid the confusion of size with importance and to invite future analysts of the epic to consider it precisely from the aspect of its actual popularity, however small or Brahminically programmed. In other words, the classic does include moral narratives and portions which became popularly known. Even if most of it remained unpopularized or its popularity was manufactured, it retains some value as a people's classic calling for ethical diagnosis. This judgment will be especially true when applied to the *Mbh*'s enduring core plot.

Before the core plot and its highly important characters are sketched, it will be convenient to examine the later Brahminized version, especially the morally didactic books twelve and thirteen. While these narratives, portions, or didactical sections never became popular in the fashion of the ancient story of the *Mbh* battle and its principal episodic insertions, they retain value precisely as people's literature, if indeed they were preached or retained to the people in various forms.

1. *Books twelve and thirteen.* The *Mbh*'s relatively inferior power to attract may be comprehended in terms of historical chance, elitist origins, or the moral ambiguity of some of its central figures.[35] Or then again, by its formidable mass alone, it might not have lent itself easily to popularization. The sheer magnitude of the world's lengthiest epic (88,000 verses in eighteen "*parvan*" sections or books) so dwarfs the mind that quantity itself help explain another curious phenomenon. Almost no one has steered ethical commentary in the *Mbh*'s direction, prescinding, of course, from remarks on the *Gītā*, which the *Mbh* eventually incorporated. Unlike the *Gītā* the *Mbh*, literally the epic of the great human forebears, the Bhārata clan, consists largely of tales rather than teaching and of events and of intricate genealogies rather than a multitude

of more immediately didactic messages.[36] From the few explorers who have entered this vast forest of verse, nonetheless, the word returns that while its contents are vast, those with ethical designs might find their most promising ventures in the more recently composed or interpolated twelfth and thirteenth sections or books, the *Śānti Parva* and the *Anuśāsana Parva.* Even in terms of those books alone, a lack of monographs prevents present determinations of the epic's specific ethos or ethoses. Nevertheless, surface probes allow the following speculations about its moral teachings in terms of general framework and particular issues.

In its general and karmic framework, the later, Brahminized *Mbh*'s ethical mirrors all four goals, four stages, and four hierarchical castes of Brahminically viewed life. The epic's focus on the goal of *moksha* and the ascetical stages pulls in tension with its accolades for the warrior rather than the priestly caste.[37] "Kashtriya duties are the foremost of all duties."[38] Characteristically Brahminic lists of trans-caste or general virtues (*sādhāraṇa dharma*) which laud ascetical and spiritual qualities like non-attached action (*niṣkāma karma*), equanimity, doing good to enemies (XII.61), and *ahimsā*[39] divulge a similar polarity in their this-worldly emphasis on the householder's (*grihastha*'s) begetting and raising children.[40] Apart from *moksha*, "diverse kinds of happiness both here and hereafter"[41] derive from *artha*, *dharma*, and *kāma* with one's spouse.

As for specific issues, the epic discloses at least three preoccupations : (1) the justification of war and other injuries, (2) coordinate and consequentialist legitimations of exceptions to scriptural principles, and (3) an ambiguous concern with the subordinate status of women socially.

First, in counterpoint with its own frequent adulation of *ahimsā*, Book XII, which stresses peace and non-violence, seems engrossed with expounding the necessity and moral ends of *ahimsā*'s various infringements through falsehood, theft, and physical violence.[42] "A *kshatriya* (in distress) may take wealth from everyone except [notice] ascetics and Brahmanas" (XII.130). The same "should take (by force) what he can, with a view to (ultimately) support or protect the people. No person in this world, O king, can support life without injuring other creatures" (XII.130). Contextual exemptions from scriptural injunctions against these and other forms of injury are also vindicated on the presupposition that the *śrutis* did not pretend to deal with all situations or irregularities in the moral life, leaving these matters to human reasons (XII.109). Accordingly "that again which is virtue may, according to time and place, be sin" whereas "theft, untruth, and injury and killing may, under special circumstances, become virtue" (XII.37). Under certain conditions "acts that are (apparently) evil" can be permitted if they "produce consequences that are good" (XII.37). The terms of permission are not only divine or scriptural sanctions, but the protection of life and of "the means by which life is sustained" (XII.37).

Second, the primary phenomenon of stating exceptions to non-violence and other principles has already involved moral reasoning through consequences. This logical process is further highlighted in a passage which notes the interrelationship of several virtues, consequentially. "Anger springs from covetousness."[43] Envy "disappears in consequence of compassion and knowledge of self" (XII.163). But the goodness of compassion depends less on a circular consideration of its results than on a quasi-intuitive and affective perception akin to Mencian *jen*.[44] "Compassion proceeds from a sight of the helpless and miserable persons with whom the world abounds." "Know him for a malevolent and wicked person who quietly and alone takes comestibles and drinks and other kinds of food that are regarded choice, even when persons are standing by with wishful eyes." Those who share, however, "attain to great felicity in the next world and infinite happiness here."[45]

Third, for women, happiness was pursuable only by way of a double standard, according to the detailed research of Shakambari Jayal. She holds that the *Mbh* demonstrates the decline of women from prehistoric times to the neo-Hinduism of the *Purāṇas*, (a phenomenon which is possibly cross-cultural).[46] In the epic's redacted and didactic portions in particular, asceticism and chastity are elevated with portrayals of women as tempting possessions of men.[47] Jayal surmises that these teachings were tantamount to a denial of rights in several areas, property, sexuality, and religion included.[48] "Asceticism degraded the religious status of women so much that religious pursuits could be taken only by abandoning women."[49]

2. *The original characters and plot.* The accuracy of these judgments notwithstanding, the epic contains some sections, probably derived from earlier versions, in which women are conceived of as indispensable teachers and partners. The first two women described below, Śakuntalā and Sāvitrī, stand out in tales which are episodic or loosely related to the movement of the central military plot. The third personage, Queen Draupadī, is the leading feminine character in the ancient tale of battles between the two central groups of the one *great Bhārata* clan (*Mahābhārata, Mbh*).

Śakuntalā. In the *Mbh*'s account of Śakuntalā—later immortalized in the celebrated play of Kālidāsa—Śakuntalā is enthroned like a primeval mother figure. Her pedagogic function, like Sītā's, the heroine of the *Ry*, is unmistakable. To a husband (Duḥṣyanta Paurava) who would deny her and their Bhārata heir, she proclaims didactically : "He who knows himself to be one way and pretends it in another way is a thief who robs his own soul—what evil is beyond him? You think you are alone with your self, but don't you know the ancient seer who dwells in your heart ? Him who knows your evil deeds ?"[50]

Śakuntalā's depiction of women's roles as partners indicates that the epic inculcates more than a Brahminic ethos about *kāma* and the other ends of life :

> A husband enters his wife and is reborn from her. ... The offspring that is born to a man who follows the scriptures saves with his lineage the forebears that died before. ... The wife is half the man, a wife is better than his best friend, a wife is the root of Law, Profit, and Love, a wife is a friend in a man's extremity. ... A man with a wife is a trustworthy man. Therefore a wife is the best course. ...and a good wife follows after her husband if he has died before. This, sire, is the reason why marriage is sought by man, where a husband finds a wife for now and eternity.[51]

Sāvitri. In a second legend or episode in book five, one meets the heroine, Sāvitrī, whose undying love brings her husband back to life. Sāvitrī was a legendary goddess of supernatural birth and beauty who had become the earthly King Aśvapati's daughter. A paragon of truthfulness and fidelity, she chooses the impoverished forest dweller, Prince Satyavān ("Man of Truth"), for her husband. She adheres to this decision in spite of a priestly prediction that Satyavān would die within a year. Noble and virtuous himself, his death would be thought to be connected with or caused by a mysterious previous *karma.* When he is actually stricken with sudden illness and death in the forest, Sāvitrī's undying love moves her into clever debate with Yama, the god of death. Finally, Yama yields to her persistence, courage, and love. He restores Satyavān to life along with his wealth. Also, he heals Satyavān's father's eyesight. Interwoven with the legend's mythopoeic and primal symbols are clear affirmations of life, love, and moral virtue.

The third feminine character, Draupadī, is less susceptible to interpretations which might highlight feminine passivity and blind fidelity at the expense of more active or aggressive virtues. The five West Indian Pāṇḍava (Pandu) brothers, rightful heirs to the Bhārata kingdom, had been victimized by the East Indian villain, Duryodhana, who convinced the Kaurava clan to exile the Pāṇḍavas. The Pāṇḍava brothers emerged from Brahminic disguise to compete in the Kaurava Princess Draupadīs bestowal in marriage to whomever could lift and shoot a massive bow (as in the *Ry*). The Pāṇḍava, Arjuna (principal figure in the later *Gītā*) performed the feat and won Draupadī in marriage for *all five* Pāṇḍava brothers, although Yudhiṣṭhira ("son of *Dharma*") functioned as the principal husband and ruled with Draupadī near modern Delhi. In an intriguing theatrical device, if not an historical one, Yudhiṣṭhira gave into his compulsive gambling and lost the whole kingdom to the Kaurava Duryodhana's loaded dice. The Pāṇḍava brothers and Draupadī were condemned to slavery. Significantly, however, at Draupadī's fiery and courageous plea, her Kaurava father, King Dhṛitarāṣṭra, commuted this sentence to thirteen years of forest exile. Subsequent to this period Duryodhana refused to return to the Pāṇḍavas what was unjustly won in the first place. A "just war" thereby seemed unavoidable. The stage was thus set for a highly dramatic and pitched series of battles which displayed the superhuman courage of both sides. (By now for all practical purposes all Indians had joined one side or the other.) All the major characters, including the heroine Draupadī and the villain, Duryodhana, died courageously and entered *heaven* (*not moksha* !). The plot concludes with a moral. Just as valor and virtue like Draupadī's brought heaven for her, it will do the same for everyone. Before concluding here with a final observation about the skeletal plot, the point to be underscored is Draupadī's courage and her unique spousal position as a counterpart to the usual instances of oppressive polygamy.

The plot. In a final commentary on the sequence of events already well synopsized by others, often quite minutely,[52] three points are to be noted about the central sequence of events. First, the nearly perfect match of the war's ups and downs takes on a form so suspensefully theatrical and entertaining that one becomes immediately wary of moralization beyond the simple mythopoeic message that courage and goodness conquer over evil. Second, in my conjecture, the tale is designed to consolidate for all times the coalitions not only between Indian warring factions but between the Brahminic and *kshatriya* classes. In the latter coalition, early *kshatriya* control is textually (if not actually) subsumed by Brahminic claims to costly gifts, custody of the royal treasury, the right to anoint or confirm royalty, and legislation of social laws. Third, in addition to the *Mbh*'s absorption of popular legends about heroines, the *Ry* plot, Manu as the first man, and the universal deluge, the theme of "conflicting duties" may have universal moral significance especially as it is later developed in the *Gītā*. Warriors on both sides must fight for their clans despite their conflicting convictions. Arjuna is encouraged and aided in battle by the divine charioteer, Krishna. This venture is the take-off point for the *Gītā*'s possibly cross-cultural message that just as Arjuna decided to go to war and to action out of caste duty, so everyone must eschew inaction for action and/or for devotional activity. Yet this action must remain non-attached to its fruits,—another point with possible cross-cultural significance, at least in a future stage of human development. At the very least, in thinking of the *Mbh*'s and *Gītā*'s stress on two seemingly universal moral problems, 1) conflicting duties, and 2) non-attached action, it is reasonable to surmise that these dilemmas have roots which are mythic, primal, and unconscious. Myth like that of the *Mbh* may have "unrepressed" them with the lance of practical resolutions without settling the matters logically.

NOTES

1. *All India Ramayana Conference* : *Sree Rama Sahasranama Dasakoti Archana Festival* : (Trivandrum: Sree Seetha Ramabhakatha Sabha, 1972-73), e.g. pp. 103, 97, and 105 respectively.

2. Khan, *Concept of Dharma*, p. 11.

3. Rai Sen, *Bengali Ramaynas*, (Calcutta : The University of Calcutta, 1920).

4. Rangacharya, *Drama in Sanskrit Literature*, p. 201.

5. Macfie, U. M., trans., *The Ramayana of Tulsidas* : W. Douglas P. Hill, trans., *The Holy Lake of the Acts of Rama* : *Translation of Tulsīdas' Ramacaritamānas* (Bombay : Oxford University Press, 1952); and C. Rajagopalachari, trans., *The Ramayana as told by Kamban* (London: George Allen & Unwin Ltd., 1961, Book II only).

6. Norvin Hein, *The Rām Līlā*, p. 96 n. 8.

7. Wm. T. de Bary and Ainslie T. Embree, eds., *Oriental Classics*, pp. 130-33.

8. Ram Awadh Dwivedi, *Hindi Literature* (Gyanwapi, Banaras: Hindi Pracharak Pustakalaya, 1953).

9. Hein, *The Rām Līlā*, especially p. 98 n. 29.

10. Shakambari Jayal, *Women in the Epics*; D. P. Vora, *Evolution of Morals*; Robert Antoine, "Indian and Greek Epics", in *Approaches to the Oriental Classics*, ed. Wm. T. de Bary, pp. 95-112; and George T. Artola, "Comments on the *Rāmāyaṇa* and *Mahābhārata*," in de Bary, *Approaches*, pp. 113-18.

11. C. Rajagopalachari, trans., *The Ramayana* (Bombay: Bharatiya Vidya Bhavan, 1973), p. 312.

12. Bapu, *Valmiki's Ramayana* (Thompson, Connecticut: Inter-Culture Associates, 1975).

13. Romesh C. Dutt, trans., *The Ramayana and the Mahabharata* (1910; rpt. New York and London: Everyman's Library, 1974).

14. Sen, *Bengali Literature*, p. 65.

15. Rai Sen, *Bengali Ramayanas*, p. 61.

16. *Ibid.*, pp. 233-34.

17. J. M. Mehta, G. H. Bhatt, P. L. Vaidya, et al, *The Valmiki Ramayana* [Critical Sanskrit Ed.] 6 Vols. (Baroda: Oriental Institute, 1960-1971), I, xxxi and 424.

18. Vaidya, *ibid.*, vi, 19, and xxix.

19. Bhatt, *ibid.*, I, xxxiv.

20. *Ibid.*

21. H. D. Sankalia, *Ramayana, Myth or Reality*? (New Delhi: Peoples Publishing House, 1973), p. 62.

22. Mehta et al, *The Valmiki Ramayana* VI, xxxii and see Sankalia, *ibid.*, pp. 19 and 62.

23. Sankalia, *ibid.*, p. 62.

24. Jayal, *The Status of Women*, pp. 237 and 243.

25. *Ibid.*, pp. 244 ff.

26. See also Shantikumar Nanooram Vyas, *India in the Rāmāyaṇa Age*, p. 124.

27. D. P. Vora, *Evolution of Morals in the Epics*, pp. 95-97.

28. Vyas, *India in the Rāmāyaṇa Age*, p. 80.

29. Jayal, *The Status of Women*, p. 304.

30. Sharma, *A Socio-Political Study*, p. 60.

31. *The Mahābhārata*, 19 Vols., 1st critical ed. by V. V. Sukthankar, S. K. Belvalkar, et al, (Poona: Bhandarkar Oriental Research Institute, 1926-1966). Introducing the inaugural volume of his projected seven volume English translation, J. B. van Buitenen remarked in 1973 that no satisfactory English translation of the whole yet existed, although the Academy of Leningrad, led by U. I. Kalyanov, was working on its own popular translation of the entire epic. See his *The Mahābhārata*, (Chicago : University of Chicago Press, 1973), I, xxxvi. The translation which I have utilized directly, while consulting others, is P. C. Roy's *The Mahābhārata of Krishna-Dwaipayana Vyasa* (Calcutta : Oriental Publishing Co., n.d. [1964 ?]), Vol. VIII, *Śānti Parva* I, (=Book XII). Other "translations," some quite old, limit themselves either to synopses or selections, although one may discern in some of them the earliest core plot.

32. See D. D. Kosambi, *Myth And Reality*, p. 16. Again, genealogical charts and authorship as well as similar estimates on dates may be conferred in van Buitenen, *ibid.*, esp. xxiii-xxviii.

33. Kosambi, *ibid.*, p. 16.

34. See Adya Rangacharya, *Drama in Sanskrit Literature*, p. 201. According to Winternitz and Jhā, dramatic plots based on the *Mbh* offer little not already found in the *Ry*. See M. Winternitz, *History of Indian Literature*, trans., with additions by Subhadra Jhā (Delhi : Motilal Banarsidass, 1963), Vol. III, I, 206 and 276.

35. Synopses both of figures and events occur in the commentary and version of Chakravarthi V. Narasimhan, *The Mahābhārata : An English Version Based on Selected Verses* (New York : Columbia University Press, 1965), pp. xxi-xxiv and *passim*. For a more concise summary, see the introduction to van Buitenen's translation. It weaves together the events which were eventually utilized to background the *Gītā*'s divine teaching of Krishna to Prince Arjuna. The reconstruction of the core plot in this appendix leans both on previously mentioned sources and the pioneer, condensed translations of R. C. Dutt, *The Ramayana and the Mahabharata*. More exact "Ur" reconstructions pend further positive research in comparative mythology and epics : Roman, Indian, etc. See Alf Hiltelbeitel's long review of George Dumezil, *Mythe Et Épopée*, Vol. 2, *Types Épiques Indocuropeens : Un Héros, Un Sorcier, Un Roi*, Vol. 3. *Histories Romaines*. Bibliothèque des sciences humaines (Paris : Editions Gallimard, 1973) in *History of Religions* 15, 1 (August 1975), 90-100.

36. Primarily descriptive details of the epic's teachings are found in D. P. Vora, *Evolution of Morals*. Apparently, the most thorough ethical commentary on the *Mbh* to date exists in Surama Dasgupta, *Moral Philosophy*, pp. 19-28, summarized in her essay "The Individual in Indian Ethics," in Charles A. Moore, ed., *The Indian Mind*, pp. 342-44. Dasgupta sees the epic's samples of consequentialist, utilitarian, and situational reasoning as evidence of the individual conscience's distinct role in Hindu ethics, at least in *abnormal* situations. Otherwise, scriptures (*śruti*) and custom are to be followed. In *Moral Philosophy* she writes : "It is wrong to suppose that one can understand the nature of *dharma* from the scriptures alone" (p. 23). The social good (*lokayātrā*) may necessitate exceptions to *ahimsā* and other scriptural principles.

The house-holder stage emerges supreme in the *Āpaddharma-parva* 140-43. Dasgupta's scope of references extend beyond those of the *Śānti-parva* employed in my commentary and the *Āpaddharma-parva* to the *Udyoga-parva* 37.16, *Ajagara-parva* 180, and the *Rājadharma-parva* 15, 34, 56, 75, 101, 109, and 136. Apart from the studies of Dasgupta and Vora, other recent books on Hindu ethics refer to the epic either briefly or only in passing. A short treatment exists in S. Cromwell Crawford's clear-volume, *The Evolution of Hindu Ethical Ideals*, pp. 61 and 77. Parenthetical references are located in I. C. Sharma, *Ethical Philosophies.*

37. *Śānti Parva,* Nos. 19-32 104, and 329.

38. *Ibid.*, 64. See also 59.5, 13-30, and 93-94 where this book's divine authority on specifying the conduct of kings was apparently delegated to Brahmins. Other important *Mbh* allusions to caste refer to the lowest : "A Śūdra cannot have any wealth that is his own. Whatever he possesses belongs lawfully to his master" (*ibid.*, 37). "There is no *expiation* [emphasis added] for them that cast off the duties and practices of their order and class, country, and family, and that abandon their very creed" (*ibid.*). On expiation and for details on the moral aspect of penance (*prāyaścittas*) see P. V. Kane, *History of Dharmaśāstra*, Vol. IV.

39. XII.21 and 109. See other passages on *ahimsā* in the selections chosen by Radhakrishnan, *A Source Book*, pp. 164-65.

40. *Śānti Parva*, 60; and confer Crawford, *Hindu Ethical Ideals,* p. 212.

41. *Ibid.*, 61. Compare with two similar goals of happiness in 63 and 190; and contrast with 25, 175, and 177.

42. *Śānti Parva*, 109 and 329. Narasimhan, *The Mahābhārata*, p. xxiv, notes that while the classic claims peace as a major theme, good intentions about military conduct collapsed and episodes of violence snowballed. In the opinion of Mary Carroll Smith, "warriors had already fashioned the limits of morality and it is the priests' tampering with the warriors' code that can be traced in the [later] layers of the epic." See her "Warriors : The Originators of the Moral code in Ancient India," in *Asian Religions : History of Religion* : 1974 *Proceedings, American Academy of Religion,* ed. Harry Partin (Florida State University: AAR, 1974), p. 59.

43. XII.163. See P. V. Kane, *History* IV, 10-11 on the specification of grave sins.

44. See *Mencius* 6A6 and 2A6.

45. *Śānti Parva*, 1963-64. Raimundo Panikkar has found even more direct analogues for the golden rule of dealing with others as you would with them to deal with you in *Mbh* V. 1270. XII.5528 and XIII.5571, to quote his references in "Christians and So-Called non-Christians," 304, n. 2.

46. S. Jayal, *The Status of Women*, p. 13.

47. *Ibid.*, pp. 17, 128, 130, 252-53, 298 and, on female group suicide, 181-82.

48. *Ibid.*, pp. 253 and 301.

49. *Ibid.*, pp. 298-99. In his *Hindu Ethical Ideals*, pp. 101-02, Crawford indicates that XIII.38-39 and 40.12-13 characterize women as unequal and weak seducers.

50. Van Buitenen, *The Mahābhārata*, I, 166.

51. *Ibid.*, p. 167.

52. See note 35 above.

APPENDIX II

DIAGRAM OF TOPICAL PARALLELS

(Order of *Gītā* and *Ry* reversed for comparative purposes)

	MORALITY OR MORES ? If morality, why be moral ?	ETHICAL VALIDATION BY WORLDVIEWS OR ANTHROPOLOGIES; A) COOPERATION; B) MYSTICAL UNITY OF ALL; C) ALTRUISTIC INSIGHT OR POSTULATION.
Rv 1500-1300 B.C.E.	Some moral virtues and action with a-moral dimensions; sin is problematical in volitional sense.	(A) *Cooperative worldview. Rita* as cosmic and moral order as well as divine authority. No (B) mystical worldview or overt statements on (C) moral insight. No mystical worldview of reincarnation/transmigration.
Ups. 800-500 B.C.E.	Sin is *avidyā* or ignorance; yet virtues and general morality abound. A *rita*-like, dhārmic order prevails not only for mystics, but for all classes.	*Rita* becomes *dharma*, (B) *The worldview is highly mystical* : non-dualistic oneness is the grounds for any "moral" activity. Pre-Vedic *karma-saṁsāra* overshadows the less mystical, Vedic heavens and hells. Moksha or mystical liberation is the final, eventual goal for every individual.
Manu 200 B.C.E.-C.E.	Little volition, if any : but universal virtues for all classes; ascetical and dianoetic in content.	(B) *A mystical-moral worldview* undergoes a subtle transposition into mystical world-concern in steering all castes and stages towards Brahminic and ascetical goals. A developmental toleration of the this-worldly second stage of life runs in tension with multiple ascetical rules overflowing into that stage. *Dharma* both as caste-convention and Brahminic authority is identified both with Brahminic authority and divine authority. Thus, in one sense, a worldview (the Brahminic one) acts as the sole justification for moral activity.
Gītā 500-100 B.C.E. Brahminic version; 400 C.E.	Free will prevails over determinism, if not clearly over caste duty. Some duties are universal for all castes.	(B) *A mystical-moral worldview still prevails* in spite of the *Gītā*'s attempts to synthesize perspectives of devotional and moral activity. Both theistic and non-theistic mysticism coexist. Mysticism is more positively directed to ground a type of moral activity called non-attached *action*. Historically, it seemed to prevail, nonetheless, as *non-attached* action, or quasi-inertia (prescinding from the devotional dimension).

Ry 3d cent. B.C.E.- 2d cent. C.E.	Probable volition. Clearly universal virtues prevail over class mores—in aspiration at least.	A) Cooperative and C) altruistic worldviews. No mystical world-*moksha*. Heavens and hells prevail over karmic beliefs, even in the Brahminized versions.
Popular classics	Universal morality assumed. Some volition seems to prevail.	A) Mainly cooperative worldview, with some altruism.
Śaṅkara 9th cent. C.E.	Sin is ignorance. Volition is finally illusory. If moral goals are implied in *moksha*, they are not intended for all classes—in the present existence. Morality is in lowest possible profile.	B) Mystical worldview; each individual is really one with *Ātman*—if only this could be realized. Other forms of consciousness are to be dealt with at a practical level, including devotionalism and the offering of stipends. Gods may be worshipped. But all of these phenomena are finally illusory and unreal, a lower, dispensable level of truth. The lower, devotional, and moral life prepares for the higher rebirths necessary for *moksha*. A form of compassion may stem from *moksha*. But take care of *moksha* and everything else will take care of itself.
Gandhi, 1869-1948	*Dharma* for all prevails over *moksha* in the present life.	B) Mystical-devotional worldview. The ultimate Reality, God, is spiritual Truth and Love. Abide in love and *ahimsā* as the this-worldly path to other worldly *moksha*. Ascetical mysticism grounds activism—a highly ascetical activism.
Tagore 1861-1949	Universal moral humanist.	B) Mystical only in the theistic sense with belief in a finally harmonious worldview. Anti Av, devotional, highly talented in explaining his mystical-morality in poetry comprehensible to religious and non-religious humanists (A and C).
Mbh, Ur (Dates unknown)	Common sense morality in low profile—for all.	A) Cooperative worldview based on theistic/polytheistic beliefs in heavens. Karmic compensation is dim. Altruistic worldview (C) in some episodes (Śakuntalā and Sāvitrī).
Mbh, Bks. XII-XIII 4th cent. C.E.	General virtues for all.	(A) Cooperative and (B) mystical worldview in different sections.

APPENDIX II (*Contd.*)

	3. OTHER ETHICAL VALIDATIONS : a) collective experience; b) authority, human and divine; c) consequences of actions; d) value feeling and esthetical motivation. (Epistemological question.)	4. CENTRAL ETHOS (Substantive question).	5. BASIC ATTITUDES ABOUT RELATIONSHIPS BETWEEN INDIVIDUALS, CONVENTION, AND OTHER STRUCTURES. (Substantive question).
Rv	Appeals through a, b, and c. No analytical use of d, but *Rv* poetry moves rhetorically and esthetically.	No *moksha* or *nirvāṇa*. Giving and life-affirmation. Only one stage : householder.	*Ahimsā* lacking. Racial and sexual slavery. Detailed *varṇa* and *jāti* discriminations otherwise unmentioned.
Ups	C and d in lowest profile except for some altruism flowing from mystical sense of oneness. Appeals to divine and Brahminic authority identified and central. *Rita* is now Brahminic *Dharma*.	*Moksha* with self-restraint and *ahimsā*, esp. related to ritual sacrifice. Compassion and giving, esp. for the householder. All four stages are now present and generally necessary.	Virtues under ethos plus last 7 Jewish commands, no abortion, no alcohol. Emergence of Brahminic and ascetical prominence. Four *varṇas* are divinely legitimated.
Manu	Legitimations a and c negligible. All justification flows from clear identification of divine and Brahminic authority. *Śruti* are determined and interpreted through Brahminic *smṛti* or tradition. No *rita*.	Householder stage allowed a developmental function on the way to asceticism and *moksha*. But ascetical rules overflow into the specification of the householder's life-style. *Ups*' schema of rebirths places Brahminic stage at pinnacle. General virtues remain passive. Brahmins attempt poetic and legislative control over all via karmic and caste sanctions. (World concern).	Four stages and castes. Sexual discrimination. Caste discrimination. Priority of society over every individual. *Ahimsā* substantively qualified. Punishments most severe in theory. Castes divinely legitimated.

Gītā	Appeal (a) to reason scant. B, authoritative resort to the sanction of caste duty takes highest priority and is given divine confirmation. No *rita*, yet the trans-conceptual realization of one's identity with Brahman, devotionally or contemplatively, or through non-attached action resembles a quasi-intuitive basis for altruistic action.	*Niṣkāma karma* or NON-ATTACHED action captures the central mood. In effect, activity other than *bhakti* or devotion yields to the atmosphere of *jñāna* and yoga. A social ethic might be derived from this ethos in principle and at a later period in history.	Pro-war; pro-caste. Individual must yield to caste duty.
Ry	Divine authority prevails in some versions. The *Ur* and Vālmīki versions are Brahminized with layers which stress Brahminic authority and *karma*, but they are built mainly on appeal to reason, collective experience, and some altruistic feelings (Sītā). Rāma and especially Sītā are humanly normative models and esthetically portrayed.	Life-affirmation; *trivarga* only. No *moksha*. Some tendencies to *ahimsā* and altruistic compassion. Heaven extends this life and its loves.	Caste discrimination. Factual sexual discrimination against women censured by Vālmīki.
Popular Classics	a) collective experience of common sense (of moral consequences) prevails almost exclusively; with touches of altruistic insight.	Affirmation of human life and loves. Care for wealth, sharing, prudential cunning and common sense consequentialism. Secondary attention to *ahimsā*, compassion, and truth. High devotionalism underlies moral feeling. It merges with a generally intense feeling for the esthetical (see 3).	Four classes. Some female subordination; with females as moral heroines. Brahminic control largely ignored.
Saṅkara	b) divine and Brahminic, esp. Śaṅkara's, authority, merge as supreme, final, and canonical.	Mystical asceticism. Non-attached morality and devotion tolerated at the lower, relative, passive, and illusory level of life.	All but the final ascetical stages may be bypassed and one may live entirely on alms. Discrimination againt castes (lower) and women. Brahmins supported through devotional offerings, tax-free land grants,

	3. OTHER ETHICAL VALIDATIONS; a) collective experience; b) authority, human and divine; c) consequences of actions; d) value feeling and esthetical motivation. (Epistemological question).	4. CENTRAL ETHOS (Substantive question).	5. BASIC ATTITUDES ABOUT RELATIONSHIPS BETWEEN INDIVIDUALS, CONVENTION, AND OTHER STRUCTURES. (Substantive question).
Gandhi	A quasi-intuitive belief (d) in Kantian?) duty for its own sake, performed with *Gītā*-like non-attachment. In principle no persons are to be treated as means, just as evil or violent means would subvert good goals. Obed. to conscience has a devotional basis, not excluding respect to Gandhi himself (blind obed. acc. to R. Tagore).	Non-attached service of the lower castes, out-castes, and people in general, especially through physically non-violent resistance (with relatively few exceptions). Ascetical poverty and non-attachment seem to supercede other human or religious goals in this life, although the promise of a better consciousness or life lies in the background.	Notable exceptions to *ahimsā* militarily, and personally at the physical level; and esp. at the psychological level. Anti-caste.
Tagore	God as truth is intuitively known through love. Brahminic and human authority takes a backseat. Priests must work for a living.	Forest life and blind obedience also slip into the background. Concern for the poor and oppressed springs from powerful esthetical imagery in favor of action, life, love, and sharing. Mysticism is not excluded and can be integrated. Highly life-affirmative.	Opposed oppression of caste, poor, children, women. Fought fatalism, egoistic nationalism.
Mbh-Ur	Warrior powers claimed by Brahmins who claim rights to gifts, lands, confirmation of royalty.	Brahminic coalition with warriors/rulers. Episodic tales of life-affirmation and equality.	Some justice, *dāna*; early caste discrimination by coalition of top two.
Mbh-XII-XIII	Brahminic (only) consequentialist exceptions to rules.	Brahminic ethos of all four stages, classes, goals.	Racial, sexual, economic discrimination.

SELECTED BIBLIOGRAPHY

General Sources

Abelson, Raziel and Neilsen, Kai. "History of Ethics," *The Encyclopedia of Philosophy*. Ed. Paul Edwards. New York : Macmillan Publishing Co., Inc. and The Free Press, 1967. III, 81-116.

Adams, Charles J. *A Reader's Guide to the Great Religions*. New York : The Free Press, 1965.

Aquinas, Thomas. *Summa Theologica*. Romae : Marietti, 1948.

Beardsley, Monroe. "Aesthetics, History of," *The Encyclopedia of Philosophy*. Ed. Paul Edwards. New York : Macmillan Co., Inc. and The Free Press, 1967. I, 18-35.

Berry, Thomas. "Contemporary Spirituality : The Journey of the Human Community," *Cross Currents* 24, 2/3 (Summer-Fall 1974), 172-83.

——"A Multi-Cultural World," in *Approaches to the Oriental Classics*. Ed. Wm. T. de Bary. New York : Columbia University Press, 1959.

Bleeker, C. J., et al. *International Bibliography of the History of Religions*. 18. vols. Leiden, Netherlands : Brill, 1952-75.

Burke, T. Patrick. *The Reluctant Vision : An Essay in the Philosophy of Religion*. Philadelphia : Fortress Press, 1974.

de Beauvoir, Simone. *The Ethics of Ambiguity*. Translated by B. Frechtman. Secaucus, New Jersey : The Citadel Press, 1948.

de Rougement, Denis. *Love in the Western World*. Translated by M. Belgion. Rev. ed. Greenwich, Connecticut : Fawcett Publications, Inc., 1969.

Deeken, Max. *Process and Permanence in Ethics : Max Scheler's Moral Philosophy*. New York : Paulist Press, 1974.

Friedman, Maurice; Burke, T. Patrick; and Laeuchli, Samuel. *Searching in the Syntax of Things*. Philadelphia: Fortress Press, 1972.

Golding, M.P. "History of the Philosophy of Law," *The Encyclopedia of Philosophy*. Ed. Paul Edwards. New York : Macmillan Publishing Co., Inc. and The Free Press, 1967. VI, 254-64.

Gunn, Giles. "Threading the Eye of the Needle : The Place of the Literary Critic in Relgious Studies," *Journal of the American Academy of Religion* 43 (June 1975).

Hazard, N. *Communists and their Law : A Search for the Common Core of the Legal Systems of the Marxian Socialistic States.* Chicago: The University of Chicago Press, 1969.

Hindery, Roderick. *The Disinterested Love of God According to Eusebius Amort (diss.).* Rome : Academia Alfonsiana/ Lateran University, 1962.

—— "Exploring Comparative Religious Ethics," *Journal of Ecumenical Studies* 10, 3 (Summer 1973), 552-74.

—— "Marcuse's Eroticized Man," *Christian Century,* February 4, 1970.

—— "Muslim and Christian Ethics," *Cross Currents* 22,4 (Winter 1973), 381-97.

—— "Pluralism in Moral Theology : Reconstructing Ethical Pluralism" *CTSA Proceedings,* 1973, 71-94.

Hospars, John. "Aesthetics, Problems of," *The Encyclopedia of Philosophy.* Ed. Paul Edwards. New York : Macmillan Co., Inc. and The Free Press, 1967. I, 35-36.

Ionesco, Ghita. *Comparative Communist Politics.* London : The Macmillan Press, 1972.

Kierkegaard, Soren. *Fear and Trembling.* Translated by Walter Lowrie. Princeton : Princeton University Press, 1941.

Kitagawa, Joseph. "Primitive, Classical, and Modern Religions," in *The History of Religions : Essays on the Problem of Understanding.* Ed. Joseph Kitagawa. Chicago : The University of Chicago Press, 1967.

Lévi-Strauss, Claude. *The Savage Mind.* Chicago : The University Press, 1962.

—— "The Structural Study of Myth," in *The Structuralists from Marx to Lévi-Strauss.* Eds. R. T. and F. de George. Garden City, New York : Anchor Books, 1972.

Little, David and Twiss, Sumner B. "Basic Terms in the Study of Religious Ethics," in *Religion and Morality.* Eds. Gene Outka and John P. Reeder. Garden City, New York : Anchor Press/Doubleday, 1973.

Little, David. "Comparative Religious Ethics," in *The Study of Religion in Colleges and Universities.* Eds. Paul Ramsey and John Wilson. Princeton, New Jersey : Princeton University Press, 1970.

Little., David. "Max Weber and the Comparative Study of Religious Ethics," *Journal of Religious Ethics* 2, 2 (Fall 1974).

Machiavelli, N. *The Discourses*. Ed. B. Crick. Translated by L. J. Walker. Baltimore : Penguin Books, 1970.

—— *The Prince*. Translated by Luigi Ricci. New York : The New American Library, 1952.

Margolis, Joseph. *Values and Conduct*. New York : Oxford University Press, 1971.

Murdoch, Iris. *The Sovereignty of Good*. New York : Schocken Books, 1971.

Nagel, Thomas. *The Possibility of Altruism*. Oxford : Clarendon Press, 1970.

Neilsen, Kai. "Problems of Ethics," *The Encyclopedia of Philosophy*. Ed. Paul Edwards. New York : Macmillan Publishing Co., Inc. and The Free Press, 1967. III, 117-34.

Niebuhr, H. Richard. *The Responsible Self*. New York : Harper and Row, 1963.

Nietzsche, Friedrich. *Beyond Good and Evil*. Translated by Walter Kaufmann. New York : Vintage Books, 1966.

—— *On the Genealogy of Morals*. Translated by Walter Kaufmann and R. J. Hollingdale. New York : Vintage Books, 1969.

Northrop, F. S. C. *The Meeting of East and West : An Inquiry Concerning World Understanding*. New York : Macmillan Co., 1946.

Nygren, Anders. *Eros and Agape*. Translated by P. S. Watson. New York : Harper and Row, 1969.

O'Connell, D. P. "The Role of International Law," in *Conditions of World Order*. Ed. Stanley Hoffman. Boston : Houghton Mifflin Company, 1968.

Outka, Gene. *Agape : An Ethical Analysis*. New Haven : Yale University Press, 1972.

Panikkar, Raimundo. "Christians and So-called Non-Christians," *Cross Currents* 22,3 (Summer-Fall 1972), 281-308.

—— "Some Notes on Syncretism and Eclecticism Related to the Growth of Human Consciousness," in *Religious Syncretism in Antiquity*. Ed. Birger A. Pearson. Missoula, Montana : Scholars Press, 1975.

Peters, Richard S. *Reason and Compassion.* London and Boston: Routledge and Kegan Paul, 1973.

Philosophy East and West : Symposium on Law and Morality : East and West 21,4 (October 1971).

Pye, Michael. "Comparative Hermeneutics," in *The Cardinal Meaning : Essays in Comparative Hermeneutics : Buddhism and Christianity.* Eds. M. Pye and R. Morgan. The Hague : Mouton, 1973.

Raju, P. T. *Introduction to Comparative Philosophy.* Carbondale, Illinois : Southern Illinois University Press, 1962.

Ramsey, Paul. *Nine Modern Moralists.* Englewood Cliffs, New Jersey : Prentice-Hall, Inc., 1962.

Reiter, Seymour. *World Theater : The Structure and Meaning of Drama.* New York : Dell Publishing Co., Inc., 1974.

Rorty, Richard. "Intuition," *The Encyclopedia of Philosophy.* Ed. Paul Edwards. New York : Macmillan Co., Inc. and The Free Press, 1967. III, 204-12.

Sadler, William A. *Existence and Love.* New York : Charles Scribner's Sons, 1969.

Scheler, Max. *Der Formalismus in der Ethik und die materiale Wertethik.* Bern : A. Francke AG Verlag, 1966. Translated by M. S. Frings and R. L. Funk as *Formalism in Ethics and Non-Formal Ethics of Values.* Evanston: Northwestern University Press, 1973.

Smurl, James F. "Cross-cultural Comparisons in Ethics : A Critical Response to Sally Wang," *Journal of Religious Ethics* 4 (Spring 1976), 47-56.

—— *Religious Ethics : A Systems Approach.* Englewood Cliffs, New Jersey : Prentice-Hall, Inc., 1972.

Stace, W. T. *Mysticism and Philosophy.* London : Macmillan & Co. Ltd., 1961.

Sturm, Douglas, "The Priority of the Philosophical Question : A Response to David Little on Max Weber," *Journal of Religious Ethics* 2, 2 (Fall 1974), 41-52.

Wach, Joachim. *The Comparative Study of Religions.* New York : Columbia University Press, 1958.

—— *Sociology of Religion.* Chicago : The University of Chicago Press, 1944.

—— *Types of Religious Experience, Christian and Non-Christian.* Chicago : University of Chicago Press, 1957.

Weber, Max. *The Protestant Ethic and the Spirit of Capitalism.* Translated by Talcott Parsons. New York : Charles Scribner's Sons, 1958.

Westermarck, Edward. *Ethical Relativity.* New York : Harcourt, Brace, and Company, Inc., 1932.

—— *The Origin and Development of Moral Ideas.* London : Macmillan and Co., Limited, 1917.

Wittenstein, Ludwig. "A Lecture on Ethics,", in *Ethics : Selections from Classical and Contemporary Writers.* 3d. ed. New York : Holt, Rinehart and Winston, Inc., 1974.

—— *Tractatus Logico-Philosophicus.* London : Kegan, Paul, Trench, Trubner & Co., 1923.

General Sources, Asian

Bellah, Robert N. *Tokugawa Religion : The Values of Pre-Industrial Japan.* Boston : Beacon Press, 1970.

de Bary, Wm. T. and Embree, Ainslie T., eds. *A Guide to Oriental Classics.* 2nd ed. New York : Columbia University Press, 1975.

Ernst, Earle. *The Kabuki Theatre.* Rpt. Honolulu : The University Press of Hawaii, 1974.

Hisamatsu, Sen'ichi. *Bibliographical Dictionary of Japanese Literature.* Tokyo : Kodansha International, 1976.

—— "The Characteristics of Beauty in the Japanese Middle Ages," *Acta Asiatica,* Toho Gokkai, 1966.

Hsia, C. T. and Lau, J. S. M. *Twentieth-Century Chinese Stories.* New York : Columbia University Press, 1971.

Joshi, Lal Mani. *Brahmanism, Buddhism and Hinduism.* Kandy : Buddhist Publication Society, 1970.

Murusaki Shikibu. *The Tale of Genji.* Translated by Arthur Waley. 2 vols. Rpt. New York : Random House (Modern Library), 1960.

Nakamura, Hajime. *Ways of Thinking of Eastern Peoples : India, China, Tibet, Japan.* Rev. and ed. by Philip Weiner. Honolulu : East-West Center Press, 1964.

Nippon Gakujutsu Shinkōkai. *The Manyōshū.* Rpt. New York : Columbia University Press, 1970.

Upadhyaya, Kashi Nath. *Early Buddhism and the Bhagavad Gitā.* Delhi : Motilal Baṇarsidass, 1971.

Watson, Burton. *Early Chinese Literature.* New York : Columbia University Press, 1962.

—— *Chinese Lyricism : Shih Poetry from the Second to the Twelfth Century, with Translations.* New York : Columbia University Press, 1971.

Weber, Max. *The Religion of China.* Translated by H. H. Gerth. New York : The Free Press, 1951.

Hindu and Indian, Primary Sources

Aiyar, V. V. S., trans. *The Kural or the Maxims of Tiruvalluvar.* 3d ed. Madras : The Jupiter Press, 1952.

Archer, W. G., ed. *The Kāma Sūtra.* Translated by Richard Burton and F. F. Arbuthnot. London, 1963.

Bapu, trans. *Valmiki's Ramayana.* Thompson, Connecticut : Inter-Culture Associates, 1975.

Basu, B. D., trans. *The Yoga Sutra of Patanjali.* Sacred Books of the Hindus. Allahabad : Panini Office, 1924.

Bhattacharya, Deben, trans. *Love Songs of Vidyāpati.* Delhi : Orient Paperbacks, 1963.

Bühler, Georg, trans. *The Laws of Manu.* Rpt. New York : Dover Publications, Inc., 1961.

de Bary, Wm. T. et al, eds. *Sources of Indian Tradition.* 2 vols. New York : Columbia University Press, 1958.

Deutsch, Eliot, trans. with commentary. *The Bhagavad Gītā.* New York : Holt, Rinehart, and Winston, 1968.

Deutsch, Eliot and van Buitenen, J. A. B., eds. *A Source Book in Advaita Vedānta.* Honolulu : East West Center Press, 1971.

Dutt, Romesh C., trans. *The Ramayana and the Mahabharata* [abridged]. New York and London : Everyman's Library, 1974.

Edgerton, Franklin. *The Bhagavad Gītā : Translated and Interpreted.* Cambridge, Mass. : Harvard University Press, 1944, 1974.

Griffith, R. T. H., trans. *The Hymns of the Ṛgveda.* Rev. ed. Delhi: Motilal Banarsidass, 1973.

Hein, W. Douglas P., trans. *The Holy Lake of the Acts of Rama: Translation of Tulasī Das's Rāmacaritamānas.* Bombay : Oxford University Press, 1952.

Hume, Robert Ernest, trans. *The Thirteen Principal Upanishads.* Oxford : Oxford University Press, 1921, 1975.

Jhā, Subhadra, ed. *The Songs of Vidyāpati*, Banares : Motilal Banarsidass, 1954.

Kangle, R. P., trans. *The Kautilya Arthaśāstra*. 3 vols. Bombay : University of Bombay, 1960, 1963.

Keyt, George, trans. *Gīta Govinda*. Bombay : Kutub, 1947.

Macdonnell, Arthur A., trans. *Hymns from the Rigveda*. Oxford: Oxford University Press, 1922.

Mehta, J. M.; Bhatt, G. H.; Vaidya, P. L. et al. *The Vālmīki Rāmāyaṇa* [Critical Sanskrit Ed.] 6 vols. Baroda : Oriental Institute, 1960-71.

Narasimhan, Chakravarthi V., trans. *The Mahābhārata : An English Version Based on Selected Verses*. New York : Columbia University Press, 1965.

Poddar, H. P., trans. *The Bhagavata*. Gorakhpur : Gita Press, 1952.

Prabhupada, A. C., trans. *Śrīmad-Bhagavatam*. 10 vols. New York and Bombay : The Bhakti-Vedanta Book Trust, 1972.

Purohit, N. B., trans. *The Pratimā of Bhāsa*, Baroda : The Allied Stores, 1957.

Radhakrishnan, S. and Moore, Charles A. *A Sourcebook in Indian Philosophy*. Princeton : Princeton University Press, 1957.

Rajagopalachari, C., trans. *The Ramayana as told by Kamban*. London : George Allen & Unwin Ltd., 1961.

——*The Ramayana*. Bombay : Bharatiya Vidya Bhavan, 1973.

Ramaswamy, T. N., trans. *Essentials of Indian Statecraft : Kautilya's Arthasastra for Contemporary Readers*. Bombay : Asia Publishing House, 1962.

Roy, P. C., trans. *The Mahabharata of Krishna-Dwaipayana Vyasa*. Calcutta : Oriental Publishing Co., n.d. [1964] ?. Vol. VIII.

Ryder, A. W., trans. *Panchatantra*. Bombay : Jaico Publishing House, 1949.

——*Shakuntalā and other Writings*. New York : E. P. Dutton and Co., 1959.

Sangal, J. M., trans. *The Srimad-Bhagavatam of Krishna-Dwaipayana Vyasa*. Calcutta : Oriental Publishing Co., 1951.

Shamasastry, R., trans. *Kautilya's Arthasastra*. 7th ed. Mysore : S. Srinivas, 1961.

Shastri, Hari Prasad, trans. *The Ramayana of Valmiki.* 3 vols. 2nd rev. ed. London : Shanti Sadan, 1962-1970.

Sternbach, Ludwik, trans. *Cāṇakya Nīti Text Tradition.* Vol. II, I. Hoshiarpur : Vishveshvaranand Vedic Research Institute, 1970.

——*Maxims on Rāja-Nīti.* Madras : The Adyar Library and Research Center, 1963.

Sukthankar, V. V.; Belvalkar, S. K., et al. *The Mahabharata.* 19 vols. [Critical edition]. Poona : Bhandarkar Oriental Research Institute, 1926-66.

Thibaut, George, trans. *Vedānta-Sūtras of Bādarāyaṇa with the Commentary by Śaṅkara in Two Parts* [volumes]. Rpt. New York : Dover Publications, 1962.

Thomas, Edward J. *Vedic Hymns, Translated from the Rigveda.* (Wisdom of the East). London : John Murray Publishers Ltd., 1923.

Van Buitenen, J. B., trans. *The Mahābhārata* I. Chicago : The Chicago University Press, 1973.

——*Two Plays of Ancient India : The Little Clay Cart ; The Minister's Seal.* New York : Columbia University Press, 1968.

Wells, Henry W., trans. *Six Sanskrit Plays.* New York : Asia Publishing House, 1964.

Hindu and Indian, Secondary Literature

All India Ramayana Conference : Sree Rama Sahasranama Dasakoti Festival. Trivandrum : Sree Seetha Ramabhaktha Sabha, 1972-73.

Banerjee, N. V. *The Spirit of Indian Philosophy.* New Delhi : Arnold-Heinemann Publishers, 1974.

Basham, A. L. *The Wonder That Was India.* New York : Grove Press, 1954.

Bhargava, Dayanand. *Jain Ethics.* Delhi : Motilal Banarsidass, 1968.

Bhattacharya, K. C. *Search for the Absolute in Neo-Vedānta.* Honolulu : University of Hawaii Press, 1975.

Bhattacharya, S. et al. *The Encyclopedia of Indian Philosophies.* Delhi : Motilal Banarsidass, 1970.

Bhave, Vinoba. *Talks on the Gitā.* New York : The Macmillan Company, 1960.

Cenkner, Wm. *The Hindu Personality in Education : Tagore, Gandhi, Aurobindo.* New Delhi : Manohar, 1976.

Chaitanya, Krishna. *A New History of Sanskrit Literature.* New Delhi : Asia Publishing House, 1962.

Chand, Tara. "The Individual in the Legal and Political Thought and Institutions of India," in *The Indian Mind.* Ed. Charles A. Moore. Honolulu : East-West Center Press, 1967.

Chatterjee, Margaret. ed. *Contemporary Indian Philosophy,* Series II. London : George Allen and Unwin, 1974.

Crawford, Cromwell. *The Evolution of Hindu Ethical Ideals.* Calcutta : Firma K. L. Mukhopadhyay, 1974.

Creel, Austin B. "The Reexamination of Dharma in Hindu Ethics," *Philosophy East and West,* 25, 2 (April 1975).

Dasgupta, Surama. *Development of Moral Philosophy in India.* New York : Frederick Ungar Publishing Co., 1965.

Dasgupta, Surendra Nath. *A History of Sanskrit Literature, Classical Period.* Calcutta : University of Calcutta, 1947.

De, Sushil Kumar. *Ancient Indian Erotics and Erotic Literature.* Rpt. Calcutta : Firma K. L. Mukhopadhyay, 1969.

——*Aspects of Sanskrit Literature.* Calcutta : Firma K. L. Mukhopadhyay, 1959.

de Bary, Wm. T., ed. et al. *Approaches to the Oriental Classics.* New York: Columbia University Press, 1959.

Derrett, J. M. Duncan. Dharmaśāstra and Juridical Literature in *A History of Indian Literature,* Vol. IV., Ed. Jan Gonda. Wiesbaden : Otto Harassowitz, 1973.

——*History of Indian Law* (*Dharmaśāstra*). Leiden und Köln : E. J. Brill, 1973.

——"Rajadharma." *The Journal of Asian Studies* 34, 4 (August 1976).

Deutsch, Eliot. *Advaita Vedānta : A Philosophical Reconstruction.* Honolulu : East-West Center Press, 1969.

Devaraja, N. K. *Hinduism and Christianity.* New York : Asia Publishing House, 1969.

——*The Mind and Spirit of India.* Delhi : Motilal Banarsidass, 1967.

Dwivedi, Ram Awadh. *Hindi Literature.* Gyanwapi, Banares: Hindi Pracharak Pustakalaya, 1953.

Erikson, Erik H. *Gandhi's Truth : On the Origins of Militant Nonviolence*. New York : W. W. Norton & Company, Inc., 1969.

Gandhi, M. K. *Autobiography : The Story of My Experiments with Truth*. Translated by Mahadev Desai. Washington D.C. : Public Affairs Press, 1948.

Goodwin, Wm. F. "Mysticism and Ethics." *Ethics* 67, 1 (October 1956), 25-41.

Hiriyanna, Mysore. *Outlines of Indian Philosophy*. London : George Allen & Unwin Ltd., 1932.

Hopkins, E. W. *The Ethics of India*. New Haven : Yale University Press, 1924.

Iyer, Raghavan N. *The Moral and Political Thought of Mahatma Gandhi*. New York : Oxford University Press, 1973.

Jayal, Shakambari. *The Status of Women in the Epics*. Delhi : Motilal Banarsidass, 1966.

Kanakasabhai, V. *The Tamils : Eighteen Hundred Years Ago*. 2nd ed. Madras : The South India Saiva Siddhanta Works Publishing Society, Tinnelvelly Limited, 1956.

Kane, P. V. *History of Dharmaśāstra*. 4 vols. Poona : Bhandarkar Oriental Research Institute, 1930-53.

——*History of Sanskrit Poetics*. 4th ed. Delhi : Motilal Banarsidass, 1971.

Karmarkar, R. D. *Bhavabhuti*. Charivar : Karnatak University, 1963.

Kaveeshwar, G. W. *The Ethics of the Gītā*. Delhi : Motilal Banarsidass, 1971.

Khan, Benjamin. *The Concept of Dharma in Valmiki Ramayana*. Delhi : Munshi Ram Manohar Lal, 1965.

Kosambi, D. D. *Myth and Reality : Studies in the Formation of Indian Culture*. Bombay : Popular Prakashan, 1962.

Lacy, Creighton. *The Conscience of India*. New York : Holt, Rinehart, and Winston, 1965.

Larson, Gerald G. "The *Bhagavad Gītā* as Cross Cultural Process," *Journal of the American Academy of Religion* 43, 4 (December 1975), 651-70.

Lefever, Henry. *The Vedic Idea of Sin*. London and Travancore : Mission Press, 1935.

Mathur, D. C. "The Concept of Action in the *Bhagavad Gītā*,"

Philosophy and Phenomenological Research 35, 1 (September 1974), 34-43.

McDermott, Robert A. "The Legacy of Sri Aurobindo," *Cross Currents* 22,1 (Winter 1972), 2-8.

——*Sri Aurobindo : An Introduction to the Major Works of Sri Aurobindo.* Chambersburg, Pa. : Wilson Books, 1974.

Mehta, Ved. *Mahatma Gandhi and his Apostles.* New York : The Viking Press, 1966.

Naipaul, V. S. *India : A Wounded Civilization.* New York: Knopf, '77.

Narasimhan, C. V. *The Mahābhārata.* New York : Columbia University Press, 1965.

Nayagam, X. S. Thani. *The Tamil Culture and Civilization : Readings; The Classical Period.* New York : Asia Publishing House, 1970.

Nikhilananda, Swami. "Hindu Ethics," in *Moral Principles of Action.* Ed. Ruth Nanda Anshen. New York : Harper and Brothers, 1952.

——*Vedāntasāra or the Essence of Vedānta.* Of Sadānanda. Rpt. Calcutta : Advaita Ashrama, 1968.

O'Connor, June. *The Quest for Political and Spiritual Liberation: A Study in the Thought of Sri Aurobindo Ghose.* Rutherford, New Jersey : Fairleigh Dickenson University Press, 1976.

Panikkar, R. "The Silence of the Word," *Cross Currents* 24/2-3 (Summer-Fall 1974), 154-63.

Plott, John C. *A Philosophy of Devotion.* Delhi : Motilal Banarsidass, 1974.

Potter, Karl H. *Presuppositions of India's Philosophies.* Englewood Cliffs, New Jersey : Prentice Hall, Inc., 1968.

Raghavan, Venkatarama. "Hinduism," in *Historical Atlas of the Religions of the World.* Ed. Isma'il Rāgī al Fārūqī. New York : Macmillan Publishing Co., Inc., 1974.

Raju, P. T. *The Philosophical Traditions of India.* London : George Allen & Unwin Ltd., 1971.

Rangacharya, Adya. *Drama in Sanskrit Literature.* 2nd ed. Bombay : Popular Prakashan, 1967.

Rangacharya, M. *The Hindu Philosophy of Conduct : Lectures on the Bhagavadgitā.* 2 vols. Madras : The Educational Publishing Co., 4th ed., 1957.

Rao, M. V. Krishna. *Studies in Kautilya.* 2nd ed. Delhi : Munshi Ram Manohar Lal, 1958.

Ray, Benoy Gopal. *Gandhian Ethics*. Ahmedabad : Navajivan Publishing House, 1950.

Ray, Sibnarayan, ed. *Gandhi, India and the World*. Philadelphia: Temple University Press, 1970.

Rayapati, J. P. Rao. *Early American Interest in Vedanta : Pre-Emersonian Interest in Vedic Literature and Vedantic Philosophy*. New York : Asia Publishing House, 1973.

Renou, Louis. *Études des Grammaire Sanskrite et Monographies Sanskrites*. Paris : Adrien-Maisonneuv, 1936.

Sankalia, H. D. *Ramayana : Myth or Reality* ? New Delhi : People's Publishing House.

Schweitzer, Albert. *Indian Thought and its Development*. Translated by C. E. B. Russell. Boston : The Beacon Press, 1936.

Scott, Roland W. *Social Ethics in Modern Hinduism*. Calcutta: YMCA Publishing House, 1953.

Sen, Rai S. D. *The Bengali Ramayanas*. Calcutta : The University of Calcutta, 1920.

Sen, Sukumar. *History of Bengali Literature*. Rev. ed. New Delhi : Sahitya Akademi, Rabindra Bhavan Publishers, 1971.

Sharma, I. C. *Ethical Philosophies of India*. Rev. and ed. by Stanley M. Daugert. New York and Evanston : Harper & Row, 1965.

Sharma, Ramashraya. *A Socio-political Study of the Vālmiki-Rāmāyaṇa*. Delhi : Motilal Banarsidass, 1971.

Singer, Milton. "The Great Tradition in a Metropolitan Center : Madras," in *Traditional India : Structure and Change*. Ed. Milton Singer. Philadelphia : The American Folklore Society, 1959

Sinha, Purnendu. *A Study of the Bhāgavata Purāṇa*. 2nd ed. Madras : The Theosophical Publishing House, 1950.

Smith, Mary Carroll. "Warriors : The Originators of the Moral Code in Ancient India," in *Asian Religions : History of Religion*; 1974 *Proceedings*, AAR. Ed. Harry Partin. Florida State University : AAR, 1974.

Sternbach, Ludwik. *Subhāṣita, Gnomic and Didactic Literature* in *A History of Indian Literature*, Vol. IV. Ed. Jan Gonda. Wiesbaden : Otto Harassowitz, 1974.

Tagore, Rabindranath. *Gitanjali and Fruit-Gathering*. New York : Macmillan, 1916.

Tagore, Rabindranath. *The Religion of Man.* Boston : Beacon Press, 1961.

Thakur, Shivesh. *Christian and Hindu Ethics.* London : Allen & Unwin, 1969.

Underwood, Frederick B. "Notes on Conscience in Indian Tradition," *Journal of Chinese Philosophy* 2, 1 (Dec. 1974).

Vora, D. P. *Evolution of Morals in the Epics : Mahābhārata and Rāmāyaṇa.* Bombay : Popular Book Dpeot, 1959.

Vyas, Shantikumar N. *India in the Rāmāyaṇa Age : A Study of the Social and Cultural Conditions in Ancient India as Described in Vālmīki's Rāmāyaṇa.* Delhi : Atma Ram, 1967.

Warder, A. K. *Indian Kāvya Literature.* Delhi : Motilal Banarsidass, 1972.

Weber, Max. *The Religion of India.* Translated by H. H. Gerth and D. Martindale. Glencoe, Illinois : Free Press, 1958.

Winternitz, Moriz. *A History of Indian Literature.* Vol. I. Translated by S. Ketkar. Calcutta : The University of Calcutta : 1959.

——*History of Indian Literature.* Vol. III, II. Translated by Subhadra Jhā. Delhi : Motilal Banarsidass, 1967.

Buddhism in Asia, Primary Sources

Chang, Garma C. C., trans. *The Buddhist Teaching of Totality.* University Park and London : The Pennsylvania State University Press, 1974.

——*The Hundred Thousand Songs of Milarepa.* New York : Harper/Colophon Books, 1962.

Complete Catalogue of the Tibetan Buddhist Canons. Tibetto daizōkyo somokoroku. Eds. Ui, Suzuki, Kanakura, and Tajo. 2 vols. Sendai : Tokyo Imperial University, 1934.

Conze, Edward, trans. *Buddhist Wisdom Books Containing the Diamond Sutra and the Heart Sutra.* New York : Harper Torchbook, 1972.

——*The Perfection of Wisdom in Eight Thousand Lines and its Verse Summary.* Bolinas : Four Seasons Fd., 1973.

Cowell, E. B. et al, trans. *Buddhist Mahāyāna Texts* [including the three Pure Land Sūtras]. Sacred Books of the East, 49. Oxford: Clarendon Press. Rpt.; New Delhi : Motilal Banarsidass, 1968; and New York : Dover, 1969.

Cowell, E. B. et al, trans. *Jātakas or Stories of the Buddha's Former Births*. Vol. I. Pali Text Society. London : Routledge, Kegan & Paul, Ltd., 1895.

de Bary, Wm. T., Wing-tsit Chan and Watson, Burton, eds. *Sources of Chinese Tradition*. 2 vols. New York : Columbia University Press, 1964.

de la Vallée-Poussin, L., trans. *Vasubandhu's Abhidharma-Kośa-bhāṣya* [in French]. 5 vols. Bruxelles : Institute Belge des Hautes Études Chinoises, 1971.

Hakeda, Yoshito S., trans. *The Awakening of the Faith*. New York : Columbia University Press.

——*Kūkai : Major Works*. New York : Columbia University Press, 1972.

Hare, E. M., trans. *Woven Cadences of Early Buddhists*. London: Oxford University Press, n.d. preface, 1944.

Inada, Kenneth K., trans. *Nāgārjuna : Mūlamadhyamakakārikā*. Tokyo : The Hokuseido Press, 1970.

Keene, Donald, trans. *Chūsingura : The Treasury of Loyal Retainers*. Columbia University Press, 1971.

——*Major Plays of Chikamatsu*. New York : Columbia University Press, 1961.

——*Twenty Nō Plays of the Nō Theatre*. New York : Columbia University Press, 1970.

Kennett, Jiju, trans. *Selling Water by the River : A Manual of Zen Training* [incl. part of Dogen's *Shōbōgenzō*, Sōtō Ceremonials, and Keizan Zenji's *Kyoju-Kaimon*. New York : Vintage Books, 1972.

Kern H., trans. *The Lotus of the True Law* (*Saddharma-pundarīka*). Sacred Books of the East, 21. Rpt. New York : Dover Ed., 1963.

Masunaga Reiho, trans. *Shōbōgenzō Zuimonki or A Primer of Sōtō Zen*. Honolulu : University Press of Hawaii, 1971.

Ñaṇamoli, Bhikkhu, trans. Buddhaghosa's *The Path of Purification* (*Visuddhi-magga*). Colombo : R. Semage, 1956.

Nikam, N. A. and McKeon, Richard, trans. *The Edicts of Ashoka*. Chicago : The University of Chicago Press, 1958.

Nishiyama Kosen and Stevens, John, trans. Dogen's *Shōbōgenzō* (*The Eye and Treasury of the True Law*). Sendai : Daihokkaikaku Publishing Co., 1975.

Otani Kōshō Ko-nyo and Suzuki, D. T., trans. *Tannisho, A Tract*

Deploring Heresies of Faith. Kyoto : Higashi Hongenzi, 1962.

Rhys Davids, C. A. F. and T. W., trans. *Digha Nikāya* (*The Long Dialogues of the Buddha*). London : Pali Text Society, 1951.

Rhys Davids, C. A. F., trans. *Manual of Psychological Ethics* (*Dhamma-sangani*). London : Pali Text Society, 1885.

Suzuki, D. T., trans. *The Kyōgyōshinshō* (*The Collection of Passages Expounding the True Teaching, Living, Faith, and Realization of the Pure Land.* Kyoto : Shinsho Ōtaniwa, 1973.

Thera, Narada, trans. *The Dhammapada.* London : John Murray, 1954.

Tsunoda Ryusaku; de Bary, Wm. T.; and Keene, D., eds. *Sources of Japanese Tradition.* 2 vols. New York : Columbia University Press, 1964.

Waddell, Norman and Abe Masao, trans. Parts of Dogen's *Shōbōgenzō* in *The Eastern Buddhist*, New Series, IV, VI.

Wei Tat, trans., Hsūan Tsung's *Ch'eng Wei Shih Lun, Doctrine of Pure Consciousness.* Hong Kong : The Ch'eng Wei Shih Publication Committee, 1973.

Woodward, F. L., trans. *The Book of the Kindred Sayings* (*Saṃyutta Nikāya*). London: Pali Text Society. Vol. V., 1930.

Yamamoto Kōshō, trans. *The Private Letters of Shinran Shoten.* Tokyo : The Okazakiya Shoten, n.d., preface 1956.

Buddhism in Asia, Secondary Literature

Abe Masao. "Man and Nature in Christianity and Buddhism." *Japanese Religions* 7, 1 (July 1971), 1-10.

Bastow, David. "Buddhist Ethics," *Religious Studies* 52 (December 1969), 195-206.

Bibliographies of Asian Studies. Universities of Illinois and Michigan. Annual.

Bloom, Alfred. *Shinran's Gospel of Pure Grace.* Tucson: University of Arizona Press, 1965.

Blofeld, John. *The Tantric Mysticism of Tibet.* New York : E. P. Dutton & Co., Inc., 1970.

Bohn, W. *Die Psychologie und Ethik des Buddhismus.* München und Wiesbaden, 1921.

Butr-Indr, Siddi. *The Social Philosophy of Buddhism.* Bangkok : Mahamut Buddhist University, 1973.

Ch'en, Kenneth K. S. *The Chinese Transformation of Buddhism.* Princeton : Princeton University Press, 1973

Conze, Edward. *Buddhism : Its Essence and Development.* New York : Harper and Row/Harper Torchbook, 1959.

——*Buddhist Thought in India.* London : George Allen and Unwin, 1962.

de la Vallée-Poussin, Louis. *La Morale Bouddique.* Paris : Nouvelle Librairie Nationale, 1927.

Gard, Richard, ed. *Buddhist Text Information.* New York : The Advanced Studies of World Religions (from 1964).

Hanayama Shinsho. *Bibliography on Buddhism.* Tokyo : Hokuseijo Press, 1961.

Hisamatsu, S. "Zen : Its Meaning for Modern Civilization." Translated by Richard DeMartino and G. Tokiwa. *Eastern Buddhist,* New Series I, 1, 22-47.

Hsia, C. T. *The Classic Chinese Novel.* New York : Columbia University Press, 1968.

Japanese Religion : A Survey by the Agency for Cultural Affairs. Tokyo : Kodansha International, Ltd., 1972.

Joshi, Lal Mani. *Studies in the Buddhistic Culture of India.* Delhi : Motilal Banarsidass, 1967.

King, Winston. *In the Hope of Nibbana : An Essay on Theravada Buddhist Ethics.* Lasalle, Illionois : Open Court, 1964.

Kohler, Werner. *Die Lotus-Lehre und die Modernen Religionen.* Zurich : Atlantis Verlag, 1962.

Lalou, Jean M. et al. *Bibliographie Bouddique.* Paris : Maisonneuve, 1934-61.

Love, Thomas T., "Theravada Buddhism : Ethical Theory and Practice," *JBR* 33, 4. pp. 303-13.

Nishida Kitarō. *Art and Morality.* Translated by David Dilworth and W. Viglielmo. Honolulu : University Press of Hawaii, 1973

——*A Study of Good.* Translated by W. H. Viglielmo. Government Printing Bureau, 1960.

Saddhatissa, H. *Buddhist Ethics : Essence of Buddhism.* New York : George Braziller, 1970.

Smith, Bardwell. "Toward a Buddhist Anthropology : The Problem of the Secular," *Journal of the American Academy of Religion* 34, 3 (September 1966), 203-16.

Soothill, Wm. E. and Hodous, Lewis. *A Dictionary of Chinese*

Buddhist Terms. London : Kegan, Paul, Trench, Trubner, and Co., Ltd., 1938.

St Shayer. "Pre-canonical Buddhism," *Archivi Orientali* 7 (1935), 121-37.

Streng, Frederick L. *Emptiness : A Study in Religious Meaning*. New York : Abingdon Press, 1967.

Suzuki, D. T. *Collected Writings on Shin Buddhism*. Ed. by the Eastern Buddhist Society. Kyoto : Shinshu Ōtanika, 1973.

——."Eastern Ethical and Social Practice," in *Readings in Eastern Religious Thought, Vol. III, Chinese and Japanese Religions*. Ed. A. M. Frazier. Philadelphia : The Westminster Press, 1969.

——*Essays in Zen Buddhism, First Series*. New York : Grove Press, 1961.

——*Manual of Zen Buddhism*. New York : Grove Press, Inc., 1960.

——*Outlines of Mahayana Buddhism*. New York : Schocken Books, 1963.

Swearer, Donald. *Buddhism in Transition*. Philadelphia: Westminster Press, 1970.

Tachibana, S. *The Ethics of Buddhism*. London : Oxford University Press, 1926.

Takakusu Junjirō. *The Essentials of Buddhist Philosophy*. Eds. Wing-tsit Chan and Moore, Charles A. 3d ed. Honolulu : Office Appliance Co., Ltd., 1956.

Thera, Nyanaponika; Thera, Ñāṇamoli ; Jackson, H. Essays in *The Wheel Publications*. Kandy : Buddhist Publication Society. 1970-76.

Warder, A. K. *Indian Buddhism*. Delhi : Motilal Banarsidass, 1970.

Welch, Holmes. *Buddhism under Mao*. Cambridge, Mass. : Harvard University Press, 1972.

Yamamoto Kōshō. *An Introduction to Shin Buddhism*. Oyama : The Karinbunko, 1963.

Ying, Hsu. "Why the Criticisms of the 'Water Margin' ?", *China Reconstructs* [Peking] (April 1976), 31-33.

INDEX

This index includes Appendix I and major headings of Appendix II